The ULTIMATE FOOD LOVER'S GUIDE TO HOUSTON

A THIRD EDITION

THE ULTIMATE FOOD LOVER'S
GUIDE TO HOUSTON

ISBN: 978-1-931193-00-9

Written, edited, designed and printed in Houston, Texas
Third edition

Copies of this book are available at special discounts when purchased in bulk
for premiums and sales promotions as well as for fund-raising or educational use.
To buy books in quantity, contact Jane Kremer at (713) 973-0207 or
jane.kremer@my-table.com.

EDITOR/PUBLISHER Teresa Byrne-Dodge

ASSOCIATE EDITOR Amber Ambrose

ASSISTANT EDITOR Rebecca Wright

DESIGN Jennifer Blanco & Joe Ross, spindletopdesign.com

DIRECTOR OF DISTRIBUTION Jane Kremer

my-table.com
houstonculinaryawards.com

Find us on Facebook, Twitter, Instagram and Pinterest: @mytablemagazine

PHOTOGRAPHY/ILLUSTRATION CREDITS

JENNIFER BLANCO Canino's Produce p. 15 ·Kraftsmen Baking p. 61 ·Vintners Own p. 123 | CHUCK COOK
Bansuri Indian Food Corner p. 83 · Coreanos p. 81, 83 · Fat Cat Creamery p. 46 · Greenway Coffee p 75
Kris Bistro p. 213 · L'Olivier p. 220 · Lucille's p. 222 · Mélange Crêperie p. 86 · Oxheart p. 238 · The Pass and
Provisions p. 241 · The Pastry War p.107 · The Rice Box p. 89 · The Waffle Bus p. 91 · Uchi p. 273 | JOHN
EARLES Agora p. 73 · Amazing Cake Supplies p. 41 · Araya Artisan Chocolate p. 51 · B&W Meats p. 32
Chocolat Du Monde p. 52 · Crave Cupcakes p. 44, 54 · French Riviera Bakery & Cafe p. 71 · India Grocers
p. 26 · Moeller's Bakery p. 63 · Phoenicia Specialty Foods p. 11-13, 43 · Raja Sweets p. 67 · Té House of
Tea p. 80 | WILLIAM HARDIN · Anvil p. 96 · Avalon Diner p. 146 · Balkan Market p. 24 · Bistro Le Cep
p. 153 Brasserie 19 p. 8 · Down House p. 101 · Jerusalem Halal Meat Market p. 34 · Olive & Vine p. 18 · Pete's
Fine Meats p. 36 · Plonk p. 6, 114 · Reef p. 252 · Revival Market p. 21 · Spec's p. 119 | KEVIN MCGOWAN Urban
Harvest Farmers' Market p. 29 · Zelko Bistro p. 279 | MICHAEL PAULSEN Eleven XI p. 184 | DEBORA SMAIL
Brasserie 19 p. 157 · Coppa Ristorante Italiano p. 171 · Mr. Peeples p. 231 · Punk's Simple Southern Food p. 248
Sparrow p. 262 | ERIC ZIMMERMAN Prego p. 246 | Courtesy of Del Frisco's Grille p. 178 | Courtesy of Gigi's
Asian Bistro p. 193 | Courtesy of The Grove p. 198 | Courtesy of Hearsay Gastro Lounge p. 200 | Courtesy of
SWEET p. 68 | Courtesy of Tony Mandola's p. 270

The ULTIMATE FOOD LOVER'S GUIDE TO HOUSTON

A THIRD EDITION

☛ COMPLETE WITH MAP INSIDE BACK COVER FLAP

FROM THE
EDITORS OF **MY TABLE** MAGAZINE

TABLE of CONTENTS

Brasserie 19

INTRODUCTION

Forks Ready?

by Teresa Byrne-Dodge

IN EARLIER EDITIONS OF THIS GUIDEBOOK, I FELT IT NECESSARY TO PUT THE HOUSTON FOOD SCENE INTO CONTEXT FOR READERS. MANY PARAgraphs of this Introduction were devoted to explaining how the city's food scene had come to be such a crazy-delicious stew. I wrote about a culinary tradition that incorporated the influences of Mexico from the south, Southern cooking from the east, cowboy cuisine (including barbecue) from the western part of the state and, most recently, the flavors and cooking styles of our enormous and ever-growing immigrant community.

Today our readers are well aware of Houston's role in the national food scene. After all, the American media has been singing the city's food praises for the last two years. In 2013 *The New York Times* called Houston "one of the country's most exciting places to eat" and *Food & Wine* magazine described Houston as "America's newest capital of great food."

This means I can skip the lecture and just tell you that we couldn't be more excited by this third edition of *The Ultimate Food Lover's Guide to Houston*. Its purpose is to lead you to Houston's most notable sips and bites, more than 725 places in all. We've updated everything, plus added 175 new entries.

Let this book be your guide to all that's classic, nationally recognized, quirky, exotic, unexpected, down-home and downright delicious—not to mention beloved local gems—in one of the most vibrant, food-loving cities in America.

Note that we do not use a numeric or letter grading system. We believe the simplified shorthand of scoring shortchanges both restaurants and diners. Restaurants do not operate in a vacuum, and every meal is a little different. What we've tried to do is give you a summary of our experiences. If a place is included in the book, you may assume there are reasons we find it worthy, even if a few blemishes give character to the overall quality. Each listing has a black oval containing a map quadrant that refers to the fold-out map inside the back cover. The restaurants chapter also has a knife-fork-spoon pricing code.

As always, we welcome word of noteworthy openings and closings. Please email me at info@my-table.com.

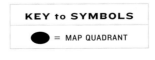

KEY to SYMBOLS

⬤ = MAP QUADRANT

☞ SEE INSIDE BACK COVER FLAP FOR MAP

Acknowledgements

BOUQUETS OF THANKS TO FREELANCE FOOD WRITER AMBER AMBROSE, WHO SPENT AN ENTIRE SUMMER'S DAYS AND NIGHTS EDITING THIS book. If you see Amber out and about, buy her a well-deserved cocktail. Special thanks, too, to our intern Rebecca Wright, who stepped up to assist in the research, fact-checking and proofreading.

I'm indebted to many of the writers who contribute to *My Table* magazine and to our twice-weekly blog, *SideDish*. They scour the city for the best, and their input keeps each edition of this guidebook as fresh as it can be. Thank you, Phaedra Cook, Dennis Abrams, William Albright, Robin Barr Sussman, Eric Gerber, Sarah Bronson, Jodie Eisenhardt, Mai Pham, Layne Victoria Lynch, Jenny Wang, intern Nadia Tazehzadeh and photographer Kevin McGowan. We wouldn't be able to cover this sprawling city without your input. And a big kiss to photographer Chuck Cook. He always seems able to retrieve a photo from his archives at the very moment we need it.

Just as the information contained herein should be useful, so a guidebook's design must make the material accessible. Spindletop Design principals Jennifer Blanco and Joe Ross created this beautiful, easy-to use layout.

Thanks, too, to Jane Kremer, the guidebook's director of distribution. Expediting the delivery of thousands of books is not sexy work, but it may be the single most important part of the process.

Cameron Ansari did not protest when asked to rack up countless miles on his Mini Cooper and try scores of far-flung restaurants. By way of reward he was subsequently pressed into proofreader service. He happens to be my husband, so what could he do?

Finally, I must credit Taylor Byrne Dodge, who is associate publisher of *My Table* magazine as well as my first-born child. She is the clear-headed, hard-to-impress young woman who sits across from me at our partners desk and who can always be counted on to write a snappy headline or bring in coffee. She's also wicked fun to share an office with.

Teresa Byrne-Dodge, EDITOR/PUBLISHER

MARKETS

SPECIALTY MARKETS

BELDEN'S
99 N. BRAESWOOD
at Chimney Rock & N. Braeswood
☎ (713) 723-5670 | MAP **B8**

JEWISH HOUSTONIANS FLOCK TO THIS CLEAN, BRIGHT Meyerland spot for all the supplies necessary to prepare for festivals, celebrations and other assorted celebratory occasions that require noshing. Belden's is also one of the only places in Houston that sells freshly butchered kosher meat, so those looking for fresh chicken skin to render their own *schmaltz* should inquire at the meat counter about special orders. Other attractions include a large selection of fresh produce, smoked fish and gourmet foods. The in-house bakery turns out consistently excellent baguettes, and the extensive wine selection always has a few intriguing choices, particularly of the kosher variety. Customer-service is top notch thanks to friendly, knowledgeable employees.

CANINO'S PRODUCE
2520 AIRLINE *just inside Loop 610*
☎ (713) 862-4027 | MAP **E5**
CANINOPRODUCE.COM

CANINO'S IS FRESH, INEXPENSIVE AND MONSTROUSLY large. With 20,000 square feet stocked with seasonal produce, it's easy to get excited about your fruits and vegetables here. While Canino's does try to keep the bins and bins of produce stocked with locally grown items as much as possible, the sheer volume and variety means that some must come from other sources both domestically and internationally.

Also kept in stock are eggs, dried beans, jams, pickles, salsa, honey and other packaged goodies as well as a large selection of dried chiles. Fall brings freshly roasted nuts and shelled pecans (done on the spot), while spring offers tomato and chile plants alongside buckets of fresh strawberries. Summer's crown jewel is the watermelon, which some claim is the best in town. The Airline Farmers' Market is located behind the shed-like Canino's building, but be warned that Canino's shopping carts are not to be taken off premise, and vendors must be paid separately in this area. Open 6 am to 8 pm daily minus holidays.

CENTRAL MARKET
3815 WESTHEIMER *at Weslayan*
☎ (713) 386-1700 | MAP **D6**
CENTRALMARKET.COM

IN HOUSTON, CENTRAL MARKET IS THE ULTIMATE HIGH-END FOOD market—to wit, it's the fancypants, specialized version of its parent company, H-E-B. People drive from all over the city and even from as far away as Beaumont to pick up elegant and hard-to-find comestibles in the various sections of this gourmet labyrinth. Follow the path from the entrance on the produce side and zigzag your way through the veggies, fruits, freshly prepared juices, extensive seafood and butcher cases, wine and beer selections, specialty toiletries and soaps, dry packaged goods, frozen foods, bulk items (e.g. sea salts, spices), dairy, deli/charcuterie counter, desserts, cheeses (!), olive bar and finally, the ready-to-eat section with a sandwich, salad, soup and prepared foods bar. It's mind-blowing in the best possible way. Did we mention that upstairs they host a myriad of cooking classes on any given day? Yes, they have that, too. It's nearly im-

Inside Canino's Produce

possible to leave without spending at least $50, but with all their community partnerships and conscientious business practices, it's money well spent. The only things you won't find much of here are random household items like kitty litter, hair color or laundry detergent, but stick to the gourmet goods and you'll be golden.

DOÑA TERE TAMALES

8331 BEECHNUT *west of Southwest Fwy. (Hwy. 59)*
☎ (713) 270-8501 | MAP **C7**
multiple locations
TAMALESDONATERE.NET

THIS FIVE-LOCATION MINI TAMALE EMPIRE SERVES LARGE —as in hot dog bun-sized—Mexico City-style tamales filled with a variety of meats and cheeses. The *Oaxaqueño*, an enormous banana-leaf-wrapped tamale made of creamy masa bursting with chicken, is a must-have. Most selections are perfectly complemented by a tangy and spicy

green salsa. Counter-service and a decidedly bare-bone décor style might make taking the order to-go preferable, but the super cheap prices make return visits mandatory. Save room for dessert options that are made with a special sweeter masa and filled with pineapple or raisins.

FREDLYN NUT COMPANY

9350 WESTPARK *near Fondren*
☎ (713) 781-2710 | MAP **C7**
FREDLYN.COM

LOOK FOR THE BIG PINK SQUIRREL ON THIS ANONYMOUS stretch of Westpark to mark nut heaven. Fredlyn Nut Company's huge selection of nuts, seeds and dried fruit spans raw, roasted, sweet, salty and chocolate-dipped. Patrons may sample each item to find the perfect mix for a custom creation. The sweet-and-spicy pecans and cranberry crunch are delicious, as

15

are the savory butter toffee peanuts. The new-crop pecans arrive every November, and hard-to-find black walnuts are here, too. Pick up a snacking portion for a pittance at warehouse prices or send in all the names on your holiday list to have gifts custom-packaged and delivered. Fredlyn, which has been in business for 40-plus years, stores all its raw nutmeats at 37 degrees until time to roast, usually twice a week in the off-season.

THE FRESH MARKET

2617 W. HOLCOMBE *at Kirby*
☎ (713) 592-0575 | MAP **E7**
THEFRESHMARKET.COM

THIS NORTH CAROLINA NEWCOMER TO HOUSTON IS SOMETHING LIKE Central Market crossed with Trader Joe's and boasts Old-World charm, wide sight lines and quality products, including many organic and gluten-free options. This is the ideal market for both lengthy casual browsing and quick weekly grocery shopping. While writing this book, only one Houston location has opened but expect three more Fresh Markets to be open in the Memorial, Tanglewood and River Oaks areas, all in old Rice Epicurean Market locations, by the time you read this.

GEORGIA'S FARM TO MARKET

12171 KATY FWY. (I-10 WEST)
near Kirkwood
☎ (281) 940-0990 | MAP **B6**
multiple locations
GEORGIASMARKET.COM

JUST OFF THE KATY FREEWAY LIES AN UNUSUALLY LARGE natural-foods grocery store with an added bonus. Taking up almost as much room as the aisles stocked with organic goods and produce

(some straight from the family farm of the store's owners), refrigerated cases displaying natural meats and grass-fed beef, an extensive selection of holistic medicines, herbs, vitamins, loose teas and bulk goods is a massive buffet with more than 30 salads, soups, fresh breads and more. Specialty coffees and teas round out the tastiness and make it feel like Sunday dinner at Grandma's house as you relax at the quaint antique-looking tables with mismatched chairs in the cafe area. Namesake Georgia Bost recently passed on, but her legacy lives on through the two Houston locations. In addition to the large well-established West Houston spot is a newer, hipper Downtown location with prepared-to-order breakfasts, lunches and dinners, a small market, cellar bar and custom coffee/tea/juice/smoothie creations.

THE GRATEFUL BREAD

☎ (832) 651-2636
THEGRATEFULBREAD.COM

THE NAME SUGGESTS THIS MIGHT BE A BAKERY, BUT IN fact owner Al Marcus doesn't sell bread at all. Rather, he offers a collection of his own artisan products that range from vanilla extract to small-batch mustards (try the cherry mustard) to Worcestershire sauce to gianduja (like homemade Nutella). What The Grateful Bread is probably most famous for, however, is the bacon, pâté and sausages that launched the company. There is no storefront as of this writing, but Marcus is a regular presence at the Urban Harvest farmers' markets. In addition, he offers free local delivery within 10 miles of downtown for orders greater than $35.

GREENLING
GREENLING.COM

AUSTIN-BASED FOOD-DELIVERY SERVICE GREENLING TAKES every excuse for not buying fresh, local produce and throws it out the window. Live far away from the farmers' markets? Greenling delivers weekly. Not sure where your vegetables are coming from? Greenling sources many of the products from small Houston-area farmers, including Wood Duck Farm, Gundermann Acres, Animal Farm and others. Don't know what vegetables to try? Options at Greenling include pre-made combinations of seasonal vegetables, which take all the guesswork out of it, and there are other specialty combinations available as well. For customers more decisive in nature, the option of choosing your own personal combinations is available: produce, dairy, meat, groceries, prepared foods and even some non-food items. It's a simple trip to the website that will get you started. The only downside is the delayed gratification of it all.

HOUSE OF COFFEE BEANS
2348 BISSONNET *at Morningside*
☎ (713) 524-0057 | MAP **E7**
HOUSEOFCOFFEEBEANS.COM

HOUSE OF COFFEE BEANS WAS ROASTING COFFEE BEFORE most Starbucks baristas were even born. That's 1973 to be exact. Also vintage is the pre-World War II German coffee roaster lovingly nicknamed Madame Hasbean that started it all. Every roast is hand-tended and done in small batches with beans from small, family estates that are verified as fair trade. Available for purchase online or in-store are blended and unblended coffees, dark and espresso roasts, flavored or decaffeinated. While a cup of joe is certainly available for purchase, House of Coffee Beans is first and foremost a whole-bean purveyor for those making their own brew at home or work.

HOUSTON DAIRYMAIDS
2201 AIRLINE *at Nadine*
☎ (713) 880-4800 | MAP **E5**
HOUSTONDAIRYMAIDS.COM

THE HOUSTON DAIRYMAIDS ARE PIONEERS OF CHEESEMONGERING here in the Bayou City. Small, local and, not surprisingly, passionate about good cheese, the maids spread it on thick when it comes to small-batch Texas-made cheeses on both a wholesale and retail level. Working closely with Texas cheese makers like Pure Luck Dairy, Veldhuizen Family Farm and more, the Dairymaids offer their carefully curated selections to local restaurants as well as the dairy-loving public at their warehouse on Airline, which is open Tuesday through Sunday. (Yes, sampling is encouraged.) In addition to Texas cheeses and cheeses from other artisan dairies across the U.S., you'll find olives, jams, freshly baked breads, cured meats and other snack-y things as well as beer and wine to accompany it.

HOUSTON PECAN COMPANY
7313 ASHCROFT *at Evergreen*
☎ (713) 772-6216 | MAP **D7**
HOUSTONPECAN.COM

SINCE 1942, THIS HOUSTON INSTITUTION HAS SUPPLIED customers with all the nuts and fruits necessary to turn out top-tier baked items. The selections range from whole nuts to wasabi peas, along with an enticing array of glazed fruits. The store makes its own mixes of nut and nut/fruit blends. It's all kosher, too, which is always a plus. You can order online, but the staff is so friendly and helpful it would be a shame to miss that and the toasty, sweet smell of warm pecans.

HUBBELL & HUDSON

24 WATERWAY AVE.
near Lake Robbins Dr.,
The Woodlands
☎ (281) 203-5600
HUBBELLANDHUDSON.COM

THOUGH MUCH SMALLER THAN CENTRAL MARKET, HUBBELL & Hudson brings its own brand of culinary grocery delights to The Woodlands. An immaculate butcher shop with dry-aged beef hanging for all to see, intense cheese and charcuterie selection, along with stellar prepared foods that can be taken home or eaten on the patio, make for an epicurean experience worthy of the swanky master-planned community. You might also enjoy dining in the Bistro where the ingredients from next door are utilized in dishes like seared foie gras with miso consommé, tofu, edamame and enoki mushrooms or their famous dry-aged steaks. In addition to the Bistro and the market is the upstairs Viking Cooking School where you can learn to create dishes on restaurant-grade equipment. Also in The Woodlands is a smaller satellite version of the

Olive oil options at Olive & Vine

mothership called Hubbell & Hudson Kitchen that focuses on prepared, take-out or dine-in options with its most important benefit being easier parking.

KITCHEN INCUBATOR

907 FRANKLIN *west of Main*
☎ (713) 581-0609 | MAP **F6**
COOKEATCREATE.COM

WHAT STARTED OUT AS A COMMERCIAL KITCHEN-rental facility in Downtown has evolved into its own unique gathering place over the years. Cycling through several iterations that included a coffee shop out front, an outpost of a popular burger restaurant (The Burger Guys) and a few others, Kitchen Inc. is now still a commercial kitchen-rental facility but with yet another recent twist: Brewery Incubator. Funded by a Kickstarter campaign, the newest offshoot of Kitchen Inc. provides a health department-inspected facility for home brewers to take it to the next level. With beers on tap, local entrepreneurs in the kitchen and occasional events, Kitchen Inc. is multifaceted in all the right ways.

LEIBMAN'S WINE & FINE FOODS

14529 MEMORIAL
near N. Dairy Ashford
☎ (281) 493-3663 | MAP **B6**
LEIBMANS.COM

SINCE 1979, NATIVE SOUTH AFRICANS ETTIENNE AND Ralph Leibman have operated this gourmet grocery, deli and gift store that's become an essential go-to for Memorial residents in search of chocolates, hostess gifts and other luxurious treats. The store's deli, a sort of mini version of the one found at Spec's downtown, turns out delicious sandwiches made of top-notch

ingredients. The Captain's Choice sandwich, made with turkey and cranberry chutney, and the petite Reuben are among the favorite lunch options, as is the Chicken Salad Afrique. When perusing the wine aisles, keep an eye out for South African selections, which are the specialty here.

OLIVE & VINE

795 TOWN & COUNTRY BLVD.
in CityCentre
☎ (832) 377-1610 | MAP **B6**
OLIVEANDVINESHOP.COM

HOME COOKS LOOKING TO MOVE BEYOND THE GIANT JUG of no-name EVOO should consider the 40-plus olive oils, vinegars and specialty oils at Olive & Vine. In addition to single-origin olive oils, the store offers sweet and savory infusions such as blood orange and roasted garlic. Just when the selection seems overwhelming, owners Susan and Wayde Burt will offer assistance and allow anyone to sample each of the oils prior to purchase. (The oils are stored in stainless steel fusti containers that fill the store.) Other gourmet treats include infused salts and whole peppercorns, which make this the perfect spot to find a gift for the person who loves to cook and wants to try something new.

PENZEYS SPICES

516 W. 19TH ST.
east of N. Shepherd
☎ (713) 862-6777 | MAP **E5**
PENZEYS.COM

PENZEYS SPICES IS GREAT AT WHAT IT DOES. THE SINGULAR focus of this national chain means quality, variety and informed salespeople at The Heights outpost. While you can buy many of their products

—which include every spice you've ever heard of, and then some—online and have them shipped, that type of shopping doesn't smell nearly as good. With faux antique decor featuring wooden crates and spice bags, the in-store experience is quaint and more conducive to impulse buys of *zatar* (a Middle Eastern spice mix of sumac, thyme, sesame seeds and salt) or any number of their signature spice blends.

RELISH FINE FOODS
3951 SAN FELIPE *at Willowick*
☎ (713) 599-1960 | MAP **D6**
RELISHHOUSTON.COM

RELISH IS A LITTLE FANCY, A LITTLE FEMININE AND A LOT local and fresh. Bathed in white and sunlight, it evokes the feeling of a New England beachside gourmet shop, but it is instead stocked with Texas items. The Houston Dairymaids, Greenway Coffee & Tea, The Grateful Bread and Atkinson Farms all have a presence, but the real draw here is the prepared foods selection. Seasonal and ever changing (depending on the local ingredients available), the menu covers all three meals with scones, breakfast tacos, salads, hot and cold sandwiches, soups and full-on entrees. Party trays and gift baskets are available with advance notice.

REVIVAL MARKET
550 HEIGHTS BLVD. *at W. 6th*
☎ (713) 880-8463 | MAP **E5**
REVIVALMARKET.COM

THIS GROCERY STORE/DELI/ COFFEE SHOP IS PRETTY MUCH ground zero for Houstonians who are willing to put their money where their mouths are when it comes to eating local. Lead by chef Ryan Pera and Revival Meats' founder Morgan Weber, the market sells freshly

butchered meat, local produce and a huge selection of house-made jams, vinegars and syrups. Revival is also an outlet for lots of top-shelf local producers, including Fat Cat Creamery, Fluff Bake Bar and the Houston Dairymaids. Saturday mornings are particularly exciting, as that's when Revival serves a weekly breakfast that rotates through a list of items including bagels and some of the city's best kolaches. Fishmonger PJ Stoops is there, too, with whatever by-catch came out of the Gulf that week. Get there early: The fish and most desirable treats sell out fast. The deli's lunch menu changes sea-sonally; prices are a touch high, but the quality is always first rate, par-ticularly the meatball sub. Subscribe to the shop's email list to learn about special dinners led by chef Adam Dor-ris that showcase creative ways to utilize these first-rate ingredients.

SPROUTS FARMERS MARKET
23105 CINCO RANCH BLVD.
near S. Peek Rd., Katy
☎ (281) 769-0444
multiple locations
SPROUTS.COM

A "NEIGHBORHOOD" GROCERY STORE WITH AN OLD-FASHIONED feel (if old-fashioned also means lots of vitamin supplements), Sprouts is a recent addition to Houston's suburbs: Katy, Spring Cypress Village, West Houston and Copperfield specifically. The recent and rapid expansion of the Arizona-based chain within the Houston area means more healthful, gluten-free, organic, natural staples as well as in-store prepared sau-sages, baked goods, produce, bulk items and prepared dips and sauces.

CHARCUTERIE

Coppa
Lonza
Lardo
Porchetta
di Testa
Salami
Salami
Prosciutto,
Culatello
Guanciale
Bacon
Pancetta
Shank
Pate Filia
Trotter

FRES

Pork $/
Rib Chop   13
Collar Steak 12.95
Tenderloin   17.95
Bacon   9.95
Fresh Belly   7.95

Chicken
  Breast   7.95   Sa
  Whole   6.95

Lamb   18.95

Duck, Breast 15.95
              14.95   Gu
              12.95   Gu
              16.95

Deli counter at Revival Market

TRADER JOE'S

2922 S. SHEPHERD *at W. Alabama*
☎ (713) 526-4034 | MAP **E6**
multiple locations
TRADERJOES.COM

IF YOU'VE NEVER HEARD THE TERM TWO BUCK CHUCK, NOW'S the time to initiate you into the cult that is Trader Joe's. The gourmet grocery store with snacks galore (and most of them sold under the name-sake brand) is a California import with huge appeal across the foodie world. Not only are the various frozen foods, chips, cookies, crackers and other pick-me-ups culinarily minded, but also—*gasp!*—affordable for the average Joe. Add to that the fact that the house brand means no artificial flavors, colors, preservatives, MSG, genetically modified ingredients or added trans fats, and it's like skipping the wedding and heading straight to the honeymoon. And about that Two Buck Chuck, the bargain-priced line of wines sold at the chain: Skip it and spend your money on the addictive, spicy cookie butter instead. It's basically a peanut butter-like spread but made with crushed cookies instead. Oh, yes, they did.

WHOLE FOODS

701 WAUGH *at W. Dallas*
☎ (713) 284-1260 | MAP **E7**
multiple locations
WHOLEFOODSMARKET.COM

FOUNDED IN THE CITY OF FREE LOVE, HIPSTERS AND THE Texas government, it's only appropriate that this Austin-based grocery store chain was one of the first in the trend towards organic and natural. It is also known for its (somewhat) pricey nature, thus its nickname "Whole Paycheck." Challenges to your pocketbook notwithstanding, products are aimed at satisfying the store's "whole body" commitment and include the chain's excellent 365 Brand. While health food and organic things are a major component, so are strictly tasty items like olives, cheeses, wines, beers, baked goodies, prepared foods and even barbecue. Like any self-respecting fancy grocery store should, Houston's newest Whole Foods (on Waugh) includes a sit-down bar with craft beers and wine on tap as well as a coffee bar up front for the other end of the spectrum. As we go to press in 2013, an enormous new Whole Foods is going up in BLVD Place at the corner of San Felipe and Post Oak Boulevard.

ETHNIC GROCERY STORES

99 RANCH MARKET

1005 BLALOCK *at Katy Fwy.*
(I-10 West)
☎ (713) 932-8899 | MAP **C5**
multiple locations
99RANCH.COM

THIS ASIAN SUPERMARKET— PART OF A CALIFORNIA CHAIN —is the Disney World of ethnic grocery stores. The food court is legendary as is the parking lot, though for opposite reasons (not surprisingly, the former is the positive while the latter is not). Between vendors like a Vietnamese/Cajun hybrid crawfish spot, dim sum served cafeteria style and oodles of noodles in between, it's satisfying in flavors as well as variety. As for the grocery part, it's also extensive in size and selection. Expect vast amounts of produce, both exotic and familiar, tons of fresh seafood and every Asian packaged good you could ever imagine. Bonus is the Vietnamese-French bakery stocked with everything from buttery croissants to red bean pastries.

ASIA MARKET & CONVENIENCE

1010 W. CAVALCADE
between Airline & N. Main
☎ (713) 863-7074 | MAP **E5**
ASIAMARKETHOUSTON.COM

YES, THIS CONVENIENCE STORE IN THE HEIGHTS IS ONE OF Houston's best spots for hard-to-find Thai ingredients like chile pastes and dried shrimp, but, like the Central Texas German meat markets that birthed most of the state's iconic barbecue restaurants, it's the store's cafe that is the real destination here. The tiny kitchen turns out dishes that range from the expected noodle dishes like *yum vun sen* (glass noodle salad) to authentic *som tom* (a green papaya salad with tiny dried shrimp), a dish not so commonly seen in more mainstream Thai restaurants. The food may be ordered at spice levels that range from a pleasant tingle and go up...way up. (Avoid "Thai-hot" —you've been warned.) Service is friendly, but some patience may be required when the cafe is busy, which is often. Still, it's worth the wait for the first-rate food at very reasonable prices.

BALKAN MARKET & COFFEE SHOP

10928 WESTHEIMER
at Lakeside Country Club Dr.
☎ (713) 974-0083 | MAP **B7**
BALKANMCS.COM

THIS SMALL GROCERY STORE, WHICH STOCKS MOSTLY IMPORTS from the Balkan Peninsula, is operated by the same family as seminal Bosnian restaurant Cafe Pita+ and is Houston's premier source for *ajvar*, the red pepper spread that's also known as "Serbian salsa." One wall has goods for preparing a traditional Balkan meal, including pickles and Shokata sodas; toward the back of the shop, there is a refrigerated section that features dried meats and hard sausages as well as dairy products (butter, thick creamy cheesy spreads, freshly made brined cheese). Wafer sandwiches with different flavors of nougat are popular, especially the Croatian Jadro brand. For Nutella fans, there is Eurokrem, which is similar and possibly better.

DROUBI'S BAKERY & DELI

7333 HILLCROFT
between Bellaire Blvd. & Bissonnet
☎ (713) 988-5897 | MAP **C7**
multiple locations
JDROUBERT416.TRIPOD.COM

ALONG WITH PHOENICIA, DROUBI'S HAS SET THE STANDARD FOR Middle Eastern groceries in Houston for many years. The selection of oils, olives and snacks is virtually unmatched, and curious shoppers can lose track of time reading labels and looking for new things to try. The grim lighting and cramped parking don't always make for the most welcoming environment, but the surprises contained within make it worth the trip. Add to that a deli counter that serves reference-quality falafel, hummus and shawarma. Oh, and then there's the pita bread. Try it warm, and you'll understand why it is sold all over the city. You should also try the *zatar* bread dusted with wild thyme and other herbs with a cup of hot tea.

Assorted packed meats at Balkan Market

FIESTA MART
8710 BELLAIRE BLVD.
at S. Gessner
☎ (713) 981-0858 | MAP **C7**
multiple locations
FIESTAMART.COM

DESPITE THE SHUTTERING OF ITS BELOVED MONTROSE OUT-post on W. Alabama, Fiesta remains a local institution that attracts Houston food-world heavy-hitters like Tony Vallone and Monica Pope to appear in its TV ads. They're willing to endorse it, because, since 1972, Fiesta has built a reputation as a reliable source of reasonably priced, high-quality meat, produce and international foods. Inside many of the stores, customers will find a sno-cone stand, bakery (with empanadas, pita and bagels), prepared foods section or deli and a serviceable selection of beer and wine. In the larger Fiestas, you could also come across men's work pants, religious icon candles, jewelry repair or, perhaps, a travel agent.

GOLDEN FOODS SUPERMARKET
9896 BELLAIRE BLVD.
just inside W. Sam Houston Parkway N. (Beltway 8)
☎ (713) 772-7882 | MAP **B7**

LESS INTIMIDATING THAN THE HONG KONG FOOD MARKET, Golden Foods offers an almost-as-massive selection of Chinese ingredients while feeling a little more manageable in terms of finding parking and navigating the store. Exotic produce (e.g. dragon fruit and piles of strange-looking melons and squashes), dozens of soy sauce brands and an extensive seafood counter where your fish is cleaned on the spot, are givens, but there are also powdered milk tea mixes, Japanese Ramune soda (the kind with the marble seal) and various vegan *faux*-meats. Of special note: The market's food court features Willie Barbecue & Meat, which is among the city's finest purveyors of freshly roasted ducks, chickens and *charsiu* (barbecued pork) by the pound. It's back in the left-hand corner.

HONG KONG FOOD MARKET
11205 BELLAIRE BLVD.
between Wilcrest & S. Kirkwood in Hong Kong City Mall
☎ (281) 575-7886 | MAP **B7**
multiple locations

IT MAY NOT BE THE FANCIEST OR PRETTIEST ASIAN GROCERY STORE in town, but as for ginormity, the Hong Kong Food Market on Bellaire Boulevard is definitely a contender. It's reminiscent of an Asian Sam's Club in its industrial look and feel. Grocery adventurers will find house-wares like woks, steamers, soup spoons and bowls; Asian condiments like *sambal*, soy sauces, fish sauces and dozens more sauces; Asian-style baked goods; tofu of every type; seafood galore (including a big selection of live seafood); butchered meats; herbal remedies, including dried herbs and roots; and a tremendous produce section with some great deals. Also popular are the roasted meats, specifically the whole pigs hanging in the window with their perfectly browned, crispy skins. Want even more adventure? Check out the neighboring businesses inside the Hong Kong City Mall, which this supermarket anchors.

INDIA GROCERS
6606 SOUTHWEST FWY. (HWY 59)
at Hillcroft
☎ (713) 266-7717 | MAP **C7**

WHEN YOU'VE FILLED UP ON INDIAN FARE AT NEARBY restaurants such as London Sizzler and are ready to attempt to recreate the dishes at home, head to India Grocers for all the ingredients necessary to prepare dishes that would win over even the most discriminating auntie. The small, clean store is well stocked with dried spices, pre-mixed curry powders, herbs, legumes and season-ings that are difficult to find in other parts of town. (Also, its convenient in-and-out access along the freeway feeder road means not having to deal with the sometimes-chaotic traffic along Hillcroft.) Those feeling a little lazier in the kitchen might consider the wide selection of frozen items that are better than expected. As cricket players smile down on shoppers from the posters lining the walls, peruse the rows of chut-neys, jarred sauces and British candies for additional delectables to take home.

*Assorted grains and beans
at India Grocers*

KHÔ BÒ
11209 BELLAIRE BLVD.
west of Wilcrest
in Hong Kong City Mall
☎ (281) 988-6630 | MAP **B7**
multiple locations
KHOBOHOUSTON.NET

A FAVORITE OF UNDERBELLY CHEF CHRIS SHEPHERD, THIS shop offers a virtually limitless selection of exotic cured and dried meats that range from regular ol' black pepper teri-yaki to shredded curry beef jerky, from barbecue squid (heads on) to baked pork liver jerky. The two stores—tidy and attractively laid out—have even more in the way of dried fruits, nuts and confections. Among the more interest-ing snacks and culinary ingredients are shredded preserved green mango with chili, mixed fruit chips (jackfruit, banana, pineapple, taro and yam) and Japanese candied ginger. With so many choices, it's easy to drop a lot of cash here, but at least your spoils won't go bad for a long time.

MI TIENDA
1630 SPENCER HWY.
at S. Perez, Pasadena
☎ (713) 941-7550
multiple locations

ALTHOUGH OWNER H-E-B AIMS MI TIENDA AT HOUSTON'S Latin American population, the two locations have plenty to intrigue anyone who loves the cuisines from south of the border. While the signs and magazines at checkout are all in Spanish, the employees will switch to English for confused-looking grin-gos. (They all wear nametags that include their country of origin.) Corn tortillas and tamales are among the best items here, because Mi Tienda makes all of its masa in-house. Other departments include a produce market, a *panaderia* (bakery) selling traditional flan, sweet pastries and treats and a *carniceria* (meat market) where you can buy fresh or marinated meats. The extensive prepared foods are perfect for eating in the store's cafe, and the *churro* (fried-dough pastry) vendor in the parking lot is an essential stop on any visit. Groceries are inexpensive, and the focus is on Mexican specialties. Don't leave without a refreshing agua *fresca* (fresh fruit or flower water).

NIPPON DAIDO

11146 WESTHEIMER *at Wilcrest*
☎ (713) 785-0815 | MAP **B7**

FROM SASHIMI GRADE FISH TO A SURPRISINGLY COMPLETE selection of Japanese cosmetics, magazines and music, Nippon Daido sells everything for the person who wants to bring a little piece of Japan into her home. The store is impeccably clean, with no errant fish smells. A small vegetable section is stocked with produce found in traditional Japanese cooking, and packaged goods like noodles, powdered wasabi, nori, miso, dashi and sushi rice are available as well. Daring foodies will take a peek in the freezer section for all the different varieties of *natto*, the fermented soybean breakfast food commonly enjoyed in Japan and reviled everywhere else in the world for its smell.

NUNDINI FOOD MART

500 N. SHEPHERD
between I-10 West & W. 6th
☎ (713) 861-6331 | MAP **E6**
NUNDINI.COM

WHAT BEGAN AS A WHOLE-SALE IMPORT BUSINESS FOR Italian products has evolved into a thriving retail business and, more

recently, a restaurant. With its popularity as a small, independent retail gourmet market eventually reaching critical mass, a Chef's Table opened in 2011 with a more extensive (and expensive) menu of classic Italian dishes. They feature ingredients from the large attached warehouse full of imported goodies that also serve a wholesale market. The bistro still offers panini, gelato and sorbetto like the old days but with updates in decor and caliber of cooking. The small market is still there, along with a limited deli offering items like pasta, cheeses, sweets and charcuterie.

PHOENICIA SPECIALTY FOODS

12141 WESTHEIMER
west of Kirkwood
☎ (281) 558-8225 | MAP **B7**
multiple locations
PHOENICIAFOODS.COM

HOOKAHS AND WINES AND SPECIALTY ITEMS, OH MY! And now in not one but two food-wonderland locations. Preparing a lamb couscous dinner for the family? Everything you need is at Phoenicia. Need a potted hyacinth and smoked fish for Persian New Year? This is the place to find all seven S's of the Nu-Rooz feast. Family-owned Phoenicia Specialty Foods first began enticing customers on the west side of Houston with olives, halal meats, cheeses, house-made pitas and pita chips, exotic condiments, canned items and a full-on deli with prepared foods and salads before opening up a second location in Downtown Houston with some notable additions. November of 2011 began the family's inside-the-Loop legacy with the same market items as the original but with a larger focus on prepared foods, lunch and breakfast items as well as a diet-busting bakery case and coffee bar. Also different in downtown is the attached MKT bar, where guests are offered tableside service, chef-prepared dishes, Sunday brunch, DJ sets for the late-night crowd, gelato and wine and beer. Try the breakfast pitas and you won't need lunch.

RUSSIAN GENERAL STORE
9629 HILLCROFT
at S. Braeswood
☎ (713) 721-7595 | MAP **C8**

ORGANIZED BY COUNTRY OF ORIGIN (RUSSIA, POLAND, Israel, etc), this specialty store sells everything to comfort Eastern Euro-peans longing for a taste of home. In addition to Russian beers and wines, there's an extensive selection of the mildly alcoholic, soda-like beverage called *kvass*. The deli section is a particular gold mine, with all manner of inexpensive Russian smoked ham, hunter's sausage and buttery hot-smoked mackerel. The house-made pickles come in several varieties, and packaged cookies catering to the foreign palate are always interesting little purchases. Pick up some frozen *pelmeni* dumplings—pair with a copy of *Doctor Zhivago* from Netflix for the perfect at-home, Russian-themed date night.

SUPER H MART
1302 BLALOCK
between I-10 and Westview
☎ (713) 468-0606 | MAP **C5**
HMART.COM

KOREAN FRIED CHICKEN HAS THE POTENTIAL TO CHANGE your life. In moderation, for the better; in excess, well, at least you enjoyed your life while it lasted.

Nonetheless, the food court at the "original" (i.e. first) Spring Branch Asian market is worth the trip to Super H Mart alone. Yes, that Korean fried chicken stall is awaiting you as are the vendors offering up bibimbap—the rice-egg-vegetable-and-chile-paste assemblage served in a sizzling hot bowl—along with spicy tofu stews, seafood soups, Korean barbecue plates and oh-so-much more. Clean and cheerful, the actual grocery store has some of the most vibrant, inexpensive selection of produce in town, a stellar seafood section, rice and noodle aisles that will make your head spin, house-made kimchi, pickled vegetables, seaweed salads as well as take-home-and-warm-up items like vegetable pan-cakes. Also, do not miss a visit to the lovely Tous Les Jours bakery up front.

VIET HOA INTERNATIONAL FOODS
8300 W. SAM HOUSTON PKWY. S. (BELTWAY 8) *at Beechnut*
☎ (832) 448-8828 | MAP **B7**
VIETHOA.COM

WHEN IT COMES TO FINDING THE SUPPLIES NECESSARY TO prepare Vietnamese cuisine, no store in Houston can touch Viet Hoa's selection. Especially large but one of the cleaner and better organized of the Asiatown grocery stores, Viet Hoa is easier to navi-gate than its competition, too. The seafood counter is a wall of live specimens (frogs? check!), and fish is custom-cleaned when you order. The cheap lunch counter offers a lit-tle more selection than other similar supermarkets, and, in particular, the barbecued meats are recommended. Beyond the assortment of sauces, produce and an enormous selection

Local honey at the Urban Harvest Farmers' Market on Eastside

of ramen, there are also departments for furniture and even shoes. Looking for a snack? Grab a *banh mi* at the sandwich counter.

FARMERS' MARKETS & PICK-YOUR-OWN FARMS

AIRLINE FARMERS' MARKET

(AKA FARMERS' MARKETING ASSOCIATION)
2520 AIRLINE AT SYLVESTER
behind Canino's Produce
☎ (713) 862-8866 | MAP **E5**

OPEN-AIR AND VERY MUCH LIKE WALKING ONTO A LITTLE street market in Mexico, the Airline Farmers' Market is located some-what confusingly behind Canino's Produce. The stalls are colorful and crammed with mountains of dried and fresh chiles and buckets of hominy as well as other random fruits and herbs of the season. But locavores beware: Very little here is grown locally, for this is a resale market more for bargain hunters than foodies looking for escarole and duck eggs. Come prepared with $1 bills because the vendors accept only cash, and it's easier to move with the flow of the crowds if you have exact change. After plundering for fragrant mangoes and bags of cut-up coconut, spend your leftover cash at the taco trucks parked in back.

ATKINSON FARMS

3217 SPRING CYPRESS RD.
east of Ella Blvd., Spring
☎ (832) 381-8202
ATKINSONFARM.COM

ATKINSON FARMS, WHICH ENCOMPASSES 100 ACRES OF vegetables, is old school in the best possible way. Passed down through four generations of Atkinsons and now run by a husband-wife-son team, this Spring farm has survived since the 1950s by way of smart decision-making and necessary adaptations. In its current form, Atkinson Farms operates a retail market for the public (open seasonally) with estate-grown vegetables, pick-your-own strawberries, pasteurized whole milk, sweet cream butter and whatever else happens to be in stock that day.

CENTRAL CITY CO-OP

2515 WAUGH
at Missouri | MAP **E6**
CENTRALCITYCO-OP.COM

WHILE THE "CO-OP" PART OF CENTRAL CITY IS A BIT confusing to those not familiar with the CSA model, the fresh fruits and vegetables from local purveyors are anything but. The only difference between this co-op and the other farmers' markets in town is paying a very modest "entry fee" or buying a membership. In addition to supporting local farmers, one of its benefits is planning ahead. Members can pick up shares of fruits and vegetables each week, assembled from the freshest produce available. Ordering online is also a convenient option, but pick-up is always done in person at the Wednesday market. Meat is the only thing missing, though eggs and dairy are available for purchase.

CHMIELEWSKI'S BLUEBERRY FARM

23810 BAUER HOCKLEY RD.
east of Becker Rd., Hockley
☎ (281) 304-0554
CHMIELEWSKI-BLUEBERRY.COM

LOCATED APPROXIMATELY 30 MILES NORTHWEST OF DOWN-town Houston, Chmielewski's has eight acres of Southern Highbush and Rabbiteye blueberries. It's strictly a pick-your-own operation, and, during the season from May to July, one can find families filling buckets with blueberries that have never had chemical pesticides sprayed on them. Check the website for current hours and prices. Local honey—the bees pollinate the blueberries—is for sale, too.

E&B ORCHARDS

28268 CLARKE BOTTOM RD.
west of Hwy. 6, Hempstead
☎ (979) 826-6303
EANDBORCHARDS.COM

TELL YOURSELF THAT YOU'RE DRIVING TO HEMPSTEAD TO pick peaches, nectarines and blackberries for homemade cobblers and pies. Tell yourself you're driving to Hempstead because fruit picking is a fun family activity that kids will remember for a long time. Tell yourself whatever you like, but we know the truth. You're driving all the way for the homemade peach and blackberry ice creams made with fresh fruit. It's okay. Your secret is safe with us.

FARM STAND AT PETROL STATION

985 WAKEFIELD | MAP **E5**
at Golf near American Legion Park
FACEBOOK: THE FARM STAND AT PETROL STATION

LED BY MARKET ORGANIZER MICKEY MORALES, THIS SMALL farm stand offers Garden Oaks/ Oak Forest residents an alternative to the more frenetic Urban Harvest Saturday market. There's a good selection of fresh meat, eggs and produce, but it's Morales' breakfast tacos that make the market worth visiting by those from outside the neighborhood. The secret, of course, is the super fresh eggs that go into each one.

FARMERS' MARKET AT IMPERIAL

198 KEMPNER ST.
near Brooks St., Sugar Land
☎ (281) 677-7996
IMPERIALSUGARLAND.COM/ FARMERSMARKET

HELD EVERY SATURDAY IN THE SHADOW OF THE OLD IMPERIAL sugar factory, the Farmers' Market at Imperial offers Sugar Land residents the opportunity to purchase fresh meat, poultry and produce, along with a large selection of prepared foods and locally made goods. As a relatively new venture, the number of vendors might be smaller than the Urban Harvest market, but it's definitely on the upswing. If nothing else, there are delicious Berryhill breakfast tacos available.

FROBERG'S FARM

3601 WEST HWY. 6
near Cardinal Dr., Alvin
☎ (281) 585-3531
frobergsfarm.com

LOOKING FOR THOSE PERFECT STRAWBERRY-SHAPED SUN- glasses to complete your summer outfit? Lucky for you, Froberg's Farm in Alvin sells those. They also sell strawberries—the kind you pick all by yourself and bring home proudly in your Froberg's branded bucket. It's actually a very endearing and family-friendly experience to visit a working farm that's been around since 1936. Conveniently open seven days a week from 9 am to 6 pm, their out-post also offers seasonal farm-grown produce like peas, tomatoes, egg-plant, okra and various greens. The strawberry on top of this farmstand sundae is Greak's Smoke House with house-cured meats like boudin, jerky and Italian sausage.

MATT FAMILY ORCHARD

21110 BAUER HOCKLEY RD.
west of Angeli Dr., Tomball
☎ (281) 351-7676
MATTFAMILYORCHARD.COM

WHEN FALL ARRIVES, PEOPLE FLOCK TO MATT FAMILY Orchard to raid the pumpkin patch and Asian persimmons that grow on the farm's 40 acres. Gather a group of 15 together to participate in a Harvest Festival that includes the chance to dress a scarecrow and take a hayride.

Pork saugage at B & W

RICE UNIVERSITY FARMERS' MARKET
2100 UNIVERSITY
at Montclair | MAP **E7**
FARMERSMARKET.RICE.EDU

NOT QUITE AS DEPRESSING AS MONDAYS, BUT NOT NEAR AS exciting as Thursdays, Tuesdays are like the middle children of the week: forgotten and ripe for therapy later in life. Luckily for Tuesdays, the Rice University Farmers' Market came along and made Tuesdays feel special again—wanted even. You'll find it in action 3:30 to 7 pm, set up in the south stadium lot at Rice University. Some 20 to 30 regular vendors want to sell you their fresh fruits and vegetables, prepared foods, organic dog biscuits, non-toxic cleaning supplies, pimiento cheese, baked goodies, goat cheeses, soaps and pasture-raised beef—even sharpen your knives, if you so please. With this much goodness on Tuesdays, even Fridays may have a hard time competing.

URBAN HARVEST FARMERS' MARKETS
3000 RICHMOND *at Eastside*
☎ (713) 880-5540 | MAP **E7**
multiple locations
URBANHARVEST.ORG

THIS POPULAR AND LARGE FARMERS' MARKET FROM NON-profit Urban Harvest is held Saturdays on Richmond (in Upper Kirby) from 8 am to noon and, more recently, Sundays. Though four hours may seem like plenty, with the crowds and all the vendors selling locally grown produce, humanely and pasture-raised meats, soaps, cheeses, fresh-cut flowers and take-away prepared food, live music, chef demonstrations, knife sharpening and other fun surprises, it may seem like the fastest four hours of your life. If you need even more incentive to get there early, just know that popular stands do run out on occasion, so the early bird does really get the proverbial worm.

DOWNTOWN

URBAN HARVEST AND THE MAYOR'S OFFICE ALSO support the seasonal City Hall Farmers' Market that's literally held on the lawn of City Hall. Stationed around the gorgeous oak-shaded walk and reflection pool, vendors here lean more towards fresh prepared foods for the weekday lunchtime crowd, as it's held Wednesdays 11 am to 2 pm during spring and fall. (Check the website for start and end of seasons.) There are some produce stands and provisions for home use on sale, but lunch is the real reason worker drones emerge from their Downtown hives and come out into the fresh air.

THE WOODLANDS FARMERS' MARKET
7 SWITCHBUD PLACE
off S. Millbend Dr. in Grogan's Mill Center, The Woodlands
GROGANSMILLVILLAGE.COM

NOW OPEN YEAR-ROUND, WOODLANDS RESIDENTS CAN visit this market every Saturday 8 am until noon to purchase an array of artisan food, local produce and humanely raised meats. The combination of high-quality goods and live music attracts a crowd, particularly when the weather's nice. Get there early for the best selection.

BUTCHERS

B&W MEAT CO.
4801 N. SHEPHERD
a couple blocks north of W. 43rd
☎ (713) 697-2844 | MAP **E5**
BWMEATCOMPANY.COM

IF THE STEER ON THE SIGN OUT FRONT DOESN'T GIVE YOU AN indication of what goes on inside the walls of B&W, the "Meat Co." part of its name definitely does. Over a half-century old and basically a large meat emporium, B&W's butcher cases are stocked for anyone's carnivorous tastes: alligator, house-made sausages and links, lamb, chicken, beef, pork, frog, venison and every cut of those imaginable. Wide aisles and a roll of numbered tickets portend crowds, though lines move fast here. While waiting, feel free to peruse the cookout-ready sides and supplies on shelves. Custom processing is also a popular service of B&W for hunters and those who have a whole hog or cow to "tend to" and don't have the necessary butchering skills or equipment.

BURT'S MEAT MARKET
5910 LYONS AVE.
between Shotwell & Hoffman
☎ (713) 674-0064 | MAP **F6**
BURTSMEATANDDELI.COM

THIS FIFTH WARD STAPLE SELLS SOME OF HOUSTON'S BEST PAN sausage and boudin. Then there are the various "meat packs" that combine items such as turkey wings, pork chops and chuck steak into one giant bundle of freezer-filling meaty goodness. Still, it's the daily lunch counter that causes people to line up at Burt's every day. One can find boudin balls, pork chops, turkey legs, greens, red beans and other soul-food favorites among the selections at this old-fashioned Southern meat market.

GUY'S MEAT MARKET

3106 OLD SPANISH TRAIL
at Telge
☎ (713) 747-6800 | MAP **E7**

LET US CUT TO THE CHASE. YES, YOU COULD GO TO GUY'S FOR slabs of beef or Cajun-style stuffed chickens, but, for the past 25 years, the real reason Houstonians have sought out Guy's is the smoked burgers. No one's Houston burger bucket list is complete without sampling one. Each morning the store puts 200 partially cooked burgers in its smoker, and all of them sell out before noon. Be sure to arrive in time because other menu items, like the ribs and brisket, get low marks.

HEBERT'S SPECIALTY MEATS

4714 RICHMOND
just inside Loop 610
☎ (713) 621-6328 | MAP **D7**
multiple locations
HEBERTSSPECIALTYMEATS.COM

ONE WORD COMES TO MIND WHEN HEBERT'S (PRONOUNCED the Cajun way, "A-Bears") Specialty Meats is mentioned: turducken. Granted it is a made-up word, but that's okay, because it is also a marvel of meat engineering with a dirty rice-stuffed chicken stuffed inside a duck stuffed inside a turkey. Along those lines, Hebert's strengths lie in deboning and stuffing practically anything that walks, flies or swims. The lengthy product list includes everything from an especially good shrimp-stuffed chicken to stuffed

rabbit, stuffed bell peppers to stuffed brisket. Non-stuffed items like boudin, étouffée, crawfish pie and a gumbo stock sell out regularly inside the simple storefront, with plenty of friendly staff on hand to give instructions when needed. The mothership is located in Maurice, La., so there's plenty of Cajun credibility to their claim that all the recipes are "straight from Louisiana."

JERUSALEM HALAL MEAT MARKET

3330 HILLCROFT
south of Richmond
☎ (713) 784-2525 | MAP **C7**
JHMEATS.COM

THIS MARKET IS A ONE-STOP SHOP FOR MIDDLE EASTERN grocery items and cut-to-order meats that comply with Islamic law. The shelves are piled high with tons of dry goods—snacks, sweets, herbs, dried legumes and cooking mixes, plus kettles, cooking pots and tableware. A counter tucked into the back serves a mix of kabobs, hummus and a daily rice special. The falafel is particularly tasty.

LA BOUCHERIE

3323 FM 1960 WEST
near TC Jester
☎ (281) 583-8177 | MAP **C2**
CAJUNMEATS.COM

JUST BECAUSE LA BOUCHERIE IS BEST KNOWN FOR ITS TUR-ducken doesn't mean that's the only reason to visit. Naturally, the tur-ducken is first rate, but you shouldn't miss the five-chicken sampler (each chicken stuffed with a different dressing), crawfish pie, stuffed quail and side dishes. Cooking instructions are practically foolproof, thankfully, and the store also sells *maque choux*

Sweet treats at Jerusalem Halal

Prepacked quail at Pete's Fine Meats

(kind of a Southern-style succotash), seafood gumbo and tasso, which make holiday meals a snap.

LA MICHOACANA MEAT MARKET

1348 N. SHEPHERD *at W. 13th*
☎ (713) 862-6129 | MAP **E5**
multiple locations
LAMICHOACANAMEATMARKET.COM

THIS HOMEGROWN MEXICAN MEAT MARKET IS JUST SHY OF 30 years old and the largest independent Hispanic grocery store chain in the country. Growing to nearly 100 locations throughout Texas, more than half of them are located in the greater Houston area. The grocery section includes Hispanic items like *queso fresco* (fresh cheese) and the dark cones of sugar known as *piloncillo*, Mexican sodas and

everyday staples like milk and baked goods as well as house-made salsas and bases for *mole poblano* that are exceptionally good. Noted for their inexpensive cuts of meat that include *Milanese*-style cutlets of pork and beef (thin and boneless), fajitas, ribs, whole tilapia and whatever else is on special that week, it's also popular for a super casual lunch or dinner with tasty, traditional Mexican tacos, chicken mole plates and the like.

PETE'S FINE MEATS

5509 RICHMOND
east of Chimney Rock
☎ (713) 782-3470 | MAP **D7**
PETESFINEMEATS.NET

PETE'S FINE MEATS IS A THROWBACK TO THE DAYS when butcher shops were fixtures in local communities. It even has a red-checkered floor to remind you it first opened in 1962. Still run by the original family, Pete's is known for quality, variety and selection of exotic meats. And "exotic" is not hyperbole when you consider that on any given day you'll find python, bear, kangaroo, ostrich, turtle or moose meat in-store. Of course there are the classics like beef, pork and chicken as well as a deli with jerky, sandwiches and barbecue beef ribs that keep regulars coming back. Pete's is also popular during hunting season for processing, and it's a good choice if you bid on and win, say, a hog at the rodeo.

STANTON'S
219 N. TAYLOR
north of W. Willis, Alvin
☎ (281) 331-4491
STANTONMEATS.COM

IF YOU ARE OLD ENOUGH, YOU MAY FONDLY REMEMBER SMALL-town general stores, and Stanton's is a funny, funky holdover. They stock everything from bulk garden seed to household hardware, from live baby chicks to rat traps, from groceries to a little eat-in cafe. But the reason you should come here is all the meats: jerky, smoked sausages, boudin (liver-free and made with local Tex-mati rice), at least eight kinds of beef sticks, buffalo and elk. They also offer deer and hog processing.

TEXAS RANCHER'S NETWORK
6317 N. ELDRIDGE PKWY.
north of W. Little York
☎ (281) 331-4491 | MAP **B4**

WHAT STARTED AS A SMALL PIG FARM KNOWN AS BLACK Hill Meats near Katy has grown to encompass what may be one of the country's largest collections of heritage breed pigs in the U.S. With a network of independent pig farmers raising hogs on the 10-acre ranch, former Brennan's wine guy Felix Florez heads it all up, ensuring every animal is fed an all-natural diet sans hormones or chemicals. Breeds include Berkshire, Red Wattle, Swabian and more, all of which equate to more flavor, much more humane conditions for the animals (they're free range) and a better product overall. Texas Rancher's Network is the butchering and distribution arm of it all, where Florez works with his network of ranchers to provide locally grown and custom-packed pork, goat, rabbits, lamb and beef to Houston restaurants. There will be a retail counter for the public, too. It's set to open Fall 2013.

FISHMONGERS

AIRLINE SEAFOOD
1841 RICHMOND
between Hazard & Woodhead
☎ (713) 526-2351 | MAP **E7**

ALTHOUGH AIRLINE SEAFOOD IS PRIMARILY IN THE WHOLE-sale/restaurant supply side of the business, the market is open to the public for retail purchases. That means a killer selection of fresh seafood at prices that are usually cheaper than grocery stores. It also means the friendly staff, lead by owner Steve Berreth, can offer expert advice on the proper way to prepare the wide variety of finfish and shellfish that are sold at the store. While there are varieties from all over the world, Airline specializes in Gulf Coast options, including drum, flounder, grouper, snapper and cobia. Aside from the raw fish selections, Airline also makes its own *campechana* rife with seafood and avocado as well as offering smoked salmon, gumbo, stuffed crabs and crabcakes.

CONNIE'S SEAFOOD MARKET

2525 AIRLINE *at Aurora*
☎ (713) 868-2144 | MAP **E5**
multiple locations

A HOUSTON ICON FOR MANY REASONS, CONNIE'S NOT ONLY offers the best *micheladas* (beer, lime juice, seasonings and hot sauce) in town but also some of the freshest seafood. The you-buy-we-fry concept is popular here, but the actual seafood available for take-home consumption is impressive as well. Buy raw or cooked seafood by the pound; that may mean frog legs, mussels, tilapia, crawfish tails, snapper, trout, shrimp and whatever else is in stock that day. Family-friendly for dining, Connie's is also known for its cross-cultural shrimp fried rice offered as a side to the mostly Mexican-style seafood. Grab some while you're at the market, and dinner will be ready in no time.

J&J SEAFOOD MARKET

3825 WOODVALLEY
north of Loop 610 near Stella Link
☎ (713) 661-6102 | MAP **D8**
JANDJSEAFOODMARKET.COM

A YOU-BUY-WE-FRY OPERATION TUCKED INTO AN ANONYMOUS, shabby strip center, J&J serves some of Houston's best fried shrimp and catfish. Owned and operated by the Ong family for more than 30 years and two generations, employees will fillet any fish on display on the spot, be it catfish, salmon, gar, perch, drum, flounder, bass or red snapper, mostly from the Gulf. Let them know if you want to take home the bones and heads for stock. Also on the ice are fresh crabmeat, oysters and shrimp. The cooked menu is full of tasty sides, including hushpuppies, shrimp fried rice, crabcakes and fried okra, mushrooms and zucchini. Prices are excellent. Try the boudin.

LOUISIANA FOODS

4410 W. 12TH ST.
east of N. Post Oak Rd.
☎ (713) 957-3476 | MAP **D5**
LOUISIANAFOODS.COM

J IM GOSSEN IS THE UNDISPUTED GODFATHER OF THIRD COAST seafood. Lucky for Houston, his largely wholesale seafood operation is located right here in the Bayou City. Recently bought by world food distributor, Sysco (also headquartered here in Houston), Louisiana Foods is still helmed by Gossen and acts as a stand-alone company, just with more distribution possibilities expanding from Texas and Louisiana into Oklahoma and Arkansas. As for us common folk, Gossen oversees a retail counter and deli in an industrial office park just north of The Galleria with fresh Gulf shrimp, meaty red snapper and whatever else happens to come off the boat that week. Take it home for dinner preparations or have them fry it up for a take-out lunch. Either way, it's fresh and delicious. Hours are very limited from 10 am to 3 pm on weekdays, and it's always best to call ahead just in case.

KITCHEN OUTFITTERS

ACE MART

3500 KATY FWY. (I-10 WEST)
at Studemont
☎ (713) 861-4582 | MAP **E6**
multiple locations
ACEMART.COM

FOR COOKS, ACE MART IS LIKE A COSTCO, BUT ONLY FOR kitchen-, catering- and entertaining-related gadgetry. Words that come to mind are "overwhelming," "vast" and "exhilarating" for first timers. Convenient for hard-to-find-in-regular-stores supplies like squeeze bottles, cotton candy machines, chafing dishes or anything else your little entertaining heart desires, Ace Mart does not require membership, so it's easy access. Online ordering is available and convenient, though not nearly as exciting as an in-store visit to one of Houston's four locations.

ALLIED KENCO SALES

26 LYERLY *at Airline*
☎ (713) 691-2935 | MAP **E4**
ALLIEDKENCO.COM

ALLIED KENCO SELLS EVERY-THING A PERSON NEEDS TO make sausage or jerky. Home cooks and professional chefs alike flock to Allied Kenco for grinders, dehydrators and all sorts of brining products. Owner Cody Brown didn't set out to operate a meat-lover's nirvana back in 1982; he originally catered to professional butchers' equipment needs. But serious backyard meat guys kept coming in, and today Brown oversees an enormous retail outlet and even publishes a 160-page catalog. What else will you find here? Tenderizers, sausage casings, various seasonings and cures, bottled spices, turkey-frying kettles, smokers, cutting boards and knives. Lots of knives.

AMAZING CAKE SUPPLIES

5611 BELLAIRE BLVD.
west of Chimney Rock
☎ (713) 665-8899 | MAP **D7**
AMAZINGCAKESUPPLIES.COM

RECENTLY EXPANDED TO A NEW LOCATION WITH HUNDREDS OF new items, this specialty shop sells everything that pastry chefs and serious home bakers need to ply their craft. Those who do not belong to that group of cooks might be confounded by some of the things found here: airbrushes, edible "disco dust," oil-based candy colors, rolling pins of various textures, fondant and isomalt sticks. Thousands of items needed to make and decorate pastries and candies line the shelves or hang from hooks, from the gay newlywed cake-toppers to jungle cookie cutters to a collection of books and DVDs. The store often hosts classes ("Intro to Gum Paste," anyone?), which might inspire anyone set on reenacting their own episode of *Cupcake Wars*.

BERING'S

6102 WESTHEIMER
near Fountain View
☎ (713) 785-6400 | MAP **C7**
multiple locations
BERINGS.COM

FROM WEDDING INVITATIONS TO HAMMERS, FROM CERAMIC smokers to fine china, Bering's packs a huge variety of products (including garden tools and hardware) into its two locations. For the purposes of this guidebook, it's the kitchen supplies and hostess gifts that make Bering's special. There's a whole range of appliances, knives and specialty tools. Then there are the European ceramics, coffee contraptions, whimsical trivets, cloth napkins, high-end glassware and fine coffees sold by the pound. Combine that with cookbooks, aprons and first-rate customer service, and it all adds up to a store that's become a beloved Houston institution since its 1940 founding.

BUFFALO HARDWARE COMPANY

2614 WESTHEIMER *at Kirby*
☎ (713) 524-1011 | MAP **E6**
buffalohardwarehouston.com

"**A** HARDWARE STORE FOR PEOPLE WHO LOVE TO COOK" COULDN'T be a more accurate description of this 60-plus year old River Oaks institution. Gift shopping for home cooks here is ideal as there are single-duty items for the person who seems to have it all. Examples include a brioche mold or meatball grilling baskets along with upscale cutlery, cookbooks, small appliances, baking ware, cutting boards, melon knives, strawberry corers and much more.

DeFALCO'S HOME WINE & BEER SUPPLIES

9223 STELLA LINK
just inside Loop 610
☎ (713) 668-9440 | MAP **D8**
DEFALCOS.COM

FOR HOUSTON HOME BREWERS, DEFALCO'S IS A ONE-STOP SHOP for hops, malts, yeast and all the other ingredients necessary to turn water into beer. Want to brew an IPA that's so hoppy it makes a grown man cry? Or a coffee-infused porter that's filling enough to serve as breakfast? The friendly staff has heard it all before and can offer advice to both novices

and experts. For those looking to step up from the "everything you need to brew in a box" kit, there's a full range of kettles, kegs and coolers. The expertise and equipment also extends to those who want to make wine. Yes, they sell gift cards: Giving one to a home brewer is the perfect way to say, "Please make me beer."

KITCHEN DEPOT

2118 LAMAR *near St. Emanuel*
☎ (713) 224-2822 | MAP **F6**
KITCHENDEPOT.NET

THIS HOUSTON-ONLY RESTAURANT SUPPLY STORE IN EADO/ Old Chinatown carries just about anything needed to run a restaurant, specifically an Asian restaurant. The industrial-looking warehouse is slightly cluttered with plates, bowls, smocks, cookware and many things that might look familiar if you've ever dined at a Korean barbecue restaurant or Chinese buffet. In addition to detail-type items, Kitchen Depot also carries hardcore restaurant equipment like a giant duck smoker, deli slicers, ice machines, fryers and anything else found in a commercial restaurant facility. Not to be confused with the national chain, Restaurant Depot, there is no need to buy a membership to shop here.

PAYAL

5615 SAVOY DR. *off Harwin*
☎ (713) 782-2150 | MAP **C7**

TUCKED INTO AN OBSCURE-LOOKING WAREHOUSE OFF Harwin, this store sells a huge selection of Indian stainless steel kitchenware: thali dishes, teapots, cups, pressure cookers, bowls, pans, woks and tiffins (India's famous stacked food carriers). They're all piled high throughout the shop. Browse at your leisure, but don't expect much in the way of service.

PITTS AND SPITTS
10016 EASTEX FWY. (HWY.59)
north of Tidwell
☎ (281) 987-3474 | MAP **F4**
PITTSANDSPITTS.COM

CUSTOM PITS, GRILLS AND TRAILERS ARE THE INVENTORY of choice at the aptly named Pitts and Spitts. Texas proud in a land where barbecue is practically a religion (any surprise that churches are major players in the weekend barbecue tradition?) these pits are the type you buy when ready to invest full weekends tending to a wood fire and ve-r-r-r-y slowly smoking meats. However, there are regular ol' grills available, too, as well as gallons of sauces, pounds of spices, charcoal, wood, accessories and cookbooks.

TONY'S BAR SUPPLY
5201 S. WAYSIDE DR. *at Long*
☎ (713) 641-2277 | MAP **F7**
TONYSBARSUPPLY.COM

PUTTING THE FINISHING TOUCHES ON YOUR POOLSIDE bar or perhaps throwing a tiki-themed party? Tony's bar supply

Tart pans at Amazing Cake Supplies

is the answer to your very specific home bar needs and have plenty of inventory built up. They've been around since 1963 after all. For instance, glassware and bartender kits will make you look like a solemn professional, while the cocktail swords and Jell-O shot syringes shout party. Either way, there's plenty here for bar managers and aspiring home mixologists alike, from sinks to refrigerators to tiny umbrellas. It's like a party just waiting to happen.

FOODIE TOURS

FARMERS' MARKET BIKE RIDES

☎ (713) 524-3567
BAYOUCITYOUTDOORS.COM

CHECK YOUR TIRES AND STRAP ON A HELMET TO JOIN A SATurday morning Farmers' Market Tour, sponsored by Bayou City Outdoors. Bikers meet at 8 am at Onion Creek on White Oak and proceed to ride 12 to 15 miles while visiting three to five markets. When the weather's nice, the number of participants can run to 50 or more. Bring your backpack and plenty of water. Participation is free.

FOODIE FLOATS

☎ (713) 752-0314
BUFFALOBAYOU.ORG

BUFFALO BAYOU IS A REFUGE OF NATURE IN THE MIDST OF urban Downtown Houston. Add to that refuge a twilight pontoon boat cruise and beer/cheese tastings, Spanish tapas or perhaps some wine and chocolates for Valentine's Day. Combine all, and you have the Buffalo Bayou Partnership-hosted series,

Foodie Floats. Offered seasonally (before mosquitoes become a nuisance), the tours typically begin at 6 pm and last about 90 minutes.

WHERE THE CHEFS EAT

HOUSTONCULINARYTOURS.COM

IN A WORLD WHERE CHEFS HAVE BECOME THE MOST POPULAR celebrities in town, getting to ride on an air-conditioned shuttle bus, drink beer and eat ungodly amounts of food with them has become a popular Houston pastime. Themes that center around genres or locales, like Korean, Indian or the Long Point corridor (a street in Spring Branch with a wide variety of ethnic restaurants) keep guests interested, as do the chefs who lead the tours. Underbelly's Chris Shepherd, Reef's Bryan Caswell, Fluff Bake Bar's Rebecca Masson and many others lead several tours a year, which meet up at Central Market on the scheduled Sunday. While tickets are a pricey $180 per person, the proceeds benefit Foodways Texas, and there's never, ever anyone still hungry at the end of the tour.

Feta & Spinach Pie

Beef Sambosay
Meat with ground beef
onion & pine nuts
$100

Chicken Puff
Filled with chicken, pickles
& garlic sauce
$100

Bee

Pies and puffs at Phoenicia

BAKERIES & SWEET SHOPS

Fat Cat Creamery

FROZEN CONFECTIONS

AMY'S ICE CREAMS

3816 FARNHAM *at Greenbriar*
☎ (713) 526-2697 | MAP **E6**
AMYSICECREAMS.COM

Amy's MAY HAVE STARTED IN AUSTIN, BUT IT'S BEEN IN Houston long enough to be considered Houstonian, too. The ice cream menu includes a mix of staples like Mexican vanilla, coffee and Belgian chocolate along with a rotating mix of specials that includes the beer-flavored Shiner. When available, the mint chocolate chip is particularly awesome. Mix-in options go beyond the usual candy and fruit with Girl Scout Thin Mints. Whether you are seated inside or on one of the picnic tables in front of the restaurant, it's a pretty great day at Amy's.

BERRIPOP

3825 RICHMOND *at Weslayan*
☎ (713) 960-1940 | MAP **D7**
multiple locations
BERRIPOP.COM

RIDING THE POPULARITY OF THE CALIFORNIA-STYLE TART FRO-zen yogurt wave, Berripop is one of the many froyo chains to "pop" up. Originating here in town, it's grown to eight locations throughout the city and suburbs since its inception in 2007. Popping with neon color as well as flavor from its not-too-sweet soft serve (with active live cultures and a miniscule calorie-count), the interiors are reminiscent of a tween girl's interior design scheme. Completing the youthful theme, pop music videos and modern, fun decor keep things lively as do flavors like watermelon and açai berry. Fresh fruit is a popular topping on the swirl-y cups of yogurt, but also delicious is the shaved ice concoction that marries a snow cone with a parfait.

CLOUD 10 CREAMERY

5216 MORNINGSIDE *at Dunstan*
☎ (281) 310-1662 | MAP **E7**
CLOUD10CREAMERY.COM

EX-KATA ROBATA/BOOTSIE'S HERITAGE CAFE PASTRY CHEF Chris Leung has jumped into making ice cream full time. The shop features an open kitchen where diners can watch Leung turn fresh ingredients into ice cream that's low in air and high in flavor. The menu mixes a slightly off-center list of standard flavors (Vietnamese-style *cafe sua da* instead of regular coffee, for example) with a rotating seasonal menu that utilizes eccentric ingredients, such as tomatoes and beets. Thankfully, it all works. Can't make it to the shop? Cloud 10 is served at The Hay Merchant and on a few food trucks around town. It's set to open Fall 2013.

CONNIE'S FROZEN CUSTARD

12545 JONES *at McCracken Circle*
☎ (281) 469-3444 | MAP **B2**
CONNIESFROZENCUSTARD.COM

WHY FROZEN CUSTARD ISN'T A "THING" IN TEXAS, WE'LL never know, but its rarity in town is certainly a positive for Connie's Frozen Custard. Folks who have been exposed to the ultra rich and creamy less-air-whipped-into-it-than-ice-cream dessert almost always want more, even if that means driving north of Beltway 8 for the treat. Making only two flavors—chocolate and vanilla—but making them once an hour to keep it ultra fresh, Connie's also turns that custard into malts, shakes, sundaes, banana splits and

"concretes" that are blended with various toppings. In typical custard-stand tradition, cones are sold out of a tiny hut with little seating area.

FAT CAT CREAMERY

1901 SHEPHERD *near W. 20th*
☎ (713) 974-2956 | MAP **E5**
FATCATCREAMERY.COM

ORIGINALLY A WHOLESALE/ FOOD CART-ONLY AFFAIR, Fat Cat has expanded to a larger brick-and-mortar location near the crowded West 19th Street shopping area. It's a full-service affair with old-fashioned sundaes, malts and ice cream treats available to satisfy just about any craving. All of the flavors use locally sourced, high-quality ingredients that pack tons of flavors into each spoonful. Fat Cat's core flavors of Mexican vanilla, milk chocolate stout and strawberry buttermilk are also available for retail purchase at Revival Market and other locations.

GELATO CUP

9889 BELLAIRE BLVD. *at W. Sam Houston Parkway S. (Beltway 8)*
☎ (713) 271-1082 | MAP **D7**

IF YOU EVER FIND YOURSELF DOUBTING THE INGENUITY, THE possibilities of fusion or just the general awesomeness that is the Houston food scene, think of Gelato Cup. The Asian gelateria serves up some of the best Italian-style gelato in all of Houston and also makes custom flavors that cater to the Asian palate. Stinky durian and black sesame flavors are a few you probably won't find in Italy, but feel right at home inside the gelato case that also holds more traditional flavors like chocolate, pistachio and coffee. A number of other desserts—

including a delectable sesame ball in ginger soup, shaved ice and a wacky ice cream burrito wrapped in Vietnamese rice paper—are reason to experiment. Just be sure to bring cash for said experimenting, as they don't take cards.

HANK'S ICE CREAM PARLOR

9291 S. MAIN *between Murworth & Buffalo Speedway*
☎ (713) 665-5103 | MAP **E8**
HANKSICECREAM.COM

AS THE SIGNED CELEBRITY PIC-TURES ON THE WALL ATTEST, no other ice cream shop in the city matches Hank's for overall charm and friendliness. Flavors are well-executed versions of traditional classics; Eater Houston named the butter pecan one of Houston's most iconic dishes. Banana pudding is also a must-try. In a time when specialty ice creams might cost $1 per ounce, Hank's old-fashioned prices are also part of the place's appeal.

JUICE BOX

9889 BELLAIRE BLVD. *at W. Sam Houston Parkway S. (Beltway 8)*
☎ (713) 484-8085 | MAP **B7**

AMONG THE MOST RELIABLE DESSERT SPOTS IN CHINA-town, Juice Box serves a variety of snacks, juices and smoothies, but it's the milk shaved ice that keeps it constantly crowded. These treats combine ice cream, fresh fruit and condensed milk in portions that are big enough to share but are so tasty you might not want to. Fruit choices include the obvious strawberry, kiwi and water-melon alongside the more unexpected avocado. It might require multiple visits to determine a personal favorite, but that's part of the fun.

LA PALETERA

5720 BELLAIRE BLVD. *at Renwick*
☎ (713) 667-8311 | MAP **D5**
multiple locations

ONE OF THE MOST REFRESHING TREATS ON A HOT SUMMER day is a *paleta*, or a Mexican-style popsicle usually made with fresh fruit and sometimes spiced up with chile powder and lime juice. At one of the dozen La Paletera locations across Texas (all designed with appropri-ately tropical color schemes), you'll find those refreshing paletas with ingredients like strawberry and mango/chile as well as slightly more daring mixtures that include pecans and even frozen rice pudding. With a snack bar of sorts, there are also plenty of fresh fruit cups, smoothies, exceptionally good ice cream, chunky ice snow cones known as *raspas* and corn cups—also known as *elotes*—spruced up with sour cream, lime juice, cheese and chile powder. Oh, and did we mention tortas, frito pies and hot dogs?

MORELIANA NATURAL ICE CREAM

10181 WESTVIEW
east of Conrad Sauer
☎ (713) 932-6262 | MAP **C5**

IT'S ONE OF THOSE PLACES YOU MAY HAVE PASSED 100 TIMES and never noticed. Located in a generic strip mall (next to a kimchi factory) with a very generic interior, Moreliana Natural Ice Cream does not attract with flashy decor. It does attract with fresh ice creams that rely more on the essence of the fruit rather than sugar. There are the token vanilla and chocolate flavors, but the real gems are found in seasonal selections like sweet corn or the brightly flavored mango. With fresh berries bulging out of their angular edges, the popsicles here are also worth a try as well as a refreshing option for those not on friendly terms with lactose. Bonus: occasional availability of homemade tamales and other traditional Mexican items available to go, but don't get your hopes up.

PINKBERRY

3838 WESTHEIMER
just west of Weslayan
☎ (713) 622-3401 | MAP **D6**
multiple locations
PINKBERRY.COM

PINKBERRY IS THE EPITOME OF THE CALIFORNIA FROZEN yogurt movement, yet it only recently made its debut here at one of three Houston-area locations. Headquartered in Los Angeles and garnering a cult-like following since opening in 2005, the brand is known for its signature tart froyo and assortment of fresh fruit, granola, candy and other toppings. Flavors vary widely with less tart varieties like cookies and cream, coconut, gingerbread and chocolate hazelnut that also go into smoothies, shakes and cones. On the cusp of the trend in Greek yogurt obsession, Pinkberry also added the non-frozen version to its menus; it's available with toppings and mix-ins both savory and sweet.

TAMPICO REFRESQUERIA

4520 N. MAIN *at Edsee*
☎ (713) 880-3040 | MAP **E5**
multiple locations

FROZEN WATER CRYSTALS PLUS SUGAR-Y SYRUPS PLUS a gentle drizzle of condensed milk on top equals greatness. Tampico Refresqueria, with its blue and yellow color scheme beckoning to the sweat-stained souls in the middle of a Houston summer, offers such greatness. Ordering an *agua fresca*, *licuado* or *raspas* (the Latin American versions of refreshing drinks, smoothies or sno-cones respectively), guests order their treats and head outside to the picnic tables to partake. There are dozens of high-fructose-heavy sno-cone flavors like strawberry cheesecake and peach, but the unique or natural flavors like *tamarindo*, *chamoyada* (which is all at once sour, salty and sweet) or *limón* (lemon) are the way to go. On the savory side, Tampico also serves snacks like frito pies and *elotes* (corn cups spruced up with *crema*, chile powder and lime). Open late for the dog days of summer and beyond.

CHOCOLATE & CANDY

ARAYA ARTISAN CHOCOLATE

2013 W. GRAY
just east of S. Shepherd
☎ (832) 967-7960 | MAP **E6**
multiple locations
ARAYACHOCOLATE.COM

HAILING FROM VENEZUELA, OWNERS STEFANO ZULLIAN, wife Carla Susi and her sister Silvana took a big risk in leaving their home country to sell chocolates to Houstonians. That risk has proven as fruitful as their chocolates are beautiful, with two upscale boutiques in Uptown Park and River Oaks in addition to their "laboratory" and original store in Katy. With a base of Venezuelan El Rey chocolate, considered to be among the world's greatest, the trio dream up combinations like Irish cream, chai spice, Manhattan (infused with bourbon, vermouth and cherry) and salty caramel rum, and that's just a sampling of their bonbons. Araya also sells a variety of truffles, French macarons and chocolate bars both in-store and through other retail outlets like Central Market and Phoenicia. Their limited-edition sets make thoughtful, tasty gifts with the added bonus of a jewel-box-like presentation to contain all that luscious chocolate.

CACAO & CARDAMOM
☎ (832) 659-7821
CACAOANDCARDAMOM.COM

OWNER ANNIE RUPANI MAY HAVE ONLY LAUNCHED HER business in 2012, but her exotic flavor combinations have already made her a household name among Houston's chefs and foodies. Intricately designed and consistently beautiful, the treats that contain guava tamarind or mango caramel may look too pretty to eat, but denying oneself the pleasure of tasting the treats would be an even greater sin. As an online-only store, the chocolate makes the perfect gift for someone far away who needs a sweet treat.

CANDYLICIOUS
1837 W. ALABAMA *at Driscoll*
☎ (713) 529-6500 | MAP **E7**
multiple locations
CANDYLICIOUSCANDY.COM

WHEN YOU CRAVE CANDY BUT A REGULAR MILKY WAY OR Snickers won't do, Candylicious can satisfy even the most obscure craving. The treat that grandpa gave you that probably isn't made anymore? Left wall, next to the gobstoppers. Gummy bears, spiders, worms, colas? All that and more. Foreign candies

that taste kind of gross? They're all here, too. Add to that every conceivable color of M&M's, and it's easy to understand why this place is such a go-to for sugar junkies. Bring your nieces and nephews for a visit, and you'll instantly become their most popular aunt or uncle.

CHANTAL & DRAGANA'S GOURMANDISES
☎ (832) 444-2233
CDGOURMETHOUSTON.COM

DRAGANA AREŽINA HARRIS MAY BE FAMILIAR TO REGULAR *MY Table* magazine readers from her how-to cooking articles. She's partnered up with friend Chantal Duvall for this business that uses great ingredients to make delicious chocolates and snacks. Only available by online order, they sell three flavors of truffles: Grand Marnier, Ginger and Texas Pecan along with a chocolate "salami" and peanut brittle. The salami is particularly delicious; it combines Belgian chocolate with a stout reduction, peanuts, pretzels and a hint of ancho chile.

THE CHOCOLATE BAR
1835 W. ALABAMA *at Driscoll*
☎ (713) 520-8599 | MAP **E7**
multiple locations
THEORIGINALCHOCOLATEBAR.COM

CHOCOLATE BARS. CHOCOLATE-COVERED FRUIT. CHOCOLATE turtles. Giant chocolate bars. Chocolate-based ice creams. Chocolate cakes. Even listing them out like that doesn't begin to describe how many different delicious chocolate items are packed into these two shops. All of the desserts are no-apology, full-calorie and full-flavor, so save a trip for a "cheat" day when you're

A gift box of chocolates at Araya

Chocolat du Monde's display of chocolates

in the mood to indulge. By the way: The made-daily chocolate-covered fruit is half-off after 8 pm. See? The best things really do come to those who wait.

CHOCOLAT DU MONDE
5302 MORNINGSIDE
at Rice Blvd.
☎ (713) 520-5600 | MAP **E7**
CHOCOLAT-DU-MONDE.COM

IT'S A CHOCOLATE BOUTIQUE IN RICE VILLAGE. ARE YOU GIDDY yet? Understanding that his customers are there for pure pleasure seeking, owner David Heiland is almost always on hand to steer smiling clients toward something inside the fully stocked glass case that they'll be dreaming about long after the chocolate shell has melted. Specialties here include Belgian varieties; Du Monde is the exclusive Houston retailer for the posh Neuhaus and Leonidas brands. Dagoba chocolates also line the shelves, as do increasingly rare candies like the Charleston Chew, Clark bars and Zero bars. If you want something messier and house-made, Chocolat Du Monde's fudge is thoroughly indulgent.

CHOCOLATE PIZAZZ
9055 GAYLORD
just east of Campbell
☎ (713) 932-0991 | MAP **C6**
CHOCOLATEPIZAZZ.COM

THE "PIZAZZ" PART OF CHOCO-LATE PIZAZZ COULD POSSIBLY refer to the playful or chic packaging of their chocolate drizzled, covered or dipped goodies, or perhaps the goodies themselves. Either way, there is plenty of pizazz to go around this Memorial Village shop with its endless combinations of chocolate-dipped cookies, potato chips,

popcorn, marshmallows, pretzel rods and some of the most decadently adorned pretzels you'll ever see. There's even chocolate-drizzled matzoh. Mazel tov! In addition to individual goodie bags, Pizazz caters to larger endeavors like weddings, baby showers, corporate gift giving and, of course, seasonal treats. Buy in-store or online and ship anywhere in the U.S.

KEGG'S CANDIES
8168 WESTPARK *at Braxton*
☎ (713) 784-3000 | MAP **D7**
multiple locations
KEGGSCANDIES.COM

NOT EVERY MANUFACTURER OUT-SOURCES TO CHINA THESE days, and Kegg's is proof. Yes, a real live candy factory exists in Houston, and it is inside the Beltway. Drop in anytime during the week between 9 am and 3 pm for a self-guided tour of the 67-year-old company and see exactly how your candy is made (if the machines are running) or gather a group of 10 or more, make reservations and have a guided tour set up. Ending serendipitously—and of course purposefully—in the retail portion of the factory, tour-goers can gather up free samples and purchase confections for take-home or in-the-car-on-the-way-home consumption. One of Kegg's biggest bonuses might be their fresh-made frozen custard: This is one of very few retailers offering such in all of Houston, much less inside the Beltway. If anything, at least give their famous pecan crisp a try: sweet, brittle-like candy made with butter, sugar and pecans.

BAKERIES & SWEET SHOPS

Rows of cupcakes at Crave

POPARAZZI'S GOURMET POPCORN

8236 KIRBY *at Old Spanish Trail*
☎ (713) 667-4767 | MAP **E8**
multiple locations
POPARAZZISPOPCORN.COM

POPARAZZI'S MISSION IS LASER-FOCUSED: TAKING POPCORN and coating it with flavors you'd never thought possible. It boggles the mind to toss a piece of lemon cake-, Froot Loops-, frito pie-, sweet pickle-, baked potato- or BLT club-flavored popcorn in your mouth and have it taste just like the real thing. While a bit confusing at first, it quickly turns into an addictive snack. There are about 100 different flavors available at any given time, and while visitors at either The Galleria or Med Center-area store enjoy sampling, ordering is also available online. Hilariously divided up into categories labeled breakfast, appetizers, fruits & sweets, snacks, entrees, desserts, drinks and healthy choices, the online shopping might almost be as fun as the real thing.

BAKERIES

THE ACADIAN BAKERS

604 W. ALABAMA *at Audubon*
☎ (713) 520-1484 | MAP **E7**
ACADIANBAKERS.COM

THERE'S NOT MUCH THE ACADIAN BAKERS CAN'T do. Churning out quality king cakes during Mardi Gras season, liqueur-spiked party cakes all year long and wedding cakes just about every weekend, they also maintain a popular lunch counter with tasty hamburgers and simple sandwiches.

Billed as "Baker to the Stars," owner Sandra Jean Bubbert is rightly proud of serving the likes of Elizabeth Taylor, Margaret Thatcher and even a few celebrities who are still of this world. The specialty cakes are usually elaborately decorated for various events, and after paying a delivery fee, your precious cowboy boot-shaped Brownie Chocolate Mousse cake will make it to the reception intact.

ALPHA BAKERY & DELI

11209 BELLAIRE BLVD.
inside the Hong Kong City Mall
☎ (281) 988-5222 | MAP **B7**

PRE-PACKAGED GOODS OF ALL COLORS, TEXTURES AND INGREdients are for the discovering at this little gem inside the Hong Kong City Mall. Jellied mixtures in neon hues sit inside cups. Shrink-wrapped steamed buns, Styrofoam trays of spring rolls and other various unidentifiable goods are all up for grabs by those who like a low-risk gamble. While the treasure-seeking is fun here, the real specialty is Alpha's made-to-order *banh mi* sandwiches prepared on house-baked French bread, stuffed full of cilantro, jalapenos, pickled carrots, pâté, French butter, various meats and practically given away for the prices they charge. Counter service is not particularly warm, but it is efficient, which helps move along the line that extends outside the door during peak hours.

ANGELA'S OVEN

204 AURORA *at Harvard*
☎ (832) 239-0437 | MAP **E5**
ANGELASOVEN.COM

WHILE THE SMALL STOREFRONT IN THE HEIGHTS is relatively new, anyone who regularly patronizes any of Houston's farmers' markets will be very familiar with the breads, pastries and croissants produced by Angela's Oven. The baguettes are good, but it's the croissant—flakey, crumbly and (optionally) chocolate-filled—that are particular favorites. Everything's preservative free, so eat them quickly and buy extra for the next time the craving strikes.

CELEBRITY CUPCAKES

2343 UNIVERSITY
just east of Morningside
☎ (713) 667-2253 | MAP **E7**
CELEBRITYCUPCAKES.COM

I T CAN BE HARD TO DISTINGUISH ONE FANCY CUPCAKE SHOP FROM another, but Celebrity separates itself in a few ways. First, its location slightly away from the occasionally maddening parking hassles of Rice Village makes getting in and out painless. Second, and more importantly, organic ingredients and small batches mean everything tastes great. The menu rotates daily, but anything is available by special order. The red velvet in particular nails the soft, chewy texture while avoiding the cupcake trend of being too sweet.

CHEZ BEIGNET

10623 BELLAIRE BLVD. *at Wilcrest*
☎ (281) 879-9777 | MAP **B7**

L ET'S CUT TO THE CHASE. AFTER TRYING TO BE IMPARTIAL FOR years, we have come to the conclusion that Chez Beignet is a more consistently excellent source of beignets than the sainted Cafe de Monde in New Orleans. It is the perfect conclusion to a meal in Chinatown when elevated salt levels may leave you craving something sweet. Fried to order and served with the appropriate chicory coffee, it always hits the spot. Yes, it's cash-only and the service can be—uh, shall we say?—indifferent, but none of that matters when hot beignets hit your table, and you have to wait for them to cool just enough to eat.

COCO'S CRÊPES & COFFEE

218 GRAY *at Valentine*
☎ (713) 521-0700 | MAP **E6**
multiple locations
COCOSCREPES.COM

O NE OF HOUSTON'S FIRST PLACES TO CONSISTENTLY offer crêpes was Coco's, nestled in among the hustle and bustle of young and hip Midtown. With a European feel permeating the place, neighborhood residents wander in at all times of the day to take advantage of WiFi and grab breakfast, lunch or dinner. The service also has a French feel to it—i.e. it can be slow and disorganized at times. Despite the hiccups, the main attraction, filled with savory or sweet combinations, are made in front of customers on special crêpe pans before they get a good slathering of Nutella or a filling of Moroccan sausage, caramelized onions and mozzarella. Beverages are also in ample supply with a glut of specialty coffees, loose-leaf teas, smoothies and Italian sodas adorning the menu.

COMMON BOND

1704 WESTHEIMER
at Dunlavy | MAP **E6**
WEARECOMMONBOND.COM

A FTER STINTS AT EL BULLI AND BOUCHON BEVERLEY HILLS (among several other stops), pastry chef Roy Shvartzapel returns to Houston with the goal of opening the city's first true world-class cafe and bakery. While the building is still under construction as this book is being written, expect a place that opens early and stays open late for coffee or dessert. During the day, fresh baguettes will emerge from the ovens on an hourly basis.

CRAVE CUPCAKES

1151-06 UPTOWN PARK
near Post Oak Blvd.
☎ (713) 622-7283 | MAP **D6**
multiple locations
CRAVECUPCAKES.COM

CLEAN, CUTE AND STYLISH LIKE A SPREAD FROM A 1950S magazine, Crave is a go-to for girl's day excursions, mother's day outings and other occasions when a lady just needs something sweet. Flavors rotate daily, but there's always a gluten-free option. The color-coded candy button sitting atop the icing is the signature element that identifies each flavor. The coffee here is particularly good, and those feeling especially indulgent can have a latte mixed with frosting.

CROISSANT BRIOCHE

2435 RICE BLVD. *at Morningside*
☎ (713) 526-9188 | MAP **E7**

BRAVELY CLAIMING NOT ONE, BUT TWO OF THE MOST ICONIC French pastries as their moniker proves to be a fair choice as the mini brioche muffins and massive croissants are two of this bakery's most popular and quality items. Filling up its quaint wooden tables that evoke the feeling of a French countryside with Rice students, retired couples and random visitors through most of the day, there's a lazy feeling as customers relax with a dessert and sip expertly prepared European coffees. Not everything is *très bon*, but most pastries like the éclair and the ham and cheese croissant have that certain *je ne sais quoi* that keeps regulars coming back for more.

DACAPO'S PASTRY CAFE

1141 E. 11TH *at Studewood*
☎ (713) 869-9141 | MAP **E5**
DACAPOSPASTRYCAFE.COM

FOR MORE THAN 15 YEARS, THIS SMALL SHOP LOCATED IN A HISTORIC building has been The Heights' go-to bakery for home-made sandwiches, cakes and cookies. We're particular fans of the chicken salad on house-made bread. The bakery also turns out very reasonably priced wedding cakes that will please brides on a budget; they even include a fresh cake top to celebrate a one-year anniversary.

DESSERT GALLERY

3600 KIRBY *at Richmond*
☎ (713) 522-9999 | MAP **E7**
DESSERTGALLERY.COM

THIS SHOP PREDATES THE TRENDY CUPCAKE BOOM, and that's definitely a good thing. In addition to decadent, enormous, old-fashioned cakes and cupcakes, the cafe offers a full range of sandwiches that make a light-enough lunch to justify a treat afterwards. Some of the flavors—for example, the old-fashioned diner cake—are sweet enough that splitting is practically mandatory. Dessert Gallery also prepares special treats for Jewish holidays, including unleavened baked goods for Passover. Screened cookies and cakes—the staff can replicate your logo or a photo—are another specialty often ordered for birthdays and corporate events.

EL BOLILLO

2517 AIRLINE *at Aurora*
☎ (713) 861-8885 | MAP **E5**
multiple locations
ELBOLILLO.COM

THERE ARE MEXICAN BAKERIES, AND THEN THERE'S EL BOLILLO. Setting the standard by which most other Houstonian-created *pan dulces* (sweet pastries) are measured, it's one of the best in the city. Using the traditional method of piling baked goods onto metal trays with tongs as the vehicle for shopping and pay stations where cashiers tally up purchases with cat-like speed, it rarely requires a wait despite the weekend crowds that flock here. Customers leave with the spoils of *dulce de leche* (milk-based caramel)-filled churros, sugar-dusted seashell-shaped *conchas*, properly filled empanadas and cream-filled cones for dreamy desserts or coffee accoutrements. Namesake *bolillos* are worth their marquee exposure, and *telera* bread is the perfect texture for homemade tortas. But wait, there's more: Fresh tortillas are spat out of the *tortilleria* in front of your very eyes. To top it off, El Bolillo also creates custom cakes with virtually no limits on decor. Ridiculous or elegant, they've seen and done it all.

EPICURE CAFE

2005-C W. GRAY *at McDuffie*
☎ (713) 520-6174 | MAP **E6**
EPICURE-CAFE.COM

IF THE MEANING OF LIFE COULD BE SUMMED UP WITH A SMELL, it might be freshly baked cinnamon rolls. Existentialism meets breakfast as that very aroma greets guests entering this quirkily bedecked River Oaks cafe with buttercup-yellow walls. Often crowded with families during the day and after-movie canoodlers coming by for an evening dessert post-River Oaks Theatre dates, the bistro-style cafe serves up some of the best pastries in town. Chewy chocolate chip cookies are worth repeated visits as are the gorgeous napoleons, Linzer cookies and princess tortes. And while it's hard to get past the pastry case in front, there are plenty of quality dishes with European flair for all three meals, including daily specials.

FLUFF BAKE BAR

☎ (832) 374-8340
FLUFFBAKEBAR.COM

FORMER *TOP CHEF: JUST DESSERT* CONTESTANT REBECCA Masson should be very familiar to *My Table* readers: She's a regular contributor to the *My Table* Houston Culinary Awards banquet, and the publication sponsors her semi-annual dinners where chefs from across the city and state help raise money for the Lucky Dog rescue organization. Fluff Bake Bar treats can be found around town at places like Revival Market, Southside Espresso and the Eatsie Boys Cafe. They're usually classic desserts with an intriguing twist, such as her takes on Mallomars or Oreos. On one Saturday morning each month, she shows up at Southside Espresso with a limited run of specialty offerings (kolaches, brioche, croissants) that are a must-try for pastry fans. Note that Masson has not yet settled on her own storefront location, but she's actually looking.

FLYING SAUCER PIE CO.

436 W. CROSSTIMBERS
at Garden Oaks
☎ (713) 694-1141 | MAP **E5**
FLYINGSAUCERPIESHOP.COM

NOT TO BE CONFUSED WITH THE PIZZA RESTAURANT OF THE same name, the block-long lines that occur at this Independence Heights institution every Thanksgiving are sufficient testimony to the quality of the baked goods. The decor is simple: fresh-baked pies piled high and a wall sporting a mural of astronauts with pies for heads. Everything's good, but we're particular fans of the strawberry cream pie that features whole strawberries and the signature pecan pie that combines a smooth interior with a properly caramelized shell.

FOODY'S GOURMET

1400 ELDRIDGE
north of Briar Forest
☎ (281) 496-3663 | MAP **B6**
FOODYSGOURMET.COM

AN OFFSHOOT OF REVERED FRENCH RESTAURANT, LE Mistral, Foody's Gourmet is a much more casual bakery and deli. While Foody's does a large wholesale business, supplying hotels and restaurants around Houston, common folk are welcome inside the retail store, which is located right next door to Le Mistral. The bakery and deli offers croissants, baguettes and other loaves, macarons and quiches, soups, salads, sandwiches, coffees and even Le Mistral entrees to-go along with gourmet packaged goods for off-premise snacking. Custom wedding cakes are also on the list of things Foody's can do.

BAKERIES & SWEET SHOPS

Fresh pastries at French Riviera

FRENCH GOURMET BAKERY & CAFE

2250 WESTHEIMER *between S. Shepherd & Kirby*
☎ (713) 524-3744 | MAP **E6**
FGBAKERY.COM

MORE A BAKERY THAN A CAFE (THOUGH THEY DO OFFER savory lunch items), French Gourmet is ideal for specialized cakes. The Moka Rum is exquisitely beautiful with thin layers of yellow cake laced with rum and sandwiched with coffee buttercream. Other notables include thumbprint cookies endowed with generous chocolate centers, pecan macarons and almond croissants that send the pleasure centers of the brain soaring into a beautiful sugar coma. A recent building update gave this River Oaks bakery a fresh look, though the freshly baked rolls haven't changed a bit. And that's a very good thing.

FRENCH RIVIERA BAKERY & CAFE

3100 CHIMNEY ROCK
between Westheimer & Richmond
☎ (713) 783-3264 | MAP **D7**

MY TABLE EDITORS ARE STRONG ADVOCATES FOR this Houston institution where French-trained Louis Wu and his brother Robert turn out some of Houston's best baguettes, croissants and éclairs. The "farmhouse loaf" is sold wholesale to restaurants all over town. Get there early to purchase one before the day's production sells out and then try to spot it at other places around town. Whereas the old location could feel cramped, the new bakery (about a block south) is bright and expansive, and the new patio makes a perfect spot for sipping a cafe au lait or lingering over the ever-popular chicken salad.

The BLT at Kraftsmen Baking

FROSTED BETTY BAKESHOP

833 STUDEWOOD *at E. 9th*
☎ (713) 862-4500 | MAP **E5**
FROSTEDBETTY.COM

FURTHER PROOF THE CUPCAKE FAD WAS NOT A FAD AT ALL: the continued success of businesses like Frosted Betty. Not only did owner Nicole Mora and her family maintain a mobile food truck operation spreading cupcake love all over town, but they turned it into two brick-and-mortar locations. The Katy location has since closed after the coffee shop it was located in shuttered, but The Heights location is still going strong. Mature flavor combinations like salted caramel, pistachio cardamom and almond ricotta raspberry are great for the discerning palate, but chocolate and vanilla are always available for traditionalists. Non-cupcake goodies include cake balls, cakes, brownies, macarons, tarts, cookies and pies.

GLUTEN FREE NATION

1014 WIRT *just north of the Katy Fwy. (I-10 West)*
☎ (713) 784-7122 | MAP **D5**
GLUTENFREEHOUSTON.COM

WHAT BEGAN AS A GLUTEN-FREE BUSINESS CATERING to the needs of Houstonians has grown to more than 14,000 "likes" on Facebook and a switch of names from *Gluten Free Houston* to *Gluten Free Nation*. Owner Randi Markowitz took matters into her own hands after suffering from a severe sensitivity to gluten known as celiac disease and opened the store and online business after her own unsuccessful search for quality gluten-free items. After much experimentation, Gluten Free Nation is growing exponentially, selling products like gluten-free hamburger buns, breads, dinner rolls, pies, cupcakes, muffins and cakes. There's even an entire holiday menu with items like gluten-free stuffing, jalapeño cornbread and biscotti. The website is a convenient way to order products.

HOT BAGEL SHOP

2009 S. SHEPHERD *near Welch*
☎ (713) 520-0340 | MAP **E6**
HOTBAGELSHOP.WEBSTARTS.COM

THERE ARE ACCEPTABLE PLACES TO BUY BAGELS IN HOUSTON, and Hot Bagel is the only one that's inside The Loop. It seems that lots of people know that, because it's almost impossible not to encounter a long line that wraps through the cramped shop on weekends. Don't worry; there are lots of people behind the counter to take orders and keep everything moving. The standard poppy/rye/everything varieties are all good here, and the clever twists, including four different bagel-wrapped hot dogs and breakfast sandwiches, offer some variety (and protein) for people looking for more than just a bagel and *schmear*.

HOT BREADS

5700-A HILLCROFT *at Harwin*
☎ (713) 785-1212 | MAP **C7**
HOUSTONHOTBREADS.COM

ONE OF ONLY THREE U.S. LOCATIONS OF THE MADRAS, India-based global chain lures customers from all over the city for the outstanding, unique Indian-European fusion pastries. Eggless, halal and vegetarian options abound, but it's the mini-pizzas with chicken tikka or paneer instead of tomatoes that are an absolute must-try. Finish off a bargain *channa* (seasoned chickpea) lunch wrap spread with mint chutney by ordering a salty, sweet masala shortbread cookie. Wash down a chicken croquette or goat curry croissant with a lassi or chai.

JODYCAKES

☎ (832) 722-4123
JODYCAKES.COM

JODY STEVENS HAS BUILT A BUSINESS AS ONE OF HOUSton's go-to sources for both vegan and gluten-free baked goods. Her twitter feed (@jodycakes) documents her adventures around the city as she provides gluten-intolerant children with their first taste of chocolate cake and elaborately decorated wedding cakes to Indian families. She's adept with traditional baked goods, too. Her red velvet and salted caramel flavors are always delicious. Online only, and orders usually require one week notice.

KRAFTSMEN BAKING

611 W. 22ND
between Shepherd & Lawrence
☎ (713) 426-1300 | MAP **E5**
KRAFTSMENBAKING.COM

DESPITE THE SHUTTERING OF ITS MONTROSE LOCATION, Scott Tycer's Kraftsmen Baking continues to be one of Houston's premier commercial bakeries. From baguettes to hot dog buns, the products can be found in restaurants all over the city. This cafe in The Heights serves breakfast and lunch everyday. All of the sandwiches are solid; it helps that the bread is really, really good.

LA VICTORIA BAKERY

7138 LAWNDALE *at S. 75th*
☎ (713) 921-0861 | MAP **G7**
LAVICTORIABAKERY.NET

RUN BY TWO SISTERS, LA VICTORIA IS A BUSINESS OF contrasts. Everyday purchases like Mexican-style breads, pastries and *pan dulces* (sweet breads) bring in the regular East Enders who've also come to grab a quick, simple breakfast of gorditas stuffed with egg, potato and bacon or crisp flautas with green sauce for lunch. More elaborate orders might include La Victoria's signature wedding and special occasion cakes, of which the detail work and extravagance knows no bounds. The ambiance and parking are lacking, service can be abrupt and the tamales are pricier than most, though the moist masa convinces some that they might just be worth it.

MAISON BURDISSO PARISIAN MACARONS

MAISONBURDISSO.COM

AS ANYONE WHO'S TRIED TO MAKE THEM AT HOME CAN attest, macarons are an extremely temperamental treat to create, especially given Houston's humid climate. It's easy to wind up with dough that's undercooked and spongy or overbaked and crumbly, which is what makes Maison Burdisso so remarkable: Among the dozen or so rotating flavors that are sold at local farmers' markets, the texture and flavor of the macarons are always spot-on. Check the website for the full roster and don't hesitate to order them for your next party.

Moeller's delicate petit fours

MICHAEL'S COOKIE JAR

5330 WESLAYAN *at Bissonnet*
☎ (713) 771-8603 | MAP **D7**
MICHAELSCOOKIEJAR.COM

TUCKED INTO THE BACK CORNER OF A SHOPPING CENTER AT Bissonnet and Weslayan, CIA-trained pastry chef Michael Savino turns out a mix of classic (chocolate chip, oatmeal raisin, etc) and decorated cookies. The intricate designs and attention to detail make them a popular choice for bridal showers, baby showers and other special occasions when impressing guests with your fabulous taste is of vital importance. For the truly cookie-obsessed, Michael's will create elaborate "cakes" out of a variety of carefully arranged cookies. Best of all: These cookies not only look good, they *taste* good.

MOELLER'S BAKERY

4201 BELLAIRE BLVD.
at Stella Link
☎ (713) 667-0983 | MAP **D7**

MOELLER'S IS MOST DEFINITELY AND UNABASHEDLY old school. In business since 1930, this is *the* place for petit fours in the city of Houston. Preciously small, bite-sized squares of light-as-air cake, topped with pastel flower decor sit in cases ripe for an afternoon tea or simply a midweek pleasure. Custom cookies and cakes are also available through advance ordering, but walk-ins may find molasses cookies, coconut snowballs and addictive orange rolls alongside those tiny French cakes for take-home goodness. "Old-school" also describes the service, helped along by some of the most affable staffers in town.

NOTHING BUNDT CAKES

5000 WESTHEIMER *just west of Post Oak Blvd.*

☎ (713) 552-9100 | MAP **D6**

multiple locations

NOTHINGBUNDTCAKES.COM

IF EVER A PUN WERE MORE APT FOR THE NAME OF A BAKERY, we'd like to know. This national chain relies on the nostalgia of bundt cakes and the moistness of its recipe. With five Houston-area locations, its method seems to be working pretty well. Each store has 10 flavors and 40 bundt designs to choose from along with a choice of two sizes: the mini cakes are perfect for splitting with a special someone and the larger are appropriate for a small gathering. The lemon bundt cake doesn't sing with tons of lemon flavor, but the cake itself is moist enough to excuse the subtlety. The heavenly butter cream cheese frosting comes standard on all flavors, which include chocolate chocolate chip, pecan praline, aforementioned lemon, white chocolate, white chocolate raspberry, marble, red velvet and cinnamon swirl.

OOH LA LA

23920 WESTHEIMER PKWY.

west of the Grand Pkwy., Katy

☎ (281) 391-2253

multiple locations

OOHLALASWEETS.COM

PASTRY CHEF AND OWNER VANESSA O'DONNELL IS A DRIVEN woman. Driven to increase the waistline of every Houstonian through her adorably decorated softball-sized cupcakes. Driven to succeed with now three locations throughout the Houston area since Ooh La La's founding in 2009. Driven to achieve extreme success before she turns 30. She's doing a great job on all fronts so far. The ironically cute, young and petite O'Donnell has baked up some funky yet approachable flavors like Margaritaville and Boston cream pie along with monthly specials like strawberry lemonade for June and grasshopper mint for March. The kitschy storefront also offers a great deal more than cupcakes, the pies and cake truffles being the most popular alternatives.

PANADERIA CENTRAL

12788 VETERANS MEMORIAL

bet. W. Richey and Bammel North Houston

☎ (281) 866-7630 | MAP **D2**

JUST WHEN YOU'VE HAD YOUR FILL OF MEXICAN BAKERIES AND their *pan dulces*, try something new and wander over to Panaderia Central for some Colombian treats. If available—we suggest getting there early—try the *roscon de guayaba*, a super-sized guava donut and a side of *arequipe*, their version of caramel that's soft and luscious. For savory, there are breakfasts of eggs and *arepas* (small, griddled corn flatbreads) with cheese or *calentado de frijoles* (a traditional Colombian breakfast consisting of beans and rice from the night before). Also available for purchase are a myriad of frozen Colombian products like the *arepas*, various sausages and tropical fruit pulp for making juice.

PARISIAN BAKERY

8300 W. SAM HOUSTON PKWY. S.
(Beltway 8) at Beechnut
☎ (281) 776-0503 | MAP **B7**
multiple locations

IF THERE EVER WERE A BETTER COMBINATION THAN *BANH MI* with a subsequent dessert of macarons and gelato, please do tell. A little slice of heaven on earth, Parisian Bakery is a place where such magical combinations happen daily. Cream puffs and a *cafe sua da* (Vietnamese iced coffee)? *Bo kho* (beef stew) and beignets? No problem. As an added bonus, everything is quick and inexpensive, and you can find an equally abundant offering of packaged spring rolls as you can fresh baked croissants and brioche. Guests rave about the *pâté chaud*, a puff pastry stuffed with pork, as well as the steamed pork buns, and the green-tinged *pandan* (a Thai leaf) waffle has its own cult-like following. The dining room isn't particularly cozy, but the decor is fresh and modern, which is all you need when there's magic in the air.

PÂTISSERIE JUNGLE CAFE

9889 BELLAIRE BLVD. *at W. Sam Houston Parkway S. (Beltway 8)*
☎ (713) 272-6633 | MAP **B7**

THE ELABORATELY DECORATED CAKES AND PETIT FOURS AT Pâtisserie Jungle Cafe may not always be sweet or creamy enough for a Western palate, but they are incredible to look at. Both the full and individual-sized cakes are beautiful and will certainly draw *oohs* and *aahs*. The mango cake is a signature item that should appeal to most customers. The macarons and coffee make for a nice snack after a meal at one of the many restaurants located in the same shopping center. For those not interested in sweets, the cafe carries an entertaining, if somewhat pricey, selection of Japanese toys and coffee/tea brewing equipment.

PETITE SWEETS

2700 W. ALABAMA *west of Kirby*
☎ (713) 520-7007 | MAP **E6**
PETITESWEETSHOUSTON.COM

WHEN YOU NEED TO SUPPLY DESSERT FOR A BIG GROUP that's somewhat fussy, Petite Sweets is the perfect choice. Pastry chef Susan Molzan prepares a variety of small desserts: cookies, mini-cupcakes, cake balls, frozen custard and a dozen-plus varieties of macarons. It's truly a something-for-everybody bakery where multiple visits are a must in order to try all the tasty treats. It's hard to go wrong here, but the salted caramel cake balls are particularly delicious.

THE PIE FACTORY

5611 BELLAIRE BLVD., *west of Chimney Rock*
☎ (713) 666-8501 | MAP **D7**
THEPIEFACTORYHOUSTON.COM

IF PHRASES LIKE "10-INCH ROUND, DEEP PAN" MEAN ANYTHING TO you, it's possible that you're an avid home baker or perhaps it's time to admit that you're addicted to pie. In any case, this is the size of the 35 varieties of pies produced at The Pie Factory. Banana cream, apple walnut raisin, black bottom, buttermilk, peach and pineapple cream are just a smattering of the flavors available—all you have to do is place the order. This isn't a sit-down-grab-a-slice cafe; it's a place-your-order-and-pick-it-up operation, and they also (quietly) supply desserts to many a Houston restaurant.

BAKERIES & SWEET SHOPS

While the name is all about pie, the company also specializes in custom cakes, cookies, cupcakes and tarts.

RAJA SWEETS

5667 HILLCROFT *at Harwin*
☎ (713) 782-5667 | MAP **C7**

FOR MORE THAN A QUARTER CENTURY, RAJA SWEETS HAS been a reliable source of syrup-soaked *gulab jamun* (doughnut balls, four kinds!) and other Indian sweets. The *burfi*, colorful desserts made with condensed milk and sold in a variety of flavors, are also worth trying. For those without a sweet tooth, the menu features a variety of savory snacks such as samosas, curries and vegetable-filled pakoras. Prices are very inexpensive, so acquiring a habit for this place won't break the bank.

RAO'S BAKERY

6915 CYPRESSWOOD
at Southampton Dr., Spring
☎ (281) 251-7267
RAOSBAKERY.COM

NOT EVERYTHING STARTS IN THE BIG CITY AND EXPANDS OUT TO the small ones. Take Rao's for example. Founded in Beaumont in 1941, Rao's is practically a household name there now after serving the smaller community with some of the best king cakes outside of Louisiana. With plenty of experience and seven flavors of king cake in tow, they opened a location in Spring serving their famous pastries, cakes, tarts, cream puffs, muffins, croissants and anything else that involves flour, butter and sugar. It's a dine-in type of cafe where breakfasts, lunches and dinners are almost as popular as the gelatos and coffees. The familial crowd peaks on Sundays for post-church chow and the occasional

sinful indulgence of the six-layered Dobasche—a cake armed with a triple serving of fudge, vanilla and walnuts. Can we get an "amen"?

RUGGLES CAFE BAKERY

2365 RICE BLVD. *at Chaucer*
☎ (713) 520-6662 | MAP **E7**
RUGGLESCAFEBAKERY.COM

NOT TO BE CONFUSED WITH THE OTHER RUGGLES—THE one that was bulldozed in 2012 or the totally separate chain, Ruggles Green—this Ruggles is a place to find casual, inexpensive fare with counter service. Basic deli dishes like salads, sandwiches and pastas are given a little something sophisticated to help them stand out from the crowd: mango salsa brightening a veggie wrap or chipotle mayo spicing up a pork loin sandwich. With "bakery" in the actual name, there's a certain expectation for the desserts, which range from *tres leches* to the Charlotte's Web (a chocolate cake melded with espresso pudding and Heath bar bits), and those are certainly met with ease. The portions are generous, the patio is pleasant and the BYOB policy is just the icing on top.

RUSTIKA BAKERY

3237 SOUTHWEST FWY. (HWY. 59)
at Buffalo Speedway
☎ (713) 665-6226 | MAP **D7**
RUSTIKACAFE.COM

RUSTIKA'S COMBINATION OF MEXICAN AND JEWISH SPE-cialties may seem like an unlikely combination, but anyone who's ever had the chance to pair an order of migas with cheese blintzes for dessert understands that these are two great tastes that taste great together. The lunch menu offers similar genre-hopping: matzah ball

Burfi in Raja Sweets

French macarons at Sweet

soup comfortably shares the menu with the chicken tortilla option. The homemade challah makes a sweet, sturdy platform for one of the many sandwiches. Empanadas are also good, with a solid, flaky crust and tasty fillings.

SIX PING BAKERY

9384 BELLAIRE BLVD.
near Ranchester
☎ (713) 773-0658 | MAP **D7**

APPARENTLY CHINATOWN IS MUCH MORE THAN DIM SUM restaurants and noodle houses, because Six Ping is yet another quality bakery to be found within the confines of this little city within a city. We should warn you now that the cheap prices will have you grabbing just about everything in sight whether it be the foot-long bacon-sprinkled breadsticks, taro-filled buns or cake rolls. Or perhaps it will be the curry pork rolls or airy chocolate sponge cake that tickles your fancy. Either way, grab a tray and make some decisions. There's not much to regret here. Don't forget to stop and admire the small, decorated cakes in the case. There's

usually a "Hello Kitty" version alongside other cute creatures that look like they jumped right out of a Japanese cartoon.

SLOW DOUGH BREAD CO.

8728 WESTPARK *at Fondren*
☎ (713) 568-5674 | MAP **C7**
SLOWDOUGHBREADCO.COM

THE WORD "ARTISAN," WHEN USED IN REFERENCE TO FOOD products has almost become cliché. But Slow Dough Bread Co. really means it when describing its product. Trust us when we say you can taste the difference. Whether it's the killer combinations of chewy and soft in the famous soft pretzels or pretzel buns, the richness of the brioche loaf, the perfect crumbs falling from a thin and wispy baguette or the mouth-watering challah, Slow Dough produces some of the best bread in the city. When not supplying its wholesale customers (an "A" list of Houston restaurants), the bakery's bread can be found delivered fresh to places like Revival Market and Georgia's Market.

SPRINKLES

4014 WESTHEIMER *at Drexel*
☎ (713) 871-9929 | MAP **D6**
SPRINKLES.COM

SPRINKLES LITERALLY STARTED AN ENTIRE GENRE OF BAKED goods: the fancy cupcake. The posh Los Angeles-based business began the trend-turned-norm in its home state before spreading its icing-coated tentacles to a tiny storefront in Highland Village. Well-heeled shoppers stop in for a sweet treat pick-me-up after exhausting themselves browsing the racks of designer clothing and accessories in nearby shops. Just like the steady stream of customers rotating in and out holding their beautifully decorated cupcakes, the flavors also rotate with options like Belgian chocolate, Madagascar Bourbon Vanilla, ginger lemon or chai latte. Mainstays like dark chocolate and red velvet always grace the menu.

STONE MILL BAKERS

2518 KIRBY *at Westheimer*
☎ (713) 524-6600 | MAP **E6**
multiple locations
STONEMILLBAKERS.COM

STONE MILL BAKERS DOESN'T PLAY AROUND WHEN IT COMES to the ingredients that go into its breads. In fact, the shop grinds its own wheat, and no bread—aside from the jalapeño cornbread, which has a bit of butter in it—has any added fats, oils or preservatives. When not grinding away, the bakers are mixing up dough, letting it rise and making the signature round loaves of old-fashioned white, cinnamon raisin walnut, whole wheat sourdough, honey whole wheat, Dakota bread, seeded rye, Texas herb and the aforementioned cornbread,

all of which are available daily. For all the other varieties, there's a bread schedule, with different loaves available on different days of the week. (Thursdays are made much more exciting with a loaf of cheddar parmesan.) Sandwiches are also available, with the unique and harmoniously sweet-savory curried chicken salad on cinnamon raisin walnut bread being one of the best in its class.

SWEET

801 TOWN & COUNTRY BLVD.
in CityCentre
☎ (713) 647-9338 | MAP **B6**
SWEETHOUSTON.COM

YOU REALLY CAN'T GO WRONG AT THIS SMALL, TIDY SHOP IN CityCentre. The rotating menu features cupcakes in both traditional and adventurous flavors that simultaneously have a moist texture and avoid the trap of being too sweet. Macarons are similarly appealing and run the gamut from traditional fruit flavors to s'mores. Add properly made Greenway coffee and Sweet becomes the perfect respite to a shopping adventure or a destination in its own right.

TAKE THE CAKE

5424 HWY. 6 N
at Timber Creek Place Ln.
☎ (281) 550-8448 | MAP **B9**
HOUSTONTAKETHECAKE.COM

OWNER/PASTRY CHEF ANABEL TRUDEAU WENT TRAIPSING ALL around Europe after graduating from the Culinary Institute of America making fancy desserts inside Michelin-rated hotels. Coming full circle, she eventually realized her true calling was one of entrepreneurship and American-style layer cakes.

So in 1991, Take the Cake was born here in Houston. The hummingbird cake is renowned across the city, being hand-mixed and made with bananas, pineapples and cinnamon and perfectly iced with pecan cream cheese frosting. There are 15 additional flavors available for custom orders as well as cheesecakes, pies and tarts.

THREE BROTHERS BAKERY

4036 S. BRAESWOOD
at Stella Link
☎ (713) 666-2253 | MAP **D8**
multiple locations
3BROTHERSBAKERY.COM

FOR HOUSTON'S JEWISH COMMUNITY, THREE BROTHERS' breads, pastries, cookies and cakes are an essential element to any celebration. From bar mitzvahs to bridal showers, it simply wouldn't be an occasion without rye bread, challah or the chocolate-dipped ladyfinger cookies. Many items are *pareve* (dairy-free), and the bakery is certified kosher. Even Gentiles will enjoy the whimsically decorated icing-topped cookies or a chocolate pecan Danish. Bringing a checkerboard cake to a family gathering will make your loved ones *verklempt*.

TIFF'S TREATS

3800 SOUTHWEST FWY. (HWY. 59)
between Edloe & Weslayan
☎ (832) 232-5200 | MAP **D7**
multiple locations
COOKIEDELIVERY.COM

THERE'S A TIME IN EVERY PERSON'S LIFE WHERE THEY simply need to experience a fresh-baked, still-warm, straight-out-of-the-oven chocolate chip cookie. Enter Tiff's Treats: a genius concept that has itself just freshly arrived in Houston straight from the bosom of Austin. Tiff's supplies freshly baked cookies of all sorts—though the chocolate chip is the favorite—to those who stop by to purchase them at one of three Houston locations. Just call ahead 30 minutes so they can bake those lovelies. More important, though, is Tiff's delivery service, which allows for those freshly baked cookies to come directly to you, still somehow magically warm and incredibly good. Don't forget the milk (they'll deliver that, too).

ZEYAD BAKERY & SWEETS

8261 RICHMOND *at Dunvale*
☎ (281) 564-1120 | MAP **C7**
ZEYADBAKERYANDSWEETS.COM

THIS MIDDLE EASTERN BAKERY AND "PIZZA" SHOP LOOKS, smells and sounds just as you might imagine—the scent of dough and enticing meat waft outside through the little pergola as you enter. Through the door, you immediately spot a small selection of pantry basics, such as rice, dried herbs, spices and pickled vegetables. Then you see the packages of bread and pita and trays of desserts. The baklava is fantastic, but we most love the little pita-bread pizzas called *manakish*, which are about $2.50 each. Much of the city's Middle Eastern population regularly comes here for bread and pastries.

COFFEEHOUSES & TEA SHOPS

AGORA

1712 WESTHEIMER *at Park*
☎ (713) 526-7212 | MAP **E6**
AGORAHOUSTON.COM

WITH JUST THE RIGHT MIX OF YOUNG HIPSTERS LISTENING to the latest indie bands on their iPods whilst sipping coffees and older Greek men sprawling out on the patio during mild weather, Agora is the ultimate in lounging. With plenty of "perfect spots" and cozy nooks, whether upstairs, downstairs or on the wooden outdoor deck, there's always a fluid crowd partaking in various activities. Meetings over pastries and wine, solo writers penning the great American novel, couples snuggled up in the inviting corner table or the random dude reading *War and Peace* with an imported bottle of beer alongside a plate of Greek cheeses, this creaky, converted house welcomes all walks of life and all manner of activity.

ANTIDOTE COFFEE

729 STUDEWOOD *at 8th St.*
☎ (713) 861-7400 | MAP **E5**

BRINGING A BIT OF CREATIVE JUICES OF THE CAFFEINATED sort to The Heights is Antidote Coffee. With potent drip coffee and all manner of barista-made drinks, including a much raved-about *cajeta latte* made with Texas goat's milk caramel, patrons come as much for the drinks as they do the free WiFi and multiple electrical outlets. Taking the coffee shop out of the stereotypical shadows are large windows that let in lots of natural light and vintage furniture that's actually comfortable. Snacks are well sourced with cheese plates from Houston Dairymaids, baked goods from Michael's Cookie Jar and even some vegan options

that include tamales. Additional creative juices include beer and wine, which are included in a generous daily happy hour. Drawbacks are a lack of parking spaces and over-crowding during peak hours, but a small patio helps expand the capacity during decent weather.

BLACK HOLE COFFEE HOUSE

4504 GRAUSTARK *at Castle Court*
☎ (713) 528-0653 | MAP **E7**

HIDDEN AWAY IN A NEIGHBOR-HOOD STRIP CENTER, BLACK Hole, owned by the same group as Antidote, offers a secluded spot for the student-heavy crowd that can typically be found here working quietly on their computers. There's a full range of coffee options, including the highly addictive *cajeta latte*. As with Antidote, Black Hole serves a small food menu and a full range of desserts: cupcakes, cookies, full-size cake slices, etc. There's even ice cream from the recently launched Whipped and Licked line. For those who aren't trying to finish a paper, the couches and adjacent patio pro-vide comfortable spots for catching up with friends, and the availability of beer and wine makes it as solid a spot to finish a night as it is to start a morning.

BLACKSMITH

1018 WESTHEIMER *at Yoakum*
☎ (832) 360-7470 | MAP **E6**

GREENWAY COFFEE OWNERS DAVID BUEHRER AND ECKY Prabanto partnered with The Clumsy Butcher group to launch this coffee shop in the space formerly occupied by Mary's. The iconic gay bar has been completely transformed, with large front windows that provide

Second floor seating in Agora

lots of light and a small adjacent patio that's a fun spot in temperate weather. Baristas here are among the best in the city, which means that lattes and flat whites made with the house-roasted beans always feature cool art in the milk foam. Blacksmith makes its own syrups and almond milk, showing a dedication to craft that's unusual even among top-level coffeehouses. Chef Erin Smith's food menu helps set Blacksmith apart from its competition, elevating it from a simple coffeehouse to a truly useful breakfast and lunch cafe. Once a month, the shop stays open late on a Sunday for intriguing pop-ups that have showcased some of China-town's best restaurants.

phenomenon of *boba*, or marble-sized, chewy tapioca pearls added to various drinks and smoothies, is not going anywhere. That's great news for Boba Zone, which puts those chewy boba into all sorts of liquids. Flavored iced teas, milk teas, slushies, smoothies, iced coffees and "snow smoothies" all have the option of adding boba. Though many are creamy, almost all of the blends are made with a dairy-free creamer rather than milk. Boba Zone also caters to the younger crowd with WiFi, later hours, shaved ice and savory snacks, which include crispy squid nuggets, popcorn chicken or beef, fried rice, chicken wings and other deep fried salty things.

BOBA ZONE
10613 BELLAIRE BLVD. *at Wilcrest*
☎ (281) 983-5700 | MAP **B7**
BOBAZONEDRINKS.COM

BOOMTOWN COFFEE
242 W. 19TH *between Yale & Rutland*
☎ (713) 862-7018 | MAP **E5**
BOOMTOWNCOFFEE.COM

THE ADDICTIVE AND SOME-
WHAT STRANGE—IF YOU'VE
never experienced it before—

STARTING OUT AS A SMALL-
BATCH COFFEE-ROASTING
operation, Boomtown eventually

COFFEEHOUSES & TEA SHOPS

spread its wings, took flight and built its permanent nest in the quaint area along W. 19th Street in The Heights. With house-roasted coffees available (they also service the wholesale market), vibrant art on the walls and some impressive latte art, it keeps guests happy on many fronts. Couches are available for snuggling or just casual lounging, but the tables are best when ordering things like the tasty breakfast tacos full of eggs, black beans and avocado. Typical pastries, breakfast sandwiches, quiche and other edibles are also available to please just about anyone when it comes to the most important meal of the day. Free WiFi and friendly service just add to the appeal.

CAFE LA TEA
9102 BELLAIRE BLVD.
near Ranchester
☎ (713) 988-3188 | MAP **C7**
CAFELATEA.COM

CAFE LA TEA IS A MODERN AMERICAN COFFEE SHOP with a Chinatown twist. That means there's a full range of coffee, tea and smoothie options. Comfortable furniture and free WiFi make it a popular spot for students to study or for couples to finish a date. In addition to pastries and frozen yogurt, Cafe La Tea has a full menu of Chinese food and pastas. The house pork chop garnished with pickled mustard greens is top notch and comes with unlimited coffee at lunch. Prices may seem slightly high for the neighborhood, but generous portions offer solid value.

CATALINA COFFEE
2201 WASHINGTON *east of Sawyer*
☎ (713) 861-8448 | MAP **E6**
CATALINACOFFEESHOP.COM

ONE OF THE FIRST IN A WAVE OF HOUSE-ROASTED COFFEE purveyors, Catalina Coffee was also one of the first to brave the early gentrification of Washington Avenue. Both gambles have paid off handsomely for owner and coffee roaster extraordinaire Max Gonzalez, who also sells his small-batch beans through Amaya Roasting Co. Among the best coffeehouses in the city in terms of quality and passion, Catalina is frequently crammed with people in search of a *Cubano* (espresso with sugar and half-and-half), *cortado* (espresso cut with milk) or *doppio* (espresso double shot). There are also loose-leaf teas, regular ol' cappuccinos, French presses and espresso available as well as fresh pastries delivered daily. With a seat at the window overlooking Washington Avenue, and a newspaper, croissant and *Cubano* at hand, Saturday has never looked so bright.

DIRK'S COFFEE
4005 MONTROSE *at Branard*
☎ (713) 526-1319 | MAP **E7**

DIRK'S QUIRKY MARQUEE QUOTATIONS (E.G. "SLEEP IS FOR the weak") are almost as admired as their interestingly named coffee drinks. Neither on the cusp of the handcrafted, house-roasted coffee movement nor apologetic for it, Dirk's is sandwiched somewhere between the wide appeal of Starbucks and the narrower focus of serious coffee obsessives. Recently adding free WiFi after pressure from customers, there are still some things that haven't changed much:

Ecky Prabanto and David Buehrer of Greenway Coffee

large pastries for sale, hit-or-miss booth seating that may or may not be clean from the person before and an oddly satisfying patio for Montrose traffic gazing. The service can waffle from surly to sweet, but what barista isn't known for having a little bit of attitude?

DOUBLE TROUBLE CAFFEINE & COCKTAILS

3622 MAIN *north of Alabama*
☎ (713) 874-0096 | MAP **E7**

THOUGH ITS NAME IMPLIES TWO GREAT THINGS, DOUBLE Trouble is actually a triple threat: coffee, cocktails and cute tiki throw-back decor. The origin of all Double Trouble's caffeinated concoctions is locally roasted Greenway coffee, and the origin of their cocktails is from the creativity of their multi-faceted baristas/bartenders who work double time making both coffees and cock-tails during shifts. Depending on your preferences, there's not much you can go wrong with here since the house-made cocktails are usually fairly priced and very tasty, as is the coffee. Live music and lively crowds make for fun lounging on a week-night or weekend with either—or both—poison(s).

FIOZA CAFE

9002 CHIMNEY ROCK
at Caversham
☎ (713) 729-8810 | MAP **D8**
FIOZA.COM

THIS SLIGHTLY-UNDER-THE-RADAR MEYERLAND COFFEE shop is quietly one of Houston's most reliable places for lattes, brewed coffee and milk tea. Craving a tea with tapioca balls but can't make it to Chinatown? Fioza's got you cov-ered. Fioza also offers a fun range of

sweet specialty lattes (e.g. chocolate covered cherry, mint mocha) that are satisfying desserts in their own right. In addition to better-than-expected pastries, there's a short, well-executed panini and deli-sandwich menu. It's a real hangout spot, and patrons frequently linger here playing board games and consuming generously sliced, high-quality cake.

GREENWAY COFFEE & TEA

5 GREENWAY PLAZA *at Richmond*
☎ (832) 382-3466 | MAP **D7**
GREENWAYCOFFEE.COM

ONE OF HOUSTON'S BEST COFFEE SHOPS CAN BE FOUND IN AN underground food court in Greenway Plaza. Yes, really. While the location can seem difficult to find the first time, if you enter the underground parking from the Highway 59 feeder road and park in the adjacent visitor parking (they validate), locating the shop is pretty straightforward. From this shop, owners David Buehrer and Ecky Prabanto launched a local coffee empire that now includes Blacksmith and other locations that serve their house-roasted coffee beans. Lattes always arrive topped with artistic designs and feature house-made syrups. The best part of being underground? Phone reception can be spotty, so it's a nice place to unplug and get a little respite during the workday.

INVERSION COFFEE HOUSE

1953 MONTROSE *at W. Gray*
☎ (713) 523-4866 | MAP **E6**
INVERSIONCOFFEE.COM

SILENCE YOUR CELL PHONES AND TIPTOE INTO INVERSION so as not to disturb the library level of quiet that is so often found here, especially on weekdays. The shot-gun-style coffeehouse is adjacent to the Art League of Houston and plays host to many a student or worker silently typing or studying away at their computers. You will find them sipping barista-pulled coffees, drip coffee from local roaster Katz Coffee or something on the sweeter side like the "Honey Badger" (espresso flavored with cinnamon and honey). Things do tend to pep up around lunchtime or evenings, especially when a food truck (often Bernie's Burger Bus or another popular vendor) is parked outside. The symbiosis works best when patrons buy liquid refreshments inside Inversion, allowing them a table inside as well as air conditioning to chow down on food truck fare.

JAVA COFFEE & TEA CO.

2727 FONDREN *at Westheimer*
☎ (713) 974-0443 | MAP **C7**
JAVACOFFEE.COM

AT THIS STOREFRONT WEST OF THE GALLERIA, JAVA OFFERS consumers the chance to purchase beans that are typically sold to large, wholesale accounts. For more than 30 years, Bill Lawder's business has acquired and roasted beans from around the world. It's where the coffee novice can begin to understand what "wet processed" and shade-grown really mean for his morning cup of joe or where the aficionado can pick up that rare bag of Tanzanian Peaberry. A variety of teas are also in stock, and a number of sample blends are brewed each day for taste testing.

KATZ COFFEE

1003 W. 34TH *west of Shepherd*
☎ (713) 864-3338 | MAP **E5**
KATZCOFFEE.COM

YOU MAY HAVE BEEN DRINKING KATZ COFFEE AT YOUR FAVORITE restaurant for years and never known. A small-batch custom roaster located in The Heights, Avi Katz has been supplying Houstonians—through restaurants, grocery stores and more—since 2003. Before the local-is-better movement really took root and coffee-is-the-new-wine was a thing, Katz was working on finding beans that were Fair Trade Certi-fied, of which all the coffee sourced and roasted there is now. Always entrenched deeply in the community through partnerships, sampling or a presence at farmers' markets, Katz is known for their special blends often named after a charity their proceeds benefit. Bags of whole-bean coffee are available to the public through the online store as well as Whole Foods and Central Market.

MINUTI COFFEE

909 TEXAS *at Main*
☎ (713) 226-7500 | MAP **F6**
MINUTICOFFEE.COM

SURPRISING OR NOT, THERE'S A LACK OF DECENT INDEPEN-dently owned coffee establishments in downtown Houston. Minuti is a welcome oasis in this coffee desert, splashed in a chic red-and-black color scheme with sleek, modern furnishings. Italian-inspired with Molinari brand beans sourced from Modena, drinks range from the clas-sic dark espresso shots to the odd-sounding "Shakerato," "Ice-O" and "Creamicinos." The cheesy names are forgivable enough, however, as you find yourself sitting on the ample

COFFEEHOUSES & TEA SHOPS

patio in a beautiful part of downtown sipping a latte or glass of wine, enjoying a house-made pastry, listening to live music and soaking in the energy of city life.

THE PATH OF TEA

2340 W. ALABAMA
just east of Kirby
☎ (713) 252-4473 | MAP **E7**
THEPATHOFTEA.COM

LIKE MOST "HIDDEN" GEMS IN HOUSTON, THE PATH OF TEA is in plain sight in a strip mall. The small store is stocked with exclusively organic loose teas from caffeine-free rooibos chai to heavy-hitting Scottish breakfast tea. Founder and tea master Thia McKann passed away recently, but the shop's commitment to providing Houstonians with a huge variety of organic teas continues on. Thia's widower, Chris, continues to offer tea tastings and classes several times a month, carrying on the legacy of education his wife had been so passionate about. Brewed teas are also available for consumption at a few tables inside, which can be great for intimate conversations or a refreshing change-up for remote officing from the coffeehouses stuffed with hipsters and angry baristas.

PEARLAND COFFEE ROASTERS

4106 W. BROADWAY *between the railroad tracks & S. Texas, Pearland*
☎ (281) 485-6670
PEARLANDCOFFEEROASTERS.COM

AS ITS NAME SUGGESTS, PEARLAND COFFEE ROASTERS roasts its own coffee. But it also serves it in brewed forms to those that visit the coffeehouse in Pearland. The most sophisticated coffee served in

Pearland, and perhaps some of the most sophisticated coffee served in the greater Houston area, can be found here along with specialty Fat Cat Creamery ice cream selections, Rise cupcakes and baked goods from local businesses. The owners love gadgetry in all forms, which shows on the website, where house-roasted coffee is sold alongside fancy grinders, Chemex coffee makers and even a specialized scale for those who value precision in their home brewing techniques.

SALENTO

2407 RICE BLVD. *at Morningside*
☎ (713) 528-7478 | MAP **E7**
SALENTOWINECAFE.COM

PART OF RICE VILLAGE'S APPEAL AS A WALKABLE SHOPPING destination is cafes like Salento where one can pop in for a coffee, quick bite or glass of wine. Free WiFi makes it popular with Rice students, who can make finding a seat difficult at peak times. There's a full range of breakfast items and also sandwiches, salads and shareable apps that are perfect for later in the day. During the daily happy hour, mini pizzas and house wines are discounted. Weekly live music and tango draws a cosmopolitan crowd.

SOUTHSIDE ESPRESSO

904 WESTHEIMER *just east of Montrose*
☎ (713) 942-9990 | MAP **E6**
SOUTHSIDEESPRESSO.COM

LOCATED NEXT TO UCHI, SOUTHSIDE PACKS A LOT OF OPTIONS into its small space. There are usually three or four types of beans available, all of which are roasted by owner Sean Marshall. The staff takes its lead from Marshall's friendly demeanor and can always answer questions about what each bean tastes like. Food options include treats from Fluff Bake Bar, and pastry chef Rebecca Masson hosts a monthly pop-up with limited batches of specialty baked goods and pastries. A well-chosen list of beers and wines by the glass makes it a solid after-dinner spot, too. For those with a little time to spare, the slightly hidden upstairs patio offers a nice view down Westheimer.

STAR SNOW ICE #1
9188 BELLAIRE BLVD.
between S. Gessner & Ranchester
☎ (713) 988-8028 | MAP **C7**

(see next)

STAR SNOW ICE & TERIYAKI
9889 BELLAIRE BLVD. *at W. Sam Houston Pkwy. S. (Beltway 8)*
☎ (713) 779-8886 | MAP **B7**

STAR SNOW ICE SERVES TREATS MADE WITH SHAVED ICE TOPPED with fresh fruit, lychee jelly, mango pudding or almost anything else you can imagine that makes it the perfect place to seek respite on a hot day. In addition to desserts, staples like milk tea with tapioca are excellent but for a little adventure try adding the egg pudding. The second location (with "& Teriyaki" in the name) also has a full lunch menu with cheap and delicious Taiwanese dishes, including fried silken tofu cubes and a generous fried pork chop with a fried egg and bok choy. Lines are often out the door at both locations. Cash only.

TAFT STREET COFFEE
2115 TAFT *at Welch*
☎ (713) 522-3533 | MAP **E6**
TAFTSTREETCOFFEE.ORG

IS IT A COFFEE SHOP ATTACHED TO A CHURCH OR A CHURCH attached to a coffee shop? From any perspective, the two are definitely intertwined. Taft Street is literally and figuratively attached to Ecclesia Church in Montrose, a non-denominational, contemporary Christian church, though it's mostly just a coffeehouse for the community that happens to be convenient for churchgoers. Inside is an art gallery, lots of open space and free WiFi along with drip coffees, espresso, lattes and other caffeine fixes that are all certified as Fair Trade Organic. As for food, there's a small menu of baked goods, pizzas and sandwiches that get good reviews, though depending on the day and the mood of the staff, there is also the slight possibility of proselytizing.

TAPIOCA HOUSE
9104 BELLAIRE BLVD.
between S. Gessner & Ranchester
☎ (713) 272-6468 | MAP **C7**

TAPIOCA HOUSE SETS ITSELF APART FROM OTHER CHINA-town bubble tea spots with the ability to add multiple enhancements to your drink and an addictive food menu. Drinks can be doctored with tapioca, of course, but also with jellies and gusher-style fruit snacks. There's a full range of drink options: cold and hot, coffee and tea, juices and smoothies. The Taiwanese-style chicken nuggets are a house specialty and highly recommended.

COFFEEHOUSES & TEA SHOPS

TÉ HOUSE OF TEA
1927 FAIRVIEW *at Woodhead*
☎ (713) 522-8868 | MAP **E6**
TEHOUSEOFTEA.COM

IT'S COZY, CALM AND SERENE: PRETTY MUCH EVERYTHING you'd want in an off-the-beaten-path teahouse in Montrose. The added bonus here is that the tea is actually very good, too. Around 130 varieties of tea ranging from a pretty pink hibiscus mint to a smoked Earl Grey are available in different teapot sizes, and once the tea arrives at your table, you'll be instructed to let it steep properly. Té also makes its own version of chai with a pungent accent of fresh ginger and a rich creamy consistency totally unlike the pre-made sugar bombs served by most other coffee and teahouses. Weekend breakfast is lively, with couples and friends lined up for crêpes or Asian-influenced salads and rice bowls. By day, this tea house is usually full of quietly studying students or fervently working freelancers.

THE TEAHOUSE
2089 WESTHEIMER *at S. Shepherd*
☎ (713) 526-6123 | MAP **E6**
multiple locations
TEAHOUSEBEVERAGE.COM

FOR THOSE SEEKING A TAPIOCA-SPIKED BUBBLE TEA FIX, THIS local chain is pretty much the only option in the River Oaks area. The menu includes countless drink options from strawberry green tea to taro coconut cream blend along with plenty of sinker options beyond tapioca, like almond pudding and lychee gelatin. A simple black cream tea is a safe bet, but the vivid red cherry ice blend is tempting on hot days, and there are also more authentically Taiwanese flavors, such as longan and red bean. Board games are available if you want to make a night out of it.

Hot tea served at Té House of Tea

FOOD TRUCKS

BANSURI INDIAN FOOD CORNER

LOCATION: 11468 S. WILCREST
outside Southwest Grill & Light
HOURS: *6:30-9 pm Monday through Thursday and until 9:30 pm Friday & Saturday*
☎ (713) 624-2009
BANSURIFOOD.COM

THE AFFABLE OPERATORS OF BANSURI ARE USED TO explaining the contents of their signature dishes like *dabeli* and *ragda* (we'll get to that later) to those curious enough to stop by and ask. After all, they've been selling vegetarian Mumbai street food known as *chaat* out of this truck since 2009. As promised: *Dabeli* is a popular dish here, consisting of two "Indian sliders" of spicy potato patties infused with pomegranate seeds and peanuts on sweet and buttery toasted buns. The stew-like *ragda* is a bowl of two potato patties nestled in a hearty broth of white peas, rice, onion chutney, mint-coriander chutney and date-tamarind chutney. Be warned that Bansuri's notion of "spicy" may not match up with yours. We suggest you try "medium" first and gradually work your way up. Hours are limited to evenings so don't plan on stopping by for lunch.

BERNIE'S BURGER BUS

TWITTER: @BERNIESBURGERS
FACEBOOK: /BERNIESBURGERS
HOURS AND LOCATIONS: *Check the website and Twitter/Facebook*
☎ (281) 386-2447
BERNIESBURGERBUS.COM

WHAT MAKES BERNIE'S BURGER BUS SO MAGICAL? THERE'S the fresh-ground, organic, grass-fed beef that goes into every patty. Then there are the homemade condiments —the ketchup is an experience unto itself. Or perhaps the fresh, local buns are what sprinkle that bit of pixie dust around. Even the hand-cut French fries leave nothing more to desire. Add to that line-up the fun school-themed names, and it's a winning formula. Traditionalists will want the "Principal": a classic burger topped with mayonnaise, mustard, ketchup, pickles, onions, shredded lettuce and roasted garlic tomatoes. Need to spruce it up? Add an "elective" like Texas cheddar, bacon or Bernie's caramelized "tipsy" onions for an additional price. There's so much magic in those buses that Bernie's is now up to three, serving all over the city and suburbs.

CHOCOLAT D'ARTE

TWITTER: @CHOCOLATDARTE
FACEBOOK: /CHOCOLATDARTE
HOURS AND LOCATIONS: *Check Twitter/Facebook*
☎ (281) 989-6464
CHOCOLATDARTE.COM

CHOCOLAT D'ARTE'S FOOD TRUCK IS A MERGING OF two worlds: The world of casual food truck service and fancy handcrafted chocolates. Bringing jewel-like creations to the masses from her air-conditioned, artfully-wrapped, custom van (not unlike an elegant ice cream truck), owner Nancy Burke is found sporadically at various events and locations around town. Her truffle and bonbon flavors are always fascinating with ingredients like violet, blueberries, goat cheese and anything else Burke thinks will combine well with quality chocolate. More snack-y things like dipped Oreos, pretzel rods and potato chips are also available depending on the occasion and season.

Top: Bansuri Indian Food Corner, Bottom: Coreanos

COREANOS

TWITTER: @COREANOSHTX
FACEBOOK: /COREANOSHOUSTON
HOURS AND LOCATIONS:
Check Twitter/Facebook
COREANOSTX.COM

WHILE INTUITIVELY IT MAKES SENSE THAT Mexican-Korean fusion would be delicious, it still takes a bit of convincing. And convince us Austin-based Coreanos food truck did with standards like their OG burrito stuffed with short ribs, French fries, slaw, cilantro, kimchi, sesame vinaigrette and garlic spread. The ubiquitous kim cheese fries have already stolen hearts with toppings of pork belly, caramelized kimchi, cheese and hot sauce along with their simpler tacos finished with a drizzle of sesame vinaigrette.

EL ULTIMO TACO TRUCK

LOCATION: 7403 LONG POINT
at Antoine
HOURS: *8 am-10 pm Monday through Friday and until midnight Saturday*

NOT AMONG THE "NEW WAVE" OF FOOD TRUCKS TO EMERGE in recent years, El Ultimo is one of the original standbys for mobile eating. Considered by some to be the best taco truck in the Long Point area—and some go as far as to say the entire city of Houston—its secret is simplicity and food made to order. Moist chicken tacos are garnished with sautéed onions and poblano peppers, cilantro and queso fresco; barbacoa, with its rich, fatty shreds of meat, comes with caramelized onions and cilantro; beef fajita tacos are topped with a creamy slice of avo-cado for extra oomph. Many also trek here for the selection of offal tacos, which include *cabeza* (head), *tripa* (tripe) and *mollejas* (sweetbreads).

FLIP 'N PATTIES

TWITTER: @FLIPNPATTIES
FACEBOOK: /FLIPNPATTIES
HOURS AND LOCATIONS: *Check the website and Twitter/Facebook*
☎ (832) 409-7580
FLIPNPATTIES.COM

IF THERE WERE ONE WORD TO DESCRIBE FLIP 'N PATTIES, IT would be diverse. Not only does their cuisine combine Filipino and American, but it also utilizes mostly local, organic, humanely-raised meats in dishes like the *siopao*, a soft steamed bun filled with a savory mixture of pork or chicken. There's also an addictive fried chicken *pupu* smothered in a secret sauce that's sweet, sticky and salty all at once, made with free-range chicken. For fusion, there are grass-fed beef burgers served on steamed buns and topped with a spicy signature sauce and other variants that include Spam and pork. As if that weren't enough, Flip 'n Patties also boasts a karaoke machine on board for those brave enough to belt it out for a well-rounded, truly one-of-a-kind experience.

GOLDEN GRILL

TWITTER: @GOLDENGRILLHTX
FACEBOOK: /THEGOLDENGRILL
HOURS AND LOCATIONS: *Check the website and Twitter/Facebook*
☎ (602) 321-0423
GOLDENGRILLHTX.COM

ALL MANNER OF GRIDDLED SANDWICHES CAN BE FOUND here. Combinations include buffalo chicken, cheddar, garlic ranch and sourdough on the "Buff Chic," or prosciutto, American cheese, jalapeño jam and sourdough for "The Hamlin." However, the most popular item on this truck is their build-your-own grilled cheese, which will go as far as your imagination (and pocketbook, since all toppings are priced a la carte) can take you. Choose from six different cheeses, two different breads and 15 different add-ons, which can include bacon jam, arugula, kimchi or pickled onions. There's even a side of tomato soup for those who dip.

HAPPY ENDINGS
TWITTER: @HAPPYENDINGSHTX
FACEBOOK: /HAPPYENDINGSHTX
HOURS AND LOCATIONS:
Check Twitter/Facebook
HAPPYENDINGSHTX.COM

CHEEKY NAMES ABOUND IN THE WORLD OF FOOD TRUCKS, and Happy Endings follows suit. We'll leave its interpretation up to you, but we will say the toppings on their hot dogs are very happy indeed. Most are Asian-inspired and include an array of umami in things like Japanese mayo, seaweed, *bonito* (smoked, dried fish) flakes that can blow away in a nice breeze if you're not careful, kimchi, *katsu* sauce and more. Recently added to their line-up: bao-style tacos, steamed buns filled with shrimp tempura, Thai chili sauce and eggrolls. Barbecue pork bao is also on the menu and mighty satisfying after a few pints of cold beer.

H-TOWN STREATS
TWITTER: @HTOWNSTREATS
FACEBOOK: /HTOWNSTREATS
HOURS AND LOCATIONS:
Check Twitter/Facebook
☎ (832) 605-2009

HALF THE FUN OF HUNTING DOWN H-TOWN STREATS

is finding out what they're serving that particular day. The menu is never set and changes seasonally or upon the whims of chefs/co-owners Jason Hill and Matt Opaleski who aim to serve "soul-satisfying, globally-inspired street food." While some items may come and go, there are categories in which most dishes fall: balls (usually fried and served with a sauce), tacos, sandwiches, burgers and desserts. Items past have included creamy, decadent risotto balls with tomato jam; macaroni and short rib grilled cheese; barbecue pork tacos with pineapple pico; bacon-wrapped hot dogs with kimchi; whoopie pies and brownies of every kind. It's like fast food on steroids but made with better ingredients and prepared by chefs—all from inside a little truck adorned with strangely endearing cartoon illustrations.

IT'S A WRAP
TWITTER: @ITSAWRAPTRUCK
FACEBOOK: /ITSAWRAPTRUCK
HOURS AND LOCATIONS:
Check Twitter/Facebook
☎ (713) 307-5403

WHAT'S IN A NAME? WELL, FOR THIS FOOD TRUCK, almost everything. Selling wraps of all sizes and ingredients—which mostly include ethnically diverse fillings like chicken tikka masala, Thai steak and falafel—it's not as wild or "out there" as other food trucks, but it's consistently spotted around town catering to the hungry masses nonetheless. After all, there are only so many crazy hot dogs one can eat in a given week. Aside from the namesake wraps, the truck also dabbles in some fried goodness (as any self-respecting food truck should) that includes macaroni and cheese balls.

FOOD TRUCKS

JARRO CAFE

LOCATION: 1521 GESSNER
near Long Point
HOURS: *8 am-11 pm Monday
through Thursday and until
midnight Friday & Saturday*
☎ (713) 365-0373
JARROCAFE.COM

CURIOUSLY SITUATED IN THE
PARKING LOT OF A RESTAURANT
bearing the same name, this taco
trailer acts more as an expedited
to-go arm of the cafe than a mobile
truck. Serving all of the same tacos
that exist on the cafe's expanded
menu inside the actual building,
there's *bistec* (beef), *carnitas* (roasted,
shredded seasoned pork), *campechano*
(beef and chorizo), *cochinita pibil*
(slow-roasted pork) and more—all
cheaper than you'd find inside. Part
of the appeal here is trying out all
of the salsas, which range from
mild and fruity to lip-melting, all
made from an abundance and
variety of chilies.

KOAGIE HOTS

TWITTER: @KOAGIEHOTS
FACEBOOK: /KOAGIEHOTS
HOURS AND LOCATIONS:
*Check the website and Twitter/
Facebook*
☎ (602) 321-0423
KOAGIEHOTS.COM

IF THERE WERE AN UNDERLYING
THEME TO THE HOUSTON FOOD
truck scene, it very well might be
kimchi. And so it is with Koagie Hots
that this theme continues. Korean-
influenced junk food is this truck's
specialty, with several variations on

Mélange Crêperie

the cheesesteak as well as the hot dog, and yes, most contain some form of kimchi—from an infused mayo to the traditional fermented cabbage condiment on its own. The korndog is worth every calorie as are the Koagie fries, topped with Korean barbecued ribeye, scallions and the so-wrong-it's-right Cheese Wiz.

L'ES-CAR-GO

TWITTER: @LES_CAR_GO
FACEBOOK: /LESCARGOINC
HOURS AND LOCATIONS:
Check Twitter/Facebook
☎ (281) 256-5791
LES-CAR-GO.COM

PROVING THERE IS APPROACH-ABLE FRENCH FOOD FOR THE masses are Jean-Philippe and Genevieve Guy, owners of Bistro Provence, a long-standing brick-and-mortar restaurant in the Memorial area. In the cleverly named L'es-Car-Go, you'll find dishes like snails gone wild, aka escargot poppers doused in hot wing sauce, salad Niçoise, *cuisse de grenouille* (frog legs), soups and salads. French snootiness be damned, this is just good food that happens to be served from a truck.

MAM'S HOUSE OF ICE

TWITTER: @MAMSHOUSEOFICE
FACEBOOK: /MAMSHOUSEOFICE
LOCATION: *Corner of 20th and Rutland, in The Heights*
HOURS: *Seasonal, 1-7 pm Wednesday through Sunday, check Twitter/ Facebook before visiting*
MAMSHOUSEOFICE.COM

MOVE OVER CRUNCHY SNOW CONES: THIS SEASONAL NEW Orleans-style sno-ball stand is ready to freeze the competition. Mam's serves up cups of fluffy "snow" drenched with syrup, and it has

amassed a loyal following over the years. Always parked in an empty lot in The Heights, Mam's doesn't offer many comfortable spots to sit or loiter, except at one of the few grotty picnic tables. Sno-ball flavors include Tiger's Blood (berries and coconut), wedding cake, watermelon and cotton candy as well as Creole cream cheese, *dulce de leche* and Cajun red hot, and it's always hard to decide. Taking it up a notch are optional toppings like gummy bears, condensed milk or even a scoop of ice cream.

MÉLANGE CRÊPERIE

TWITTER: @MELANGECREPERIE
FACEBOOK: /MELANGE.CREPERIE
LOCATION: *Corner of Westheimer and Taft, outside Mango's Cafe*
HOURS: *7 am-1 pm Thursday, Friday & Monday; 10 am-2 pm Saturday & Sunday*
☎ (713) 291-9933
MELANGECREPERIE.COM

IT'S THE TYPICAL LOVE STORY: BOY MEETS GIRL, THEY FALL IN LOVE, get married, go to Paris on their honeymoon and come back to Texas to open a street corner crêpe stand. Okay, maybe not typical but impassioned for sure. That passion for great crêpes shines through in founder Sean Carroll's made-to-order combinations, which range from Nutella and bananas to curried carrots (though not in the same crêpe, of course). With almost a constant queue—especially around peak weekend breakfast hours—guests wait with a peaceful patience as they watch the methodical technique of crêpe-making on the traditional griddles before being smeared and stuffed with the freshest of ingredients. Expertly folded into perfect little portable pockets,

FOOD TRUCKS

they're then handed off before the whole process starts all over again.

MUIISHI MAKIRRITOS

TWITTER: @MUIISHITRUCK
FACEBOOK: /MUIISHIMAKIRRITOS
HOURS AND LOCATIONS:
Check Twitter/Facebook
☎ (832) 868-6777
MUIISHIMAKIRRITOS.COM

SOME FOOD TRUCKS ARE TAKING MACARONI AND CHEESE TO A whole new level by forming it into a ball and deep-frying it. Muiishi Makirritos ups the ante by making macaroni and cheese from scratch (with Dairymaids' sourced cheeses, no less), adding bacon and ground beef to it and stuffing it inside an eggroll. Unafraid to go where others haven't, Muiishi founder Matthew Mui (previously at Soma Sushi) also makes a variety of _nori_ (seaweed) rolls with ingredients like sous-vide pork belly, grilled oyster mushrooms and avocado. More substantial entree-like dishes are surprisingly gourmet, such as the "pork belly Don Juan" with its sous-vide pork belly, soft-boiled egg, kimchi, oyster and shiitake mushrooms, pickled cucumbers and pickled daikon.

PAPOU JERRY'S

TWITTER: @PAPOUJERRYS
FACEBOOK: /PAPOUJERRY
LOCATION: WEST ALABAMA ICE
HOUSE, 1919 W. ALABAMA
HOURS:_Opens daily at 11 am, check Facebook for nightly closings_
☎ (713) 253-0432

THERE WAS A SMALL REVOLT WHEN PAPOU JERRY'S MOVED INTO Tacos Tierra Caliente's usual spot at the West Alabama Ice House, but things have since quieted down. Partially because Tacos Tierra

Caliente moved to a spot just across the street and is still close enough for loyal patrons to get their taco fix and partially because Papou Jerry's serves something altogether different. Gyros, fries, salads and pizzas are the stars of this Greek truck, where icehouse patrons meander for a meal to soak up all the suds. The pizza and the gyros are both amply portioned but can get a little messy. Luckily, the outdoor environment is most forgiving.

PHAMILY BITES

TWITTER: @PHAMILYBITES
FACEBOOK: /PHAMILYBITES
HOURS AND LOCATIONS:
Check Twitter/Facebook
☎ (832) 598-8746
PHAMILYBITES.COM

PHAMILY BITES SERVES VIETNAMESE FOOD WITH ATTITUDE, WITH a touch of Hawaiian thrown in for good measure. As for the latter, the _musubi_—a popular snack in Hawaii that is similar to sushi with rice on the bottom, usually Spam on top and wrapped together with a band of seaweed—is popular here and in variations that include egg and spicy sauce additions. But most folks come for the Vietnamese grub like cups of pho, that delicious and fragrant broth-based noodle soup, or banh mi sandwiches stuffed with lemongrass tofu, pork or Chinese sausage and egg. The Vandalizer is also a popular choice and features savory filet mignon chunks served on a baguette with Vietnamese mayonnaise, pickled red onions, watercress and jalapeños.

The Rice Box

PI PIZZA

TWITTER: @PIPIZZATRUCK
FACEBOOK: /PI.PIZZATRUCK
HOURS AND LOCATIONS:
Check Twitter/Facebook
☎ (832) 513-9453
PIPIZZATRUCK.COM

FEW TRUCKS IN HOUSTON UNDER-
STAND THEIR AUDIENCE BETTER
than Pi Pizza Truck: The Four Twenty
slice is a stoner's dream topped with
Chili Cheese Fritos. And to celebrate
its one-year anniversary, the truck
offered free slices for life to anyone
who got a Pi-themed tattoo. Yet,
there's nothing gimmicky about the
pizzas, which feature freshly made
dough and quality ingredients such
as sopressata, fresh arugula and
some of the best meatballs anywhere
on a menu that rotates weekly. If
its frequent parking spot at Catbirds

is a little divey, that's just part of
the charm.

THE RICE BOX

TWITTER: @RICEBOXTRUCK
FACEBOOK: /RICEBOXTRUCK
HOURS AND LOCATIONS:
Check Twitter/Facebook
☎ (832) 643-7994
RICEBOXTRUCK.COM

WITH ITS BRIGHT RED PAINT
AND SHINY WHEELS, OWNER
John Peterson's ode to Chinese-
American food is among Houston's
best-looking trucks. The food consists
of well-executed versions of staples
such as General Tso chicken, Kung
Pao chicken and fried dumplings.
They can turn up the spiciness on
the dishes, which makes the sesame
chicken particularly craveable. Add
fried rice or a fried egg for a little

extra money. Even by food truck standards, service is always friendly, particularly when the crowds are lighter and Peterson has a chance to engage his customers in conversation. Don't pass up the fortune cookie.

ST. JOHN'S FIRE

TWITTER: @FIRETRUCKTX
FACEBOOK: ST. JOHN'S FIRE
HOURS AND LOCATIONS:
Check Twitter/Facebook
☎ (713) 502-1188
STJOHNSFIRE.NET

WITH A MENU THAT WOULD BEFIT ANY NEIGHBORHOOD bistro, St. John's Fire is igniting a whole lot of appetites around Houston. Chef Joel St. John's New Orleans background shines through in dishes like his Cajun eggrolls, which combine shrimp, crawfish, tasso, spinach, onions, peppers and celery, served with a guava mustard dipping sauce. It's not all Cajun food—note the pulled-pork sandwich, the hot and crunchy chicken sandwich (with bacon, brie and fig preserves) or the tortilla-crusted fish—but it is all satisfying. As seems to be the trend in the world of Houston food trucks, St. John's does its own version of fried macaroni and cheese, but St. John's Fire includes crawfish tails in the mix.

TACONMADRE

LOCATION: 905 EDGEBROOK
HOURS: *10 am-3 am Monday through Friday, 10 am-5 am Saturday & Sunday*
☎ (832) 875-9377
multiple locations
TACONMADRETAQUERIA.COM

THE CHEERY GREEN BUS IS THE FIRST INDICATION THAT YOUR meal will probably be fun, at least.

The enormity of the burritos is the second. After all, who doesn't need a giant burrito the size of a schnauzer once in a while to really, truly experience life in general? The menu also encompasses other street foods like Mexican hamburgers, *piratas* (tacos that are folded over and then toasted on a griddle), tortas, quesadillas, gorditas and sopes. Not all are as big as the burritos, but they are equally as fun (and tasty).

TACOS TIERRA CALIENTE

TWITTER: @TACOS_TAQUERIA
FACEBOOK: TACOS TIERRA CALIENTE
LOCATION: *Across the street from* WEST ALABAMA ICE HOUSE, 1919 W. ALABAMA
HOURS: *Opens daily at 9 am for breakfast tacos until 11 am, then lunch, dinner and late-night*
☎ (713) 584-9359

THERE WAS ALMOST A RIOT WHEN TACOS TIERRA CALIENTE MOVED from the parking lot of the West Alabama Ice House to the lot across the street, but in the Montrose-y spirit of tolerance and coexistence, things have calmed significantly. While Papou Jerry's took over the coveted icehouse location, true regulars have no problem walking briskly across the street for their cheap tacos and fiery hot sauces. Just a simple truck with quality street tacos like *barbacoa* (moist, shredded beef), *al pastor* (crispy chunks of pork with sautéed pineapple), beef and chicken, their strongest asset is usually tucked in between a soft, folded corn tortilla. All tacos come with raw onions and cilantro unless you request otherwise, and the homemade salsas are considered legendary by some fans. There are also other items available, such as tortas, but the real magnet is the tacos.

TANDOORI NITE DHABA

FACEBOOK: /TANDOORINITEDHABA
LOCATION: 7821 HWY. 6 SOUTH
between Bellaire & Beechnut
HOURS: *5 pm-midnight Wednesday*
through Monday. Closed Tuesday
☎ (713) 852-7642
TANDOORINITEDHABA.COM

PERHAPS IT SEEMS ODD THAT ONE OF HOUSTON'S MOST RELIABLE, reasonably priced Indian restaurants is a truck located in the parking lot of a rundown gas station in Alief. Perhaps it is surprising, but Tandoori Nite is a must-try dining destination for West Side residents. The namesake tandoori chicken is delicious, and the garlic bullet naan has an addictive, spicy kick. Add in well-executed staples like chicken tikka masala and a full range of vegetarian options, and there really is something for everybody. Plus, the truck's location outside the Houston city limits means it has permanent seating under a tent to offer customers some shade.

THIRD COAST STEAK SANDWICHES

TWITTER: @THIRDCOASTHTX
FACEBOOK:
/THIRD-COAST-STEAK-SANDWICHES
HOURS AND LOCATIONS: *Check*
Twitter/Facebook
☎ (832) 589-7868

ORIGINALLY THIS WAS KNOWN AS STICK IT TRUCK, FULL OF FOODS that—you guessed it—came impaled on tiny stakes. After realizing the concept was not optimal for late-night interactions, owner Ruth Lipsky decided to rebrand. This little red truck now makes steak sandwiches, but there's much more to your

The Waffle Bus

FOOD TRUCKS

decision than provolone or Cheez Whiz. The recently debuted menu includes steak sandwiches with global inspirations including Greek, Mexican (topped with chilaquiles) and Vietnamese (topped with basil, bean sprouts, jalapeño and hoisin sauce, plus actual pho for dipping à la French dip-style). All sandwiches come on Slow Dough bread, giving even more compelling reasons to try it out.

THE WAFFLE BUS

TWITTER: @THEWAFFLEBUS
FACEBOOK: /THEWAFFLEBUS
HOURS AND LOCATIONS:
Check Twitter/Facebook
☎ (832) 640-5494
THEWAFFLEBUS.COM

MAKE A GOOD WAFFLE, AND IT'S ALMOST IMPOSSIBLE TO FAIL. The purveyors of The Waffle Bus found that out early in the game and recently expanded to a fleet of two trucks after a very warm reception by the food truck-loving Houston community. With waffles that act as sandwiches or burger buns as well as vehicles for some sweet treats, there's variety enough to please the luncher or the in-between-meals-dessert-hunter and, of course, the after-a-few-drinks-snacker. Popular combos include the buttermilk-fried chicken and waffle, the smoked salmon waffle, waffle fries and the s'mores dessert that is rich enough to share. Who knew waffles could be so versatile?

WHAT'S UP CUPCAKE?

TWITTER: @WHATUPCUPCAKE
FACEBOOK:
/WHATSUPCUPCAKEHOUSTON
HOURS AND LOCATIONS:
Check Twitter/Facebook
☎ (832) 409-6931
WHATSUPCUPCAKE-HOUSTON.COM

JUST WHEN YOU THINK HOUSTON'S CUPCAKE MARKET CAN'T BE ANY more saturated, think again. (Not that it's a bad thing.) What's Up Cupcake? brings their own take to the tiny cake sensation in a 1954 silver trailer, usually parked somewhere in The Heights. Classics like vanilla bean, chocolate ganache, red velvet and strawberry can be found on the menu alongside more daring flavors like the orange dreamsicle (orange cupcake filled with vanilla cream topped with orange buttercream) or the chocolate chili mango. Try more than one by ordering a mini-cupcake or just sink your teeth into one of their regular sized beauties. Bonus: What's Up Cupcake? also serves New Orleans-style sno-balls in a myriad of flavors.

WINE, BEER & SPIRITS

BARS

ALICE'S TALL TEXAN
4904 N. MAIN *at Walling*
☎ (713) 862-0141 | MAP **E5**

Sometimes an old-fashioned Texas beer joint is the cure for what ails you. Between one of the best jukeboxes in all of Houston—spouting songs of heartbreak, Tejano and rocking oldies—and the schooners of Texas beer like Lone Star and Shiner Bock, Alice's Tall Texan is the cure-all for many. How else will you give your drinking arm a decent workout for the evening? On certain nights, the community-minded regulars gather with their crockpots, plug them in on a folding table and share in a neighborhood potluck. If you get lucky, they might even share with the newer folks (just offer to buy them a round as a polite reciprocation). As for Alice, she's around on certain nights, and it's highly likely she'll ask who you are if you've not been in before. Don't be intimidated, just roll with the introduction and order another schooner.

The bar in Anvil

ANVIL BAR & REFUGE

1424 WESTHEIMER
east of Mandell
☎ (713) 523-1622 | MAP **E6**
ANVILHOUSTON.COM

ANVIL BAR & REFUGE IS FEARED, RESPECTED, LOATHED, LOVED, worshipped and always watched by just about everyone in the local drinks industry. Setting off a firestorm in the way of artisanal cocktails, it set the bar not only locally but nationally with its approach to handcrafted drinks. Owner and founder Bobby Heugel has since become one of the most active advocates for the Houston food and beverage industry, but his original love of making a damn good drink lives on through his first-born, Anvil. Drinks here impress even the most jaded of cocktail lovers with original recipes like the Ethel Groves—a combination of gin, lemon, St. Germaine and thyme—or The Brave—always on the menu and a mixture of mezcal, sotol, amaro, curaçao and angostura bitters. There are the old standbys like Manhattans and negronis as well as a carefully curated beer and wine selection, but why not try something new and original while you're there? Pro tips: Don't call the mad-scientist bartenders "mixologists" or expect a quick drink during peak hours.

BAKER STREET PUB & GRILL

5510 MORNINGSIDE
north of University Blvd.
☎ (713) 942-9900 | MAP **E7**
multiple locations
SHERLOCKSPUBCO.COM

IT'S NOT FANCY, BUT IT'S NOT A DIVE. SOMEWHERE IN BETWEEN those two designations is Baker Street, family member in a national chain of English pub-style establishments catering to young professionals who enjoy low-priced happy-hour beverages, the occasional live band and decent pub food. The menu is nothing to write home about, but it gets the job done while attractive young waitresses and bartenders mix drinks, pour beers and smile for tips. Clientele at this Rice Village location consists largely of Rice University students, young professionals and Medical Center employees who often pay a much-needed visit after their shifts. It can get unruly on occasion, especially around St. Patrick's day, but those are the most interesting times to visit.

THE BIG EASY

5731 KIRBY *at Robinhood*
☎ (713) 523-9999 | MAP **E7**
THEBIGEASYBLUES.COM

THIS BARE BONES DIVE DOES NOT ATTRACT WITH SIGNAture cocktails, lounge-y tables or chic bathrooms. Its character lives in the shabbiness of pool tables, the grizzled regulars, the dark corners and most of all, the reputation for giving some of the best talent around a stage to perform. Genres cover mostly blues, rock or zydeco, and there's plenty of dance floor for all those inclined—which is usually enough to fill it up. Cover charges are typically relegated to the weekends, and there's a decent beer and liquor selection. Bathrooms can lean a little toward the unkempt side, and tables are often hard to come by if you don't get there early.

BIG JOHN'S ICE HOUSE

12640 BRIAR FOREST
west of S. Dairy Ashford
☎ (281) 497-3499 | MAP **A6**
BIGJOHNSICEHOUSE.COM

EVERY NEIGHBORHOOD NEEDS ITS ICEHOUSE, AND BIG JOHN'S fills the void in West Houston. Flanked in wooden railings, mismatched televisions and an older crowd that can range from Harley gangs (friendly ones) to empty nesters, this is definitely a laidback, relax-and-watch-the-game-with-a-bucket-of-beers kinda place. In addition to plenty of televisions to watch are theme nights that encompass trivia, live music, the ever-popular steak nights and poker lessons. The food menu is surprisingly extensive with decent Tex-Mex, sandwiches, typical wings and burgers. During crawfish season, weekends can get a little crazy as people order platters the size of manhole covers of the boiled mudbugs.

BLACK LABRADOR PUB

4100 MONTROSE *at W. Main*
☎ (713) 529-1199 | MAP **E7**
BLACKLABRADORPUB.COM

THERE'S NOTHING COZIER AND MORE ENGLISH THAN AN IVY-clad edifice. Conveniently located in such an ivy-clad edifice is English-themed Black Labrador Pub, which plays the part very well with its low ceilings, fireplace, worn wooden floors and even a giant chess set in the courtyard that would seem right at home in a Harry Potter book. While you won't find any butter beer or pumpkin juice here, there's plenty of drink in the form of Bass, Harp, Boddington's, Guinness, hot toddies and at least five variations on Irish coffee. Pub classics like bangers and mash, shepherd's pie and fish and

chips are popular pairings for the very English/Irish beer selection. Food runs a little on the pricey side, but comparatively, it is much cheaper than a plane ticket to London.

BOHEME

307 FAIRVIEW *at Taft*
☎ (713) 529-1099 | MAP **E6**
BARBOHEME.COM

THERE'S NOT MUCH BETTER ON A LAZY SUNDAY THAN MOSEY-ing down to Boheme, ordering one of their famous thin-crusted pizzas and a glass of good wine (frozen mojitos are somewhat of a specialty here if a cocktail is more suited to your tastes) and grabbing a booth on their chill patio. There's something about the vibe here that makes people want to stay for hours discussing religion and philosophy and politics—in a friendly, cerebral way of course—and just soaking in the creative oxygen that flows so well in Montrose. Bartenders can be a little aloof at times, but with such a relaxed environment, it's really hard to get bent out of shape. Happy-hour deals are worthy of a trip, as are the special Vietnamese fries, which are topped with garlic mayo, sriracha, hoisin sauce, cilantro flecks and crushed peanuts.

BONEYARD DOG PARK & DRINKERY

8150 WASHINGTON *north of Katy Fwy. (I-10 West)*
☎ (832) 494-1600 | MAP **D6**
BONEYARDHOUSTON.COM

PROFESSIONALS WHO OWN DOGS CAN ASSUAGE THEIR guilt in wanting to grab a drink after work with friends by meeting up at Boneyard Dog Park & Drinkery. Bringing Fido along is not only an option, it's encouraged. Dogs get a much-needed reprieve from their lonely days, while owners can wind down with a craft brew. Everybody wins. Most of Boneyard's real estate is just that: a yard with plenty of puppy play space and picnic tables for the humans. There's additional space inside, but it's not ideal for lingering. Food trucks often park nearby, and happy hour runs all day during the week for added bonuses.

BOONDOCKS

1417 WESTHEIMER *at Windsor*
☎ (713) 522-8500 | MAP **E6**

THERE'S SOMETHING STRANGELY COMPELLING ABOUT BOONDOCKS that's hard to pin down. In fact, it might even lose a bit of that mysterious something if overanalyzed, so we'll just say this: It's nigh impossible to *not* have a memorable experience here. Dive-y in all the right ways, or perhaps it could just be considered "quirky" overall, Boondocks attracts a diverse crowd that ranges from hipster to mature bachelorettes. Downstairs you'll find a nice-sized bar with delightfully inexpensive drinks; upstairs you'll find plenty of fine young things shaking it to the DJ's themed music (everything from 60's garage band rock to dirty South rap). Always you'll find excellent people-watching.

CAPTAIN FOXHEART'S BAD NEWS BAR & SPIRIT LOUNGE

308 MAIN *between Congress & Preston* | MAP **F6**

THE NAME IS LONG, BUT THE PREMISE IS SIMPLE: QUALITY cocktails, beers and wines in a comfortable but uniquely Houston setting. Heading upstairs to the bar's entrance almost feels like finding a hidden speakeasy, but once inside, the interior is elegant and understated, the bar is deep, the lounge area is comfortably vintage and the streetside balcony is quite possibly the best in town. With founder/bartender Justin Burrow at the helm (a graduate of the ever-popular cocktail haunt, Anvil), a prime location in the budding downtown area and some amazing cocktail creations, this new member (circa 2013) of the Houston cocktail scene is headed for glory. Also notable: Burrow's title of "Favorite Mixologist" from *My Table*'s 2011 Houston Culinary Awards.

CHRISTIAN'S TAILGATE

7340 WASHINGTON
just north of Katy Fwy. (I-10 West)
☎ (713) 864-9744 | MAP **E6**
multiple locations
CHRISTIANSTAILGATE.COM

THE ORIGINAL LOCATION OF CHRISTIAN'S TAILGATE WAS famous for its burgers long before the rise and regentrification of the other side of Washington Avenue. Though it has since branched out to include locations in Midtown and The Heights, this stalwart definitely contains the most grit of the three. Perhaps it's age or perhaps it's the slightly sassy waitstaff, but the burgers they're so famous for seem to just taste better at this location. Between the dozens of flatscreen TVs and shuffleboard, all your sporting needs should be met. At the shinier, newer spots, the college nights, karaoke and Jäger bombs bring in a younger crowd looking for a romping good time.

THE CONTINENTAL CLUB

3700 MAIN *at Winbern*
☎ (713) 529-9899 | MAP **F6**
CONTINENTALCLUB.COM

THERE'S MORE KITSCH HERE THAN YOU CAN SHAKE A STICK at—velvet-lined stage, Elvis' name in lights, etc.—but it all combines for a venue that has more character in one square foot than many do in an entire building. It's a second location of the original famed music venue in Austin, but it takes on its own Houston character. Live music acts usually fall within the categories of rockabilly, folk, country, blues or local...and, frankly, so do most of the patrons. The ever-present Lone Star bottles are always popular, but the occasional mixed drink or Corona makes the rounds as well. Cover charges are reasonable, especially considering the regional and sometimes national popularity of the bookings, and the patio is comfortable. Add in the room in the back with its pool tables, shuffleboard and occasional food vendor, and this is one bar that (by Houston standards) could quite possibly be considered a standard.

COTTONWOOD

3422 N. SHEPHERD *near W. 34th*
☎ (713) 802-0410 | MAP **E5**
COTTONWOODHOUSTON.COM

GARDEN OAKS IS THE NEWEST "HOT" NEIGHBORHOOD IN Houston for residential pursuits as well as recreational. Adding to its hotness is Cottonwood, an Austin-style, mostly outdoor bar and gastropub founded by the industry veterans behind Liberty Station and Raven Grill. A huge covered patio lined with picnic tables is often filled with families from the neighborhood in the earlier hours (beware of wild children), while the chic interior and more intimate side patio fills up later in the evening. Food is above average with items like barbecued oysters, salmon deviled eggs, chicken potpie and stuffed quail. Cocktails are original and refreshing, while the beer selection is laudable. Outdoor games like cornhole and bocce complete the playful setting.

D&T DRIVE INN

1307 ENID *at W. Cavalcade*
☎ (713) 868-6165 | MAP **E5**
DANDTDRIVEINN.COM

LOTS OF CRAFT BEER HANDLES ADORN THE TAP WALL IN THIS non-traditional "icehouse." Modernizing the icehouse concept to include 50 draft beers instead of only bottled and canned beverages, the founding team knows plenty about running a successful concept: They're from the ever-crowded Down House in The Heights. The food menu is very beer-friendly with items like smoked pimiento cheese, sausage plates, a variety of po'boys and plenty of meat and cheese platters. Decor is refreshingly low-key, making for an unpretentious neighborhood watering hole.

THE DOGWOOD

2403 BAGBY
between Webster & Tuam
☎ (281) 501-9075 | MAP **E6**
THEDOGWOODMIDTOWN.COM

MODERN, MULTI-LEVELED DOGWOOD MARRIES A SOUTHERN sensibility with a clean contemporary aesthetic in Midtown. The Austin transplant from former *Bachelor* contestant and entrepreneur Brad Womack is a chill spot to catch games via ESPN, play a game of cricket

Glasses at Down House

on one of the many dartboards or enjoy the panoramic vista from the rooftop patio. Southern-inspired food includes such gems as sweet potato tater tots, risotto lollipops, a namesake burger topped with fried green tomatoes, bacon and queso and pork belly fritters. Drinks range from craft beer to creative cocktails to Deep Eddy Sweet Tea Vodka (an Austin-made spirit) on its own tap.

DOWNING STREET PUB

2549 KIRBY *at Westheimer*
☎ (713) 523-2291 | MAP **E6**
DOWNINGSTREETPUB.COM

IF YOU HAVE AN URGE TO SLIP INTO A SMOKING JACKET, SPEAK with a slight British accent and peruse the *Financial Times*, you're at the right place. Downing Street Pub is a discerning establishment that celebrates cigars and whiskey. (There are also wines and even some milquetoast cocktails to please the fruity-drink lovers.) The underlying appeal is its huge selection of high-quality Scotch, bourbon, rye and various whiskeys from around the globe as well as its humidor. Sit on a leather chair and loiter the evening away with your fellow connoisseurs. There's a small menu of pub grub for the peckish.

THE EIGHTEENTH

2511 BISSONNET
between Morningside & Kirby
☎ (713) 533-9800 | MAP **E7**
THEEIGHTEENTH.COM

HOUSTON'S OBSESSION WITH PROHIBITION-ERA STYLE cocktail bars continues, and The Eighteenth, which opened in 2013, is an obvious product of the trend. Named after the amendment that established the now-romanticized

period of American history known for illegal speakeasies, cocktails here boldly carry names like Al Capone, bootlegger's punch and bathtub gin. The interior evokes the bygone era but maintains modern touches amid the distressed look of the furniture and walls. The father-son team, Frank and Erick Ramirez respectively, are no strangers to the industry. The former spent 20 years with the Cordúa group previously, which explains the menu's penchant for upscale bites like fancy deviled eggs, tuna tartare, chimichurri chicken panini and an impressive charcuterie and cheese platter.

EL GRAN MALO

2307 ELLA BLVD. *at 23rd*
☎ (832) 767-3405 | MAP **E5**
multiple locations
ELGRANMALO.COM

EL GRAN MALO, SPANISH FOR "THE BIG BAD," IS BIG AND bad when it comes to infused tequila but otherwise not nearly as intimidating as it sounds. Festively decked out in Mexican folk art and a gorgeous mural, it gets an "A+" for funky atmosphere. The custom cocktails (mostly made with those tequilas) are just as creative as the decor, with simple but tasty Tex-Mex favorites to accompany. The ceviche is light and refreshing, while the torta burger and pork belly tacos are more apropos for a day of drinking. If tequila makes you squirm—you should probably work on getting over that, you know—you can just try a Mexican or Texas beer or sangria. Rumor has it this original Oak Forest El Gran Malo may close so that management can focus on their recently acquired downtown location at 419 Travis—to be called El Big Bad—but there's no official confirmation as of press time. Here's to hoping the owners keep the same feel as the original and double their capacity for tequila infusions.

FLYING SAUCER DRAUGHT EMPORIUM

705 MAIN *at Capitol*
☎ (713) 228-9472 | MAP **F6**
multiple locations
BEERKNURD.COM

AS FAR AS HOUSTON CRAFT BEER BARS GO, THE FLYING Saucer—though a national chain—was one of the original meccas where local beer nerds flocked for their pint of draught. With a giant wall crammed with beer taps from a mind-blowing number of breweries, "beer goddesses" dressed in plaid, pleated skirts and knee-high socks and a simple food menu that's meant to accompany any of their innumerable suds, the Flying Saucer is a great example of the new American-style pub. Between heavy wooden tables, a few couches and plenty of plates on the wall adorned with the names of proud beer drinkers (you must drink a large amount of beer to earn your plate, and it generally takes years), it's an overtly masculine environment but still comfortable for the brew-loving ladies who enjoy a pint of their own. Pre- and post-downtown events, especially of the sporting variety, see a surge in crowds here so plan accordingly or just get used to the roaringly loud environment.

THE GINGER MAN

5607 MORNINGSIDE
north of University Blvd.
☎ (713) 526-2770 | MAP **E7**
GINGERMANPUB.COM

A CHAIN OF CRAFT BEER PUBS WITH LOCATIONS THROUGH-out Texas, the Rice Village iteration of The Ginger Man is a fixture not only in its own neighborhood but among the Houston craft beer community as well. Pouring quality beers from an entire wall of taps since 1985, it's any beer-loving Houstonian's rite of passage to visit this cozy, no-frills institution. Creaky wooden floors are an endearing part of the experience as is the extensive outdoor area in the back with plenty of shade from the big ol' trees and lots of long tables for sharing on a crowded afternoon. Adding to the appeal is an old school jukebox and the extensive selection of Old World beer styles (try something Belgian). Food is minimal, but most alcohol content is not, so prep by eating something before you pay a visit.

GOODE'S ARMADILLO PALACE

5015 KIRBY *near Westpark*
☎ (713) 526-9700 | MAP **E7**
GOODECOMPANY.COM/PALACE

IT'S EVERY STEREOTYPE OF TEXAS ROLLED INTO ONE OVER-THE-TOP, unapologetically hyperbolic bar and restaurant from the famous Goode family. For one, there's an enormous 14-foot, super shiny armadillo out front; for another, it's an entire interior of Texas memorabilia, such as Western saddles in place of regular barstools. Somewhere among the everything's-bigger-in-Texas theme are actual food dishes, decent margaritas, beer and lots of live music—most of it Texas country. About that food: It's actually pretty good with very tasty *campechana* (Mexican-style seafood cocktail), venison chili with nary a bean in sight, chicken-fried steak (of course!) and plenty of burgers. As if that weren't fun enough, there are games of shuffleboard, pool and dominoes just waiting on the patio. If you've got cowboy boots, this is the place to wear them.

GRAND PRIZE BAR
1010 BANKS *at Montrose*
☎ (713) 526-4565 | MAP **E6**

ADEFINITE "INDUSTRY" BAR, WHICH BASICALLY MEANS A place that off-shift bartenders like to drink themselves, Grand Prize is a bit of an enigma. It's not seedy enough to fall into the dive category, but it's not squeaky clean, either. It is an excellent place to sip refreshing and moderately priced cocktails like the Aviation (sometimes you can catch it frozen—highly recommended) or the Vieux Carre, or perhaps even an original creation on the whim of a bartender. There's also plenty of craft or non-craft beer available ... ahem, Lone Star anyone? Food choices, namely gourmet sandwiches, have recently been added as Grand Prize's kitchen now provides a home to Sandy Witch (from the owners of Pi Pizza food truck) every night of the week. Ample seating, a surprisingly diverse jukebox and just the right amount of low lighting make this a great mid-week refuge.

HANS' BIER HAUS
2523 QUENBY *at Kirby*
☎ (713) 520-7474 | MAP **E7**
HANSBIERHAUS.COM

IT COULD ALMOST BE SAID THAT HANS' IS AS POPULAR FOR ITS breezy back patio and bocce ball court as it is for its worldly beer selection. An occasional complaint about the freshness of their product or the cleanliness of the tap lines can be heard from intense beer snobs, but usually everyone is just happy to be here. While there's nothing special about the creaky old house Hans' exists in, it does hold a certain dingy quality that makes for an authentic beer joint. There's no food to speak of, but pizza delivery is at your disposal if needed. Bonus: trivia and open mic nights.

THE HAY MERCHANT
1100 WESTHEIMER *at Waugh*
☎ (713) 528-9805 | MAP **E6**
HAYMERCHANT.COM

THE HAY MERCHANT WINS THE CATEGORY OF HOUSTON'S MOST cerebral beer bar. Located in the space formerly known as Chances (a legendary lesbian bar), it's owned by Anvil founder Bobby Heugel and former-bartender-turned-beer-obsessive, Kevin Floyd. It was created with as much attention to detail as possible with two separate coolers so different types of beer can be stored at their respective optimum temperature; specific glassware for different types of beer; an interior adorned with bricks dating back to the 1840s; individually sourced tap handles; a vintage "City of Houston" manhole cover set into one wall; custom wooden table tops; and one of the most prolific cask programs in the country. Even the food here doesn't take the easy road; the menu executed by Dax McAnear includes wagyu beef jerky, Vietnamese chicken wings, Parisian gnocchi, crispy pigs' ears and a cheeseburger made with house-butchered beef.

JULEP
1919 WASHINGTON
between Sabine & Sawyer | MAP **E6**

JULEP IS YET ANOTHER OF THE VARIOUS RESTAURANTS AND bars loosely associated with cocktail juggernaut Anvil Bar & Refuge. Announced in August of 2012, the project is slated to be headed up by Anvil alum and award-winning bartender, Alba Huerta. The cocktail bar, to be housed in the former Corkscrew location, has experienced multiple delays since its announcement. It will feature a softer decor than Anvil, much more space for patrons and plenty of original and classic cocktails with its most popular presumably being the julep itself. No official opening date has been announced as of press time.

KAY'S LOUNGE

2324 BISSONNET *near Greenbriar*
☎ (713) 528-9858 | MAP **E7**

IT'S THE DIVE BAR EVERYONE LOVES TO BRAG ABOUT BEING A regular at. Located on the border of West U, this old-school bar has been a landmark for the past five decades. (Back in the day, it's where the *Houston Post* reporters and editors unwound.) Seedy, grimy and dark in all the right places, you'll find as many good ol' boys here as frat boys. Beer is, and should be, the wise choice as liquor pours can be inconsistent and surprisingly pricey considering the surroundings. Pitchers are a staple here as is the jukebox, which we suggest you get to as soon as possible unless you're an abnormally enthusiastic Allman Brothers fan. Filling in the entertainment gaps are dartboards and a pool table with a few outdoor picnic tables for the smokers.

KELVIN ARMS

2424 DUNSTAN
between Morningside & Kirby
☎ (713) 528-4730 | MAP **E7**
KELVINARMSPUB.COM

SCOTCH WHISKY SELECTION EXTRAORDINAIRE, A SEAN Connery shrine and plenty of beer from the UK make this pub officially "Scottish." With a low-key happy hour, great draft beer selection (Scottish or not) and a room that once was the vault of a bank, Kelvin Arms is an experience worth having. There's plenty of low lighting along with sunken couches and armchairs in this intriguing vault lounge, while the bar itself provides a more personal relationship with the usually responsive bartenders. Bar entertainment like darts and board games can be in high demand some days, while others it's just a laid-back, sink-into-a-couch-with-your-Scotch kind of watering hole.

KENNEALLY'S IRISH PUB

2111 S. SHEPHERD *at Indiana*
☎ (713) 630-0486 | MAP **E6**
IRISHPUBKENNEALLYS.COM

KENNEALLY'S IS PROBABLY THE CLOSEST HOUSTON GETS TO A Boston-style Irish pub. Established in 1983, it's a jolly neighborhood watering hole with plenty of Guinness on draught, sports on the televisions and only a few darkened windows looking out from the grimy painted façade. In addition to draught beers, a little rowdy Irishness and lots of regulars, you'll find very good thin-crust Chicago-style pizzas that are made in-house. There's even a corned-beef-topped "Shamrock Special" that is way better than it sounds. It should go without saying that the signature pizza and beer taps get plenty of action on March 17 when the place turns into bonkersville—did you notice the big green shamrocks painted in the street north and south of the pub?—and everyone is seeing green by the end of the night.

KUNG FU SALOON

5317 WASHINGTON
slightly east of TC Jester
☎ (713) 864-0642 | MAP **E6**
KUNGFUSALOON.COM/HOUSTON

IT'S TRENDY. IT'S OFTEN LOUD. IT GETS VERY CROWDED ON THE weekends. It's one of the hotspots in an entire avenue of hotspots. Yet it continues to be one of the most amusing bars in town. Despite its penchant for attracting the young and tragically hip, it still leaves enough room for those neither young nor hip to enjoy 17 vintage arcade games, 24 draft beers, cocktails, sake bombs, upbeat music, giant Jenga, board games, bar food and private karaoke rooms. The adjacent patio is just shielded enough from the hustle and bustle of Washington Avenue but full of other action nonetheless.

LEON'S LOUNGE

1006 MCGOWEN *at Fannin*
☎ (713) 659-5366 | MAP **F6**

LEON'S LOUNGE WAS ONCE A DIVE BAR. AND WHILE IT HAS kept a bit of its grizzled character, it is decidedly much more pleasant on the eyes, nose and, with a new cocktail menu, presumably the palate as well. Taking it over in 2010, the owners of Under The Volcano transformed Leon's over the course of one year into a chandelier-ed, Gothic masterpiece of lush red drapes and pin-tucked furniture. With a

steady stream of hipster-y clientele, weekends here are usually packed with people wearing some form of pearl snaps, sipping craft cocktails, listening to the sounds of vinyl and enjoying the reincarnation of Leon's.

LIBERTY STATION

2101 WASHINGTON *at Henderson*
☎ (713) 640-5220 | MAP **E6**
LIBERTYSTATIONBAR.COM

ON THE QUIETER END OF WASHINGTON AVENUE IS LIBERTY Station. A modern icehouse with quality beer on tap and a few good cocktails in their arsenal, it's become a laid-back bar where people come to enjoy a very tasty beverage. Inside are a few quiet tables, a nice-sized bar and even a couch or two for comfy seating, but the bulk of space is on the covered patio of this converted gas station. Cornhole and the token giant Jenga entice even more outside, as do the food trucks parked out front almost every evening.

LITTLE DIPPER

304 MAIN *between Congress & Preston* | MAP **F6**

THIS NEWEST BAR FROM THE TEAM BEHIND BLACK HOLE Coffee and Poison Girl has yet to open as of our deadline, but when it does expect the same casual feel and unpretentious atmosphere as its siblings. Just bordering on divey but leaning more toward comfortable, owners Scott and Dawn Repass hope it finds a niche with the after-work crowd looking for something chill or the "interesting souls" who call downtown home. As a tribute to its location along the Metro line, the bar top is made from the flooring lumber of old boxcars. There will be a few booths for quiet conversation

The Pastry War

and tones of black, blue and gold. As fans of Poison Girl might be happy to note, there will be a pinball machine as well. No obvious themes or fancy cocktails, just a laid-back place to grab a drink.

LITTLE WOODROW'S
5611 MORNINGSIDE
north of University
☎ (713) 521-2337 | MAP **E7**
multiple locations
LITTLEWOODROWS.COM

LET'S JUST GO WITH "WOOD-ROW'S" SINCE NOT ALL OF them are actually "Little." But they all are very popular, often packing in the crowds for sporting events (football season is chaos), turtle races (at the Midtown location) and special events. Crawfish season is also a siren song to day drinkers in any of Woodrow's five Houston neighborhoods—Bellaire, Heights, EaDo, Midtown and Rice Village respectively—though most don't need an excuse to hit up the large patios and grab a Texas craft beer from the tap.

LOCAL POUR
1952 W. GRAY *at Driscoll*
☎ (713) 521-1881 | MAP **E6**
LOCALPOURHOUSTON.COM

IN A MAKEOVER ALMOST AS DRAMATIC AS JULIA ROBERTS' character in *Pretty Woman*, Sherlock's Baker St. Pub in the River Oaks Shopping Center was transformed into Local Pour. After an incident in its parking lot after a day of $1 drink specials and a double shooting, the parent company (which operates all of the establishments in the national chain) intelligently decided to rebrand. As a result, Local Pour is an upscale pub with a sleek, polished look, down to the massive bar with 48 taps, high-backed banquettes in sage green and a high ceilinged dining area. Shareable plates, creative salads and somewhat pricey entrees make for an interesting menu.

MARFRELESS

2006 PEDEN *at McDuffie*
☎ (713) 528-0083 | MAP **E6**
MARFRELESSHOUSTON.COM

IT WAS, AND THEN IT WASN'T, AND THEN IT WAS AGAIN. AFTER the Spring 2013 announcement of its imminent closing due to a rent hike, patrons decried the injustice so loudly that new ownership stepped in and announced its imminent re-opening later that summer. All of it was to take place in the same location and under the same name with the same darkened corners and seedy upstairs lair where much more goes on than just sipping drinks. Things will be changing, however, in a renovation, from the wiring to the carpet to the "furniture you…sit on," the new owners announced via Facebook. As of press time, the bar has not reopened, but timelines indicate it will before long. Classic cocktails, wine by the bottle and canoodling to re-commence as soon as possible.

McGONIGEL'S MUCKY DUCK

2425 NORFOLK *between Kirby & Morningside*
☎ (713) 528-5999 | MAP **E7**
MCGONIGELS.COM

THE SUPPER CLUB IS NOT DEAD. MCGONIGEL'S MUCKY DUCK IS proof that the model is viable and thriving, entertaining and enlightening. The intimate bar—which usually books acts in the genres of Texas country, folk, singer-songwriter, Irish and acoustic—serves as a reminder that bigger isn't always better. Even on nights when the performers are average Joes out for an open mic, the atmosphere feels welcoming and artistic, even sometimes downright cozy. As for food and drink, both are also surprisingly high quality with plenty of draft beers (sometimes even rare cask finds), wines and English pub fare that's actually tasty. Call ahead if you're planning a visit, as there are often sold-out shows with well-known acts coming through that may prevent you from entering without a ticket on certain nights.

MONGOOSE VS COBRA

1011 MCGOWEN
between Fannin & Main
☎ (713) 650-6872 | MAP **E6**
MONGOOSEVERSUSCOBRA.COM

IT'S A BIT UTILITARIAN AS FAR AS DECOR GOES, WITH A MASCULINE interior that features clean lines and a merging of metal and wood. The overall simplicity allows for more focus on the cocktails, the craft beer and the small batch spirits—some of which even appear on one of their 42 rotating taps. Food is scarce and snacky, though of high quality with suitable charcuterie, cheese and house-pickled comestibles. The owners, who are also behind wine bar 13 Celsius, are justly proud of the building's heritage, which dates back to 1915 and housed Auditorium Grocery until the 1940s. Literary types might enjoy MVSC's poetry nights, which provide a dose of culture alongside a great glass of sipping bourbon.

NOUVEAU ANTIQUE ART BAR

2913 MAIN *at Tuam*
☎ (713) 526-2220 | MAP **E6**
ART-BAR.NET

IN THIS CASE, "NOUVEAU ANTIQUE ART BAR" COULD EASILY TRANSlate to "hundreds of Tiffany-style lamps as our main form of interior design." Add in some alcohol, some furniture from the Art Nouveau period and you've got a real bona fide antique bar on your hands. Earlier in the evening—particularly during happy hour—the scene is much less frenetic with softer music that befits the gorgeous collection of softly glowing lamps, but as the night progresses, so does the loud, clubby music. Either way, the space is breathtaking and the drinks decent, with enough space and seating areas for larger groups or cozy corners for couples out on a date.

THE ORIGINAL OKRA CHARITY SALOON

924 CONGRESS *west of Main*
☎ (713) 237-8828 | MAP **F6**
FRIEDOKRA.ORG

DRINKING ALCOHOL FOR CHARITY. IT'S A TOUGH JOB, BUT somebody's got to do it. That's the concept behind this saloon, which is a cooperative-owned non-profit that donates proceeds from the bar to a different charity each month. While you do a double take, let us explain: Guests get to vote on which charity will be the month's beneficiary as they sip their sommelier-chosen glass of wine, a craft beer or a simple but tasty classic cocktail. There's also some fantastic food in the mix including panini, seasoned fries and even baked-to-order cookies. So drink up and do good.

THE PASTRY WAR

310 MAIN *between Congress & Preston* | MAP **F6**

BOBBY HEUGEL AND HIS BAND OF MERRY BAR AND RESTAUrant founders are at it again. This time in one of the hottest blocks in the city: Main Street in Downtown. (We know you're wondering: The curious name comes from a historical event in which France invaded Mexico in the 1830s.) The bar focuses on family-produced, small-batch mezcals and tequilas from Mexico, many of which have never been tasted on Texas soil, while a selection of Mexican longneck beers is also a part of the mix. Pesos accepted (seriously).

PETROL STATION

985 WAKEFIELD *east of Ella*
☎ (713) 957-2875 | MAP **E5**

THE BEARD TO NON-BEARD RATIO HERE IS ABOUT 3:1, with a majority of those sans facial hair being women. Not that it has anything to do with the very expertly compiled beer selection, the better-than-average pub food or the very good burgers, but it's worth noting if you're into statistics of random things. Also random is Petrol Station's location in the middle of a residential neighborhood in Garden Oaks, but that doesn't stop the beer-loving crowds from flocking here every evening. Since our last edition, the converted gas station has undergone a kitchen revamp to increase capacity and an expansion of their outdoor seating areas. More space for more pints, and ultimately, more beards.

POISON GIRL

1641-B WESTHEIMER *at Dunlavy*
☎ (713) 527-9929 | MAP **E6**

IT'S BEEN CALLED A HIPSTER BAR. IT'S BEEN CALLED A PSEUDO-DIVE bar. It's been called a whiskey bar. But it often defies any particular label because it is such an amalgam of things, much like its Montrose neighborhood. Whiskey is a popular spirit here, but there's also plenty of craft beer and Lone Star, and all of it priced reasonably. Just gritty enough to seem legit but clean enough to take a first date for after-dinner drinks, it's got just the right mix of everything: statues of a life-size Kool-Aid man and Cabbage Patch doll out back, sweet pinball machines and an all-Texas jukebox. Literary types may enjoy the Poison Pen series, a monthly event featuring three local authors and samples of their work.

PORCH SWING PUB

69 HEIGHTS BLVD. *at Washington*
☎ (713) 880-8700 | MAP **E6**
PORCHSWINGPUB.COM

PORCH SWING PUB IS JUST A REGULAR BAR – THAT IS, THE kind of bar where there's no particular overarching theme, no pretentiousness, no reason to get dressed up. It's just a comfortable neighborhood bar with plenty of drink options to please everyone in the group—beer (tons on tap), cocktails (frozen Bellinis for the win!) and wine—and decent pub food that tastes so good after a few beers. Decor leans toward a modern saloon look with wooden tables, wooden floors and typical bar signs. Trivia nights and NFL games are popular here, much as they are at sister location Front Porch Pub in Midtown.

PROHIBITION

5175 WESTHEIMER
in The Galleria
☎ (281) 940-4636 | MAP **D6**
PROHIBITIONHOUSTON.COM

FIGHTING THE FAMOUSLY BAD GALLERIA TRAFFIC TO GET TO this swanky speakeasy-style cocktail lounge shouldn't spoil the evening's fun, which starts with the cocktails. Prohibition is so serious about their "mixology" they employ various levels in the training of their bartend-

ers. It starts at "apprentice," then to "barsmith," onward to "bar chef" and finally, "mixologist." Also impressive are the burlesque shows from in-house troupe, The Moonlight Dolls, which take place every Thursday, Friday and Saturday. Topping it off is Prohibition's upscale dinner menu, which has a few hits and a few misses, but no one probably notices when the Dolls are shimmying the night away.

PROOF BAR & PATIO

2600 TRAVIS *at McGowen*
☎ (832) 767-0513 | MAP **E6**
PROOFBARHOUSTON.COM

IT'S AS IF PROOF BAR, WHICH IS ABOVE REEF RESTAURANT, TOOK all the finer things one might find at a luxury hotel bar and turned them into a freestanding bar. Decor is downright sexy, done in reds and blacks and dark wood, with the provocative wall-length sepia photo of a woman's torso hanging out by the dartboards. It only makes sense that the pretty young things of Midtown flock here on the weekends for boozy concoctions like the Pepino Diablo—a mix of jalapeño-infused tequila, agave syrup, fresh watermelon, cilantro and lime—and some quality time on the atmospheric, above-ground patio adorned in romantic twinkle lights and red furniture. The glorious view of the Houston skyline is just the cherry on top.

PUB FICTION

2303 SMITH *between Webster & McGowen*
☎ (713) 400-8400 | MAP **E6**
PUBFICTION.COM

STANDING THE TEST OF TIME – WHICH FEW TRENDY BARS IN Houston manage to do – Pub Fiction is quite possibly Houston's hottest college bar year after year after year. How do they do it? Well, it's not really a mystery: plenty of seating, upscale design but laid-back sports bar feel, solid food menu, good drinks, bar games and a great location in Midtown. If shuffling into a crowded space filled with loud music and a younger set is not your scene, avoid on the weekends at all costs.

RED LION PUB

2316 S. SHEPHERD *at Fairview*
☎ (713) 782-3030 | MAP **E6**
REDLIONHOUSTON.COM

AUTHENTICITY IS THE OVERALL APPEAL OF RED LION PUB. From the logo that looks as if it's come directly off the banners of Tudor England to the cozy wood-paneled interior and blazing hearth (winter only, of course) to the patio shaded by the gently swaying branches of willow trees, it's UK all the way. Even owner Craig Mallinson hails from jolly old England, which by default makes his curries, fish and chips, shepherd's pie, roast beef, Cornish pasties and Yorkshire pudding entirely authentic. Even the prices look as if they've been converted from pounds into dollars, but British expats don't mind paying the extra coin for their pint of Old Speckled Hen and a warming bowl of curry if it means a little taste of home.

RESERVE 101

1201 CAROLINE *at Dallas*
☎ (713) 655-7101 | MAP **F6**
RESERVE101.COM

SCOTCH, BOURBON AND RYE WHISKEYS TAKE CENTER STAGE at this surprisingly low-key establishment in Downtown. Instead of feeling like the back room of a private

club where patrons don jackets, it feels like a regular everyday kind of place...and that's a welcome thing for normal, everyday whiskey drinkers. Houston's largest collection of globally produced whiskeys offers more than 200. There's also a signature cocktail list for those not yet ready to order their spirits "neat." Check out Reserve 101's monthly tasting events if you're looking to expand your palate. The management has also recently expanded the food menu.

ROYAL OAK BAR & GRILL

1318 WESTHEIMER
between Commonwealth & Yupon
☎ (281) 974-4752 | MAP **E6**
ROYALOAKHOUSTON.COM

ROYAL OAK BAR & GRILL IS ALMOST MAINSTREAM WHEN it comes to Montrose bars (of course, just being less quirky in that neighborhood is itself a bit quirky), be it not for a few tweaks that specialize it just enough. First, it's the modern speakeasy decor theme with tufted black booths, wooden floors and a masculine palette done in warm tones, accented with deer antler chandeliers. Second, it's their extensive selection of whiskeys, particularly American-produced bourbons and variations thereof. Food is internationally inspired with crispy pizzas that please, burgers for every mood and appetizers ranging from Asian dumplings to quesadillas.

RUDYARD'S BRITISH PUB

2010 WAUGH *at Welch*
☎ (713) 521-0521 | MAP **E6**
RUDYARDSPUB.COM

RUDYARD'S ISN'T PARTICULARLY BRITISH, BUT IT IS A PUB, SO no harm done. It is, however, a great gathering place for fans of indie local musicians, comedians, poets and the performing arts in general. There's also lots of great craft beer, decent bar food—in addition to a full menu, there are theme nights like "curry" and "steak," plus their burgers have inspired impassioned endorsements all their own—and plenty of games like pool, shuffleboard and darts. Rudyard's has become somewhat famous for monthly beer dinners from chef Joe Apa, pairing gourmet entrees like braised lamb shank with craft brews, all set inside the some-what grubby location, which could be a metaphor for Houston: a diamond in the rough.

SAMBUCA

909 TEXAS *at Travis*
☎ (713) 224-5299 | MAP **F6**
SAMBUCARESTAURANT.COM

AS MUCH AS HOUSTONIANS LOVE WEARING CASUAL ATTIRE to any and every level of restaurant, sometimes it's rejuvenating to dress up and hit the town. Sambuca should be one of the destinations on your list when you decide finally to show off that little black dress or break in a new sports coat. With a sultry tone set by dark woods, white linens and live music, it's the ultimate supper club for date night. Jazz is prob-ably a good bet, though the genres can range from R&B to Latin on any given night. Be warned that there is a per-person minimum at dinner, but the food is consistently well prepared with elegant entrees and tasty cock-tails and wine.

TAPS HOUSE OF BEER

5120 WASHINGTON *at Reinerman*
☎ (713) 426-1105 | MAP **E6**
TAPSHOUSEOFBEER.COM

DRIVING ALONG WASHINGTON AVENUE, IT'S HARD TO MISS this bar, which is dedicated to the brewmaster's art and looks like a ginormous beer keg. Walk in and you'll see nearly 100 draught beers on tap. As Taps is orchestrated for fans of beer, this isn't a bar that boasts about its cocktail menu. There is something to delight every beer drinker, however, even hard-to-impress aficionados. Note that the crowd tends to be younger here.

TRIGGER HAPPY

308 MAIN *between Congress & Preston* | MAP **F6**

SITED DIRECTLY BELOW THE COCKTAIL HUB CAPTAIN FOX-heart's Bad News Bar, Trigger Happy is the announced beer and wine bar from the Clumsy Butcher group (which also owns Anvil, of course). It will add another libations location to the downtown block that is making a comeback after years of construction and low foot traffic, but it is not yet open as this guidebook goes to press.

UNDER THE VOLCANO

2349 BISSONNET *at Morningside*
☎ (713) 526-5282 | MAP **E7**

IN THE MIDDLE OF THE RICE VIL-LAGE NEIGHBORHOOD IS A LITTLE hideaway that has been shaking and muddling classic and tiki cocktails for decades. Unlike John Huston's depressing 1984 film and Malcolm

Lowry's 1947 novel of the same name, this Volcano brings people together for college reunions, young professionals' happy hours and to celebrate the arrival of the weekend. Fresh-squeezed juices, jolly Day-of-the-Dead decor and Monday steak night are prime draws. Pimm's cups are also a potent recommendation and house specialty.

WARREN'S INN
307 TRAVIS *at Congress*
☎ (713) 247-9207 | MAP **F6**

THIS MARKET SQUARE DIVE BAR ISN'T JUST KNOWN FOR GEN erous pours and dark shadowy corners. What you'll notice first are the vintage neon signs on the façade and the beloved jukebox—it comes prepaid and loaded with everything from Sam Cooke to REM. The crowd is mixed, including club rats, hipsters, energy traders and attorneys burning the midnight oil.

WEST ALABAMA ICE HOUSE
1919 W. ALABAMA *near Hazard*
☎ (713) 528-6874 | MAP **E7**

IF YOU CAN VISIT ONLY ONE HIS-TORIC BAR IN HOUSTON, MAKE IT the West Alabama Ice House. It is an institution, reminiscent of an über-cool open-air garage and has been a gathering spot for bikers and Montrosians since 1927. While there have been new covered seating areas added in recent years, the attitude hasn't changed at all. Patrons regularly bring their dogs to the shady patio where they (the owners, not the dogs) enjoy a longneck and a round of horseshoes. You'll even see the occasional child throwing a basketball up at the lone hoop. While there isn't any food served at the icehouse

itself, there are two good food trucks parked just a few feet away, and usually after 8 pm you'll spy the tamale man peddling from a loaded tray of fragrant foil-wrapped tamales. Beer offerings range from local craft beers such as Saint Arnold and Karbach to Abita and Six Point.

WINE BARS

13 CELSIUS
3000 CAROLINE *at Anita*
☎ (713) 529-8466 | MAP **E6**
13CELSIUS.COM

IT USED TO BE THE SITE OF A DRY CLEANERS, BUT TODAY 13 Celsius is a chic, dimly lit wine bar just inside Midtown. Exposed brick and cozy couches make for the ideal environment to chat privately with an attractive companion. Or sidle up to the bar and get adventurous with a cheese tray—the employees are great about pairing the cheeses to the wine you've ordered. On Sundays, all open bottles are 50 percent off, and if you don't know what to order just ask your friendly bartender. They'll offer you tastes and suggest options that you might not have picked for yourself.

CAMERATA AT PAULIE'S
1834 WESTHEIMER *at Driscoll*
☎ (713) 807-7271 | MAP **E6**
PAULIESRESTAURANT.COM/CAMERATA

HOUSTON RESTAURATEUR PAUL PETRONELLA AND SOMMELIER David Keck built out the industrial space next door to Paulie's in record time in Summer 2013 and decked it out with unusual selections of beer and wine at this neighborhood wine bar across the street from Lanier Middle School. While the wine bar isn't promoting budget-friendly flights or half-price bottles, it is showcasing staff favorites and interesting wines you've probably never heard of. Get adventurous and ask for a rosé suggestion, as Camerata is one of few places in town that always has four or five available by the glass. If you're hungry for a meal, you'll need to pop in next door at Paulie's, but if you're fine with nibbling on a platter of charcuterie, they've got one of the best selections of regionally made cheese in town.

The burger at Plonk

D'VINE WINE BAR
25202 NORTHWEST FWY.
at Skinner, Cypress
☎ (281) 213-4656
DVINE-WINEBAR.COM

THIS UNDERSTATED SPOT SELL-
ING FAIR-PRICED WINES BY THE
glass and by the bottle is camou-
flaged in a mixed-use development in
the Northwest suburbs. Come here
to test-drive various wine flights—
who knows what you might discover?
Then buy a bottle (or a case) to take
home. The real surprise is the food:
Chef Clarence Alexander dishes up
lamb chops, seafood dishes, great
pizzas (e.g. wild boar sausage with
pepperonata) and much more. The
staff is especially gracious.

LA CARAFE
813 CONGRESS *at Milam*
☎ (713) 229-9399 | MAP **F6**

LA CARAFE IS HOUSED IN A
DOWNTOWN BUILDING THAT
was built in 1847—that's practically
prehistoric by Houston standards. It
was originally a bakery owned by an
industrious Irish immigrant named
John Kennedy, and the structure later
served as a Pony Express station.
With its original 19th-century brick
walls still more or less intact, La
Carafe is listed on the National Register of Historic Places. Civil War era
portraits and other historical artifacts
hang from the chippy plastered walls,
and the tables are rickety. But we
forgive the creaky floorboards: After
all, the building is almost as old as
Houston itself. In this rustic—and,
some would argue, romantic—setting, the bar serves beer and wine
only. If you ever enjoyed a visit to
Lafitte's Blacksmith Shop Bar in
New Orleans, you would enjoy La
Carafe. Cash only.

PLONK BEER & WINE BISTRO
1214 W. 43RD *at Ella*
☎ (713) 290-1070 | MAP **E5**
PLONKBISTRO.COM

GARDEN OAKS IS FINALLY COM-
ING INTO ITS OWN, AND THAT
includes good food and drink worth
the drive. Intimate spots like Plonk
that are favorites among the locals
and manage to produce a high-
quality product without losing their
homespun charm are becoming the
norm in this part of town. Wander up
to the bar to place your order—the
ordering style is very casual. There
may be some misses on the menu,
but the burger piled high with caramelized onions and the muffaletta
are both spot on. Owner Scott Miller
was once the wine director at Pappas
Bros. Steakhouse, so while cheap
glasses of wine are available, if
you move up the price ladder just a
notch or two, you'll find some truly
interesting options.

SIMONE ON SUNSET
2418 SUNSET *between Kirby
& Greenbriar*
☎ (713) 636-3033 | MAP **E7**
SIMONEONSUNSET.COM

WINE IS LARGELY BY-THE-
BOTTLE (FROM $20 TO
$300) and is supplemented by
dozens of beers in this little West
University nook. The selection won't
inspire a true oenophile, but there are
enough good choices to satisfy most.
While the cocktails and parking
availability aren't the strongest trait
of the tiny bar, the super-thin crust
house pizzas are a plus, as is the
brick-paved patio that people seek
out when the weather behaves.

SONOMA RETAIL WINE BAR & RESTAURANT

2720 RICHMOND *west of Kirby*
☎ (713) 526-9463 | MAP **E7**
multiple locations
SONOMAHOUSTON.COM

THIS COMFORTABLE WINE BAR AND ITS NEW (CIRCA 2012) sibling in The Heights are both great choices for a glass of wine and a hungry appetite—the menu has more than just nibbles. Sliders, Caprese salad, cheese and meat platters, hand-tossed thin-crust pizza (on Thursday, that pizza is half price) and more are all served in generous portions. The Heights location is quieter than the original on Richmond, and you can sit on the intimate rooftop patio next to the fireplace on a crisp evening. Views include the downtown skyline, which is especially nice at twilight. Be sure to try Sonoma's house sangria in the summer, as it has a cult following. Note: This is one of the best happy hours in Houston.

THE TASTING ROOM

1101-18 UPTOWN PARK
at S. Post Oak Blvd.
☎ (713) 993-9800 | MAP **D6**
multiple locations
TASTINGROOMWINES.COM

OFFSHOOTS OF THIS SLEEK WINE BAR CONCEPT ARE NOW established in four neighborhoods across the greater Houston area, each a little different from its siblings. An enormous wrapping patio defines the CityCenter location, for example, while the recent renovation at the Uptown Park location provides more space for indoor diners. The handkerchief-sized River Oaks flagship is an intimate wine bar with an air-conditioned patio and open cellar, and the Kingwood version has a

stunning water view of King's Harbor. Management regularly schedules live acoustic music on the patios, and TTR often hosts tastings and other special events. The dining menus are impressive, too.

VINE WINE ROOM

12420 MEMORIAL *west of Gessner*
☎ (713) 463-8463 | MAP **C6**
VINEWINEROOM.COM

WITH WINE DINNERS EVERY MONTH, WINE TASTINGS every Saturday and a variety of wine from regions around the world offered every day, it is no surprise that Joe Rippey's Vine Wine Room has become a second home for its Memorial-area patrons. Inside the setting is cozy and comfortable, with antiques and artwork to accentuate the living room style. Outside you can participate in the "Pairings on the Patio" event every Tuesday, with wine, pizza and live jazz 6 to 9 pm. There are about 200 wines from small and unique estates around the world to purchase by the bottle. Hungry? Pick out a bottle or two and head across the shopping center to Two Saints, the BYOB restaurant also owned by Rippey.

CRAFT BREWERIES

8TH WONDER BREWERY

2202 DALLAS *at Hutchins*
☎ (713) 229-0868 | MAP **F6**
8THWONDERBREWERY.COM

THE LOCALLY ESTEEMED EATSIE BOYS—A GROUP OF CHEFS, entrepreneurs and now brewers, with Aaron Corsi as brewmaster—have waited to start large-scale production until their coveted East Downtown location was ready to brew. With a background in the restaurant industry, Corsi recently became a brewing science educator, so he brings a scientific approach to the company thanks to a formal education and advanced degrees in distilling. Eventually, 8th Wonder will likely be in cans, and there are several recipes in the works to build upon their current lineup of three foundational brews: Alternate Universe, Hopston and Intellectuale. Many of their planned brews will pair to the food served at their Eatsie Boys Cafe on Montrose.

BUFFALO BAYOU BREWING CO.

5301 NOLDA *at Detering*
☎ (713) 750-9795 | MAP **E6**
BUFFBREW.COM

WITH NINE OF BUFF BREW'S FIRST 12 BEERS HAVING been collaborations, you can guess how founder Rassul Zarinfar feels about the controversial new trend to join forces with local retailers and fellow breweries to produce specialty beers. Zarinfar's "weird-ass beers" include 1912, a red ale aged on live oak wood from the Rice University campus, and Smoke on the Bayou, a wee heavy brewed with malts smoked at Goode Co. Seafood, Rockwell and Beaver's. Another shouldn't-have-worked success story is Buffalo Sunset, a coffee-infused IPA (India Pale Ale), as coffee is more commonly used in porters and stouts. It was a long shot to pair hops with coffee beans, but it seems to have worked since Sunset sold well around town. Buff Brew is currently more than doubling its capacity.

FORT BEND BREWING CO.

13370 S. GESSNER *between S. Cravens & Pike, Missouri City*
☎ (281) 769-8618
FORTBENDBREWING.COM

ANOTHER BREWERY THAT OPENED WITH DEEP POCKETS, Fort Bend was started by a former software tycoon who sourced out beer expertise from as far away as Philadelphia. Despite the big budget, "down-to-earth, grassroots and hard-working" are the terms brewmaster Christopher Leonard hopes to conjure when consumers taste his beer. Hailing from the Northeast, Leonard has fully embraced the Southern culture with his beer, made to suit Houston's hot summers and Texan palates. He is more interested in making beer that is technically sound than palate-shocking adjunct brews. A fan of the mathematical and scientific aspect of brewing, Leonard taps into his extensive professional brewing history to make technically correct beer.

KARBACH BREWING CO.

2032 KARBACH
between Mangum & Hempstead
☎ (713) 680-2739 | MAP **D5**
KARBACHBREWING.COM

WITH A HEFTY ROLL-OUT BUDGET AND A COMPANY FULL of beer distribution-savvy founders (they previously owned a distribution company), you can be sure that this company hit the ground running when it launched in 2011. They poached Eric Warner, who graduated from a prestigious brewing program in Germany and obtained his brewmaster degree in 1990, and they self-distributed until they couldn't meet the market's demand any longer, at which point they signed Silver Eagle Distributors. Brewmaster Warner is a fan of well-executed classic styles, but he is open to move in the direction of more adjunct beers if that's what the market demands. They offer the cherry bourbon-barrel-aged Hellfighter along with their flagships and a few other small batches.

LONE PINT BREWERY
507 COMMERCE
near 6th, Magnolia
☎ (281) 731-5466
LONEPINT.COM

THIS BREWERY HAS BEEN HOST-ING TASTING EVENTS AT WELL-regarded pour spots since March 2013. The brewmaster is a longtime home brewer who creates his own recipes from "daydreaming and spontaneous inspiration." A sour-mash wheat and a smoked habanero ale are their small-batch offerings with staples to include 667, Neighbor of the Beast, Gentleman's Relish, Jabberwocky and Pioneer Yellow Rose.

NO LABEL BREWING
5351-A 1ST ST.
near Pin Oak Rd., Katy
☎ (281) 693-7545
NOLABELBREW.COM

ENTERING THIS KATY BREWERY, NEIGHBOR TO SILOS IN HOUS-ton's far-west suburb, it initially looks more like a drafthouse cinema because of its projector and stage. On weekends there is food, live music, movie screenings and children's moonwalk obstacle courses. No Label's claim to fame isn't just the beer they release to the market—they're also pros at attracting visitors. With their tours being amongst the most successful in the local beer scene, it's no secret that this brewery

puts on a good party every Saturday. It's also the only local brewery with two women running the company alongside their husbands. The original impetus was to open a brewery in the founders' backyard in order to sample co-founder and brewmaster Brian Royo's homebrew.

SAINT ARNOLD BREWING COMPANY
2000 LYONS *east of Hardy*
☎ (713) 686-9494 | MAP **D5**
SAINTARNOLD.COM

THE PIONEER OF THE CRAFT BREWERY SCENE IN HOUSTON is facing steep competition with all of the new breweries we've welcomed lately. But the city's established brewery, coming up on its 20th anniversary in 2014, is doing more than keeping up; it's staying ahead of the curve with different series, and the brewmaster is giving many of the best-selling brews the barrel-aged treatment. (Yes, Pumpkinator is a part of that lineup.) The most recent addition to the company was a full kitchen with chef Ryan Savoie serving up weekday lunch. The seasonal menu changes every day and offers beer-infused dishes to pair to whichever brews are on tap.

SOUTHERN STAR BREWING COMPANY
1207 N. FM 3083 RD E.
near Airport Parkway, Conroe
☎ (936) 441-2739
SOUTHERNSTARBREWERY.COM

EVERY YEAR THIS CONROE BREW-ERY'S SEASONAL PRO-AM OFFER-ing changes because every year the brewery hosts a home-brewing competition wherein the winner's recipe is scaled up to commercial production and distributed to retailers all over our area. There is no set style or rules—whichever wins, wins. Apart from including fans in their brewing process, the brewery is also known for frequently putting on fundraisers in an effort to give back to the community. Founded in 2007, the brewery isn't the oldest, but it has a good track record with local retailers for having amongst the most consistent quality kegs compared to their competitors. Cans of Pine Belt Ale, Buried Hatchet Stout and Bombshell Blonde are distributed all over Texas and in several other states.

RETAILERS

FRENCH COUNTRY WINES

2433 BARTLETT *just east of Kirby*
☎ (713) 993-9500 │ MAP **E7**
FRENCHCOUNTRYWINES.COM

YOU COULD EASILY MISS THIS GEM, AS THE LITTLE BOUTIQUE blends right into the Rice Village

neighborhood and is shy with its signage—look for a French flag on the window. French Country Wines trades only in French wines, importing them directly from small family-owned, estate-bottled and (often) organically grown vineyards throughout France. Not just a retailers of wine, owners Phyllis Adatto and Tim Smith also serve as distributors, selling wine to French bistros all over the greater Houston area. Curious? Plan to come to one of the free tastings from noon to 6 pm on Saturdays or 5 to 7 pm on Wednesdays. (During that time you'll usually spot a food truck out front, too.) Buy a case and receive a 10 percent discount.

GOODY GOODY LIQUOR

2680 HWY. 6 SOUTH
north of Richmond
☎ (281) 497-1862 │ MAP **A7**
multiple locations
GOODYGOODY.COM

FAMILY-OWNED GOODY GOODY LIQUOR OPENED ITS FIRST TWO Houston-area locations in 2013, but

Wine shopping in Spec's

they've been a dominant wine, beer and liquor retailer in the Dallas-Fort Worth area for nearly 50 years. Now they intend to take on Houston hometown favorite, Spec's. Goody Goody has already announced a third Houston location to open in 2013 and at least one in 2014. The story is that young and near-broke Joe Jansen bought the tiny Goo Goo Liquor Store on Greenville Avenue in Dallas in 1964 and simply added "dy" to the signage in order to avoid buying an entirely new sign. The family's Houston stores, which are a roomy 28,000 square feet each, combine a handsome ambiance (e.g. wood flooring, wide aisles, rare wines in their own walk-in wine room, even a few chandeliers) with bargain pricing.

HOUSTON WINE MERCHANT

2646 S. SHEPHERD
south of Westheimer
☎ (713) 524-3397 | MAP **E6**
HOUSTONWINES.COM

HOUSTON WINE MERCHANT – FOUNDED AS WINES OF AMERICA in 1984—is still owned and operated by Scott Spencer, one of the most erudite wine pros in the city. The single-location shop now carries a finely curated selection of spirits as well, but let's face it: It's the wines for which it is best known. The staff offers free wine tastings twice a week, often with the winemaker in attendance, in an effort to educate its loyal clientele. (If you come to all of them, you'd try more than 500 new wines a year.) Our favorite thing about Houston Wine Merchant is the case subscription program that delivers a dozen bottles to your home or office every other month. There's nothing like it for getting you out of your wine rut.

RICHARD'S LIQUORS & FINE WINES

2545 KIRBY *at Westheimer*
☎ (713) 523-7405 | MAP **E6**
multiple locations
RICHARDSLIQUORS.COM

SINCE 1949, RICHARD'S HAS BROWN-BAGGED BOOZE FOR YOUR mother and your mother's father. As the business grew, its stock and trade became more diversified with fine wines, fine cigars and upscale gift items. The staff, some of whom have worked with the company for decades, are knowledgeable and eager to offer recommendations with commendable professionalism, and many are on first-name terms with customers. All four locations are perfect for finding just the right chilled Champagne impromptu or choosing from in-store specials. The ambience is boutique rather than warehouse, and the wine is always premium quality, whether modestly priced or rare vintage. Customers in neighborhoods surrounding each of the locations can call for home delivery.

SPEC'S WINES, SPIRITS & FINER FOODS

2410 SMITH *at McGowen*
☎ (713) 526-8787 | MAP **F6**
multiple locations
SPECSONLINE.COM

THE SPECTACLE-WEARING RABBIT THAT IS THE SPEC'S BRAND mascot has become one of Houston's most beloved icons. The company's 60-plus stores are where locals go for wine and spirits, sure. But Spec's also carries Riedel barware, gifts, mixers, snack foods, cigars and much more. At the mothership location on Smith, there are close to two acres of store to explore, every square foot crammed with some 40,000 labels of wine, spirits, liqueurs, beer and gourmet food including an impressive selection of cured meats and imported cheeses in the deli. You can even pick up a juicy roasted duck to take home for dinner. Don't be surprised if you arrive to purchase a few bottles of wine and depart with a week's worth of groceries and a new set of martini glasses. The walk-in humidor houses 900 cigar varieties, and the Smith Street megastore often has tasting tables set up throughout the store on Saturdays. Satellite locations are smaller and less generously stocked, but the staff can get you anything you need from the main store. Pay with cash and receive a five percent discount.

DISTILLERIES

RAILEAN DISTILLERS

341 5TH STREET *near Avenue D, San Leon*
☎ (713) 545-2742
RAILEAN.COM

LOCATED IN SAN LEON DOWN ON GALVESTON BAY SINCE 2007, Railean Distillers uses only Gulf Coast sugar cane molasses and produces rum in small batches. Currently three styles of rum are made: white rum, dark rum and aged Reserve Single Barrel Rum. More recently, in 2010, namesake Kelly Railean introduced a line of 100% Blue Agave spirits made from blue agave from Jalisco, Mexico. Railean is careful not to call this spirit tequila, though others sometimes do. She told *My Table* magazine in Summer 2013 that she is playing around with

some other spirits, too, but cannot talk about those yet.

YELLOW ROSE DISTILLING

1224 N. POST OAK RD.
north of Katy Rd. | MAP **D5**
YELLOWROSEDISTILLING.COM

SINCE THEY FOUNDED YELLOW ROSE DISTILLING ABOUT THREE years ago, partners Troy Smith and Ryan Baird have outgrown their whiskey distillery in Pinehurst, Texas, and are in the process (as we go to press with this book) of relocating to a larger venue in Houston near Spring Branch on North Post Oak Road. The new facility, which they hope to open in Fall 2013, will welcome visitors, provide tours and—yes!—have a tasting room. Yellow Rose Distilling will be the first whiskey distillery located within the city limits of Houston. Their first two products are Outlaw Bourbon and Straight Rye Whiskey.

WINERIES

DIONISIO

2110 JEFFERSON *near Hutchins*
☎ (713) 906-2499 | MAP **F6**
DIONISIOWINERY.COM

JIMMY ARANDA AND WIFE CLARICE ARANDA ARE THE OWNERS, wine experts and juice experimenters who love to talk about wine with their customers. Dionisio, which is named for Jimmy's paternal grandfather, produces some traditional red and white wines, but it's the fruit wines that set this winery apart in the market. If you're curious to try something completely different, something different is what you'll get: Green

Apple Riesling, Cranberry Malbec, Pomegranate Zinfandel and Black Cherry Pinot Noir, to name a few. Dionisio also offers Wine 101 classes and is available for private parties.

HAAK VINEYARDS WINERY

6310 AVENUE T
1.8 miles south of Hwy. 6, Santa Fe
☎ (409) 925-1401
HAAKWINE.COM

A DREAM BROUGHT TO FRUITION BY OWNERS RAYMOND HAAK and Gladys Haak, the vineyard started in 1969 when Raymond began experimenting with grape varietals that would thrive in our humid coastal Texas climate. He found success with a white hybrid called Blanc du Bois, and today the little winery makes several styles from the juice. Located about 10 miles from the Gulf of Mexico, this three-acre vineyard boasts a 11,000-square-foot stone winery where scores of events take place—some on a grand scale like the summer concert series and some on a more casual note like the pruning day that's paired with an oyster fry. A petite open-air chapel is a quaint venue for weddings.

LA FUENTE WINERY

10606 HEMPSTEAD *north of Antoine* | MAP **D5**
☎ (713) 269-4489
LAFUENTEWINERY.COM

W INES ARE BLENDED AND AGED IN THIS TINY WINERY that is buried in an industrial park in near-Northwest Houston. It's bland-looking from the outside, but warm and even charming inside, a cozy place for a group tasting. White wines are made in steel tanks, so there is no oakiness; the reds are 100 percent

of their varietal. Some of the wines have done very well at the annual Rodeo Uncorked! International Wine Competition.

THE NICE WINERY

2901 W. SAM HOUSTON PKWY. N. (BELTWAY 8) *at Kempwood*
☎ (713) 744-7444 | MAP **B5**
THENICEWINERY.COM

T HE NICE WINERY MIGHT BE BEST DESCRIBED AS A VINTNER'S laboratory—its home is in a generic strip-center space rather than a traditional winery. The two owners Ryan Levy and Ian Eastveld both trained at Le Cordon Bleu, and they are certified sommeliers as well as certified wine educators. (Nice wines are also produced in Argentina and Napa as well as here in Houston.) Levy and Eastveld offer wine classes, wine-and-food-pairing classes, guided wine tastings, wine flight tastings and a wine club.

VINTNERS OWN

3482 W. 12TH *west of Ella*
☎ (713) 880-3794 | MAP **D5**
VINTNERSOWN.COM

H OW PURPLE DO YOU WANT YOUR HANDS TO GET? JUST kidding. But those who want to be hands-on in the winemaking process should take a trip to Vintner's Own and take a look at the specialized crush facility that focuses on small-lot barrel production. You choose how much or how little you want to contribute in the crushing, blending, aging, bottling and labeling process. The grapes are shipped here from California, and you'll make a barrel, which is about 24 cases. Cost depends on the grapes you select, as well as some other variables, so consider forming a "wine consor-

Wine barrels in Vintners Own

tium" with a couple of like-minded friends. Your wine stays in the barrel in the Vintners Own warehouse for aging, but you can visit and taste as often as you like. When it's time to bottle your own custom blend, you can also personalize your label. Interestingly, some Houston restaurants have begun bottling their own house wines here.

WATER 2 WINE

3331 WESTPARK *just west of Buffalo Speedway*
☎ (713) 662-9463 | MAP **D7**
WATER2WINE.COM

THIS FUN LITTLE CUSTOM WINERY IS OWNED AND OPERATED BY husband-and-wife team Al and Vickie King along with their partners, Sandra and Juan Mangini. Customers choose which wine they will make from a list of some 70 different wines, made from 100 different musts (grape juices) from 13 different countries. All of these wines are available to taste before you begin. Once you choose the wine you'd like to make, you work side-by-side with the staff to combine the must with a selection of yeasts, oak chips, grape skins and other ingredients. At this point the fermentation begins. In 45 to 60 days your batch of approximately 29 bottles will be ready for bottling. Customers are able to check in on their wine's progress as much or as little as they desire. Come bottling time, many clients make it a wine-tasting party. A wide variety of stock or custom labels and foils are available, with many appealing options. The per-bottle price from a 29-bottle batch varies from $9.50 to $17.50.

RESTAURANTS

WE HAVE INCLUDED A FEW NATIONAL CHAIN RESTAU-
RANTS IN THIS CHAPTER, BUT MOSTLY WE DID NOT. YOU
will certainly find those places by yourself. Instead, we want to guide
you to 440 of Houston's best independent restaurants and locally
grown chains, funky holes in the wall and ever-variable ethnic trea-
sures. We take particular delight in directing you to a hallmark of
Houston dining—the casual fine-dining spots where you will eat
exquisite food and dressing up is not required. So please be seated,
tuck a napkin under your collar, pick up a fork, and get ready to dig in.

KEY to SYMBOLS		
⟈ = CHEAP	⟈⟈ = MODERATE	⟈⟈⟈ = EXPENSIVE

AMERICAN CONTEMPORARY

024 Grille
*17
51Fifteen Restaurant
  & Lounge
Backstreet Cafe
Benjy's
Bird & the Bear, The
Blackfinn American
  Grille
Cafe Benedicte
Cafe Express
Canopy
Cullen's Upscale
  American Grill
Daily Review Cafe
Eleven XI
Flora & Muse
Glass Wall
Grove, The
Haven
Hearsay Gastro Lounge
Line & Lariat
Lucio's

Mark's American
  Cuisine
Masraff's
Max's Wine Dive
Mockingbird Bistro
  Wine Bar
Monarch
Mr. Peeples
Olivette
Paulie's
Rainbow Lodge
Raven Grill
RDG + Bar Annie
Remington, The
Seasons 52
Shade
Sorrel Urban Bistro
Sparrow Bar +
  Cookshop
Tiny Boxwood's
Tony's
Triniti
Two Saints
Underbelly
Up

AMERICAN TRADITIONAL

Baba Yega
Bohemeo's
Barbecue Inn
Barnaby's Cafe
Beaver's Ice House
BRC Gastropub
Brasil
Brooklyn Athletic Club
Buffalo Grille, The
Cleburne Cafeteria
Del Frisco Grille
Down House
Dry Creek Cafe
Facundo Cafe
Federal Grill, The
Fielding's Wood Grill
Fountain View Cafe
Frank's Americana
  Revival
Funky Chicken
Gratifi Kitchen + Bar
Hollister Grill
Jasper's

Jax Grill
Jonathan's The Rub
Jus' Mac
Just Dinner
Katch 22
Lankford Grocery
Laurenzo's Prime Rib
Liberty Kitchen &
  Oyster Bar
Local Foods
Lola
Mia's
Natachee's Supper
  'N Punch
Noe Restaurant
Ogden's Hops &
  Harvest
Onion Creek
Triple A
White Oak Kitchen
  + Drinks
Zelko Bistro

ARGENTINE
Argentina Cafe
Manena's Pastry Shop
Original Marini's
  Empanada House
Tango & Malbec

ASIAN ECLECTIC
Bodard Bistro
Blu
Doozo Dumplings
  & Noodles
Golden Dumpling
Hollywood Vietnamese
  & Chinese
Hot Pot City
Jasmine Asian Cuisine
Little Sheep Mongolian
  Hot Pot
Nara
Sandong Noodle
  House
Shabu House
Sinh Sinh
Straits
Tan Tan

BAR BITES
Batanga
Benjy's
Coppa Ristorante
  Italiano
Cove
Danton's Gulf Coast
  Seafood Kitchen
Del Frisco's Double
  Eagle Steak House
Eddie V's Prime
  Seafood
Eleven XI
Etoile Cuisine et Bar
Goode Co. Texas
  Seafood
Max's Wine Dive
Mockingbird Bistro
  Wine Bar
Queen Vic Pub
Piola
Pistolero's
Poscól Vinoteca
  e Salumeria
Osteria Mazzantini
RDG + Bar Annie
Reef
Shade
Sorrel Urban Bistro
Uchi

BARBECUE
Barbecue Inn
Burns Bar-B-Q
Corkscrew BBQ
Gatlin's BBQ
Goode Co. Texas
  Bar-B-Q
Killen's Steakhouse
Oak Leaf Smokehouse
Pierson & Co. BBQ
Pizzitola's Bar-B-Cue

BELGIAN
Cafe Brussels

BEST HANGOVER
CURE
Aladdin
Hubcap Grill

Lankford Grocery
Pho Binh I
Spanish Flowers
Torchy's Tacos
Triple A

BOSNIAN
Cafe Pita+

BREAKFAST
*Many bakeries and
Mexican restaurants
also serve breakfast.*

59 Diner
Avalon Diner
Barnaby's Cafe
Brasil
Breakfast Klub, The
Buffalo Grille, The
Canopy
Down House
Empire Cafe
Fountain View
  Cafe
Flora & Muse
Gilhooley's
Goode Co. Taqueria
  & Hamburgers
Harry's
House of Pies
Kenny & Ziggy's
Lankford Grocery
  & Market
Lola
Natachee's Supper
  'N Punch
New York Bagel &
  Coffee Shop
Onion Creek
Ouisie's Table
Niko Niko's
Pho Ga Dakao
Pondicheri
Snap Kitchen
This is it!
Tiny Boxwood's
Triple A

BRITISH

Queen Vic Pub & Kitchen

BRUNCH

Many more restaurants serve breakfast or lunch on the weekend.

Backstreet Cafe
Beaver's Ice House
Benjy's
Brasserie 19
Brasserie Max & Julie
BRC Gastropub
Brennan's of Houston
Brooklyn Athletic Club
Danton's Gulf Coast Seafood Kitchen
Eleven XI
Hugo's
Indika
Laurenzo's Prime Rib
Le Mistral
Max's Wine Dive
Mockingbird Bistro Wine Bar
Original Ninfa's, The
Ouisie's Table
Quattro
RDG + Bar Annie
Rioja
Shade
Tiny Boxwood's
Zelko Bistro

BUSINESS LUNCH

Brasserie 19
Brennan's of Houston
Da Marco
Masraff's
Mark's American Cuisine
Morton's
Olivette
Osteria Mazzantini

Palm, The
Quattro
Rainbow Lodge
RDG + Bar Annie
Restaurant Cinq
Tony's

BYOB

Most of the following charge a corkage fee of $5 to $12, but some are free.

Aladdin
Bistro Des Amis
Cafe Pita+
Collina's Italian Cafe
Corkscrew BBQ
Dry Creek
Doshi House
Fadi's Mediterranean Grill
Himalaya
Hollister Grill
Huynh
Istanbul Grill
Jonathan's The Rub
Just Dinner
Kanomwan
Korean Noodle House
La Guadalupana
La Vista
Lola
Lucio's
Pasha
Pizaro's Pizza Napoletana
Reginelli's Pizzeria
Two Saints
Vieng Thai
Zabak's

CAJUN & CREOLE

BB's Cafe
Bistro, The

Brennan's of Houston
Cajun Stop, The
Danton's Gulf Coast Seafood Kitchen
Jimmy G's
Pappadeaux Seafood Kitchen
Ragin' Cajun
Tony Mandola's
Treebeards
Willie G's
Zydeco Louisiana Diner

CHARCUTERIE

Brasil
Brasserie 19
Chez Nous
Coppa Ristorante Italiano
Grove, The
Kenny & Ziggy's
Kris Bistro
L'Olivier
Mezzanotte
Mockingbird Bistro
Oporto Cafe
Poscól Vinoteca e Salumeria
Rainbow Lodge
Sorrel Urban Bistro
Tango & Malbec
Triniti
Underbelly

CHEF'S TABLE

Artisans
Brennan's of Houston
Damian's Cucina Italiana
Eleven XI
Haven
Le Mistral
Oxheart
Pass & Provisions, The
Quattro
Triniti
Uchi

CHINESE

Aling's Chinese Hakka
   Cuisine
Arco Seafood
Bistro 888
Cafe Chino
China Garden
Dim Sum King
E-Tao
Fat Bao
Fufu Cafe
Fung's Kitchen
Gigi's Asian Bistro &
   Dumpling Bar
Golden Dumpling
Hollywood
   Vietnamese &
   Chinese
Hunan Garden
Mala Sichuan Bistro
Ocean Palace
Peking Cuisine
Sandong Noodle
   House
Sichuan King
Sinh Sinh
Tan Tan
Yum Yum Cha

CHURRASCARIA

Fogo de Chao
Nelore Churrascaria
Tradiçao Brazilian
   Steakhouse

COCKTAILS

*Creative and
well made*

Backstreet Cafe
Beaver's Ice House
Benjy's
Brasserie 19
Brennan's of Houston
Cuchara Mexico City
   Bistro
Eddie V's Prime
   Seafood

Eleven XI
Grove, The
Haven
Hugo's
Indika
Kata Robata
Latin Bites Cafe
Mockingbird Bistro
   Wine Bar
Pass & Provisions, The
Philippe Restaurant
Queen Vic Pub
Shade
Soma Sushi
Sparrow Bar +
   Cookshop
Tony's
Triniti
Truluck's
Uptown Sushi

CUBAN

Cafe Piquet
El Meson
Flor de Cuba

DIM SUM

Arco Seafood
Dim Sum King
E-Tao
Fung's Kitchen
Gigi's Asian Bistro &
   Dumpling Bar
Golden Dumpling
   House
Ocean Palace
Yum Yum Cha

DINERS

59 Diner
Avalon Diner
Bradley's Fine Diner
Harry's
House of Pies
Triple A

DOG-FRIENDLY PATIO

*Our favorites,
among many:*

Barnaby's Cafe
Becks Prime
BRC Gastropub
Canopy
Down House
Hugo's
Gratifi Kitchen + Bar
Mia's
Natachee's Supper
   'N Punch
Pico's Mex Mex
Tila's Restaurante
   & Bar
Tiny Boxwood's

DRAMATIC INTERIOR DESIGN

*17
Américas
Armando's
Artista
Bistro, The
Brasserie 19
Brennan's of
   Houston
Brenner's
Capital Grille
Da Marco
Del Frisco's Double
   Eagle Steak House
Downtown Aquarium
El Real Tex-Mex
Flora & Muse
Gigi's Asian Bistro &
   Dumpling Bar
Grove, The
La Casa del Caballo
Les Givral's
Mark's American
   Cuisine
Masraff's
Mr. Peeples
Ouisie's Table

Oxheart
Pappas Bros.
   Steakhouse
Pass & Provisions, The
Perry's Steakhouse
   & Grille
Philippe Restaurant
Quattro
Ra Sushi
Rainbow Lodge
Restaurant Cinq
Ristorante Cavour
Straits
Tony's
Trevísio
Triniti
Uchi
Underbelly
Up
Uptown Sushi
Vic & Anthony's

ECLECTIC MENU

Al's Quick Stop
Baba Yega
Backstreet Cafe
Benjy's
Bohemeo's
Cafe Benedicte
Cafe Express
Charivari
Conscious Cafe
Costa Brava Bistro
Cove
Cullen's Upscale
   American Grill
Eatsie Boys Cafe
Empire Cafe
Fat Bao
Fusion Taco
Goro & Gun
Gratifi Kitchen + Bar
Grove, The
Hungry's
La Vista
Max's Wine Dive
Mockingbird Bistro
   Wine Bar
Mr. Peeples

Natachee's Supper
   'N Punch
Oxheart
Pass & Provisions, The
Paulie's
Pistolero's
Radical Eats
Restaurant Cinq
Roost
Tiny Boxwood's
Underbelly

ENTERTAINMENT

*Includes live music,
flamenco, blues
brunch, movies,
games and open-
mic nights. Check
websites.
Our favorites,
among many:*

Batanga
Brasil
Breakfast Klub, The
Brennan's of
   Houston
Brooklyn Athletic Club
Carmelo's
Danton's Gulf Coast
   Seafood Kitchen
Eddie V's Prime
   Seafood
El Hidalguense
El Meson
Flor de Cuba
Flora & Muse
Grappino di Nino
Hugo's
Last Concert Cafe
Mo's A Place for
   Steaks
Ouisie's Table
Pico's Mex Mex
Rainbow Lodge
Rioja
Rudi Lechner's
Tango & Malbec
The Tasting Room

Tony's
Truluck's
Vic & Anthony's
Vine Wine Room

ETHIOPIAN

Blue Nile Ethiopian
   Restaurant

FARM-TO-TABLE MENU

Brennan's of Houston
Down House
Grove, The
Haven
Hugo's
Ogden's Hops &
   Harvest
Oxheart
Radical Eats
Restaurant Cinq
Roost
Ruggles Green
Shade
Sorrel Urban
   Bistro
Sparrow Bar +
   Cookshop
Underbelly
Zelko Bistro

FRENCH

Artisans
Au Petit Paris
Aura Brasserie
Bistro Des Amis
Bistro des Arts
Bistro Le Cep
Bistro Provence
Brasserie 19
Brasserie Max &
   Julie
Cafe Rabelais
Chez Nous
Etoile Cuisine et Bar
Kris Bistro
La Balance
Le Mistral
L'Olivier
Philippe Restaurant

Salé-Sucré
Sweet Paris Crêperie
  & Cafe

FRIED CHICKEN
Barbecue Inn
Cleburne Cafeteria
Frank's Americana
  Revival
Federal Grill, The
Frenchy's Chicken
Funky Chicken
Haven
Liberty Kitchen
Lucille's
Max's Wine Dive
Spanish Village
Triple A
Zelko Bistro

GERMAN
Charivari
Rudi Lechner's

GARDEN
*Restaurants that
grow some of the
kitchen's produce*

Coltivare
Daily Review Cafe
Haven
Laurenzo's Prime Rib
Patrenella's
Rainbow Lodge

GREAT VIEW
Dramatic vistas

Artista
Brenner's
Del Frisco Double
  Eagle Steak House
Grove, The
Monarch
Rainbow Lodge
RDG + Bar Annie
Trevisio
Up

GREEK
Al's Quick Stop
Alexander the
  Great
Niko Niko's

HAMBURGERS
BRC Gastropub
Becks Prime
Bubba's Texas Burger
  Shack
Burger Guys
Christian's Tailgate
Dry Creek Cafe
Eleven XI
Facundo Cafe
Fielding's Wood Grill
Goode Co. Taqueria
  & Hamburgers
Hubcap Grill
Jax Grill
Lankford Grocery
Little Big's
Little Bitty Burger
  Barn
Mia's
Mockingbird Bistro
  Wine Bar
Rainbow Lodge
Sammy's Wild Game
  Grill
Shepherd Park
  Draught House
Tookie's
Underbelly

HOT DOGS
Burger Guys
Good Dog Hot Dogs
Max's Wine Dive
Moon Tower Inn
Sammy's Wild Game
  Grill

HOTEL
RESTAURANTS
*17/The Sam Houston
  Hotel
Bistro, The/Hotel
  Sorella

Grille 024/Westin
  Houston Memorial
  City
Line & Lariat/Hotel
  Icon
Monarch/Hotel
  ZaZa
Noe Restaurant/
  The Omni
Olivette/The
  Houstonian
Quattro/The Four
  Seasons
Remington, The/St.
  Regis Hotel
Restaurant Cinq/La
  Colombe d'Or
Ristorante Cavour/
  Hotel Granduca
White Oak Kitchen +
  Drinks/Westin Hotel
  Galleria

HOUSTON
INSTITUTIONS
Avalon Diner
Barbecue Inn
Brennan's of Houston
Cleburne Cafeteria
Damian's Cucina
  Italiana
Goode Co. Texas
  Bar-B-Q
Irma's
Lankford Grocery
Last Concert Cafe
Molina's
Nielsen's Delicatessen
Original Ninfa's, The
Spanish Village
Taste of Texas
This Is It!
Tony's
Triple A

INDIAN
Bismillah Restaurant
Hot Breads
Indika
Kerala Kitchen

Khyber North Indian
  Grill
Kiran's
London Sizzler
Madras Pavilion
Maharaja Bhog
  Restaurant
Narin's Bombay
  Brasserie
Pondicheri
Queen Vic Pub
Raja Sweets
Shiva Indian
  Restaurant
Trenza
Udipi Cafe

INDONESIAN
Straits

ITALIAN
Amerigo's Grille
Antica Osteria
Arcodoro
Arturo Boada
  Cuisine
Arturo's Uptown
  Italiano
Bellissimo Ristorante
Carmelo's
Carrabba's Italian
  Grill
Ciao Bello
Ciro's Italian Grill
Collina's Italian
  Cafe
Coppa Ristorante
  Italiano
Costa Brava Bistro
Crapitto's Cucina
  Italiana
Crisp
D'Amico's Italian
  Market Cafe
Da Marco
Damian's Cucina
  Italiana
Divino
Dolce Vita Pizzeria
  Enoteca

Frenchie's
Giacomo's Cibo
  e Vino
Grappino di Nino
Grotto
La Griglia
La Vista
Mezzanotte
Mia Bella Trattoria
Osteria Mazzantini
Nino's
Piola
Quattro
Palazzo's Trattoria
Patrenella's
Perbacco
Piatto Ristorante
Piola
Poscól Vinoteca
  e Salumeria
Prego
Pronto Cucinino
Ristorante Cavour
Sorrento
Tony's
Trevisio
Vincent's

JAMAICAN
Reggae Hut

JAPANESE
Azuma
Blue Fish, The
Blue Fish House
Kaneyama
Kata Robata
Kubo's Sushi Bar & Grill
MF Sushi
Michiru Sushi
Nippon
Oishii
Ra Sushi
Shabu House
Soma Sushi
Sushi Jin
Sushi Miyagi
Uchi
Uptown Sushi

JEWISH DELI
Katz's Deli
Kenny & Ziggy's
New York Bagel &
  Coffee Shop

KID-FRIENDLY
*Most Asian restau-
rants, bakeries,
Tex-Mex cafes,
barbecue joints and
burger bars also
welcome children.*

59 Diner
Avalon Diner
Barnaby's
Breakfast Klub, The
Buffalo Grille, The
Cafe Express
Cleburne Cafeteria
Downtown Aquarium
Fountain View Cafe
Goode Co. Taqueria &
  Hamburgers
Hobbit Cafe
House of Pies
Jus' Mac
Kenny & Ziggy's
Lankford Grocery
Niko Niko's
Pappadeaux
Piola
Torchy's Tacos

KOREAN
Arirang Korean
  Restaurant
Jang Guem Tofu
  House
Korean Noodle House
Nam Gang
Nara

LADIES WHO
LUNCH
Brasserie Max & Julie
Crapitto's Cucina
  Italiana
Etoile Cuisine et Bar

Kiran's
La Griglia
Monarch
Ouisie's Table
Philippe Restaurant
Raven Grill
Seasons 52
Tiny Boxwood's
Up

LATIN AMERICAN

Amazón Grill
Américas
Artista
Batanga
Churrascos
El Pueblito Place
El Pupusodromo
Gloria's Restaurant
Honduras Maya Cafe
   & Bar
Julia's Bistro
La Fogata
Latin Bites Cafe
Mi Pueblito
Piqueo
Pollo Bravo
Saldivia's South
   American Grill

LEBANESE

Cafe Lili
Mary'z Mediterranean
   Cuisine

MALAYSIAN

Banana Leaf

MEXICAN BREAKFAST

Our favorites,
among many:

Chiloso's Taco
   House
El Rey Taqueria
Gorditas
   Aquacalientes
Irma's
La Guadalupana

La Mexicana
Martinez Cafe
Otilia's
Spanish Flowers
Teotihuacán

MEXICAN/ TEX-MEX

100% Taquito
Armando's
Bellissimo Ristorante
Berryhill Baja Grill
Bodegas Taco Shop
Cadillac Bar
Cantina Laredo
Caracol
Chiloso's Taco House
Chuy's Comida Deluxe
Cuchara Mexico City
   Bistro
Cyclone Anaya's
El Hidalguense
El Real Tex-Mex
El Rey Taqueria
El Tiempo
Escalante's
Fusion Taco
Gerardo's Drive-In
Gloria's Restaurant
Goode Co. Taqueria
   & Hamburgers
Gorditas
   Aguascalientes
Guadalajara Bar & Grill
Hugo's
Irma's
La Casa del Caballo
La Fisheria
La Guadalupana
   Bakery & Cafe
La Mexicana
Laredo Taqueria
Last Concert Cafe
Lopez Mexican
   Restaurant
Maria Selma
Martinez Cafe
Mission Burrito
Molina's

Original Ninfa's, The
Otilia's
Pappasito's Cantina
Pico's Mex Mex
Pistolero's
Spanish Flowers
Spanish Village
Sylvia's Enchilada
   Kitchen
Tacos à Go-Go
Teala's
Teotihuacán
Tila's
Torchy's Tacos
TQLA
Trenza

MIDDLE EASTERN

Abdallah's Bakery
Afghan Cuisine
Al Aseel Grill & Cafe
Aladdin
Arpi's Phoenicia Deli
Cafe Lili
Fadi's Mediterranean
   Grill
Falafel Factory
Mary'z Mediterranean
   Cuisine
Shawarma King
Yildizlar
Zabak's

NATIONAL RECOGNITION

Recent ink or air time

Cafe Pita+
Fusion Taco
Haven
Hugo's
Kenny & Ziggy's
Killen's Steakhouse
Lankford Grocery
Niko Niko's
Oxheart
Pass & Provisions, The
RDG + Bar Annie
Reef

Sparrow Bar +
   Cookshop
Tony's
Uchi
Underbelly

OPEN LATE/
OPEN 24 HOURS
Our favorites serving
food after 10 pm

59 Diner
BB's Cajun Cafe
Brasil
BRC Gastropub
Christian's Tailgate
El Real Tex-Mex
Fufu Cafe
Gorditas
   Aguascalientes
Hollywood
   Vietnamese &
   Chinese
House of Pies
Indika
Kata Robata
Last Concert
Little Big's
London Sizzler
Mai's
Max's Wine Dive
Oporto Cafe
Piola
Queen Vic Pub
Rioja
Saigon Pagolac
Sinh Sinh
Soma Sushi
Spanish Flowers
Tacos à Go-Go
Tan Tan
Van Loc

OYSTER BAR
Brasserie 19
Danton's Gulf Coast
   Seafood Kitchen

Eleven XI
Gilhooley's
Goode Co. Texas
   Seafood
Joyce's Seafood
   & Steaks
Liberty Kitchen &
   Oyster Bar
McCormick &
   Schmick's
Oceanaire Seafood
   Room, The
Pappas Seafood House
Ragin' Cajun
Reef
Tony Mandola's

PAKISTANI
Bismillah Restaurant
Himalaya

PASTA MADE
IN-HOUSE
Ciao Bello
Coppa Ristorante
   Italiano
D'Amico's Italian
   Market Cafe
Da Marco
Dolce Vita Pizzeria
   Enoteca
Giacomo's Cibo e Vino
Osteria Mazzantini
Pass & Provisions, The
Paulie's
Poscól Vinoteca
   e Salumeria
Prego
Quattro
Ristorante Cavour
Tony's

PATIO DINING
Américas
Arcodoro
Artista
Arturo's Uptown
   Italiano
Baba Yega
Backstreet Cafe

Batanga
Becks Prime
Brasil
Brasserie Max &
   Julie
Brennan's of Houston
Brenner's
Brooklyn Athletic Club
Cafe Express
Canopy
Churrascos
Chuy's
Ciao Bello
Ciro's
Crapitto's Cucina
   Italiana
Crisp
D'Amico's Italian
   Market Cafe
Daily Review Cafe
Dolce Vita Pizzeria
   Enoteca
Down House
Eatsie Boys Cafe
El Pueblito Place
El Real Tex-Mex
El Tiempo
Eleven XI
Empire Cafe
Etoile Cuisine et Bar
Flora & Muse
Giacomo's Cibo
   e Vino
Gigi's Asian Bistro
   & Dumpling Bar
Goode Co. Taqueria
   & Hamburgers
Grappino di Nino
Grove, The
Haven
Hugo's
Ibiza
Kata Robata
Khun Kay Thai Cafe
La Griglia
La Mexicana
Last Concert Cafe
Le Mistral
Maria Selma

Monarch
Mr. Peeples
Niko Niko's
Onion Creek
Original Ninfa's, The
Osteria Mazzantini
Ouisie's Table
Pico's Mex Mex
Rainbow Lodge
Raven Grill
RDG + Bar Annie
Rioja
Spanish Flowers
Teala's
Tila's
Tiny Boxwood's

PERSIAN
Cafe Caspian
Darband Shishkabob
Kasra Persian Grill

PERUVIAN
Latin Bites Cafe
Piqueo
Pollo Bravo

PIZZA
Bombay Pizza
  Company
Candelari's Pizzeria
Ciao Bello
Crisp
Dolce Vita Pizzeria
  Enoteca
Grimaldi's Pizzeria
Osteria Mazzantini
Pass & Provisions, The
Pink's Pizza
Piola
Pizaro's Pizza
  Napoletana
Reginelli's Pizzeria
Seasons 52
Star Pizza

POLISH
Polonia

PORTUGUESE
Oporto Cafe

PRIVATE DINING ROOM
Most hotels and steakhouses also have private dining rooms.

Arcodoro
Backstreet Cafe
Brennan's
Brenner's
Carmelo's
Coppa Ristorante
  Italiano
El Meson
Kenny & Ziggy's
Mockingbird Bistro
  Wine Bar
Mr. Peeples
Ouisie's Table
Philippe Restaurant
Prego
Rainbow Lodge
Seasons 52
The Tasting Room
Trevisio
Vic & Anthony's

PUERTO RICAN
Tex-Chick

SANDWICH SHOP
Brown Bag Deli
Cajun Stop, The
Carter & Cooley
Cricket's Creamery
  & Caffe
Kahn's Deli
Kraftsmen Baking
Lee's Sandwiches
Les Givral's
Local Foods
Maine-ly Sandwiches
Nielsen's Delicatessen

SEAFOOD
Crawfish & Beignets
Cove
Danton's Gulf Coast
  Seafood Kitchen
Downtown Aquarium
Eddie V's Prime
  Seafood
Gilhooley's
Goode Co. Texas
  Seafood
Joyce's Seafood &
  Steaks
La Fisheria
McCormick &
  Schmick's
Oceanaire Seafood
  Room, The
Pappadeaux Seafood
  Kitchen
Pappas Seafood House
Reef
Truluck's

SLIDERS
Our favorites, among many:

Capital Grille
Del Frisco's Double
  Eagle Steak House
Katch 22
Little Big's
Mockingbird Bistro
Morton's
Reef
Sullivan's Steakhouse

SOUTHERN/ SOUL FOOD
Breakfast Klub, The
Conscious Cafe
Frenchy's Chicken
Lucille's
Ouisie's Table
Punk's Simple Southern
  Food
Resie's Chicken &
  Waffles
This Is It!

SPANISH
Andalucia Tapas
Costa Brava Bistro
El Meson

Ibiza
Rioja

STEAKHOUSE

III Forks
Brenner's
Capital Grille
Del Frisco's Double
  Eagle Steakhouse
Eddie V's Prime
  Seafood
Fleming's Prime
  Steakhouse
Killen's Steakhouse
La Casa del Caballo
Lynn's Steakhouse
Mo's A Place for
  Steaks
Morton's
Palm, The
Pappas Bros.
  Steakhouse
Perry's Steakhouse
  & Grille
Smith & Wollensky
Sullivan's Steakhouse
Taste of Texas
Vic & Anthony's

SUSHI HAPPY HOUR

Blue Fish, The
Blue Fish House
Kaneyama
Kata Robata
Kubo's Sushi Bar & Grill
Oishii
Ra Sushi
Sushi Jin
Uchi

TABLE FOR TWO

Date-friendly restaurants, our favorites among many

Américas
Antica Osteria
Armando's
Artisans

Au Petit Paris
Backstreet Cafe
Brasserie 19
Brasserie Max & Julie
Brennan's of Houston
Brenner's
Brooklyn Athletic Club
Cafe Rabelais
Da Marco
Damian's Cucina
  Italiano
Danton's Gulf Coast
  Kitchen
Dolce Vita
Etoile Cuisine et Bar
Fung's Kitchen
Indika
Just Dinner
Killen's Steakhouse
Kiran's
Kubo's Sushi Bar
  & Grill
La Casa del Caballo
Le Mistral
Mark's American
  Cuisine
Mockingbird Bistro
Oporto Cafe
Original Ninfa's, The
Ouisie's Table
Pass & Provisions, The
Patrenella's
Queen Vic Pub
RDG + Bar Annie
Seasons 52
Shade
The Tasting Room
Tony's
Vic & Anthony's

THAI

Kanomwan
Khun Kay Thai Cafe
Nidda Thai
Thai Sticks
Vieng Thai

TURKISH

Empire Turkish Grill
Istanbul Grill
Pasha

VEGAN- OR VEGETARIAN-FRIENDLY

A Moveable Feast
Aladdin
Baba Yega
Batanga
Cafe TH
Canopy
Cricket's Creamery
  & Caffe
Dolce Vita Pizzeria
  Enoteca
Doshi House
Fadi's Mediterranean
  Grill
Field of Greens
Giacomo's Cibo e Vino
Green Seed Vegan
Haven
Hobbit Cafe
Indika
Khun Kay Thai Cafe
Kiran's
Local Foods
London Sizzler
Loving Hut
Madras Pavilion
Maharaja Bhog
Mission Burrito
Narin's Bombay
  Brasserie
Oxheart
Pondicheri
Radical Eats
Ruggles Green
Shade
Shiva
Snap Kitchen
Sparrow Bar +
  Cookshop
Tiny Boxwood's
Udipi Cafe

Vieng Thai
Zabak's

VIETNAMESE

Cafe TH
Crawfish & Beignets
Hollywood
    Vietnamese &
    Chinese
Huynh
Jasmine Asian
    Cuisine
Kim Son
Lee's Sandwiches
Les Givral's
Mai's Restaurant
Pho Binh 1
Pho Danh
Pho Ga Dakao
Saigon Pagolac
Tan Tan
Thanh Phuong
Van Loc

WATCH THE GAME

Blackfinn American
    Grille
El Real Tex-Mex
Blu
Katch 22
Little Big's
Ragin' Cajun
Sammy's Wild Game
    Grill
Shepherd Park Draught
    House
Sorrel Urban Bistro

WHOLE FISH ON THE MENU

Our favorites, among many:

Blu
Hugo's
Jasmine Asian Cuisine
L'Olivier
Lucille's
Mala Sichuan Bistro

Osteria Mazzantini
Tony's
Underbelly

WILD GAME ON THE MENU

Brennan's of Houston
Eleven XI
Masraff's
Mockingbird Bistro
    Wine Bar
Pass & Provisions, The
Rainbow Lodge
Restaurant Cinq
Sammy's Wild Game
    Grill
Thanh Phuong

WINE LIST OF NOTE

Well-chosen, well-written

III Forks
Américas
Amerigo's Grille
Arcodoro
Au Petit Paris
Backstreet Cafe
Brasserie Max &
    Julie
Brennan's of
    Houston
Brenner's
Cafe Rabelais
Capital Grille
Chez Nous
Coppa Ristorante
    Italiano
Da Marco
Del Frisco Double
    Eagle Steak House
Divino
Dolce Vita Pizzeria
    Enoteca
Eddie V's Prime
    Seafood
El Meson
Giacomo's Cibo e Vino
Glass Wall

Haven
Hugo's
Ibiza
Killen's Steakhouse
Kiran's
Le Mistral
Lynn's Steakhouse
Mark's American
    Cuisine
Max's Wine Dive
Mockingbird Bistro
    Wine Bar
Osteria Mazzantini
Oxheart
Pappas Bros.
    Steakhouse
Pass & Provisions, The
Perry's Steakhouse
    & Grille
Philippe Restaurant
Poscól Vinoteca
    e Salumeria
Prego
Quattro
Rainbow Lodge
RDG + Bar Annie
Reef
Rioja
Seasons 52
Shade
Smith & Wollensky
Taste of Texas
The Tasting Room
Tony's
Truluck's
Vic & Anthony's
Underbelly
Zelko Bistro

024 GRILLE
945 GESSNER
just south of Katy Fwy. (I-10 West)
in the Westin Hotel
☎ (281) 501-4350 | MAP **C6** | ⟦🍴⟧
024GRILLE.COM

TAKING OVER THE SPOT BRIEFLY OCCUPIED BY TRATTORIA II Mulino (a New York landmark that didn't translate well in the given setting), 024 Grille has a broader spectrum, which makes much more sense for its location and function as a hotel restaurant. Serving breakfast, lunch and dinner, it's fashioned as an American bistro with global touches. Dinner brings a menu of steakhouse-inspired fare like the 18-oz cowboy ribeye, sides like parmesan risotto and creamed spinach as well as entrees of glazed short ribs, Berkshire pork chops and baked tilefish. Lunch is definitely more casual with burgers on brioche and "composed salads," and breakfast is as upscale (smoked salmon Benedict) or as casual (blueberry protein smoothie) as you'd like.

III FORKS
1201 SAN JACINTO *at Dallas,*
in GreenStreet
☎ (713) 658-9457 | MAP **F6** | ⟦🍴⟧
3FORKS.COM

JOINING THE RANKS OF STEAKHOUSES LOCATED IN DOWNtown Houston is III Forks, one of a chain of restaurants founded in Dallas. While many Houstonians like to down-talk their northern neighbors, wagging tongues are soon silenced when they get a taste of the restaurant's famous bread pudding. Also impressive are the 1,500 bottles of wines housed in a temperature-controlled glass cellar. Of course there are also the standard steaks and seafood and sides like sweet potato hash or off-the-cob creamed corn. Throw in the elegant dining room of white wood paneling and brass bead chandeliers, private rooms and professional service and you've got the formula for a great executive lunch or dinner. Weekday happy hour is more approachable for non-business related munching and martini-ing.

*17
1117 PRAIRIE *at San Jacinto,*
in the Sam Houston Hotel
☎ (832) 200-8888 | MAP **F6** | ⟦🍴⟧
17FOOD.COM

ALTHOUGH IT'S NEARING THE 10-YEAR MARK, *17'S DINING room (inside the boutique Sam Houston—formerly Alden—hotel) is still one of the most aesthetically modern dining rooms in Houston. White wingback chairs contrast dramatically with red brocade walls and dark tabletops while a sort of crystal fringe hangs from the ceiling. The menu is not as dramatic as the decor, but considering its mission of servicing downtown clientele and hotel guests, it makes sense. Breakfast is fairly extensive with a few large plates like eggs Benedict and steak and eggs; lunch is a punctuated version of the dinner menu but with sandwiches and salads; dinner brings entrees of local red snapper, crabcakes with a Latin twist, short ribs or rack of lamb alongside decadent desserts like crème brûlée cheesecake. Though the menu plays it safe, they do change it up seasonally and use local produce and meats when available.

51FIFTEEN RESTAURANT & LOUNGE

5115 WESTHEIMER *inside Saks Fifth Avenue, in The Galleria*
☎ (713) 963-8067 | MAP **D6** | ¶¶¶
51FIFTEEN.COM

THE ULTIMATE IN LUXURY MEANS HAVING A GOURMET restaurant in the middle of a Saks Fifth Avenue inside one of the most high-end shopping centers in the country. That restaurant and lounge is 51Fifteen, full of golds and taupes and ladies who lunch alongside luminous rose-shaped wall sculptures that undulate with various colors. It's like a trippy secret garden that turns into a sexy lounge at night (often with live entertainment). Champagne is practically a requirement here—you are dining inside a Saks Fifth Avenue restaurant after all. As for food, it's all fairly predictable with dishes like barbecued salmon, filet mignon, lamb chops, snapper, etc. But it is nicely done and satiating after a hard day of shopping.

59 DINER

3801 FARNHAM
between S. Shepherd & Greenbriar
☎ (713) 523-2333 | MAP **E7** | ¶
multiple locations
59DINER.COM

IT'S LIKE A TIME WARP TO WALK INSIDE ANY LOCATION OF 59 Diner, with its vinyl booths, sassy waitresses, milkshakes and jukeboxes. Short of the free WiFi and a lack of poodle skirts, it is everything you'd expect of a traditional American diner, right down to the greasy, utterly habit-forming curly fries. Clientele varies mostly on the location, but any given day you'll find families out for breakfast, college students studying after-hours or late-night revelers recharging after an evening on the town. The milkshakes are worth the calories, and blue-plate lunch specials are downright homey, but breakfast is the foundation for everything else served here and rightly so. It is a diner after all.

100% TAQUITO

3245 SOUTHWEST FWY. (HWY. 59) *at Buffalo Speedway*
☎ (713) 665-2900 | MAP **E7** | ¶
100TAQUITO.COM

A VETERAN IN THE WORLD OF FOOD-TRAILER-GOES-BRICK-and-mortar, 100% Taquito started selling Mexican street foods in a parking lot in 1996 before moving into its now strip-center locale. Decor is colorful and even includes a lime green taxicab parked inside as well as murals and tiles and a faux food truck facade where orders are placed. The menu is rather extensive and packed with traditional Mexican street foods like tacos, sopes, tostadas, tortas, *flautas* (rolled-up, deep-fried tacos) and *molletes* (open-faced sandwiches). Sides like *chicharrón* (crispy pork rinds) con guacamole are a tasty treat and coincidentally a perfect accompaniment to the margaritas, which are available by the pitcher. Rounding out the appeal is a kids' menu for the little ones under five.

A MOVEABLE FEAST

9341 KATY FWY. (I-10 WEST) *at Echo Lane*
☎ (713) 365-0368 | MAP **C6** | ¶
AMOVEABLEFEAST.COM

THERE'S A MELLOWNESS ABOUT A MOVEABLE FEAST, UNLESS it's a busy lunch hour. It's a restaurant inside a health food store that stocks its shelves with vitamins and supplements, gluten-free goods, organic meats and the like. The restaurant follows the theme with nary a fried item on the menu and a smattering of Mediterranean, Asian and Southwestern-influenced dishes like quesadillas, tabouli and grass-fed beef burgers. For convenience, there's free WiFi and bulk items like their chicken salad are prepackaged and ready to take home. Saturday brings a guilt-free brunch from 9 am to 3 pm with organic eggs, healthful low-fat sausage and pancakes. If the weather's right, patio seating is very pleasant with a naturally landscaped buffer of plants and flowers.

ABDALLAH'S BAKERY

3939 HILLCROFT
at Westpark
☎ (713) 952-4747 | MAP **C7** | 🍴
ABDALLAHS.COM

EXCEPT FOR ITS INCLUSION IN THIS BOOK, ABDALLAH'S WOULD qualify as a "hidden gem." Part cafeteria, part grocery, part bakery, it's one of the places on Hillcroft that you need to set aside preconceived notions to visit. In other words, get out of your inside-the-Loop comfort zone and have an adventure. The pita bread is legendary and even sold wholesale to Whole Foods as well as at other Middle Eastern grocers, but fresh is always best. Fill one up with their equally legendary chicken shawarma at the steam table lunch (which comes with a side) and you'll be hooked. Save room for dessert, which comes in the form of traditional and fresh-baked Lebanese pastries like baklava, bird's nests and shortbread cookies.

AFGHAN CUISINE

11920 HWY. 6 SOUTH
at Voss, Sugar Land
☎ (281) 879-0945 | 🍴

"WHAT EXACTLY IS AFGHAN CUISINE?" YOU MAY ASK yourself one rainy afternoon. Find out with an immersive experience at the very literally named Afghan Cuisine in Sugar Land. If you can get past the sparse dining room and sometimes aloof service, you're in for a culturally delicious treat. Dishes range from curries to kabobs and are often served alongside house-made yogurt, which helps equalize the heat in dishes like *borani bademjan*—chunks of tender eggplant stewed in tomatoes, garlic and spices. There's even a platter of the national dish of Afghanistan, *quabili pallow*, with a layer of spiced brown basmati rice covering a fork-tender lamb shank, topped with sautéed raisins and shredded carrots.

AL ASEEL GRILL & CAFE

8619 RICHMOND *at Dunvale*
☎ (713) 787-0400 | MAP **C7** | 🍴
ALASEELGRILL.COM

AL ASEEL HAS BEEN TOUTED RECENTLY BY LOCAL FOODIES as having one of the best variations of fried chicken in town, but that's not all they have. While the chicken may be the hook that reels you into the modest strip-center storefront, it's the uniquely cylindrical-shaped falafel, the tomato casserole—bubbling tomatoes with chunks of ground meat and warming spices—and the musakhan chicken (grilled, dusted with sumac and smothered in sautéed onions) that keep us coming back. Also of note is the fact that their most expensive dish, a mixed grill, levels out at only $13.99.

AL'S QUICK STOP

2002 WAUGH *at Welch*
☎ (713) 522-5170 | MAP **E6** | ❚

AL'S MAY BE THE ONLY CONVE-
NIENCE STORE IN TOWN WITH
cafe-like sidewalk seating, and there's
no better place to plunk down and
peel open a freshly prepared falafel
pita (provided it's not raining, of
course). You can even do so until
3 am on the weekends when it's
open late to serve weekend revelers,
especially those emerging from the
next-door pub of Rudyard's after a
live show. Also lauded are their gyros
with mountains of tender, moist lamb
inside a warm pita with tomatoes,
onions and *tzaziki* (yogurt and cucumber), though the food counter
serves a myriad of cuisines, of
which tacos are even included.

ALADDIN

912 WESTHEIMER *at Montrose*
☎ (713) 942-2321 | MAP **E6** | ❚
ALADDINHOUSTON.COM

IF YOU'VE NEVER TASTED A PITA
THAT'S LITERALLY JUST BEEN
pulled from the hearth it was baking on, you haven't been to Aladdin.
Accompanying that über-fresh pita
are a variety of hummus, salads,
vegetables and meats like chicken
shawarma, braised lamb shanks or
baked red snapper. Served cafeteria-
style from some of the friendliest restaurant employees in Houston, it's an
all-around satisfying meal. To sample
the most items (and you'll want to
pile on as many as you can), get the
combo, which gives you a choice
of three sides—the grilled vegetable
salad is always a hit as is the roasted
cauliflower or the creamy hummus—
and one meat. House-prepared juices
like mango or watermelon are also
always available and highly recom-

mended. Otherwise feel free to BYOB
as there's no corkage fee.

ALEXANDER THE GREAT

3055 SAGE *at Hidalgo*
☎ (713) 622-2778 | MAP **D7** | ❚❚
ALEXANDERTHEGREAT.CC

UPSCALE GREEK DINING IS
UNCOMMON IN HOUSTON,
with this exception. Alexander
the Great is the remedy for those
occasions that require a live belly
dancer performing as you have an
appetizer of Greek cheese flambéed
tableside. There are also excellent
and traditional Greek dishes like
moussaka, gyro plates and seafood
specialties like whole grilled snapper (served bone-in) and octopus
that simply shine. The pace can
be slow at times, but sit back and
enjoy the scene. If enough ouzo
is flowing, you may find yourself
dancing alongside the live enter-
tainers while you wait.

ALING'S CHINESE HAKKA CUISINE

15425 SOUTHWEST FWY.
(HWY. 59) *at William Trace exit,*
Sugar Land
☎ (281) 242-0432 | ❚
ALINGSHAKKA.COM

EVER HEARD OF "CHINDIAN"
FOOD? IF NOT, IT'S TIME TO
educate yourself at Aling's. Also known
as Indo-Chinese, the style originated
when Chinese immigrants brought
their comfort food to India, which
then took on a life of its own through
Indian chefs' interpretations. Resulting dishes are quirky but full of flavor
like the chilly chicken—boneless
marinated chunks of chicken stir-fried
with soy, onions and chiles—and the
ironic but delicious American chop
suey made with crunchy chow mein

noodles, chicken and crisp vegetables served in a spicy sauce with a hint of tomato. The dining room is eerily lit with a piping of neon, but your attention will be diverted quick enough by the oddly delicious combinations of Indian spices and Chinese technique.

AMAZÓN GRILL

5114 KIRBY *between Hwy. 59 & Bissonnet*
☎ (713) 522-5888 | MAP **E7** | ⑂
CORDUA.COM

AMAZÓN GRILL IS THE ONE AND ONLY FAST-CASUAL CONCEPT under the Cordúa umbrella, which also includes the high-rolling Américas, Churrascos and Artista. Counter service makes for a less intimidating atmosphere, which in turn invites more families and also higher noise levels. But don't let that turn you off: The break in pricing alone (for some of the same Cordúa favorites) is worth braving either lunch rush or weekend breakfast. Puffy chicken tacos and empanadas are savory and satisfying, and portions are very generous. Before and after: Mojitos make for a lovely happy hour, and tabletop s'mores are a fun way to end any evening. While the atmosphere is much more casual, you may recognize some of the signature, modern, dramatic furniture pieces inside from the now-closed Galleria-area Américas, making for a slightly more elegant look.

AMÉRICAS

2040 W. GRAY *at S. Shepherd*
☎ (832) 200-1492 | MAP **E6** | ⑂⑂
multiple locations
CORDUA.COM

WITH DINING ROOMS AS WHIMSICAL AS A DR. SEUSS imagining and as elegant as any Vegas hotspot, the Cordúa family wows first with visuals. Luckily, with 25 years in the restaurant industry, they also wow equally with the food. Chef/owner/impresario Michael Cordúa made a name for himself introducing Houstonians to the flavor profiles of Latin America with menus originally built around the *churrasco*, or Latin steakhouse. There's a signature steak that never disappoints—beef tenderloin butterflied and grilled with a garlicky chimichurri sauce—but there's so much more to the extensive menu. From paella to ceviche flights to crawfish taquitos, it's almost as fun to order as it is to walk in and see the swooping surrealist shapes of the interior for the first time. Pro tip: Don't skip the rich and decadent *tres leches*.

AMERIGO'S GRILLE

25250 GROGANS PARK DR.
off Sawdust, The Woodlands
☎ (281) 362-0808 | ⑂⑂⑂
AMERIGOS.COM

JUST THE FACT THAT EXECUTIVE CHEF ARTURO OSORIO HAS been running Amerigo's kitchen since it opened in 1994 should give some indication of the consistency that's made this Northern Italian steakhouse so successful. The first in a boom of upscale restaurants to hit The Woodlands, it maintains an authenticity rarely found in the highly polished master-planned community these days. Beef carpaccio, *pappardelle capesante* with sea scallops and tomato mint sauce, handmade capellini with crawfish, shrimp, roasted garlic, mushrooms, scallions and sugo rosa are just a handful of near-perfect dishes. Even the bar is hopping most evenings with a piano, excellent happy hour specials and an award-winning wine list.

ANDALUCIA TAPAS

1201 SAN JACINTO
at Dallas, in GreenStreet
☎ (832) 319-6673 | MAP **F6** | ⑀
ANDALUCIATAPAS.COM

EVEN THOUGH IT'S LOCATED IN THE VERY DEVELOPED-FEELING GreenStreet (formerly Houston Pavilions) complex downtown, Andalucia Tapas' slower pace and Old World details give it a comfortable, European feeling. Dim lighting, a matador mural, dark wooden tabletops, wrought iron and cozy booths make for a romantic setting, only enhanced by late weekend hours and flamenco guitarists and dancers performing live on stage. With an environment that invites lounging, it's the perfect spot to grab a bottle of Spanish wine, a few plates to share (the salmon tartar-stuffed piquillo peppers are nicely done as are the crispy chicken livers) and simply relax. Larger plates like paella and lamb tagine are available, but these are more suited to communal dining.

ANTICA OSTERIA

2311 BISSONNET *near Greenbriar*
☎ (713) 521-1155 | MAP **E7** | ⑀
ANTICARESTAURANT.COM

IT'S A THROWBACK TO THE DAYS WHERE A ROMANTIC DINNER meant sitting at a table for two draped in a white tablecloth and sharing a plate of pasta à la *Lady and the Tramp*-style. While health regulations forbid having actual dogs—however endearing—inside the restaurant, there are still the white tablecloths, the romantic

two-tops and a creaky old house that encapsulates a comfort unmatched in newer establishments. With Italian dishes like veal piccata, spaghetti alla carbonara, eggplant parmesan and off-menu specials like lobster ravioli, it's classic and solidly good. The wine list is just so-so, but well-priced bottles are available. Dinner only.

ARCO SEAFOOD

9896 BELLAIRE BLVD. *at W. Sam Houston Parkway S. (Beltway 8)*
☎ (713) 774-2888 | MAP **B7** | ⑀

AS STATED IN ITS NAME, SEAFOOD IS A BIG DEAL AT ARCO, located among the innumerable strip mall restaurants in Houston's "new" Chinatown. How so? Tanks of live sea creatures—oblivious to their impending doom—await as guests literally select the freshest ingredients available, which are then scooped from their tanks and made into dinner. Hand-selecting specimens will cost you extra, but it does give a sense of quality control to the meal. Other notables include one of the city's best Peking duck platters and Cantonese classics like lobster with chives and garlic, walnut shrimp and clay pots. And while dressing up is not necessary, Arco does feel a little more upscale than its Chinatown neighbors with upholstered chairs and a fancy chandelier.

ARCODORO

5000 WESTHEIMER
at Post Oak Blvd.
☎ (713) 621-6888 | MAP **D6** | ⑀
ARCODORO.COM

RIGHT IN THE MIDDLE OF THE GALLERIA AREA, ARCODORO has certain standards to uphold for its well-heeled crowds. And that it does with a polished interior of gold, brown and russet and rustic Sardinian foods inspired by owner Efisio Farris' homeland. On the menu are unique dishes found only at Arcodoro (which also has a location in Dallas) such as *gnocchetti calamaretti e bottarga*—Sardinian teardrop pasta with roasted baby calamari, squash, cherry tomatoes and shavings of delicate dried mullet roe) or *linguini su Barchile* with fresh clams and skinless tomatoes. Pizza here is also destination-worthy and prepared in a wood-burning oven, topped with ingredients like imported buffalo mozzarella, porcini mushrooms or roasted vegetables. Making it that much more authentic is the fact that Farris is author of one of the standards in Sardinian cooking, *Sweet Myrtle and Bitter Honey: The Mediterranean Flavors of Sardinia.*

ARGENTINA CAFE

3055 SAGE *at Hidalgo*
☎ (713) 622-8877 | MAP **D7** | 🍴

IT'S A CASUAL, CLEAN AND BRIGHTLY COLORED HAVEN FOR Argentine transplants craving a taste of home or looking for a place where soccer is most likely on the television. Of course, Galleria-area workers also find it a comfortable spot for quick and simple breakfasts, Argentine pastries baked from scratch, a hearty lunch of fried-egg-topped filet mignon or just a spicy *choripan* (sausage sandwich) with snappy casing. If green things are important to you, know that this is not a vegetable-loving kitchen; the only roughage seems to be the simple salads. However, a lack of veggies is balanced by an abundance of desserts, which include a *dulce de leche* cake roll gleaming with caramel and a very satisfying cup of coffee to accompany it.

ARIRANG KOREAN RESTAURANT

9715 BELLAIRE BLVD. *at Corporate*
☎ (713) 988-2088 | MAP **B7** | 🍴

ARIRANG'S BEEN THROUGH A TUMULTUOUS COUPLE OF years. It originally began as a Korean barbecue restaurant, then transformed itself into a fast-casual dumpling concept, closed for a bit and then re-opened back as a Korean barbecue restaurant. Coming full circle, you can expect to leave here smelling of smoked meats as one of their claims to fame is the all-you-can-eat Korean barbecue: marinated meats that range from pork belly to squid are served raw and grilled on your tabletop. Luckily, they've also kept the highly praised dumplings on the menu as well as Korean favorites like seafood pancakes and *bibimbap* (vegetables and meat served over rice in a hot stone bowl).

ARMANDO'S

2630 WESTHEIMER
just west of Kirby
☎ (713) 520-1738 | MAP **E6** | 🍴
ARMANDOSHOUSTON.COM

IN THE MOOD FOR TEX-MEX BUT ALSO LOOKING TO IMPRESS someone with a gorgeous Mexico City-style dining room and upscale environs? A place that meets both requirements does exist, and it's Armando's. Jest if you will about the stains that chile con queso will leave on white tablecloths, but the food is simple and authentic and actually fun to eat in such a posh locale. Besides *queso flameado* (a sizzling plate of melted cheese), fajitas, chicken mole, crabcakes, lobster enchiladas and grilled snapper, there are the legendarily potent margaritas to up the ante. Celebrity cameos are also a possibility here, so keep your discretely angled iPhone camera ready.

ARPI'S PHOENICIA DELI
12151 WESTHEIMER
west of S. Kirkwood
☎ (281) 558-0416 | MAP **B6** | ❚ ¶
PHOENICIA-DELI.COM

ADJACENT TO THE ORIGINAL PHOENICIA MARKET, THIS deli is much more than its label suggests. Named for the matriarch of the Tcholakian family (founders of the gourmet grocery), Arpi still makes sure that the Middle Eastern cuisine served in a massive cafeteria set-up is up to her standards. Any given day in the sleek and modern dining room will bring a smorgasbord of exotic salads, dips and entrees including *muhammarra*, the roasted red pepper, pomegranate and walnut dip, or a fava bean salad or even heartier Armenian-style lamb shanks and chicken shawarma. Difficult decisions are just the way it goes here, right down to the selection of gelatos for dessert.

ARTISANS
3201 LOUISIANA
a block south of Elgin
☎ (713) 529-9111 | MAP **E6** | ❚¶❚
ARTISANSRESTAURANT.COM

ARTISANS IS BROUGHT TO YOU BY THE FRENCH TRIO OF CHEF Jacques Fox (previously at area country clubs) and partners/real-life brothers David and Sylvain Denis of Le Mistral. With the whole restaurant built around an extremely large and open kitchen, the chefs' world really is a stage and all the men and women merely players, much to the delight of patrons. The rest of the dining room is done simply but elegantly with black chairs and booths, wooden tables and simple accents. Like any good French restaurant, there is a tasting-menu option that might include foie gras, pistachio-crusted *poisson* (fish), pan-seared scallops and frozen Grand Marnier soufflé.

ARTISTA
800 BAGBY *at Rusk, in the Hobby Center*
☎ (713) 278-4782 | MAP **F6** | ❚¶❚
CORDUA.COM

LOCATED INSIDE THE HOBBY CENTER FOR THE PERFORMING Arts, this Cordúa restaurant is just as dramatic as the productions that go on inside the adjacent theater. Plush, luxurious seating, a massive wall of windows overlooking the Houston skyline and a panoramic balcony terrace make for an experience for the eyes while the Cordúa-signature menu makes for a largely Latin experience for the palate. However, while there are the staples like churrasco steak with yuca, crawfish taquitos and *tres leches*, there's also a touch of Italian with dishes like a shrimp masala with polenta or sides like gnocchi bolognese. The staff is so used to getting theater-goers in-and-out in time for the first act that pre-show service is down to a very efficient science.

ARTURO BOADA CUISINE
6510 DEL MONTE
just east of S. Voss
☎ (713) 782-3011 | MAP **D6** | ❚¶
BOADACUISINE.COM

AFTER LEAVING ANOTHER EPONYMOUS RESTAURANT (that still bears the name despite his absence), chef Arturo Boada quickly found another job heading up his own place, this one also bearing his name. At his newer spot, Boada is serving a very similar cuisine to his previous incarnation (see below), with a wood-fired oven churning out blistered pizzas like the traditional margherita or the jazzed up *carnitas* with Latin-style shredded meat, asadero cheese, charred salsa, onion and cilantro. There's also a tapas-style selection of seafood-heavy small plates like ceviche, fish tacos, tuna tartare and a *camarones henesy en hamaca* (sautéed shrimp with hearts of palm, tomato and cilantro in a thick soy-ginger sauce over a bed of plantains) as well as more hearty entrees of pasta, steaks and seafood. The setting is intensely colored and on the small side, which makes the whole place feel like a cozy neighborhood bistro.

ARTURO'S UPTOWN ITALIANO

1180-1 UPTOWN PARK
at Post Oak Blvd.
☎ (713) 621-1180 | MAP **D6** | 🍴
ARTUROSUPTOWN.COM

ALTHOUGH ARTURO BOADA—THE FORMER EXECUTIVE CHEF this restaurant was named for—has since moved on to open his own restaurant (see above), the name, menu and pretty much everything else has remain unchanged. This is a good thing for the regular crowds that come here for the simple but tasty Italian pleasures like fried calamari, yellow bell pepper soup, veal *saltimbocca* (topped with prosciutto, sage and lemon butter sauce) or various pastas. The hospitality here is always pleasant, and the knowledgeable staffers are usually spot-on with their

wine recommendations. On a mild Houston day, the place to be is Arturo's Tuscan-style patio with plenty of tables, ceiling fans and elegant columns.

AU PETIT PARIS

2048 COLQUITT
just east of S. Shepherd
☎ (713) 524-7070 | MAP **E7** | 🍴
AUPETITPARISRESTAURANT.COM

OWNERS ERIC LEGROS AND DOMINIQUE BOCQUIER WEREN'T just romanticizing by naming their restaurant Au Petit Paris. This Montrose bungalow is full of burnished wood and intimate dining rooms, blurry Impressionistic cityscapes, cozy outdoor seating under the trees and a menu of classic French dishes. Fish is always well prepared, whether it's the skate or the snapper, and, of course, there's foie gras and escargots as well. Braised beef cheeks cook for eight hours, making for a tender, rich dish and other entrees are equally as satisfying. Lunch is a pared-down affair but still apt with plenty of salads and French sandwiches like the classic croque madame.

AURA BRASSERIE

15977 CITY WALK *near Texas Dr., Sugar Land*
☎ (281) 403-2872 | 🍴
AURA-RESTAURANT.COM

THE CURRENT EDITION OF AURA BRASSERIE COMES IN A WHOLLY different location than the original. First opened to critical praise in Missouri City, chef and founder Frédéric Perrier has moved his upscale French fusion concept into the City Walk development in Sugar Land. Moving from one suburb to another, some say it's lost a little of its luster, but perhaps it's just growing pains. Small criticisms aside, Perrier's menu caters to both French and Texan tastes: braised pork cheeks, steak *au poivre* (filet mignon in a cognac peppercorn sauce) and foie gras prepared according to the whims of the chef. Speaking of whims, dishes like jalapeño-chicken burger have been known to show up on the daily prix-fixe lunch menu. Desserts are always a strong point, and there's plenty of French and Californian wines to round out the meal.

AVALON DINER

2417 WESTHEIMER
just east of Kirby
☎ (713) 527-8900 | MAP **E6** | ⑂
multiple locations
AVALONDINER.COM

THE ORIGINAL AVALON DINER BEGAN AS AVALON DRUG CO. in 1938 near River Oaks. While it has moved locations since then, it's still got the feeling of bygone days when milkshakes never came with a side of guilt. (And their homemade milkshakes are so amazing, the only thing you'll feel guilty for now is not ordering another.) As at most Texas diners, Avalon's specialties include epic breakfasts mostly cooked on a griddle, homey blue-plate specials, chicken-fried steaks and all things comforting. True to form, Avalon's regulars often use the neighborhood River Oaks location as a second office, tended to by efficient and sassy waitstaff that never seem to age and always keep your coffee mug full. The suburban Avalons are less quirky, more highway diner-like.

AZUMA

5600 KIRBY *south of Sunset*
☎ (713) 432-9649 | MAP **E7** | ⑂
multiple locations
AZUMARESTAURANT.COM

THE FLAGSHIP RESTAURANT OF THE GROUP THAT HAS SINCE branched out into five restaurants—three locations of Azuma along with upscale concepts of Soma Sushi and Kata Robata—is still a solid place to find both traditional Japanese sushi as well as trendy, fun rolls catering to a more Western palate. The combination works when Azuma is on its game, especially if you're willing to spend the money to go all out and order *omakase*, a meal created and hand-picked by the chef from what's freshest that day. In addition to sushi favorites are plenty of upscale or traditional Japanese entrees ranging from tempura to seafood *nabeyaki udon*, a soup with udon noodles, shrimp, squid, white fish, clams, spinach and mushrooms. Each of the three Azuma locations has its own unique feel.

BABA YEGA

2607 GRANT *at Missouri*
☎ (713) 522-0042 | MAP **E6** | ⑂
BABAYEGA.COM

BABA YEGA IS SYNONYMOUS WITH CASUAL DINING IN Montrose. It's quirky and Bohemian with a focus on vegetarian offerings, though there are many dishes for meat lovers as well, including a very admirable rendition of the burger. The patio is surprisingly tranquil with a fountain and pond, lush greenery and colorful umbrellas for shade making it one of the most desirable locales for spring and fall happy-hour gatherings.

Inside Avalon Diner

Thursday nights bring live music, and behold, the Baba Yega Sunday brunch: a buffet full of omelets, blintzes, bagels and lox, sausage, frittatas, brisket and more.

BACKSTREET CAFE

1103 S. SHEPHERD
between W. Dallas & W. Gray
☎ (713) 521-2239 | MAP **E6** | 🍴
BACKSTREETCAFE.NET

AFTER CELEBRATING 30 YEARS OF SUCCESS, IT'S SAFE TO SAY that Backstreet Cafe is officially a Houston institution. Restaurateur Tracy Vaught and husband/James Beard-nominated chef Hugo Ortega plan the menu with a refreshing seasonal approach that utilizes farmers' market ingredients in not only their dishes but in stunning cocktails that also change frequently under the direction of sommelier/beverage director Sean Beck. The theme is more upscale comfort food than anything else, but it occasionally takes influences from Ortega's Mexican background with red corn and chicken enchiladas or jalapeño fettuccine as well as thoughtful menu selections for vegetarians and vegans. The celebrated courtyard out back is an oasis of peace, paved with bricks, lined with greenery and centered around a gently splashing fountain.

BANANA LEAF

9889 BELLAIRE BLVD. *at W. Sam Houston Parkway S. (Beltway 8)*
☎ (713) 771-8118 | MAP **B7** | 🍴
multiple locations
BANANALEAFHOUSTON.COM

THIS IS NOT ONLY THE MOST PROMINENT MALAYSIAN RES-taurant in Houston, it's now two of the most prominent Malaysian restaurants in Houston. Banana Leaf recently opened a second location, and, curiously, it just so happens to be very close to the first. Acting as more of an extension of the original, there's usually still a wait, but the spicy Malaysian dishes on the menu are the same, though the original menu is slightly expanded in the newer location. *Roti canai* (the fluffy flatbread accompanied by curry dipping sauce) is made fresh by Malaysian chefs, and sambal shrimp is spicy and slightly mysterious. More daring dishes like crispy pork intestine still satisfy the adventurous while the Hainanese chicken in a flavorful rice and the whole flounder wrapped in the eponymous banana leaf are crowd pleasers. Luckily for Houston, there's now double the seating and double the deliciousness.

BARBECUE INN

116 W. CROSSTIMBERS *at Yale*
☎ (713) 695-8112 | MAP **E5** | 🍴
THEBARBECUEINN.COM

PEOPLE COME HERE FROM ALL OVER HOUSTON FOR SOME OF the crunchiest and, arguably, best fried chicken in town. Cooked to order and served with a choice of baked potato or French fries as well as an extremely simple iceberg lettuce salad with the sole purpose of transferring their homemade ranch dressing into your mouth effectively, it is worth the wait for a table and for your piping hot food. It has a well-earned small-town retro feel: The seating consists of lots of booths, some cozy tables and a lunch counter where waitresses in throwback uniforms are always just an arm's length away to refill your iced tea. Fried shrimp is also

a homerun with fans, made even more decadent by the kitchen's homemade tartar sauce. Crazy as it may seem, the barbecue is secondary to the fried dishes, though it was the original foundation for the restaurant when the Skrehot family opened it in 1946. Third-generation Skrehots still run it.

BARNABY'S CAFE

604 FAIRVIEW *east of Montrose*
☎ (713) 522-0106 | MAP **E6** | 🍴
multiple locations
BARNABYSCAFE.COM

EQUAL PARTS HIPPIE COMFORT FOOD, CLASSIC AMERICAN and health food, Barnaby's is going strong with six locations now. Simple wholesome dishes aren't groundbreaking, but they do have their own unique touches. The salads are legendarily large and globally influenced, ranging from the all-American Cobb salad to Chinese chicken to a Lebanese chicken *fattoush*. Tasty burgers made with all-natural humanely raised beef, dressed-up sandwiches (e.g. pesto chicken salad with artichoke hearts) and veggie options are always a hit at lunch while full-on plates like Doctor Gale's meatloaf make for a hearty dinner. The various locations' breakfast schedule varies (except at Baby Barnaby's, which serves breakfast exclusively), so check the website for hours.

BATANGA

908 CONGRESS *at Travis*
☎ (713) 224-9500 | MAP **F6** | 🍴
BATANGAHOUSTON.COM

AMONG THE FRESH CROP OF DOWNTOWN RESTAURANTS and bars is Batanga, a gorgeous space with an expansive patio and

Latin tapas. Lounging either inside or outside at this comfortable spot is practically required, with live Latin music at night, pig roasts on Sundays, half-price wine bottle promotions, brunch and a happy hour already popular with after-work downtown business folks. Vegetarians and gluten-sensitive types will be pleasantly surprised by the variety of tapas sans meat and wheat, though they could stand to offer complimentary breads to soak up the delicious sauces with most dishes. Parking is surprisingly easy in this section of downtown, located just across from the newly redone Market Square Park, making for a pleasant experience all the way around.

BB'S CAFE
2710 MONTROSE
just north of Westheimer
☎ (713) 524-4499 | MAP **E6** | 🍴
multiple locations
BBSCAFE.COM

THE PO'BOYS AT BB'S ARE INCREDIBLY MESSY, SO YOU know they're legit. The Midnight Masterpiece is dripping with gravy and stuffed with roast beef and, frankly, just plain indulgent. There are the traditional fried catfish, shrimp, crawfish and oyster po'boys as well, each just as good as the next along with some surprises like the South Texas Fire with beef fajita, pepper jack cheese, avocado, sautéed peppers and onions and topped with queso, plus entrees like grillades and grits, "Tex Orleans" creations and even nachos. Luckily for revelers in the Montrose, Heights and Greenway Plaza areas, the restaurants are open late on the weekends, perfect for post-party munchies. The Montrose loca-

tion, in fact, won a 2012 Houston Culinary Award for Favorite Late Night Spot.

BEAVER'S ICE HOUSE
2310 DECATUR
south of Washington
☎ (713) 864-2328 | MAP **E6** | 🍴
BEAVERSHOUSTON.COM

BEAVER'S IS A STRONG ANCHOR TO THE QUIETER END OF WASH-ington Avenue, but inside it's anything but quiet. Weekends will find the modern icehouse full of mostly youthful diners enjoying some of the best cocktails in town like a Beaver Mary (popular at their brunches)—a take on the Bloody Mary with wasabi, infused tomato juice and a garnish that eats like a meal—or perhaps an in-your-face dinner of chicken-fried steak smothered in bacon mushroom gravy and served with equally sub-stantial cheddar mashed potatoes. Pleasantly surprising for this South-ern- and barbecue-themed menu are some real vegetarian gems like BBQ tofu or the Beaver nut burger.

BECKS PRIME
2902 KIRBY *between W. Alabama & Westheimer*
☎ (713) 524-7085 | MAP **E6** | 🍴
multiple locations
BECKSPRIME.COM

HOUSTON'S RELATIONSHIP WITH BURGERS IS ALMOST AS tumultuous as any number of Elizabeth Taylor's marriages. When it's good, it's really good; when it's bad, it can often turn ugly. Thank-fully, local chain Becks Prime is more in the "really good" stage and has been since patrons discovered their kitchen-ground and cooked-to-order burgers and real fries. Juicy and oh-so-satisfying for those inevitable burger cravings, Becks always ranks among the city's top tier in just about any burger poll. As for non-burger foods, there are also mesquite-grilled swordfish sandwiches, fancy steak dinners, salads and milkshakes served in their casual dining rooms. (Most locations also have a drive-thru.) The Augusta Drive and Memorial Park locations are especially gorgeous for outdoor dining, while the Sportatorium at Memorial City Mall doubles as a sports bar.

BELLISSIMO RISTORANTE
1848 AIRLINE DR.
near W. Cavalcade
☎ (832) 618-1168 | MAP **E5** | 🍴
BELLISSIMOHOUSTON.COM

IS IT MEXICAN OR IS IT ITALIAN? IT'S BOTH, THOUGH CHEF/OWNER Javier Machuca's Bellissimo leans slightly more towards the Italian. Namesake *pasta alla Bellissimo*, for example, is jalapeño fettuccine tossed in a white wine parmesan butter sauce then topped with grilled chicken, black beans, cilantro, more jalapeños and diced tomatoes. More traditional dishes like the pizzas, outstanding lasagne and chicken *scalloppini* stay the straight and narrow course. It's all served up in the little restaurant's latest location on Airline in a simple dining room. Prices and quality of the food more than make up for the absence of ambiance.

BENJY'S
2424 DUNSTAN *east of Kirby*
☎ (713) 522-7602 | MAP **E7** | 🍴
multiple locations
BENJYS.COM

BOTH BENJY'S LOCATIONS ARE IN HIP NEIGHBORHOODS, SPORT modern decor and attract 20- and 30-somethings like bees to pollen. Well, it's really their steal-of-a-deal happy hour that brings in the well-dressed young professionals. Intriguing dishes like cornflake-crusted Gulf shrimp and house-smoked salmon sashimi come at super-low prices between 4 and 7 pm, and the drink specials include a variety of cocktails, liquors, beer and wine. That doesn't make the rest of Benjy's hours any less happy, however, because menus are always utilizing local seasonal ingredients and meshing them with a variety of influences. Consider a hot-weather dish of buckwheat gnocchi with summer squash, slow-roasted local tomatoes, basil and corn relish.

BERRYHILL BAJA GRILL
2639 REVERE *at Westheimer*
☎ (713) 526-8080 | MAP **E6** | 🍴
multiple locations
BERRYHILLBAJAGRILL.COM

YOU CAN HEAR IT IN YOUR HEAD AS YOU CROSS ANY OF THE 11 Berryhill thresholds, a slow chant gradually building to a climax as you reach the ordering counter, "Fish tacos, fish tacos, fish tacos." To avoid ordering regrets, it's best that you stick with your gut on this one, as Berryhill's claim to fame is for this very dish. Fried or grilled, the fish filets are topped with a creamy "special sauce," thinly shredded red cabbage and cilantro and wrapped in two warm corn tortillas. It really is a marvel how it all comes together so perfectly. Casual and fun, the counter-service ordering makes it easy for groups needing to split checks, the margaritas are certainly serviceable and the salsa bar is self-serve. Tamales here are also elevated to iconic status with super moist masa, tasty fillings and large portions.

THE BIRD & THE BEAR

2810 WESTHEIMER *west of Kirby*
☎ (713) 528-2473 | MAP **E6** | 🍴
THEBIRDANDTHEBEARBISTRO.COM

THE BIRD & THE BEAR, WHICH DEBUTED IN 2011, COULD EASily double as a filming location for a modern-day version of *Alice in Wonderland*. With an interior that looks as if it were designed by the Queen of Hearts herself, there are chairs hanging from the ceiling, black walls, red tufted banquettes, white tables and chairs, black napkins and fantastical crystal chandeliers. Just as the decor has a whimsical flair, so, too, does the menu. Spanning the globe in terms of styles and flavors, it's just as likely you'll find Moroccan chicken as you will owner Elouise Adams Jones' signature Southern-styled dishes (standards at her Ouisie's Table) like chicken-fried steak, braised short ribs and her locally famous "Damn Eggplant" made with shrimp, crabmeat and oysters in a spicy brandied sauce with wild rice.

BISMILLAH RESTAURANT

5702 HILLCROFT
between Westpark & Harwin
☎ (713) 781-5000 | MAP **C7** | 🍴
BISMILLAHRESTAURANT.COM

LOCATED IN HOUSTON'S EXCITING AND TRAFFIC-CLOGGED Mahatma Gandhi district, Bismillah is an approachable Indo-Pak restaurant where the masala spices are house mixed. Most everything here is going to have some spice, so ask for recommendations if you're wary

of capsaicin. The owner is friendly, inviting and always honest when suggesting dishes to newbies, all it takes is a little trust. The popular *bun kabob* is a ground beef, egg and lentil patty topped with tamarind and mint sauces, and breakfast is served at the restaurant daily with dishes like *anda* and *paratha*, a spicy omelet and flaky flatbread or *aloo chana* and *paratha*, a spicy, potato and chickpea curry served with the same bread. Just two doors down is the cafe version of Bismillah with a selection of *chaat* (the Indian/Pakistani version of fast food) like 10-spice chicken wings, *samosas* (deep fried pastries stuffed with spiced meat or vegetables) and even their version of pizza.

BISTRO 888

16744 EL CAMINO REAL
near Bay Area Blvd.
☎ (281) 990-8888 | 🍴
southwest of MAP **H9**
multiple locations
GO888TX.COM

IT'S A BIT DISORIENTING TO PULL UP TO BISTRO 888 AND FIND A castle-shaped facade, but that's just the first of many surprises. Once inside, the dining room opens up with spacious ceilings and bistro tables with red Chinese lanterns tastefully accenting rather than overpowering. The bar area itself is lounge-y with a fully tiled wall and lighted shelves displaying an extensive liquor selection and cozy booths on the other side perfect for pre-meal drinks on date night. As for the food, Bistro 888 has built a kid-friendly foundation on American-Chinese favorites like General Tso's chicken. Not content to stop there, however, the kitchen pushes the suburban envelope by offering esoteric Chinese cuisine like clay pot dishes, Taiwanese-style rice noodles, ox tongue and tripe with chili peppers, stir-fried cuttlefish and whole snapper preparations.

THE BISTRO

800 W. SAM HOUSTON PKWY. S. (BELTWAY 8) *south of Katy Fwy. (I-10 West), in the Hotel Sorella*
☎ (713) 827-3545 | MAP **B6** | 🍴
BISTROALEX.COM

CITYCENTRE HAS SWIFTLY EVOLVED INTO ONE OF HOUSton's most sophisticated and popular developments outside of The Galleria. Part of that evolution is the posh Hotel Sorella and its in-house restaurant, The Bistro. As the generic name suggests, there's a French element to the menu, but there are touches of Italian, Southern, Cajun, Latin American and Asian in the dishes as well. Utilizing the bounty of local produce, there's always a seasonal menu that changes quarterly: A summer menu recently included a peach, heirloom tomato, plum and cucumber salad as well as chicken-fried quail with smashed potatoes, sweet corn-*cuitlacoche* (savory corn fungus) gravy with pickled watermelon salad and watercress. The menu is equal parts inventive and comforting, which is not a combination found often in a hotel-embedded restaurant.

BISTRO DES AMIS

2347 UNIVERSITY *at Morningside*
☎ (713) 349-8441 | MAP **E7** | 🍴
BISTRODESAMIS.COM

IT'S AS IF THE WORD "QUAINT" WERE CONJURED SPECIFICALLY to describe this small Rice Village cafe. Going for a French country theme, original founders Odile de Maindreville and Bernard Cuillier

excelled at rustic French fare with an environment to match. Small tables fill the modest dining room (with a pastry case filled with in-house baked goods that you'd be remiss to pass up), and a larger, covered patio provides an expansive extra dining area when the interior gets cramped. Served without pretense but with careful execution are bistro classics like garlic butter escargot, tender beef bourguignon and *ratatouille gratinee*, a cassoulet of eggplant, zucchini and tomatoes. Lunch runs a little lighter with quiches, sandwiches, soups and savory crêpes. The wine selection is modest with mostly French and American bottles, but the BYOB policy is one of the best deals in town with a small corkage fee of only $8.50 as of press time.

BISTRO DES ARTS

12102 WESTHEIMER *between S. Kirkwood & S. Dairy Ashford*
☎ (281) 597-1122 | MAP **B6** | 🍴

GEORGES GUY WEARS MANY HATS: 66-YEAR-OLD CANCER survivor, former owner/chef at Chez Georges and Bistro Provence, retiree three-times-over and, most recently, restaurateur/executive chef of Bistro des Arts. Unable to resist the allure of opening and running yet another Houston restaurant—the grandkids live here, after all—Monique and Georges Guy opened their newest bistro with a simple plan: prix fixe for both lunch and dinner. Priced modestly and prepared in a way that facilitates quick service, it's a bargain for the multiple-course meals that include dessert, coffee and tea. On any given day you may find a charcuterie platter, lamb stew, ratatouille, celeriac en remoulade or duck leg confit in addition to daily desserts. The dining room is casual and as equally suited to an intimate date as a family meal; it's where Georges himself is often found in the evenings checking on guests and catching up with friends.

BISTRO LE CEP

11112 WESTHEIMER *at Wilcrest*
☎ (713) 783-3985 | MAP **B7** | 🍴
BISTRO-LECEP.COM

A FRENCH FARMHOUSE IN WEST HOUSTON? WELL, NOT QUITE, but closer than anything else you'll find in town. Bistro Le Cep's rooster theme, pine floors and rustic wooden everything (tables, bar, barstools, doors, etc.) reiterate their variation on French country in a cozy and charming setting. Also rustic are the homey and classic French dishes like duck pâté, coq au vin, pot-roasted rabbit, steak au poivre, pan-roasted calf liver with apples, onions and bacon, plus *tarte tatin* (traditional apple tart) and strawberries Romanoff. It's easy to settle in here with 50-plus selections of wine available by the glass, and most bottles are offered at moderate prices.

BISTRO PROVENCE

13616 MEMORIAL *between Wilcrest & Kirkwood*
☎ (713) 827-8008 | MAP **B6** | 🍴
BISTROPROVENCE.US

Q UIETLY TUCKED AWAY IN A SMALL, OLDER STRIP CENTER in West Houston, Bistro Provence could easily be bypassed without a second glance. It's unassuming, with only a blue awning and simple signage to alert you to its presence. Inside, it's cozy yet colorful with contrasting blue and yellow topping the small bistro tables, a wood-beamed ceiling and open kitchen. Literally a French bistro—down to the all-French wine list—there's no fusion or highfalutin' foams, powders or infusions, just simple French home-cooking that comes from the heart. Provence being the main region of influence here, meals start with *fougasse* (a crusty twist of warm bread) and olive oil, then develop into hearty and rich bistro dishes like *confit de lapin* (rabbit confit with prunes), pig's feet in white wine, mustard, garlic and parsley sauce, grilled sausages and *boeuf cocotte* (beef stew with black olives). *Note:* You can also find Bistro Provence's cuisine aboard their food truck, L'Es-Car-Go, which can be found around town and at special events.

BLACKFINN AMERICAN GRILLE

1910 BAGBY
near the Pierce Elevated
☎ (713) 651-9550 | MAP **E6** | 🍴
BLACKFINNHOUSTON.COM

B LACKFINN FITS NICELY INTO THE YOUTHFUL, ENERGETIC landscape of Midtown with an impressively large 11,000-square-feet of restaurant and bar. A chain based in Florida, the management has tried to give it a more local feel by stocking it with historic Houston photos as well as sports and rodeo memorabilia from the home teams. Most young singles packing the place don't seem to care one way or the other as they order an array of food that ranges from sports-bar favorites like quesadillas and nachos to more upscale fare like seared ahi tuna and 16-oz ribeyes. Food is not the only draw here, though, as the bar gets its fair share of action with typical cocktails

Inside Bistro Le Cep

tweaked up a bit with their fresh-squeezed juices, a large selection of local beers on draft and a surprisingly palatable wine list.

BLU

2248 TEXAS DR. *on Town Square, Sugar Land*

☎ (281) 903-7324 | 🍴

BLUSUGARLAND.COM

SUGAR LAND IS QUICKLY BECOMING THE SUBURB FOR UPSCALE dining once only found inside the Houston city limits. Adding to its repertoire of destination-worthy restaurants is Blu, a fusion of all things Asian, Indian and a few things Mexican and European. It sounds confusing, but executive chef Junnajet "Jett" Hurapan has found a magical way to put it all together that works on most levels. From tamarind-glazed spareribs to steak au poivre, the menu's got a bit of an identity crisis, but any Asian dishes are a good bet considering Hurapan's previous position in Gigi's Asian Bistro kitchen. Interestingly, Hurapan's wife, Jiraporn, acts as pastry chef for the restaurant. *Warning:* At night the lounge turns into a full-blown nightclub including go-go dancers and wall-to-wall people.

THE BLUE FISH

5820 WASHINGTON

two blocks east of Westcott

☎ (713) 862-3474 | MAP **E6** | 🍴

multiple locations

THEBLUEFISHSUSHI.COM

BECAUSE HOUSTON CAN NEVER HAVE ENOUGH SPICY TUNA rolls, Dallas sent one of its own to contend for a spot among the myriads of sushi restaurants. Not to be confused with Blue Fish House

on Richmond (see below), this chain is much more produced in the way of interiors—which are grand and clubby with an almost Miami-feel—as well as the aesthetics of the actual food. Lunches tend to be slow, but things pick up as the sun sets, especially at the Washington Avenue location. The ahi tower is a structural marvel: Tuna tartar is molded into a tower atop layers of avocado, sushi rice and snow crab with garnishes of various fish roes. It's by far their most popular dish. Discounted sushi rolls and drinks make for a bargain happy hour, which also reels in the crowds.

BLUE FISH HOUSE

2241 RICHMOND

between Greenbriar & Kirby

☎ (713) 529-3100 | MAP **E7** | 🍴

multiple locations

BLUEFISHHOUSE.COM

DESPITE THE CRAMPED QUARTERS INSIDE THE ORIGINAL Richmond Avenue location or the awful condition of the parking lot it shares with The Hobbit Cafe, Blue Fish House has lasted 10 years as of 2013, and that's saying a lot. While not the most authentic sushi in town, it is creative and well done with usually efficient service. Combinations most likely not found in Japan include deep-fried sushi rolls with asparagus and, well, probably every roll they serve. But guess what? Guests don't care about authenticity, they care about flavor, and Blue Fish House delivers. Entrees are equally satisfying with various curries, Caribbean-influenced creations and stir-fries packed full of vegetables, proteins and served with plenty of rice. The newer Sugar Land location is more chic and less funky than the original.

BLUE NILE ETHIOPIAN RESTAURANT

9400 RICHMOND
between Fondren & S. Gessner
☎ (713) 782-6882 | MAP **C7** | ⑾
BLUENILERESTAURANT.COM

IT TAKES A LITTLE WHILE TO GET USED TO THE IDEA OF EATING with your hands, especially in a nicer restaurant with tablecloths and cloth napkins. But don't worry: You'll get the hang of using the spongy, traditional *injera*—an Ethiopian flatbread made from fermented dough—as the main vehicle for getting various stews into your mouth in no time. Heavy on the spices but not always spicy are shareable platters like *yemissir wot* (a red lentil stew) and *gomen besiga* (a mixture of collard greens and cubed beef). Vegetarian options are abundant, though there are also plenty of beef, lamb, chicken and fish stews to round it out. Coffee service is a must-try, complete with a traditional ceremony, frankincense and popcorn.

BODARD BISTRO

9140 BELLAIRE BLVD.
at Ranchester
☎ (713) 541-5999 | MAP **C7** | ⑂

THIS VIETNAMESE-CHINESE NOODLE HOUSE STAPLE HAS made its own niche in the mini ecosystem of Chinatown. That niche would be their *nem nuong*—pork meatball spring rolls with an added crunch from the addition of wonton crisps—and the turmeric-tinged rice flour pancake stuffed with pork, shrimp and bean sprouts known as *banh xeo*. Knowing what to order will help you avoid the pitfall of braving the two-hour time-limited parking nearby only to mistakenly come for the sub-standard noodle bowls and pho. And just because it is so incongruously out-of-place, take note of the waterfall fountain on one side of the restaurant.

BODEGAS TACO SHOP

1200 BINZ *in Park Plaza Professional Bldg.*
☎ (713) 528-6102 | MAP **E7** | ⑂
BODEGASTACOSHOP.COM

BODEGAS TACO SHOP—WHICH, FOR THE RECORD, IS NOT AN actual bodega—is perfect for busy Medical Center personnel or famished Museum District folks. Picky definition aside, it is a convenient place to grab some of the only Mexican food in the surrounding area with build-your-own burritos, tacos, tostadas, salads, bowls and nachos. Fillings are pretty standard and include a range of meats, rice, beans, produce, cheese, sour cream and the like. More community Tex-Mex spot than fast-food joint, the comfortable setting is enhanced by live music on the weekends, free WiFi for customers and a full-on tequila bar with tasty margaritas.

BOHEMEO'S

708 TELEPHONE *at S. Lockwood*
☎ (713) 923-4277 | MAP **F7** | ⑂
BOHEMEOS.COM

THE EAST END DOESN'T GET A LOT OF ATTENTION FROM restaurateurs and bar owners, but Bohemeo's is a bona fide hangout that any region of the city would be proud to boast. Quirky and hippie and hipster and indie all rolled into one, it's colorful on the outside as well as the inside. Locally roasted coffee forms the basis for most of the barista-made lattes and cappuccinos, while a simple menu of sandwiches, salads, tacos and snacks give guests even more reason to linger in the couches and tables. Nightfall brings live music, Beatles-only open mic nights and even the occasional hula hoop dance class as well as craft beer aficionados and wine drinkers. Bonus is its location inside the vibrant Tlaquepaque Market.

BOMBAY PIZZA COMPANY

914 MAIN *at Walker*
☎ (713) 654-4444 | MAP **F6** | ❚
multiple locations
BOMBAYPIZZACO.COM

As the name suggests, the cuisine here meets at the intersection of Italy and India: a wacky yet perfect combination of pizza and Indian food. Small thin-crust pizzas are served up via counter service in a very clean but also very bare-bones pizza joint atmosphere. Favorites include a *saag paneer* pizza topped with stewed collards and spinach, paneer, goat cheese and fontina as well as "The Slumdog," which manages to fit pepperoni, chorizo, ground beef, Canadian bacon, mozzarella, grilled chicken, jalapeños, red onion and pizza sauce all onto the small disk of dough. There are stuffed kati rolls made of Indian flatbread and served with cilantro-mint chutney (ideal for individual lunches) along with heartier Italian entrees. While parking is not ideal, there is a rear entrance from the downtown tunnels.

BRADLEY'S FINE DINER

910 HEIGHTS BLVD. | MAP **E6**
just south of Katy Fwy. (I-10 West)

Big name Las Vegas chef Bradley Ogden is branching out into other cities, and Houston is among the slate of announced expansions with three concepts (so far): Bradley's Fine Diner, Ogden's Hops & Harvest and Funky Chicken. The first will be an "upscale casual" concept featuring a menu of comfort foods with price tags under $20 and a variety of choices for all palates, vegetarian or omnivore. In addition to serving breakfast, lunch, dinner and brunch, there will also be a selection of craft beer as seems to be the trend in restaurants opened post-2012 here in Houston. Funky Chicken will be located about a block away, and Hops & Harvest will be in the Memorial City area. Estimated opening date for Bradley's hovers around Fall 2013 as of press time.

BRASIL

2604 DUNLAVY *at Westheimer*
☎ (713) 528-1993 | MAP **E6** | ❚
BRASILCAFE.NET

Brasil is quite possibly one of the "coolest" hangouts in town with shady front and back patios and a roomy interior with two rooms: one industrial-chic, the other cozy coffeehouse. It's quintessential Montrose, with a mixture of hippies, hipsters, retirees and everything in between complete with sometimes-aloof baristas and live music. The scene is enhanced by its proximity to one of the most pedestrian-friendly areas of Montrose as well as its recent addition of a tap wall to service the craft-beer-loving clientele. An improved menu of pizzas,

Steak Tartare at Brasserie 19

sandwiches, burgers, tacos and tamales adds yet another element to entice crowds, who have long been coming for the already popular weekend brunches.

BRASSERIE 19

1962 W. GRAY *at Driscoll*
☎ (713) 524-1919 | MAP **E6** | 🍴
BRASSERIE19.COM

IN THE RIVER OAKS SHOPPING CENTER, THIS CHARLES CLARK-Grant Cooper restaurant has become the place to go when you want your peer group to take notice of your new designer shoes or new companion. It also is a place where raw oysters and Champagne are an acceptable mid-week appetizer, and valets work overtime parking the latest Mercedes model. It's not surprising then that the menu is pricey but upscale with French flair and luxurious ingredients. Prime rib, whole Maine lobsters, rack of lamb, duck breast, several kinds of oysters and dry-aged ribeyes are just a sampling. On the bargain side are the wines, which are priced fairly and displayed on an iPad for a fun interactive experience. The setting—drenched in gorgeous dove gray, crisp white, carrara marble and wicker—resembles a New Orleans seafood bar that went to finishing school in Paris.

BRASSERIE MAX & JULIE

4315 MONTROSE
south of Richmond
☎ (713) 524-0070 | MAP **E7** | 🍴
MAXANDJULIE.NET

JULIA CHILD WOULD FEEL RIGHT AT HOME IN LAURENCE AND Chris Paul's white linen- and lace curtain-adorned brasserie in Montrose. In addition to the casual but slightly dressy setting, there are traditional French menu favorites like sweetbreads, steak tartar and frites, mussels, cassoulet *Toulousain* and foie gras. Making it more brasserie-like are the chilled shellfish platters (oysters come from the East Coast) and a by-the-glass French wine selection to accompany. Brunches are delightful on the treetop balcony upstairs with crêpes both savory and sweet as well as *pain perdu* (real French toast) and plenty of egg dishes. Add bubbly and you've got a mini-vacation right here in town.

BRC GASTROPUB

519 SHEPHERD
south of Washington
☎ (713) 861-2233 | MAP **E6** | 🍴
BRCGASTROPUB.COM

IT'S A PUB WITH COMFORTING AND OVER-THE-TOP FOOD WHERE beer nerds love to hang out and food nerds love to pig out. Frequently, the two genres of nerds intersect, and those are the regulars at BRC, which stands for Big Red Cock. Get your mind out of the gutter, it refers to a rooster—there's even a statue of one out front. Founding chef Lance Fegen is known for his gut-busting menus stocked with items like the charred brisket chile con queso and the cheddar biscuits with bacon jam. (Can't say we didn't tell you so.) Burgers have also gained a loyal audience here, with their thick patties and Slow Dough buns. The best part about having few to no waist-friendly options on the menu? There's no choice but to splurge. Love beer? Bring your growler to fill here.

THE BREAKFAST KLUB

3711 TRAVIS *at Alabama*
☎ (713) 528-8561 | MAP **E6** | ⑂

THEBREAKFASTKLUB.COM

IT'S RARE TO ARRIVE AT THE BREAKFAST KLUB AND NOT FIND a winding line out front. Just like the postal service, neither rain nor sleet nor snow—or in Houston's case, triple-digit temperatures—can stop dedicated fans from getting their fix. The wings and waffles plate might give you a heart attack before you finish, not because of the saturated fat, but because it takes the breath away with its magnificence. Crispy wings here could have possibly birthed the oft-used phrase "seasoned to perfection" with their salty, spicy zing; waffles are Belgian and fluffy and crisp in all the right places and a pleasure all their own. Others swear by the catfish and grits, which is just as hearty. Despite its name, The Breakfast Klub also serves lunch and some soul food classics.

BRENNAN'S OF HOUSTON

3300 SMITH *south of Elgin*
☎ (713) 522-9711 | MAP **E7** | ⑂⑂

BRENNANSHOUSTON.COM

EVEN 2008'S HURRICANE IKE COULDN'T KNOCK BRENNAN'S out. Closed for several months after a fire (caused by an electric transformer explosion in the throes of the hurricane) damaged the restaurant, Brennan's re-opened to rabid fans and an improved, updated look. The kitchen picked up right where it left off under the watchful eye of chef Danny Trace, who ensures that the Texas-accented neo-Creole cuisine is still top-notch. Bananas Foster is still flambéed tableside, turtle soup is still laced with a hint of sherry and seafood still reigns supreme with shrimp remoulade, pecan-crusted Gulf fish and so much more. Brunch is always a memorable affair, especially in the beautiful courtyard, where it feels as if you've been magically transported to New Orleans.

BRENNER'S

10911 KATY FWY. (I-10 WEST)
between Brittmoore & Wilcrest
☎ (713) 465-2901 | MAP **B6** | ⑂⑂

multiple locations

BRENNERSSTEAKHOUSE.COM

BRENNER'S WAS AND IS A CLASSIC HOUSTON RESTAURANT. It's changed hands from the original Mrs. Lorene Brenner to Landry's Restaurant Group, but it has maintained a local authenticity that many of the corporation's concepts do not. Both locations are surrounded by gorgeous landscaping—the original with a verdant outdoor area behind the restaurant and the inside-the-Loop location (which once was the first location of the Rainbow Lodge) set along a scenic bayou with adjacent gardens—making for a romantic escape. Steaks are the main attraction at both, being wet-aged and served simply in their own juices alongside crispy German-style potatoes and salads dressed in a signature blue cheese dressing. Surprising but also delicious is the wienerschnitzel à la Holstein with thinly pounded fried veal topped with anchovies, capers and a sunny-side-up egg. Service is impeccable (there are some things Landry's is very good at improving), and Brenner's on the Bayou's "Blue Bar" is one of the best balconies in town.

BROOKLYN ATHLETIC CLUB

601 RICHMOND *near Hwy. 59 spur to downtown*

☎ (713) 527-4440 | MAP **E7** | ⑪

THEBROOKLYNATHLETICCLUB.COM

IT'S NOT IN BROOKLYN, AND UNLESS YOU CONSIDER BOCCE ball, horseshoes, badminton or croquet "athletic," it's not really that either. Nor is it even a club. It's actually just a really fun restaurant with a unique name and lots of outdoor dining and playing area. There's been a buzz about their Reuben sandwiches and a dish they call "Porkobucco," a massive braised pork shank served with a pan gravy, roasted Brussels sprouts, potato/bacon hash and grapefruit gremolata, and the restaurant stays crowded even on weekdays. While the dishes can get pricey, the drinks are reasonable and are, in fact, the reason many come out to the "BACyard" on weekends.

BROWN BAG DELI

2036 WESTHEIMER *just east of S. Shepherd*

☎ (713) 807-9191 | MAP **E6** | ⑪

multiple locations

THEBROWNBAGDELI.NET

IT'S SIMPLE AND EFFECTIVE: USE A PENCIL TO MARK YOUR PREFERences on a brown bag checklist from a range of four bread choices, 12 proteins, four cheeses, eight toppings, four premium toppings, four types of chips, four fresh sides, three various desserts and, lastly, drinks. While the formula is very basic, the ingredients are of a high quality, so every combination is a winning one. Example sandwich: jalapeño cheese bread with pimento cheese, tomatoes, pickles and bacon. Bam. There's your lunch, delivered in your original order-form brown bag. Add in a fruit cup and a rice crispy treat, if you like, and there's no way your day can be anything but stellar. Brought to you from the founders of the highly successful Barnaby's chain.

BUBBA'S TEXAS BURGER SHACK

5230 WESTPARK *at S. Rice*

☎ (713) 661-1622 | MAP **D7** | ⑪

BUBBASTEXASBURGERSHACK.COM

THERE IS NO WAY YOU'RE GOING TO FIND BUBBA'S ON the first try. That's not to say you shouldn't try, but its location literally underneath a highway is not an easy destination, even with an iPhone or GPS. But finding it is made that much sweeter when you get there and "discover" Bubba's in all its grungy Texas glory. A true dive in every sense of the word, there's "Get ye to Texas" memorabilia plastered throughout the tiny space, which also includes a deck where you can see and hear and sometimes even taste the Houston traffic. Helping calm matters are some of the best thin-pattied burgers in town, mostly made with a leaner buffalo meat, which is just as tasty when topped with their thick-cut bacon. Sides are sparse, with Zapp's potato chips and a jalapeño potato salad that's nothing to write home about. Shiner and Saint Arnold are available in bottles and accompany a buffalo patty melt (with added tomatoes) like nothing else can.

THE BUFFALO GRILLE

4080 BISSONNET *at Academy*
☎ (713) 661-3663 | MAP **D7** | 🍴
multiple locations
THEBUFFALOGRILLE.COM

BREAKFAST. BREAKFAST. BREAK-
FAST. AND ALSO, BREAKFAST.
That's not all you need to know
about Buffalo Grille and their
hubcap-sized pancakes and other
ridiculously large-portioned dishes
here, but it is something every
Houstonian should experience at
least once. Selections teeter from
diner to Tex-Mex with one stunner being the chile relleno topped
with fried eggs. Zong! It's excess
at its finest when washed down
with their famous cinnamon-spiked
self-serve coffee. Beware of the
chilaquiles, which are spiced to
a deadly degree, but everything
else is fair game. Even other meals
like lunch and dinner are hearty
with more Tex-Mex and Southern
dishes on the menu that are as
satisfying—if not more—than a
trip to Grandma's house (assuming
Grandma is an incredible Southern
or Mexican cook).

BURGER GUYS

12225 WESTHEIMER *west of S.
Kirkwood*
☎ (281) 497-4897 | MAP **B7** | 🍴
THEBURGERGUYS.COM

THE BURGER GUYS AREN'T
PLAYING AROUND WHEN IT
comes to the American classic.
Marbled Texas Akaushi beef in
quarter- or half-pound hand-formed
patties is seared intently on a
buttered griddle, cooked to order
and gloriously juicy. All that juice
dripping down your arms is only a
momentary distraction as you wipe
it away with the nearest paper towel

and go in for the next bite. Themed
after major cities across the globe,
there's the Saigon, for example,
with pâté, daikon, carrot, jalapeño,
cilantro and a sriracha-lime aioli or
the Havana with dill pickles, Swiss
cheese and ale mustard. There are
also additional themes as well as
gourmet hot dogs and duck-fat fries
with various house-made dipping
sauces to take it to the next level.
Bonus: A gourmet soda fountain
with cane sugar-sweetened drinks
as well as homemade ice creams
and milkshakes.

BURNS BAR-B-Q

7117 N. SHEPHERD
just South of W. Little York
☎ (713) 692-2800 | MAP **E4** | 🍴
multiple locations

THE STORY OF BURNS BAR-B-Q
IS CONFUSING FOR SURE, BUT
here's what you need to know. First,
the barbecue style is African-Amer-
ican East Texas with a focus on
quality sauce (it's even sold in retail
establishments), homemade hot
links, pork ribs and brisket. Second,
the Shepherd location is considered
the official "original." After founder
Roy Burns, Sr. passed away in 2010,
its location (at 8307 DePriest) was
moved and daughter Kathy Braden
took over. Recently, the DePriest
location has been resurrected after
three dormant years by Burns' son,
Gary Burns, who is also in the barbecue business selling all the same
types of barbecue made famous by
his father. In short, two locations,
one run by the daughter and one
by the son, all slow-smoked over a
pit and served with a tasty sauce.
Don't leave without trying the sausage at either spot.

CADILLAC BAR

1802 SHEPHERD *just south of Katy Fwy. (I-10 West)*
☎ (713) 862-2020 | MAP **E6** | 🍴
multiple locations
CADILLACBAR.COM

MARGARITA-LOVERS, LOOK NO FURTHER. THE CADILLAC BAR, originally inspired by the Nuevo Laredo 1926 landmark (alas, now closed), is a lively place full of noise and tequila, chips and salsa, gigantic plates of Tex-Mex and the occasional mariachi band. Mesquite-roasted pork carnitas, smoked pork ribs, bacon-wrapped stuffed shrimp and *cabrito* (milk-fed baby goat) are just a handful of their specialties, with plenty of enchiladas and combo plates as well. Brunch is a lavish buffet affair with Tex-Mex favorites and breakfast dishes intermingling with those aforementioned margaritas, practically guaranteeing a Sunday afternoon nap in the near future. There's also a tortas-to-go menu for easy take-out.

CAFE BENEDICTE

15455 MEMORIAL
between Eldridge & Hwy. 6
☎ (281) 558-6607 | MAP **B6** | 🍴
CAFEBENEDICTE.COM

WEST HOUSTON IS AN UNLIKELY AREA FOR SO many charming cafes, but somehow it just works. Yet another in the area is Cafe Benedicte, right in the thick of the Energy Corridor and an ideal lunch or dinner spot for executive meals. The bright blue dining room and scenic patio stay packed with a good mixture of folks ranging from business people to families from the neighborhood. The menu is broadly Mediterranean with a touch

of Greek, Spanish, French, North African and even a little American with burgers and sandwiches for lunch. The weekend brunch is extensive and well attended, and wine flights are fun and affordable at only $10 for a sample of three.

CAFE BRUSSELS

1718 HOUSTON AVE. *at Crockett*
☎ (713) 222-6996 | MAP **E6** | 🍴
CAFEBRUSSELSHOUSTON.COM

COME HERE FOR THE TRADITIONAL BELGIAN STEAMED mussels and frites, stay for the largest selection of Belgian beers in Houston. It's a setting that's cozy and comfortable and very Belgian-feeling with vintage oak tables and straight-back chairs. It continues the Belgian-French theme all the way through the beers on tap to the beer-heavy beef stew *les carbonades à la Flamande*. Just about everything here is heavy and richly sauced, but there are a few salads on hand if you can't take the buttery, creamy sauces that come with most dishes aside from the mussels. Brunch is also an option with crêpes, omelets and those famous steamed mussels that put them on the map.

CAFE CASPIAN

12126 WESTHEIMER *between S. Kirkwood & S. Dairy Ashford*
☎ (281) 493-4000 | MAP **B7** | 🍴
CAFECASPIAN.COM

EVERY MEAL HERE STARTS WITH THE ARRIVAL OF WARM PERSIAN flatbread known as *taftoon*, alongside a plate of feta and herbs. It's a traditional start to any Persian meal, but the hospitality of the gesture does not go unnoticed. It's little touches like this, along with the interior accents of Persian tapestries hung on the walls, patterned tablecloths and a glass curio full of hookahs, that give it an upscale yet comfortable feel. Food is also traditional and hearty with seasoned ground meat *koobideh* kebabs, saffron-tinged lamb shank, a chicken, pomegranate and walnut stew called *fesenjan* and healthy portions of long-grain basmati rice served with almost every dish. Tea service is a relaxing way to finish the meal.

CAFE CHINO
3285 SOUTHWEST FWY. (HWY. 59) *at Edloe*
☎ (713) 524-4433 | MAP **D7** | 🍴
CAFECHINOHOUSTON.COM

CAFE CHINO HAS ALL THE FAVORITES OF A TAKE-OUT Chinese menu: sesame chicken, wonton soup, General Tso's chicken, dumplings and more. But they also have a few stunners that push things to another level like Chilean sea bass with Asian pesto, whole red snapper in chili sauce and curry basil lamb. It's a combination that fits well within the snazzy dining room and colorful modern bar and somehow also works with the very American dessert selection for which they've become famous. (Try the blueberry croissant bread pudding.)

CAFE EXPRESS
1422 W. GRAY *west of Waugh*
☎ (713) 522-3100 | MAP **E6** | 🍴
multiple locations
CAFE-EXPRESS.COM

A LAVISH CONDIMENT BAR IS ALWAYS THE CENTER OF MUCH attention in any location of Houston-based chain Cafe Express. How could it be anything but, stocked full of all sorts of goodies like pickled carrots, olives, breadsticks, cornichons and more? It provides the perfect accoutrement to any of their sandwiches with gourmet touches like pesto, roasted tomatoes or a creamy Parmesan dressing or their generously portioned salads. The menu also offers entrees and pastas with vaguely Mediterranean influences as well as beer and wine for lazy lunches with friends. Counter service makes things easy and efficient and officially fast-casual. (Many will tell you this was the city's first-ever fast-casual restaurant.)

CAFE LILI
5757 WESTHEIMER
west of Chimney Rock
☎ (713) 952-6969 | MAP **D7** | 🍴
CAFELILI.COM

It's a quiet little restaurant located in a strip mall like so many others. But inside are some of the best Lebanese dishes in Houston. It's family-owned and feels that way with homey sampler plates full of creamy hummus, *kibbie* (seasoned ground beef that is deep fried), spinach pie, meat pie, *tabouli* (parsley and bulgur salad) and *babaganoush* (eggplant dip) for a mere $13.99. There are also sides of fried cauliflower, lima bean salad and more that go well with their kebab dishes, shawarma sandwiches and even the occasional daily special. Beer and wine are available, and the Lebanese coffee is bottomless.

CAFE PIQUET
5757 BISSONNET
west of Chimney Rock
☎ (713) 664-1031 | MAP **C7** | 🍴
CAFEPIQUET.NET

IT'S SURPRISING HOW FEW CUBAN RESTAURANTS WE HAVE IN HOUSton, the country's fourth-largest city and one that loves Latin flavors. (The 2011 closing of Latina Cafe knocked the Cuban cafe population down one more.) Cafe Piquet, a restaurant founded in 1996 with only 10 tables that then grew so quickly it had to move to another location with much more room, does take up much of the slack. The owners are actually from Cuba and brought the love of their country's food along with them: menu favorites include *yuca frita* (lightly fried yuca), *papa rellenas* (balls of mashed potatoes stuffed with ground meat, then fried), empanadas, *picadillo* (seasoned ground beef), *masitas fritas* (fried pork chunks), *ropa vieja* (shredded seasoned beef) and *pargo entero frito* (whole fried snapper). It's a comfy space suitable for weekday lunch and relaxed evening dining.

CAFE PITA+

10852 WESTHEIMER *at Lakeside Estates Dr.*
☎ (713) 953-7237 | MAP **B7** | ❚
multiple locations
CAFEPITA.WEEBLY.COM

GILDED BY THE ONE-TIME APPEARANCE OF GUY FIERI and his signature red convertible, Cafe Pita+ has officially hit the big time with its appearance on Food Network's *Diners, Drive-ins and Dives*. While it is none of those three, really, it is a family-run Bosnian restaurant with plenty of personality. Enjoying the popularity that a national television appearance can bring, the cafe has now expanded to include a second location on Richmond and has since moved their original location to a separate space within the same shopping center, freshening things up a bit. Must try dishes: *Cevap-*

cici, the Bosnian national dish that consists of seasoned ground meat shaped to look like a hot dog and served with fluffy *lepinja* bread and *ajvar*, a bright red bell pepper and eggplant spread; any of their pizzas; fresh grilled sardines over basmati rice; and tender lamb shank.

CAFE RABELAIS

2442 TIMES *between Kirby & Morningside*
☎ (713) 520-8841 | MAP **E7** | ❚❙❚
CAFERABELAIS.COM

TWO QUIRKY THINGS ABOUT CAFE RABELAIS: NO RESERVA-tions are accepted (it's a first come, first seated situation) due to its super small but romantic dining room, and there's no print menu. Neither one of those quirks should turn you away, however, as they both contribute to the charming cafe atmosphere that really is reminiscent of France. The daily-changing chalkboard menu may offer up dishes of *moules* (mussels), quiche du jour, *merguez* (lamb sausage) sandwich, salad Niçoise and specials that depend on the fresh produce of the week and the whims of the chef. The wine list is also a thing of beauty with more than 500 French wines to sip and savor.

CAFE TH

2108 PEASE *at St. Emanuel*
☎ (713) 225-4766 | MAP **F6** | ❙
CAFETH.COM

IT'S KNOWN FOR CASUAL VIET-NAMESE FOOD, BUT IF YOU LEAVE without youthful owner Minh Nguyen chatting you up and getting to know your name, you're not doing it right. One of the most personable hosts in town, Nguyen purchased the decrepit Thiem Hung Bakery and made it his own. There's a Bohemian feel to the space with original art on the walls, patrons from diverse backgrounds and surfer-looking Nguyen himself flitting around like a bumblebee. Traditional Vietnamese comfort food like banh mi, pho and noodle bowls are popular, but there are also a few vegan items like a spicy rich curry and customized combinations named after regular customers. Great for a quick lunch. Also, dinner is served Thursday and Friday 6 to 9 pm, and it's BYOB.

THE CAJUN STOP

2130 JEFFERSON *at Hutchins*
☎ (713) 222-8333 | MAP **F6** | ⏍
THECAJUNSTOP.COM

FORMERLY KNOWN AS CALLI-OPE'S PO-BOY, OWNER LISA Carnley changed the cafe name in late 2012 to The Cajun Stop after a legal battle. But it turned out to be a sensible decision, seeing as how the little po'boy shop is known for its Louisiana-style cuisine. It's nothing fancy, just a little fried seafood shack with real heart and a former New Orleanean at its helm. There are salads and full-on plates, but the reason people flock here is because of the aforementioned po'boys. They cover just about every critter that swims—crab, crawfish, shrimp, catfish and oysters—as well as roast beef, turkey, sausage and fried chicken, if seafood isn't your thing. There's also a party room available, so grab your beads and get to downtown for some real Cajun food.

CANDELARI'S PIZZERIA

6002 WASHINGTON
east of Westcott
☎ (832) 200-1474 | MAP **E6** | ⏍
multiple locations
CANDELARIS.COM

THE VARIETY IN PIZZA CRUST OPTIONS IS WHAT ATTRACTS many diners to Candelari's, which has come a long way since its founding by two Bellaire High graduates. It's now in multiple locations across town, servicing each neighborhood with its brand of low-key pizza joint atmosphere, which can get crowded, noisy and have the occasional lax service but for the most part is pretty pleasant. Back to those crusts: Five-grain is nutty and studded with flax seeds, white is typical and gluten-free is available for those poor souls with an intolerance to wheat. The crusts are also available thin (recommended), thick or deep-dish, depending on your whims of the day. As for toppings, these might be anything from the house-made Italian sausage to goat cheese, rustic capicola to roasted grape tomatoes. Carry out or dining in, pizza is the thing to get. Lunch turns into a pizza buffet, which is great for those who love variety but bad for those who lack self-control.

CANOPY

3939 MONTROSE *at Sul Ross*
☎ (713) 528-6848 | MAP **E6** | ⏍
CANOPYHOUSTON.COM

A FAUX VERDANT INTERIOR, BY WAY OF TREE BRANCH MURALS wrapping around the dining room walls, gives this Montrose gem its name. It also has to do with the fact its sister Heights restaurant's name is Shade. Tree themes notwithstanding, chef-owner Claire Smith is known for her solidly satisfying dishes with touches of spice and personality. Tandoori-style salmon is served with a lentil basmati pilaf, oven roasted tomatoes, spinach and a ginger-mango chutney, while the buttermilk-fried pork loin comes with a jalapeño andouille gravy. Parking is pretty much valet-only, though lucky ones may find a spot along the street. As an added bonus, Canopy is open for breakfast Mon-day through Friday and for brunch on weekends. In fine weather, ask to be seated on the lovely side patio.

CANTINA LAREDO

11129 WESTHEIMER *at Wilcrest*
☎ (713) 952-3287 | MAP **B7** | 🍴
CANTINALAREDO.COM

IT'S A CORPORATE CHAIN WITH JUST A SINGLE LOCATION IN Houston that somehow manages to feel authentic in our Mexican-food-savvy town. The upscale Tex-Mex/Mex-Mex restaurant offers the token enchiladas like the Veracruz, which combines spinach, chicken and Monterrey jack cheese as well as the fancy tableside-prepared guacamole that's become a staple in many an upscale Mexican dining room. However, their take on taqueria classics sets them apart. The kitchen's *torta de carnitas*, for example, combines the traditional slow-roasted pork with goat cheese and apricot spread, topping it all with a fried egg. Be warned that live music is often part of the experience in the evenings, so there's not much room for quiet conversations.

CAPITAL GRILLE

5365 WESTHEIMER
between Sage & Yorktown
☎ (713) 623-4600 | MAP **D7** | 🍴
THECAPITALGRILLE.COM

THERE'S STILL A STEAKHOUSE FORMULA WHERE OPULENCE and expense are key elements. Ritzy national chain Capital Grille's Houston outpost is one that still adheres to that theme with a sort of grand masculinity, thick-cut dry-aged steaks and butler-like service.

This is where business executives and those admiring classic carnivorous dining take clients and friends they want to impress. It's done in clubby dark wood and cushy Oriental carpeting with accents of hunting trophies along the walls. With nothing but the best, there's a crispness about the white napery, the heavy flatware and the delicate wine glasses (often filled with selections from the award-winning wine list). But know that all these things come at a price. Capital Grille has among the highest check averages of any restaurant chain in the country. *Note:* A second Capital Grille location is set to open in CityCentre a few months after this book goes to press.

CARACOL

2200 POST OAK BLVD. | MAP **D6**
between Westheimer & San Felipe

A PEDIGREED RESTAURANT IS CURRENTLY IN THE WORKS (though not open as of deadline) featuring the cuisine of chef Hugo Ortega (of Hugo's and Backstreet Cafe) as well as former Vegas chef Daniel Bridges. Ortega's wife and serial restaurateur, Tracy Vaught is also involved in the project. The name refers to sea snails found along the coast of Mexico, so perhaps it's going to focus on seafood? Management has been mum on details, but we do know it should be open sometime in late 2013 on the ground floor of the new BBVA Compass Tower near The Galleria.

CARMELO'S

14795 MEMORIAL
west of Dairy Ashford
☎ (281) 531-0696 | MAP **A6** | ¶¶

CARMELOSRESTAURANT.COM

IF IT'S GOOD ENOUGH FOR WEST HOUSTON TEENS ON PROM NIGHT, it's good enough to be considered an upscale Italian restaurant. You know the type: white tablecloths, pasta dishes, veal, steaks and seafood catering to a broad audience but done with heart and soul. It's hard to go wrong with Carmelo Mauro's classically prepared veal marsala or even the dramatic presentation of steak Diane, which is cooked tableside. Surprisingly, perhaps, there are also thoughtful additions of vegan, vegetarian and gluten-free items to cater to dietary concerns in a very delicious way. Look for the occasional wine dinner, book-signing or special-occasion (Mother's Day) buffets for something off-menu.

CARRABBA'S ITALIAN GRILL

3115 KIRBY *south of W. Alabama*
☎ (713) 522-3131 | MAP **E7** | ¶¶
multiple locations
CARRABBAS.COM

THERE'S ALMOST ALWAYS A WAIT AT ANY LOCATION OF Houston-founded Italian restaurant chain Carrabba's but especially at the original on Kirby. That's because it's still owned and operated by the famous Johnny Carrabba—he and his clan also still own the location on Voss Road—who can claim titles of "PBS cooking show host" and "cookbook author" to his credit. While the founder is part of the appeal, it's mostly the solidly good Sicilian-rooted

Gulf Coast cooking that continues to draw in the crowds year after year. Wood-tended grilled items, seafood dishes, premium pastas, chewy charred-crust pizzas and a house salad that is one of the most beloved in restaurant chain history are just a few of the reasons it has remained a staple of the Houston dining scene. The Kirby location has undergone a massive re-do and expansion in 2013.

CARTER & COOLEY

375 W. 19TH *at Ashland*
☎ (713) 864-3354 | MAP **E5** | ¶
CARTERANDCOOLEY.COM

IT CLOSES EARLY AND HAS A LIMITED SELECTION OF SIDES, BUT for the most part, this Heights deli is just delightful. Located along the scenic town-square-esque area of West 19th Street between a vintage clothing store and an antiques retailer, the old drugstore outfitted with bentwood chairs, pressed tin ceilings and antique scales (for weighing deli meat) is appointed in a style that fits nicely into the neighborhood aesthetic. "Lots of crisp bacon" on the menu is no lie, and the classic Reuben, liverwurst and honey ham/brie sandwiches are just a smattering of the larger menu. Dessert is just as worthy with large slices of classic cheesecake, homemade pies and milkshakes a-plenty.

CHARIVARI

2521 BAGBY *at McGowen*
☎ (713) 521-7231 | MAP **E6** | ¶¶¶
CHARIVARIREST.COM

SILVER-DOMED DISHES PLACED CEREMONIOUSLY BEFORE DINERS in unison, thick curtains to separate the outside world from the dining room, German-style draft beers poured with a traditional technique—these are all things you'll find at Charivari. A true classic in the world of continental cuisine, chef/owner Johann Schuster's old school environment plays host to any number of New World techniques. While the evergreen dishes like "Dracula" garlic soup, escargot, beluga blinis and "Budapest-style" foie gras will remain forever on the menu, chef Schuster has been known to utilize everything from Peruvian ingredients to seasonal produce like white asparagus. The setting is conducive to mature crowds at night, but nearby executives also frequent for power lunches and the famously good apple strudel.

CHEZ NOUS

217 S. AVENUE G *just south of Main, Humble*
☎ (281) 446-6717 | ♟♟
CHEZNOUSFRENCHRESTAURANT.COM

HOUSTON'S SUBURB OF HUMBLE ISN'T EXACTLY THE PLACE you'd expect to find a charming, pedigreed French restaurant, but surprise! Founding chef Gerard Brach originally opened the place in 1984 after converting the space from its previous life as a Pentecostal church and eventually brought in husband-wife/chef-sommelier co-owners Stacy Crowe-Simonson and Scott Simonson. The same classic French dishes emerge from the kitchen every evening with house-made charcuterie, roasted beef tenderloin with a béarnaise sauce, shrimp Provençal and snails sizzling in thick garlic butter. It's like a restaurant you'd discover in the rolling hills of California wine country only much, much closer to home.

CHILOSO'S TACO HOUSE

701 E. 20TH *west of N. Main*
☎ (713) 868-2273 | MAP **E5** | ♟

HOUSTONIANS ARE VERY PASSIONATE ABOUT THEIR BREAKfast tacos and rightfully so. Breakfast tacos are definitely worthy of passion, especially the good ones. Enter Chiloso's Taco House and their Saturday morning service. A queue of people will most likely be outside the doors, all patiently awaiting their turn to order the thick flour tortillas stuffed with eggs, potatoes and bacon or chorizo. A magic combination of simple ingredients, which, when done well, can make everything right with the world—at least for a few moments of taco bliss. The front porch is ideal when the inside is chock full of folks. Although the restaurant closes mid-afternoon, you can still fit in a non-breakfast plate of enchiladas or carne guisada before it's too late and for a very moderate price, too.

CHINA GARDEN

1602 LEELAND *at Crawford*
☎ (713) 652-0745 | MAP **F6** | ♟♟
CHINAGARDENHOUSTON.COM

IN A WORLD OF FUSION CUISINE AND CELEBRITY CHEFS, SOMEtimes a comforting order of shrimp with lobster sauce is all you really need. For those days when Houston's immense and growing restaurant roster is just too, too much, it might be time to visit China Garden. Located in an ungentrified part of downtown and dating from 1969, this is a regular stop for local politicians, downtown workers and the occasional sports fan (it's near Toyota Center). It's just an old-school American-Chinese restaurant with big crunchy eggrolls, an efficient waitstaff and a familiar menu. Dinner is the real stunner here, which brings a little extra oomph to the table in dishes like the whole fried fish with hot sauce, Szechuan cabbage with beef, chicken with Chinese black mushrooms and shrimp balls with Chinese mushrooms. Curiously, everybody gets an order of hush puppies with their food.

CHURRASCOS

2055 WESTHEIMER *at S. Shepherd*
☎ (713) 527-8300 | MAP **E6** | ||
multiple locations
CORDUA.COM

THIS IS THE CONCEPT THAT STARTED IT ALL FOR MICHAEL Cordúa and his eventual restaurant empire (see also Américas, Artista and Amazón Grill). Based on the flavors of Latin America, it's still going strong after 25 years in business. The namesake dish is a quick-grilled butterflied cut from the beef tenderloin that is basted with the potent, garlicky chimichurri sauce that was so very novel when it made its debut at his restaurants. (It may be commonplace now but remains delicious nonetheless.) The plantain chips and selection of dips that start every meal have spoiled guests and also possibly spoiled appetites, but that won't stop anyone from ordering subsequent sweet plantains known as *maduros*, yucca fries, ceviche, empanadas and a full bounty of Latin-heritage beauties. Service, atmosphere, wine selection and just about everything else falls in line with the food for a well-rounded experience.

CHUY'S COMIDA DELUXE

2706 WESTHEIMER
just west of Kirby
☎ (713) 524-1700 | MAP **E6** | |
multiple locations
CHUYS.COM

PAYOFF FOR BRAVING THE CHA-OTIC PARKING LOT OUTSIDE will be a frozen, happy-hour margarita inside. It's a sure bet that any night of the week will find the interior just as chaotic and packed, though turnover is down to a science here to keep waits short and the crowds from rioting. Once you sit down inside the Austin-imported chain with a 1950s-era flair and Elvis shrine, you'll find plenty of kitschy knick-knacky decor and Tex-Mex with standout enchiladas, crispy flautas and massive burritos. The creamy jalapeño dip is exceptional, and service is friendly, thoughtful and amenable to families with small children, no matter how messy they get with the chips.

CIAO BELLO

5161 SAN FELIPE *at Sage*
☎ (713) 960-0333 | MAP **E6** | ||
CIAOBELLOHOUSTON.COM

TONY'S (FROM TONY VALLONE) MIGHT BE THE MOST INTIMI-dating restaurant in Houston. Luckily for those with fine-dining anxiety, there's a casual version of Vallone-style Italian, and its name is Ciao Bello. Geared toward a less-formal crowd usually from the nearby Tanglewood neighborhood, the food is more family friendly but still authentic and of utmost quality. And since the pomp and circumstance are turned way down here, so are the prices. Pizza is a big hit with the classic margherita or the Ciao Bello pizza with porcini and wild mushroom medley as well as rich pastas like the osso bucco ravioli. There's a very nice wine list, too. Don't be surprised to see Vallone's son Jeff on premise keeping an eye on things.

CIRO'S ITALIAN GRILL

9755 KATY FWY. (I-10 WEST)
between Bunker Hill & Gessner
☎ (713) 467-9336 | MAP C6 | 🍴
CIROS.COM

IT MAY SURPRISE SOME TO LEARN THAT THIS VERY POLISHED, LARGE restaurant off I-10 near the Memorial area of Houston is not a chain. Though it comes with some of the trappings of a corporate-run restaurant in terms of looks, it still maintains the heart of a family-owned and -run restaurant. Many pastas are made in-house, and the menu is full of delicious dishes like lasagne, pork chops, calzones, eggplant parmigiana and penne with crawfish. Pastas are conveniently available in two portion sizes, the larger version being big enough to share with the table, making for a communal meal. After dinner, grab a cigar (they're sold here) and head out to the bocce ball court to end the evening.

CLEBURNE CAFETERIA

3606 BISSONNET *at Edloe*
☎ (713) 667-2386 | MAP D7 | 🍴
CLEBURNECAFETERIA.COM

THERE'S A CERTAIN "BLAH" FACTOR THAT'S OFTEN ASSO-ciated with steam-table cafeteria-style restaurants, but that's definitely not the case with Cleburne. First, the kitchen uses quality ingredients (some sourced from the farmers' market), natural meats that aren't injected with anti-biotics, wild salmon when possible and house-butchered beef. Second, this is not a chain, therefore everything is made from scratch. Squash casserole, turkey and dressing, poached salmon in dill sauce, beef stroganoff, chicken and dumplings and other old-school classics are here on a daily basis (except for Saturdays when they're closed). Also old school are the clientele (the expected senior citizen set and families) and the payment system: cash or check only, no credit cards accepted.

COLLINA'S ITALIAN CAFE

3835 RICHMOND
just east of Weslayan
☎ (713) 621-8844 | MAP D7 | 🍴
multiple locations
COLLINAS.COM

THERE ARE SEVERAL LOCATIONS OF THIS CASUAL LOCAL CHAIN, and each one carries with it a unique neighborhood vibe. Families and groups gather every night of the week to take advantage of the long-standing BYOB policy and share one of the better pizzas in town, made with a yeasty dough with nicely charred edges and topped with a myriad of fresh ingredients. There are plenty pizza varieties to choose from, but their Mona Lisa—made with roma tomatoes, mushrooms, spinach and feta—makes a vegetarian not-as-gut-busting combination. House salads appease the need for roughage, and pastas, entrees and appetizers are all decent, too.

COLTIVARE

3320 WHITE OAK *at Arlington*
COLTIVAREHOUSTON.COM | MAP **E6**

REVIVAL MARKET CHEF RYAN PERA AND HIS PARTNER MOR-gan Weber have been working on a rustic Italian restaurant in The Heights for more than a year, and it should be ready (fingers crossed) by the time this book comes off press. Pera and Weber have rehabbed an old building for the restaurant and are develop-ing a large garden adjacent. The garden will supply produce to both the trattoria and Revival Market; any excess will be available for sale, farmers' market style. Vincent Huynh, who has spent the last year at Revival Market, has been named chef de cuisine. His menu will focus on small plates and sharable items at reasonable prices.

CONSCIOUS CAFE

2612 SCOTT *near McGowen*
☎ (713) 658-9191 | MAP **F7** | ❙
C2CONSCIOUSCAFE.NET

DIETARY RESTRICTIONS— THOUGH PLENTIFUL IN THIS Nation of Islam restaurant—are not a negative when it comes to the fulfilling dishes served here. Adhering to the guidelines placed forth in Elijah Muhammad's *Eat To Live*, the owners have come up with a satisfying menu: wild-caught salmon burgers are the most popu-lar option, and you might also enjoy the nutmeg-scented bean pie. The eggplant hoagie served on wheat bread and dressed with tomatoes, olives and a smidge of Veganaise (mayonnaise made without eggs) is also in the running for tastiest sandwich. In lieu of sugary sodas, Conscious Cafe serves organic teas

RESTAURANTS

Bolognese at Coppa Ristorante Italiano

and coffees as well as smoothies for either a jolt of caffeine or a remedy for the sweet tooth.

COPPA RISTORANTE ITALIANO

5555 WASHINGTON *at T.C. Jester*
☎ (713) 426-4260 | MAP **E6** | 🍴
COPPARISTORANTE.COM

PART OF THE CHARLES CLARK/ GRANT COOPER GROUP OF restaurants, Coppa inhabits the space formerly occupied by Catalan, where celebrity chef Chris Shepherd really made a name for himself. Shepherd left to start Underbelly, and rather than bring in another chef, Clark Cooper intelligently revamped the restaurant into an Italian concept, a move that the neighborhood has totally approved. Rustic dishes like melt-in-your-mouth meatballs in a savory tomato gravy, a rich spaghetti carbonara and handcrafted pizzas make for approachable, comforting fare alongside more sophisticated items like octopus carpaccio and brick oven sardines. The bar is always bustling, especially during the value-heavy happy hour. The entire formula has proven so successful that there's already a brand-new more casual sister location called Coppa Osteria in Rice Village.

CORKSCREW BBQ

24930 BUDDE RD. *south of Sawdust Rd., The Woodlands*
☎ (832) 592-1184 | 🍴
CORKSCREWBBQ.COM

IN THE TRADITION OF COOK-AS-MUCH-AS-WE-CAN AND SELL-until-it-runs-out barbecue stands, this family-run trailer has steadily gained a loyal following, which explains the long and very slow-moving lines on Saturdays. There's no rhyme or reason as to why they sell out when they do, but the guarantee is that they will, so call or text after 2 pm to see if there's any product left. The slow-smoked meats cover all the bases: beef brisket, turkey breast, pulled pork, sausage and ribs, and there's a remarkably huge stuffed baked potato. It's outdoor dining only, but the owners don't mind if you BYOB in the shaded area full of rustic picnic tables. As of press time, owners Will and Nichole Buckman are planning a permanent location.

COSTA BRAVA BISTRO

5115 BELLAIRE BLVD.
at S. Rice Ave. Bellaire
☎ (713) 839-1005 | MAP **C7** | 🍴
COSTABRAVABISTRO.COM

BELLAIRE FINALLY HAS A FINE-DINING RESTAURANT. NEW since our 2011 edition, this little spot by Madrid native Angeles Dueñas and Houstonian Kitty Bailey is too fancy to be deemed a true bistro; prices and service are both rarefied. But it has quickly found a niche with the Meyerland/Bellaire bourgeoisie. The accent is a little bit French, a little bit Italian, a little bit Spanish with entrees such as lamb chops, crispy salmon with tarragon buerre blanc, paella and linguine with wild mushrooms. The lunch menu is rich with entree salads.

COVE

2502 ALGERIAN WAY *off Kirby, inside Haven Restaurant*
☎ (713) 581-6101 | MAP **E7** | 🍴
HAVENHOUSTON.COM

IN A SHARP LEFT TURN FROM HAVEN'S LOCALLY SOURCED Southern comfort classics, this restaurant-within-a-restaurant offers an almost exclusively raw menu that brings in briny ingredients from around the world. Strange and wonderful dishes are created right at the mise en place station behind the bar with chefs carefully plating the dishes under the watchful eyes of hungry guests, but they keep their cool amidst the sometimes frenetic atmosphere. Flavors have roots in various parts of the globe with exotic combos from the Pacific, the Americas, Europe, the Mediterranean and North Africa. Come early to get a seat at the bar and be forgiving of the bartenders, as they're usually overextended servicing drinks for the main Haven dining room as well as the packed Cove bar.

CRAPITTO'S CUCINA ITALIANA

2400 MID LANE
north of Westheimer
☎ (713) 961-1161 | MAP **D6** | ¶¶¶
CRAPITTOS.COM

FREQUENTED BY AN OLDER CROWD IN SEARCH OF EXPENsive Italian-American food, Crapitto's is a cozy little gem inside the Highland Village neighborhood. Housed in a remodeled, historic farmhouse, the charm flows as freely as the wine here. Simple, well-seasoned dishes are the mainstays with crabcakes, lasagne, pansautéed snapper, salmon florentina and cheesecake being just a handful to choose from. The patio, shaded by century-old oak trees, often has live music and feels worlds away from the hustle and bustle of the world. Tomatoes have become somewhat of a phenomenon here, being grown in a country garden planted by owner Frank Crapitto himself and

often sold by the pound (in season) when the harvest exceeds what goes into the restaurant's kitchen.

CRAWFISH & BEIGNETS

11201 BELLAIRE BLVD. *at Boone, in Hong Kong City Mall*
☎ (281) 498-5044 | MAP **B7** | ¶

LOCATED IN THE HONG KONG CITY MALL DEVELOPMENT IN Chinatown, Crawfish & Beignets is actually not stocked with one of the items in its title. The proprietor took beignets off the menu after their unpopularity proved fatal to the previously namesake dish. As for the crawfish? During the season (February through May) the slightly grungy place remains packed with folks in for the large-sized crawfish boiled in Cajun seasonings and then tossed in a flavorful garlic butter that is the signature of Vietnamese-style boiled crawfish. Condiments and sauces make for variety, and cheap beer helps add to the dive-y and delicious experience. Off-season crawfish are from frozen stockpiles, but the restaurant is honest about which ones they're currently serving.

CRICKET'S CREAMERY & CAFFE

315 W. 19TH *at Rutland*
☎ (713) 869-9450 | MAP **E5** | ¶
CRICKETSCAFFE.COM

THIS FUNKY LITTLE GELATERIA AND CAFE IS IDEALLY SITUATED in an equally funky and charming area of The Heights, which is the closest thing Houston has to an old-timey Main Street. Cricket's is part coffeeshop, part vegetarian eatery (serving breakfast and lunch only—and obviously no meat), part gelateria. Breakfast is simple with offerings of veggie sausage, cage-free eggs, waffles and pastries, while lunch consists of soups, salads, sandwiches and the occasional daily special. Families might enjoy the convenient kids' area and seating, while students and freelancers enjoy the caffeinated beverages—both cold and hot—as well as free WiFi. And of course, don't forget the Nutella gelato or a vegan passion fruit sorbetto.

CRISP

2220 BEVIS *at West 23rd*
☎ (713) 360-0222 | MAP **E5** | 🍴
CRISPHOUSTON.COM

CRISP IS A NEW LOW-KEY CON-CEPT THAT OPENED IN 2013. IT is part vinoteca, part pub, part Italian restaurant and part neighborhood gathering spot. The Enomatic by-the-taste wine selection is fun to play around with and offers a new and different experience for those not versed in the world where wine comes from a tap. Beers are no joke either, with 24 craft brews on draft. Food is Italian with stone-deck-fired, hand-tossed pizzas like the Texas shrimp carbonara with aged provolone, bacon, sweet peas, alfredo sauce, sage and a fried yard egg. Outside seating is recommended during mild weather—and plentiful, too, with a patio that measures 5,000-square-feet.

CUCHARA MEXICO CITY BISTRO

214 FAIRVIEW *near Taft*
☎ (713) 942-0000 | MAP **E6** | 🍴
CUCHARARESTAURANT.COM

JUST IN CASE THE "MEXICO CITY" PART ESCAPES YOU, this is not a Tex-Mex restaurant. There will be no complimentary chips and salsa to start the meal,

no burritos as big as the Sunday newspaper and no frozen margaritas with a bottle of beer placed upside down in them. However more dainty the plates may be, they are sporting items from interior Mexico on a succinct but authentic menu with dishes like grilled cactus paddles stuffed with panela cheese on a puddle of salsa with spring onions and refried beans on the side. Ordering appetizers to share along with some of the quality cocktails—the serious drinks menu was devised by mixologist Chris Frankel—may be a more apt way to experience this little bistro where things can get pricey pretty quick. The *charalitos*, small deep-fried lake fish served with salsa, are good for a starter; pair them with a "Charlie's Devil" cocktail with blanco tequila, cucumber, blackberries, lemon juice and ginger beer.

CULLEN'S UPSCALE AMERICAN GRILL

11500 SPACE CENTER BLVD.
between Genoa Red Bluff & Hwy. 3
☎ (281) 991-2000 | 🍴
southwest of MAP **19**
CULLENSGRILLE.COM

CULLEN'S IS AN OVER-THE-TOP HOSPITALITY COMPLEX WITH 37,000 square feet of space and plenty of show-y features. The state-of-the-art kitchen is visible from the main dining room and trimmed out in marble and limestone, while the suspended private dining area known as Macy's Table is enclosed in glass walls and offers a panoramic view of the dining area below. The menu is just as bells-and-whistles as the restaurant itself with upscale ingredients in new American dishes. For example, a Frito pie starter uses Berkshire pork, Texas goat cheese, Oregon cheddar and crème fraîche. There are the token luxury meats like prime rib, steaks, chops and duck along with pizzas and sandwiches. Following the overall trend of extravagance, the wine list is available via a computerized tablet that allows guests to search in various categories that include vintage, origin, price and varietal. Though it is undoubtedly upscale, an attached bar is laid-back and kid-friendly for a more accessible experience. There seems to be something for everyone here.

CYCLONE ANAYA'S

309 GRAY *at Bagby*
☎ (713) 520-6969 | MAP **E6** | ⑪
multiple locations
CYCLONEANAYA.COM

CYCLONE ANAYA'S SEEMS TO HAVE A HOLD ON THE UPSCALE Tex-Mex market, where the average ticket runs higher than most other enchiladas-guacamole-margarita spots. The interior is just polished enough to give credence to those more expensive renditions, and the margaritas certainly have their place in a town where this one cocktail can make or break a place. Happy hour is the best time to visit with a special menu of small plates that run from $4 to $6. Recommended: spicy chicken wings with cilantro-jalapeño ranch, mini ceviche and tamarindo braised pulled beef sliders with spicy coleslaw and ancho-honey barbecue sauce. Brunch is rather loud but popular with the crowd that uses the label "Sunday Funday" un-ironically.

D'AMICO'S ITALIAN MARKET CAFE

5510 MORNINGSIDE
between Rice & University
☎ (713) 526-3400 | MAP **E7** | ⑪
multiple locations
DAMICO-CAFE.COM

D'AMICO'S IS A HOUSTON CLASSIC. THE NAME HAS BEEN around since the 1970s and is synonymous with home-style Italian cooking. This market/cafe/deli combination is always bustling and full of energy with market guests buying cheese from the deli case, chefs prepping a pasta dish and servers dashing around the tiny dining room. Daily steam-table lunches are popular and with good reason—they're inexpensive, large-portioned plates full of items of your choosing from a rotating menu that could include vegetable lasagne, meatballs, house salad or fish. At dinner, house-made pasta reigns over all else in dishes like the mushroom and walnut tortellini or penne with grilled chicken and asparagus. Gelato, cannolis and a ricotta cheesecake that's one of the best in town (though made by an outside supplier) make for a perfect ending to any meal. A Heights location has opened and closed since the latest edition of this book, but a Sugar Land location is scheduled to open in late 2013.

DA MARCO

1520 WESTHEIMER
between Waugh & Mandell
☎ (713) 807-8857 | MAP **E6** | ⑪⑪
DAMARCOHOUSTON.COM

IF YOU HADN'T HEARD BY NOW, DA MARCO IS A BIG DEAL. IT'S considered one of the best Italian restaurants not only in Houston but also on a national scale. Chef/

owner Marco Wiles' flagship Italian restaurant—he also has Vinoteca Poscol and Dolce Vita—sits in a converted house in Montrose and serves meals in stages that start with *antipasti* (appetizers) like creamy burrata with roasted cherry tomatoes and moves into *primi* starches of risotto, pasta or gnocchi, *secondi* meats and *contorini* (sides) like favas and tomato or the rich Brussels sprouts with guanciale. Wine is, of course, also of special importance with a huge Italian selection to stay on theme. Truffle season is a big to-do, too, with specials utilizing the luxury ingredient that is flown in from Italy and shaved onto just about every edible thing in the restaurant. You will pay a hefty price, but you only live once, right?

DAILY REVIEW CAFE

3412 W. LAMAR *at Dunlavy*
☎ (713) 520-9217 | MAP **E6** | 🍴
DAILYREVIEWCAFE.COM

A CAFE THAT INSPIRES MANY A DREAMY CONVERSATION about what it would be like to open a restaurant, Daily Review is a little charming, a little inspirational and a lot cute. The approachable menu is just exciting enough to bring in adventurers but comforting enough for more grounded palates, with plenty of Southern-inflected but modernized comfort food. No matter what they're ordering, all can agree that the bricked patio is a mini-oasis in the bustling cityscape, with enough greenery to obscure the urban surroundings. Also a way to escape: a bottle of wine and a plate of oven roasted mushroom ravioli with a rich Madeira mushroom sauce or a lobster taco garnished with yellow tomato salsa. Prices are fair for the cuisine,

but the small cafe does usually attract more than it can hold during peak hours, resulting in a wait.

DAMIAN'S CUCINA ITALIANA

3011 SMITH *at Rosalie*
☎ (713) 522-0439 | MAP **E6** | 🍴
DAMIANS.COM

A FTER 30 YEARS IN BUSINESS, DAMIAN'S HAS EARNED THE label "Houston classic." Keeping it afloat all these years probably has something to do with the name Mandola being involved (founded by Damian Mandola and now owned by Frankie Mandola and cousin Bubba Butera) but also with its upscale Gulf Coast Southern Italian-American cuisine. Portions and flavors are both plentiful, with a large representation of pastas, seafood and meat dishes on the menu. Grilled snapper is topped with tomatoes, shrimp, mint and basil in the Snapper Nino Jr., while the tortellini alla pana is stuffed with chicken, pork, mortadella and ricotta. Low ceilings and lights make for a romantic atmosphere, and the snappy waiters help move things along for people dining pre-theater. They offer a convenient shuttle to downtown's Theater District, which makes them a popular destination for pre-show dining.

DANTON'S GULF COAST SEAFOOD KITCHEN

4611 MONTROSE *just south of Southwest Fwy. (Hwy. 59)*
☎ (713) 807-8883 | MAP **E7** | 🍴
DANTONSSEAFOOD.COM

D URING OYSTER SEASON, WE'RE GUESSING THAT DANTON'S doubles its business. Though we don't have any official records, our own experience of the sublime pleasures of sitting down to a dozen raw oysters and an ice-cold martini here lead us to believe it might be true. Generous Cajun and Mexican influences guide the ship of Texas Gulf seafood that is uniquely Houston: a jumbo lump crabcake comes with a roasted poblano sauce, grilled items are wood-fired over oak and hickory and the famous gumbo is cooked for up to 18 hours to develop the robust flavor. Crawfish season is also a good time to visit, and Sundays bring a blues brunch that transports guests straight to New Orleans for the day.

DARBAND SHISH KABOB

5670 HILLCROFT
between Harwin & Westpark
☎ (713) 975-8350 | MAP **C7** | 🍴

DARBANDSHISHKABOB.COM

IT'S NOT MUCH TO LOOK AT, BUT JUST AS MANY OF THE MULTI-cultural restaurants in aesthetically run-down Hillcroft teach us: Don't judge a book by its cover. As the name suggests, shish kabobs are something of a specialty here, but the *kubideh*—cylinders of spiced ground beef—and turmeric-tinged lamb shank are among their best dishes. Fresh, warm flatbread accompanies nicely as does the simple white rice adorned with crushed grilled tomatoes. It's Houston's oldest Persian restaurant and also one of the most authentic and beloved.

DEL FRISCO GRILLE

2800 KIRBY *just south of Westheimer, in West Ave*
☎ (832) 623-6168 | MAP **E6** | 🍴

DELFRISCOSGRILLE.COM

THE LITTLE-SISTER CONCEPT TO DEL FRISCO'S DOUBLE EAGLE Steak House, Del Frisco Grille still

serves a certain type of clientele, but this time the clientele is invited to put up their feet and relax a little. The casual concept (and that term is relative) focuses on comfort food rather than luxurious steaks, with sections like "Two-Fisted Sandwiches" (there's a hefty burger calling your name), along with flatbreads and a dish in the "Knife & Fork" section that takes meatloaf to another level by using veal and topping it with a bordelaise sauce. The interior is still markedly refined and done in beiges, browns, burgundies and light-colored wood, but there is a certain image to uphold—it's located in the swanky West Ave development after all.

DEL FRISCO'S DOUBLE EAGLE STEAK HOUSE

5061 WESTHEIMER
in The Galleria
☎ (713) 335-2600 | MAP **D6** | 🍴

DELFRISCOS.COM

IN A TOWN WHERE SWANKY STEAKHOUSES ARE PLENTIFUL, Del Frisco's is one of the most beloved. Beloved by those with money (professional athletes for one) to spend and people to see, that is, as they crowd the bar in the evenings with loud, boisterous chatter. The national chain knows luxury—whether it's the lush interior with a hand-painted Italian glass ceiling, 40-foot windows featuring skyline views or the USDA prime beef they serve on a daily basis. Classics done well here include the crabcakes, oversized onion rings and any of their prime steaks, while updated classics like the jalapeño-bacon macaroni and cheese are even better than the originals. It's just the place for a prix-fixe business lunch complete with a martini or a night of fancy wine and indulgent dishes. Diet and wallets be damned.

Del Frisco Grille burger

DIM SUM KING

9160 BELLAIRE BLVD.
at Ranchester
☎ (713) 270-6788 | MAP **C7** | 🍴

DIM SUM ALL DAY, EVERY DAY. IT'S A DREAM TOTALLY ACHIEV-able at Dim Sum King, which is much less regal than it sounds. Rather modest and dull as far as the procedure goes, there's no bustling around of pushcarts loaded with plates and steamers full of dump-lings as the traditional dim sum service usually calls for. Instead, you'll order via checklist. The selec-tion is fairly standard with the usual line-up of pork *shu mai* dumplings, red bean paste sesame balls and chicken feet, but it is much more convenient without all the chaos. Just don't get a craving on Tues-days, because it's the one day the restaurant is closed.

DIVINO

1830 W. ALABAMA *near Woodhead*
☎ (713) 807-1123 | MAP **E6** | 🍴
DIVINOHOUSTON.COM

THE TELLTALE RED AWNINGS OUTSIDE DIVINO GIVE A HINT that this restaurant might be a little more neighborhood-focused than its upscale pricing might suggest. Cozy and simple, the focus is more on the food than on any grand interior elements. Chef and co-owner Patrick McCray trained in the Emilia-Romagna region of Italy, so naturally it's a big influence on the menu. House-made ravioli and lasagne, risottos and entrees that utilize many local ingredients like quail, pork and cheese sourced from the Houston Dairymaids keep regulars in the seats. The wine list is frequently updated and stocked with bottles that often fall below $60 a bottle.

DOLCE VITA PIZZERIA ENOTECA

500 WESTHEIMER *at Taft*
☎ (713) 520-8222 | MAP **E6** | ⑪
DOLCEVITAHOUSTON.COM

PIZZA HERE OFTEN WINS THE DEBATE IN THE "MOST AUTHEN-tic" wars. From seasoned restau-rateur and chef Marco Wiles (see Da Marco), this pizzeria is the type where crusts come thin and crisp, scorched appropriately in the wood-fired oven. Toppings are just sparse enough but exciting and fresh on pizzas like the *zucca* with butternut squash, pancetta, smoked buffalo mozzarella and red onion. Simple sal-ads like the shaved Brussels sprouts with pecorino are a nice counterpoint to the pizzas and just big enough to share. There are also pastas, salads and charcuterie that invite you to linger inside the creaky old converted house over a bottle of wine and some friendly conversation. Note: A 2012 fire closed Dolce Vita for a couple of months, but they seem to be back as good as ever now.

DOOZO DUMPLINGS & NOODLES

1200 MCKINNEY *at Lamar, in Houston Center*
☎ (713) 571-6898 | MAP **F6** | ⑪

THE RULES OF ORDERING AT DOOZO ARE AS FOLLOWS: 1) Know your order before reach-ing the front of the line. 2) Don't panic. 3) Have your payment at the ready. Why so much stress around a simple food-court restaurant inside a downtown office building? The Doozo Dumpling lady, now affec-tionately nicknamed "The Dumpling Nazi," is a no-nonsense and stern-faced enforcer who keeps things efficient at lunchtime when lines can

form quickly. Choose either a full order of 10 or a half order; choose pork, chicken or veggie; choose spicy or extra spicy sauce. The freshly steamed dumplings are famously good and worth the ordering anxiety.

DOSHI HOUSE

3419 DOWLING *near Holman*
☎ (713) 528-0060 | MAP **F6** | ⑪
DOSHIHOUSE.COM

WHAT STARTED OUT AS AN ART GALLERY IN THE THIRD Ward has evolved into a vegetar-ian- and vegan-friendly cafe with a rotating chalkboard menu. Offering coffees, tea, vegetarian panini and a nightly dinner, Doshi House has become a rallying point for many in the neighborhood and surrounding areas to get their fix of tasty, meat-less food. While those tasty panini, soups and salads keep lunch-goers sated, the evening's offering is a single dish that rotates weekly. From vegan fajitas to Thai red curries, it's usually something hearty and stew-like. BYOB is an option for a very small corkage fee, but you may just want to embrace their selection of non-alcoholic beverages instead.

DOWN HOUSE

1801 YALE *at W. 18th*
☎ (713) 864-3696 | MAP **E5** | ⑪
DOWNHOUSEHOUSTON.COM

DOWN HOUSE STARTED OUT AS FLAGRANTLY HIP IN BOTH decor and menu, but it has backed down slightly since. As it matures, the food has become more consis-tent, the drinks tastier and the ser-vice a little less lax. Utilizing local ingredients is a priority here and can be tasted in breakfasts like the pork hash with braised pork, home fries, feta, tomato, jalapeño and two eggs sunny side up. Dinner is equally ambitious with an array of local ingredients prepared thoughtfully and flavorfully. For beverages, Down House can boast serious coffee and cocktail programs (yes, here they're programs) that draw in just as many guests as the food and atmosphere. Since our last edition, Down House has added a shady patio for additional capacity and al fresco dining.

DOWNTOWN AQUARIUM

410 BAGBY *at Memorial*
☎ (713) 223-3474 | MAP **F6** | ¶↑↑
AQUARIUMRESTAURANTS.COM

YOU SHOULD KNOW THAT THIS RESTAURANT IS MUCH MORE apropos for entertaining (especially youngsters) than serious seafood dining. Of course, there is a large selection of seafood dishes like coconut shrimp and grilled mahi mahi—this is a Landry's restaurant after all—but the real reason to visit is riding that towering Ferris wheel: You feel like you can practically reach out and touch the cars on the adjacent I-45 overpass. Great for kids and family outings, this theme-park-disguised-as-a-restaurant has plenty to carry on about in the way of activities, from white tigers to the carnival arcade to the giant aquarium tank that's the centerpiece of the main dining room. Packed to the hilt just about every weekend, it's like dining at a local maritime version of Disney World. And sometimes, just as expensive.

DRY CREEK CAFE

544 YALE *at W. 6th*
☎ (713) 426-2313 | MAP **D5** | ¶
DRYCREEKCAFE.COM

IF IT HAS THE WORD "CREEK" IN ITS NAME, THERE ARE CERTAIN

aspects locals have come to expect. First, there is a decent selection of beer and wine; second is an Austin-style environment with plenty of patio; and third is simple, California-style food that isn't fussy. Dry Creek has almost all those points covered with the exception of the alcohol. "Dry" in more ways than one, this eatery is located in a dry part of The Heights. Inviting to BYOBers, there is a corkage fee, but there's also a scenic patio, significant salads, good burgers and veggie quesadillas. They're not doing anything that hasn't been done before, but it still seems to draw a good crowd.

E-TAO

5135 W. ALABAMA *in The Galleria*
☎ (713) 965-0888 | MAP **D6** | ¶
ETAOASIAN.COM

SOUP DUMPLINGS ARE IN SHORT SUPPLY IN HOUSTON, SO THANK goodness for E-Tao. Oddly located in a quieter wing of The Galleria, this shotgun-style restaurant houses booths on one side and a bright and open kitchen on the other, all of it clean and modern and worlds away from the typical Chinatown dive usually frequented for such iconic dishes. From that busy kitchen come some of the best soup dumplings in town. Worth the hassle of Galleria traffic and parking, this is a must if you make it all the way. Complementing these little soupy pillows are additional dishes like roast pork, lobster four ways, hot pots and crispy shrimp in a spicy sauce.

EATSIE BOYS CAFE
4100 MONTROSE *near Richmond*
☎ (713) 524-3737 | MAP **E7** | ⑂
EATSIEBOYS.COM

THE "BOYS" WHO WERE ON THE
FOREFRONT OF HOUSTON'S FOOD
truck explosion have found a home
without wheels. Located in Montrose in a quaint ivy-clad building
(next to the Black Labrador), their
cafe provides a counterpoint with
the dining area's spray-paint murals
and modern look. Offering breakfast,
lunch and dinner along with coffees
and dessert, it's a neighborhood
hangout where the WiFi is fast and
the combination of fresh sandwiches, salads and fun food-truck
fare is both eclectic and comfortable.
The counter service makes it easy
to order at will, and a few picnic
tables out front are just right on mild
days. Matzoh ball pho has proven
best-seller, as have their selection
of "Frozen Awesome" (gelato-ice
cream hybrids). Of course they still
serve their famously good food-truck
selections like the "pork snuggie," a
steamed bun stuffed with pork
belly, onion and pickle.

EDDIE V'S PRIME SEAFOOD
12848 QUEENSBURY
in CityCentre
☎ (832) 200-2380 | MAP **B6** | ⑂⑂
EDDIEV.COM

HARKEN BACK TO THE DAYS
WHEN RAW BARS AND WHITE-
waistcoated servers defined a fine
dining restaurant, and you have
Scottsdale chain Eddie V's. While
they've updated the menu to include
more Asian elements—crab fried
rice, kung pao-style calamari and
Hong Kong-style sea bass to name a
few—and have adapted their interior

design to encompass a fresh, modern
look, it still carries the soul of an old-
school, fine-dining establishment.
Fresh seafood is flown in three times
a week from both the East Coast and
Hawaii, and service is impeccable.
Retro masculine energy permeates
this refined lounge where live music
is scheduled for every evening, and
martinis go perfectly with dramatic
seafood towers stacked high with
fresh sea creatures.

EL HIDALGUENSE
6917 LONG POINT
between Silber & Antoine
☎ (713) 680-1071 | MAP **D5** | ⑂⑂

HIDALGUENSE HAS MANY THINGS
GOING FOR IT, WHICH IS GOOD
seeing as how its facade and sketchy
location on Long Point are not exactly
inviting. Their corn tortillas have
dedicated fans, and everything that
goes between them is also part of
their charm. Specialties here include
cabrito (baby goat roasted in a large
pit) and Hidalgo-style lamb, which
is great for sharing among groups.
Occasional live music gets things
going with the crowd, who whoop
along and dance if there's enough
room. Stay away from the "margaritas," which are not made with tequila
due to the restaurant's beer- and
wine-only permit. Some may be put
off by the general grubbiness here,
but many foodies swear by
its authenticity.

EL MESON
2425 UNIVERSITY *at Morningside*
☎ (713) 522-9306 | MAP **E7** | ⑂
ELMESON.COM

IT'S ALL THE SPANISH DISHES YOU
COULD WANT, AND BY "SPANISH"
we mean Cuban, Tex-Mex and
food with origins in actual Spain.

An eclectic menu attracts a large crowd pretty much any night of the week, and there's also an award-winning wine list and cute surroundings that bring in the Rice Village clientele. Garlicky shredded beef known as *ropa vieja* falls under the Cuban category while traditional tapas (read: Spanish) like *patatas bravas* (fried potatoes in a spicy tomato sauce) and serrano ham with manchego go nicely with a glass of sangria. *Enchiladas verdes* are available for those needing a Tex-Mex fix. Oh, and there are seven varieties of paella. (Owners Peter and Regina Garcia are happy to customize a paella for your special event.) Live music brings in energy but also volume, so if a quiet dinner is what you want, check their online calendar beforehand.

EL PUEBLITO PLACE
1423 RICHMOND *west of Mandell*
☎ (713) 520-6635 | MAP **E7** | ⁉
ELPUEBLITOPATIO.COM

DRINKS FROM HOLLOWED-OUT COCONUTS AND PINEAPPLES. What else do you need to know? If you must inquire further, El Pueblito Place is a quirky oasis with tropical appeal, right down to the bright paint job and the perfect patio: There's a cabana area, and the bar is decorated in bamboo for a tiki effect. As for the food? It's not the greatest in town, but it's as if something magical happens when topped with their cilantro-heavy salsa and served under fairy-light-wrapped palm trees. Fish tacos, platters of grilled chicken, black beans and fried plantains appease the masses, who are mainly just here for the scenery and the frozen drinks.

EL PUPUSODROMO
5802 RENWICK *between Hwy. 59 & Gulfton*
☎ (713) 661-4334 | MAP **D7** | ⁉
multiple locations

TACOS, BURRITOS AND EVEN GORDITAS SEEM TO HAVE earned a permanent place in the Houston vernacular, but for some reason the Salvadoran *pupusa*—fluffy maize pancakes redolent with lard and stuffed with cheese, meat or beans—haven't quite reached critical mass. It's time to remedy that, and El Pupusodromo is a good place to start if you've never experienced one. The namesake *pupusas* taste best when garnished with the pickled cabbage called *curtido*, a condiment found on every table here. If you feel like branching out, try the tamals, which are similar to their Mexican cousins, though lighter. Or perhaps the *yuca con chicharrones* (boiled or fried yucca that is dressed and sprinkled with crunchy bits of pork) is something that piques your interest. It's a casual place to experiment and is low risk as everything here is very reasonably priced.

EL REAL TEX-MEX CAFE
1201 WESTHEIMER
west of Montrose
☎ (713) 524-1201 | MAP **E6** | ⁉
ELREALTEXMEX.COM

SOME THINGS ON EL REAL'S MENU ARE MORE NOSTALGIC than they are good, but then again Tex-Mex is an incredibly subjective cuisine. Quesadillas with smoky chicken chunks sandwiched between melty cheese and soft tortillas are outstanding, not to mention the perfect foil to the bar's sweet frozen margaritas.

The cheese enchiladas #7 are also excellent. History is the main ingredient here at this converted theater, which seems enormous with its soaring ceilings, wide expanses and walls covered with Western memorabilia. That history comes from a desire to let Houstonians taste how the rest of Texas does (and did) Tex-Mex. Greasy puffy tacos dripping with picadillo beef, for example, were born in San Antonio, and the stacked enchiladas borunda smothered in guajillo chili are a West Texas phenomenon. If you want a little of everything, check out the combo menu.

EL REY TAQUERIA
910 SHEPHERD *at Washington*
☎ (713) 802-9145 | MAP **E6** | ❙
multiple locations
ELREYTAQUERIA.COM

THIS CUBAN-MEXICAN FAST-CASUAL CONCEPT OFFERS drive-thru service with restaurant quality meals. While it's not exactly an ideal situation for dining in—the chairs are uncomfortable and forks are plastic—the low prices outweigh the lack of ambiance. On the Cuban side are plates of stewed, shredded beef (*ropa vieja*) cut with sticky sweet plantains and rice as well as traditional Cuban sandwiches with ham, Swiss cheese, pickles and pork. On the Mexican side are tacos that come with a choice of tortilla—corn, flour or wheat—as well as a great selection of street-food-style tortas. Combining two cultures into one tortilla is the Cuban taco with fajitas, smoky black beans, plantains and a schmear of *crema* that is irresistible. Breakfast tacos are just as good as everything else here and go well with a steaming cup of Cuban *cafe con leche*.

EL TIEMPO
3130 RICHMOND *between Kirby & Buffalo Speedway*
☎ (713) 807-1600 | MAP **D7** | ❙❙
multiple locations
ELTIEMPOCANTINA.COM

THE LAURENZO FAMILY'S EL TIEMPO IS NOT SIMPLY A Houston Tex-Mex institution, it's a full-on experience. One of the places on the short list of where to take out-of-town guests, it's usually loud and packed and staffed with servers dressed as if they're ready to drop everything and start singing mariachi songs. The food is served in ungodly generous portions, and woe is the brave one who attempts to leave without a doggy bag. Some of their specialties include fajitas, brisket enchiladas, a "cannonball" of stuffed deep-fried avocado and giant flautas. Margaritas are worthy of praise as is the always attentive and festive service. Sure you'll pay a larger sum for dinner, but just remember how much food you have for lunch tomorrow. As of this latest edition, El Tiempo has opened a location in East Houston just one block from The Original Ninfa's, which was founded by matriarch Ninfa Laurenzo and was once owned by their family. The family, it seems, has come full circle back to their roots.

ELEVEN XI
607 W. GRAY
between Taft & Montrose
☎ (713) 529-5881 | MAP **E6** | ❙❙❙
ELEVENXIHOUSTON.COM

ELEVEN XI IS THE LATEST RESTAURANT TO TAKE OVER THIS 1940s-era building in Montrose. Previously occupied by various iterations of Bibas over the years, there's a lot of history tied up in the location. As all things evolve toward something, so has the newest tenant, with an upscale menu by chef Kevin Bryant that could be categorized as Southern Coastal. Of interest are the raw bar, baby back ribs in a Texas root beer sauce, caveman-style beef short rib, tea-brined wild game hen and Texas quail with blue corn cheese grits and mixed greens. Cocktails are fancy and the wine list is extensive, perfect to enjoy on the very inviting lounge-like patio, which makes the building's transformation complete.

EMPIRE CAFE

1732 WESTHEIMER
between Dunlavy & Woodhead
☎ (713) 528-5282 | MAP **E6** | 🍴
EMPIRECAFE.COM

I**T'S ONE OF THOSE RETRO SIDE-WALK CAFE/COFFEEHOUSES THAT** gives this area of Montrose its unmistakable charm. Empire is a cozy gathering place that gives locals (and those who don't mind driving inside the city) a spot for both bustling brunches and quiet casual dinners of pasta on the patio. In between the two extremes, lattes and coffees and giant slices of cake are served to students or those with laptops in hand and some that come just to read the paper and get a sugar rush. Helping keep those cakes fresh are half-priced cake days (Mondays) with giant helpings of Toll House, peanut butter, chocolate and hummingbird cake attracting lines at the small counter.

EMPIRE TURKISH GRILL

12448 MEMORIAL
just west of Gessner
☎ (713) 827-7475 | MAP **C6** | 🍴
EMPIRETRGRILL.COM

G**IVEN THAT ITS LOCATION IS IN THE SUBURBAN MEMORIAL** area of Houston, it's even more exciting to find this pretty little gem of a Turkish restaurant. The tables are dressed in crisp white table-cloths but don't let that dissuade you: The dress code is "Houston chic," meaning t-shirt and jeans are totally acceptable. Kebabs are the thing to get here, though the yogurt grills wherein fried bread cubes are covered in yogurt and topped with grilled meat are more intriguing. The usual Middle Eastern fare is also found here in the form of falafel, plenty of eggplant dishes—including one called *imam bayildi*, which is roasted baby eggplant with onions, tomato, parsley, garlic and olive oil served cold—and stuffed grape leaves. Warm flatbread sops up hummus and other spreads with ease and is served with every meal. Tripe soup with vinegar dressing, fried liver and a red caviar spread called *tarama* are nice to experiment with if you've got the courage.

ESCALANTE'S

4053 WESTHEIMER *at Drexel*
☎ (713) 623-4200 | MAP **D6** | 🍴
multiple locations
ESCALANTES.NET

I**F YOU CAN FORGIVE THEM FOR THEIR INCLUSION OF FAT-FREE** refried beans as an option, chances are you'll like this dressed-up Tex-Mex spot full of vibrant colors and suburban families. The local chain, placed strategically in mostly affluent neighborhoods, attracts

Eleven XI patio picnic

those who don't mind valet parking or having a menu that ranges from Greek salads to fajita *rellenos*. In fact, sometimes it's nice to visit a Tex-Mex restaurant that actually offers an intriguing selection of salads alongside gut-busting combo plates. The kitchen's classic enchiladas verdes go great with a top-shelf margarita, and guacamole is made tableside with just enough show to justify the $13 price tag. Might as well live it up while you're here, and don't forget to tip the valet.

ETOILE CUISINE ET BAR

1101 UPTOWN PARK BLVD.
in Uptown Park
☎ (832) 668-5808 | MAP **D6** | 🍴
ETOILECUISINE.COM

FRENCH RESTAURANTS IN HOUSTON ARE ALMOST AS EASY TO find these days as SUVs on Interstate 10. Which is to say, plentiful. Adding itself to the line-up is Etoile, a newcomer from transplanted San Diego celebrity chef Philippe Verpiand that still manages to hang on to a piece of the escargot-loving market in its Uptown Park location. While the location and dinner prices imply a possible swankiness, it's anything but. Portions are hearty during both lunch and dinner and include classics like the aforementioned escargots, homemade pâté, cassoulet and steak frites as well as wild boar Bolognese and rich vegetable risotto. The atmosphere is welcoming, service friendly and the dining room nicely scaled.

FACUNDO CAFE

3103 ELLA *at W. 34th*
☎ (713) 880-0898 | MAP **E5** | 🍴
FACUNDOCAFE.COM

IT'S QUIRKY, IT'S HIP, IT'S A CAFE "HIDDEN" INSIDE A CAR WASH

facility. Joke all you will about its odd location, but it does manage to turn out some impressive grub. Breakfast is a simple affair with typical American dishes like bacon and egg sandwiches or French toast for dine-in. What really grabbed the attention of Houstonians, however, is Facundo's extensive burger menu, which utilizes sourdough buns, thick juicy patties and plenty of toppings. There are other items like sandwiches, salads and a few grilled dishes, too, if you're all burgered out. Facundo has created such a loyal following they've decided to build a new location just down the road. As of press time, it is still under construction. Will it be as successful detached from the car wash? Only time will tell.

FADI'S MEDITERRANEAN GRILL

8383 WESTHEIMER *at Dunvale*
☎ (713) 532-0666 | MAP **C6** | 🍴
multiple locations
FADISCUISINE.COM

CAFETERIA-STYLE HAS NEVER LOOKED SO REGAL OR TASTED so exotic. Fadi's is universally loved in Houston, and it's easy to understand why. Large portions come at affordable prices, and the see-it-before-you-order-it format builds a certain type of anticipation before the meal. There are hills of *fattoush* (Lebanese salad), tabouli and lentil salad that lead to cumin-rich lamb shank and fried cauliflower. It's a great resource for vegetarians, but the kebabs and roasted meats are savory and fresh. Piping hot pita bread comes with every meal, and baklava awaits at the end of the line. A family-friendly atmosphere is just an added bonus.

FALAFEL FACTORY
914 PRAIRIE *at Travis*
☎ (713) 237-8987 | MAP **F6** | ❙ Ψ

THE KEYS TO THIS HOLE-IN-THE-WALL'S SUCCESS ARE efficiency and price. It's also got a great location serving falafel in a part of town where there's something of a Mediterranean food desert (with the exception of Phoenicia Specialty Foods, of course). With a recent change of ownership, there seem to be some positive changes afoot, with a better ordering system on its way and freshened versions of the falafel pitas already so famous here. There are still the same simple crispy fries that accompany each combo as well as salads, hummus and shawarma, and they all are still offered at a bargain price. Also not expected to change is the interior, which sports a shotgun kitchen and dining area the size of a closet, but most downtown orders are for take-out anyway.

FAT BAO
3419 KIRBY *at Richmond*
☎ (713) 677-0341 | MAP **E7** Ψ
FATBAOHOUSTON.COM

TO UNDERSTAND FAT *BAO*, YOU SHOULD FIRST KNOW WHAT bao is exactly. Pronounced "bow" (as in a ship) and not "bay-oh" (as in Scott Baio), these are steamed buns, fluffy and soft, stuffed with various ingredients. And when done right, they are ethereal. Now that you know what they are, it's not hard to figure out what Fat Bao specializes in. The very narrow-focused menu stuffs those buns with all manner of combinations from braised pork belly, Asian slaw and green onions in the Memphis to softshell crab, spicy mayo and

Asian slaw in the Crab Daddy. Sides are mostly variations on fast food (onion rings, fries, etc.), but there are a few salads and some astonishingly delicious little poke tuna tacos that come three to an order. Counter service is convenient and casual.

THE FEDERAL GRILL
510 SHEPHERD
south of Washington
☎ (713) 863-7777 | MAP **E6** | ❙ΨΨ
THEFEDERALGRILL.COM

WHAT ONCE WAS BRANCH WATER TAVERN IS NOW THE Federal Grill. Pretty much seamlessly transforming from one to the other, owner Matt Brice's concept is similar but updated just enough to make it different from its predecessor. While the already beautiful interiors have remained pretty much the same, the soundtrack is more Rat Pack, the service includes more niceties and the rewritten menu (executed by chefs Antoine Ware and Michael Hoffman) of upscale steakhouse classics include tuna tartare, jumbo lump crabcakes, bacon-wrapped shrimp, steaks and chops as well as such homey fare as fried chicken.

FIELD OF GREENS
2320 W. ALABAMA *east of Kirby*
☎ (713) 533-0029 | MAP **E6** | Ψ
FIELDOFGREENSCUISINE.COM

CALL IT HIPPIE, CALL IT HEALTHY, BUT DON'T CALL IT BORING. Field of Greens is the place for vegetarian, macrobiotic and vegan dishes that are filling and, most of the time, pretty darn tasty. Wild field pockets are stuffed with soy ham and chicken, shiitake mushrooms, sprouts and guacamole.

Layers of roast vegetables make up the vegan lasagne, and gluten-free spinach salad is dressed with feta, pecans and a bright vinaigrette. As a concession to the pescatarians, there are also grilled Alaskan salmon and a tuna salad sandwich with a zing of curry. It does fall short on ambiance in the utilitarian space, but just bring your food next door to The Path of Tea for a more intimate experience.

FIELDING'S WOOD GRILL

1699 RESEARCH FOREST DR., *between Six Pines & Grogans Mill, The Woodlands*
FIELDINGS.COM

NOT SURPRISINGLY, THE WOOD GRILL WILL BE A BIG FEATURE of this restaurant, which comes from specialty market Hubble & Hudson partners Cary Attar and Edel Gonçalves. Burgers will be a draw here, of course, but the menu will provide other options like salads, rotisserie items and freshly baked goods. Milkshakes will be kicked up a notch with half being traditional versions, the other half for adults—if you get our drift—all made from ice creams produced in-house. As if that weren't do-it-yourself enough, bacon will be cured on-site and meat will be ground inside their very own butcher shop. It will open Fall 2013.

FLEMING'S PRIME STEAKHOUSE

2405 W. ALABAMA *east of Kirby*
☎ (713) 520-5959
multiple locations
FLEMINGSSTEAKHOUSE.COM

THE BEST WAY TO DESCRIBE THIS UPSCALE CHAIN WOULD be classic steakhouse with a few modern, even feminine twists. There's plenty of beef as expected, including a wet-aged, hand-carved USDA Prime bone-in ribeye that satisfies the inner caveman in many of us. But then there's the small plates menu with shrimp skewers accompanied by a chimichurri dipping sauce and fennel citrus salad and the baked brie for an appetizer. Also enticing to a non-traditional steakhouse crowd are low-calorie cocktails. Of course, it usually doesn't matter how many calories you're imbibing if you take advantage of Fleming's happy-hour food menu, which includes burgers and house-made burrata for a dangerously low price.

FLOR DE CUBA

16233 CLAY *near Hwy. 6*
☎ (281) 463-8611 | MAP **B5** | ❦
FLORDECUBA.COM

FLOR DE CUBA FANS THE STEREOTYPE THAT LATINS KNOW how to party. The bar, serving up the lovely mojito, of course, keeps guests relaxed, the homey Cuban food keeps them full and the live music that plays on into the early morning hours keeps them entertained. Family-owned and authentic as they come, Flor de Cuba attracts Cubanos who travel from all over Houston to get a taste of home. For some that means the traditional Cuban sandwich; for others it's the falling-off-the-bone *pollo asado*, perfect with black beans; still others might try the *parrillada Cubana* family-style meal that includes massive portions of pork chops, *vaca frita* (fried shredded beef), fried yucca and many side dishes. But wait, there's more! The bakery part of the restaurant produces a variety of *pastelitos* (traditional Cuban puff pastries), tres leches and custom cakes.

FLORA & MUSE

12860 QUEENSBURY *at W. Sam Houston Parkway N. (Beltway 8) in CityCentre*

☎ (713) 463-6873 | MAP **B6** | ¶¶

FLORAANDMUSE.COM

FLORA & MUSE IS A TWO-FER. HALF IS A CHARMING LITTLE pâtisserie dedicated to coffee, pastries and flowers, while the other side is a full-service restaurant and bar. It's a tiny piece of Europe in a large, commercial development surrounded by highways and beltways. The tufted banquettes, sparkling chandeliers and gilded mirrors add a light feminine touch. With a large menu that covers breakfast, lunch, late night and even tea, there's a lot to consider. So far, the Turkish pies, stone-oven flatbreads (topped with pear and gorgonzola or cured salmon and capers) as well as a variety of crêpes and wild mushroom ravioli have proven tasty and consistent.

FOGO DE CHAO

8250 WESTHEIMER *between S. Voss & Fondren*

☎ (713) 978-6500 | MAP **C7** | ¶¶¶

FOGODECHAO.COM

THERE'S SOMETHING SO EXTRAVAGANT ABOUT THE way servers parade around giant skewers of meat at this opulent *churrascaria* chain. The style of service where the meat comes to you, known as rodizio, is a sure-fire way to consume more protein than you ever thought possible. Thankfully, there is a mechanism to stop the endless rotation of 15 various

cuts of beef, lamb, pork, chicken and sausage, too: a little table token that has a "stop" and a "go" side. Underrated here, mostly due to rampant meat lust, is the giant salad and vegetable bar with traditional Brazilian-style salads, heart of palm, a little bit of roughage (stock up, you'll need it this meal) and a few cheeses. Don't say no to the little cheese rolls called *pão de queijo*, which are chewy and cheesy and totally addictive.

FOUNTAIN VIEW CAFE

1842 FOUNTAIN VIEW *south of San Felipe*

☎ (713) 785-9060 | MAP **D6** | ¶

AGOOD BREAKFAST OUT IS WORTH ITS WEIGHT IN GOLD. After all, who wants to wash dishes at 10 am? Leave the cooking and the dishes to Fountain View Cafe, a neighborhood joint with a quaint interior of old school chairs and tables and counter service. Thin and buttery pancakes have a following, but there are plenty of eggs-bacon-starch combinations on the menu for anyone who appreciates a hardy American start to the day. Just because breakfast is the hallmark here, don't count lunch out just yet. Blue-plate lunch specials are hearty, and burgers are commendable. Finish it off with a banana split and you won't be sorry.

FRANK'S AMERICANA REVIVAL

3736 WESTHEIMER *at Weslayan*

☎ (713) 572-8600 | MAP **D6** | ¶¶¶

FRANKSCHOPHOUSE.COM

PREVIOUSLY KNOWN AS FRANK'S CHOP HOUSE, THIS HANDSOME neighborhood spot has changed hands since the last edition, not to mention names. It's now owned by Michael Shine and his son Chris. But not too much else has changed. There's still an abundance of contemporary American food that takes comfort classics upscale. How upscale is it? You'll pay $15 for a burger, and lunch starts at $19. For those prices you will get a pretty fine crispy shrimp BLT or a chicken-fried steak that's worthy of a hefty price tag. There are also plenty of salads for the greenery lovers and a much more approachable bar menu for those looking to snack while sipping a martini. It's nicely suited to its River Oaks location with a $56 dry-aged ribeye and extensive wine list.

FRENCHIE'S

1041 NASA PARKWAY *at El Camino Real*
☎ (281) 486-7144 | 🍴
southwest of MAP **19**
FRENCHIESVILLACAPRI.COM

BE ADVISED THAT FRENCHIE'S IS NOT ACTUALLY FRENCH. IT'S Italian, and it is full of character. From the unassuming location in a strip mall to the paper napkin dispensers on each table, it's anything but fancy. But there are white tablecloths on each, and walls full of NASA memorabilia and photos of celebrities posing with the owners/ brothers Frank and Giuseppe Camera tell a history rooted in the economy that space travel created. Cheese-stuffed manicotti, spaghetti with clams, baked lasagne and veal parmigiana seem as if they came right out of a mob movie, but don't fret about gangsters here—you're more likely to run into a retired astronaut. Lunch can be hectic with counter service, but dinner is a sit-down affair with table service and an expanded menu.

FRENCHY'S CHICKEN

3919 SCOTT *at Wheeler*
☎ (713) 748-2233 | MAP **F7** | 🍴
multiple locations
FRENCHYSCHICKEN.COM

WHEN HOUSTON NATIVE AND INTERNATIONAL SUPERSTAR, Beyoncé Knowles-Carter is a fan of something, you don't question it. Perhaps the most famous fan of Frenchy's Chicken, she is far from the only one. Sundays find Frenchy's slammed with customers loading up for family dinners, all of them hauling home boxes of freshly fried, highly spiced chicken. That's not even counting the 30,000-plus "likes" Frenchy's has racked up on Facebook. The secret lies in the New Orleans spices that came from founder Percy "Frenchy" Creuzot's family recipe. Along those lines, the Creole fast-food stop also offers sides of collard greens, dirty rice, gumbo, jambalaya, red beans and rice and buttery biscuits.

FUFU CAFE

9889 BELLAIRE BLVD. *at W. Sam Houston Parkway S. (Beltway 8)*
☎ (713) 981-8818 | MAP **C7** | 🍴

BRACE YOURSELF, YOU'RE IN FOR A BUMPY RIDE, AT LEAST in the service department. While Chinatown is notorious for less-than-friendly service, Fufu Cafe seems to have one of the worst reputations. Despite that caveat, people still venture here because of one thing: the illustrious *xiao long bao*, or soup dumplings. How is that possible, you ask? Containing hot broth as well as meat, soup dumplings are made by filling purse-shaped pouches of dumpling skin with aspic that liquifies when cooking, then splashes out and burns your tongue if not eaten with careful technique. (Use a spoon and chopsticks ... heck, just go to You-Tube to watch a demo.) Aside from their main draw, steamed and fried pork dumplings, *ma po* eggplant and the spicy beef noodle soup layered with pickled mustard greens are worth ordering. Note: Don't mix up Fufu Cafe with Fufu Restaurant, which is right down the street.

FUNG'S KITCHEN

7320 SOUTHWEST FWY.
(HWY. 59) *between Bellaire Blvd. & Fondren*
☎ (713) 779-2288 | MAP **C7** | 🍴
FUNGSKITCHEN.COM

THE LOCAL GOLD STANDARD FOR CANTONESE DINING, Fung's Kitchen is a more refined experience than most other Chinese restaurants in Houston. From the dramatic entrance with a pagoda-like facade and two lions guarding the door to the hundreds of menu items and the sea creatures swimming in tanks along the wall, any meal here is a full-on presentation. Getting back to those finny creatures swimming next to your table—these very well might be the base of your main course, and the freshness is unmistakable. Lobster is a particularly extravagant choice, sautéed and spiked with chives, while steamed scallops come still in the shell. It's not a cheap date, but you definitely get your money's worth. Dim sum is a Fung's weekend tradition, and the dining room tends to get a little hectic, while at night the red and gold dining room hosts many a special-occasion banquet for the Chinese community in Houston.

FUNKY CHICKEN

810 HEIGHTS BLVD. | MAP **E6**
just south of Katy Fwy. (I-10 West)

WHAT USED TO BE KNOWN AS A SILLY DANCE CRAZE WILL now be known as a casual restaurant from Las Vegas chef Bradley Ogden. The concept built around its namesake poultry, the chicken served here will be organic and free range and baked, fried or sautéed into any number of dishes. Examples include rotisserie chicken, buttermilk fried chicken, chicken potpie, barbecued chicken and before we start sounding like Bubba Gump, chicken fingers. Sides are homey and comforting, and the atmosphere is designed to be laid-back and family friendly. Coming Fall 2013.

FUSION TACO

801 CONGRESS *at Milam*
☎ (713) 422-2882 | MAP **F6** | 🍴
FUSIONTACO.COM

TAKING OVER THE MARKET SQUARE SPACE THAT WAS previously occupied by Les Givrals in July 2013, Fusion Taco is poised to become the hot new downtown destination. With ample seating and a view of the recently revamped Market Square Park, chef Julia Sharaby and partner-partner (it means what you think it means) chef David Grossman (formerly of Branch Water Tavern) serve Latin American-Asian fusion in the form of tacos. Fusion Taco started off as a food truck and became so popular it was nigh impossible to wait out the line during its appearances at the downtown farmers' market. The wait will be much more pleasant in the open dining room and adjoining bar with a bottle of Kirin Ichiban beer in hand. Tacos don't come cheap, but where else can you find a chicken satay-stuffed tortilla or crispy tofu with wasabi aioli and Napa cabbage?

GATLIN'S BBQ
1221 W. 19TH AT BEVIS
☎ (713) 869-4227 | MAP **E5** | 🍴
GATLINSBBQ.COM

IT'S GOT THE DECK STACKED AGAINST IT: LIMITED HOURS, only a few tables, Styrofoam plates and long waits. But Gatlin's thrives in spite of its disadvantages, which is a testament to how beloved the family's smoked meats have become to Houstonians searching for quality barbecue. The brisket gets raves as do the ribs and spicy house-made sausage. The sauce is nice and vinegary and tastes good on just about anything. Even the sides, which can be lackluster at other barbecue joints, are exemplary with dirty rice and baked beans especially worthy of consumption.

GERARDO'S DRIVE-IN
609 PATTON *just west of Irvington*
☎ (713) 699-0820 | MAP **F5** | 🍴

WHAT YOU NEED TO KNOW: GERARDO'S IS A DIVE, IT'S in a weathered neighborhood, the staff isn't particularly fluent in English and, on the weekends, they serve some of the best *barbacoa* in the country. What is that exactly? It's meat from the head of a cow, but stay with us. Steamed until it falls of the skull, the meat is rich and tender and incredibly flavorful. Topped off with some of the green salsa here, it's almost transcendent. The catch is that all components come separate, and the *barbacoa* is ordered by the pound. Pick up a

bag of tortillas on your way out, and you're good to go.

GIACOMO'S CIBO E VINO
3215 WESTHEIMER *west of Kirby*
☎ (713) 522-1934 | MAP **E6** | 🍴
GIACOMOSCIBOEVINO.COM

WITH A FOCUS ON *CICCHETTI*, OR SMALL PLATES, LYNETTE Hawkins' charming little eatery is much like that of a tapas restaurant, only Italian style. Cold dishes are on display at the counter for you to pick and choose, and hot plates are individually prepared. Panini and salads are popular lunch selections, but pastas and main courses like slow-roasted Berkshire pork have their place at the dinner table. The mosaic of colorful, asymmetrical tiles on the main wall creates a casual, cheerful environment that makes you want to stay a while, as does the very pleasant vine-lined patio. Whereas lunch is a casual affair, dinner is a more intimate experience with dimmed lights. Split checks aren't allowed, and substitutions aren't always easy to request, but it's a small price to pay for such a unique restaurant here in Houston. There's a lovely patio as well.

GIGI'S ASIAN BISTRO & DUMPLING BAR
5085 WESTHEIMER
near McCue, in The Galleria
☎ (713) 629-8889 | MAP **D6** | 🍴
GIGISASIANBISTRO.COM

IT'S A SULTRY ASIAN RESTAURANT WITH MODERN TOUCHES AND A gorgeous bar and dining area. (It's in The Galleria after all.) Just the zip code alone means there will be a certain see-and-be-seen crowd,

Gigi's Asian Bistro

but the food still stands on its own. Covering many of the staple Asian foods, the menu jumps from Vietnamese to Thai to Chinese and back again, all served in a lush dining room with special tables in the "Alley," where each cubbyhole is curtained off from prying eyes. Dinner could mean tamarind-glazed short ribs, green curry chicken or crispy whole fish with Thai basil sauce, and their house-made table condiments give it yet another gourmet touch. Casual diners might want to try the Dumpling Bar for cocktails and dim sum.

GILHOOLEY'S
222 9TH ST. *off E. Bay Shore Dr., San Leon*
☎ (281) 339-3813 | 🍴

A FEW THINGS TO KNOW BEFORE VENTURING DOWN TO THIS BAYside legend: 1) Be sure to Google the best route from your part of Houston. 2) Take along no children younger than 18, as they are not allowed. 3) Expect a smoke-filled dive bar that just happens to do grilled oysters better than anyone else on the planet. Oysters Gilhooley, the star attraction, come smoky-grilled on the half shell with parmesan and a secret sauce. Adding shrimp is allowed. We also recommend the gumbo and an excellent half-pound burger. Early risers brag about the breakfast selection, but we wouldn't know. You can't be too casually dressed to offend the locals, but a big-city attitude won't fly here. Just sit back, order a couple dozen of those delicious bivalves along with a beer or two, and thank your designated driver.

GLASS WALL
933 STUDEWOOD *at E. 10th*
☎ (713) 868-7930 | MAP **E5** | 🍴🍴
GLASSWALLTHERESTAURANT.COM

THE GLASS WALL IS STILL AT THE TOP OF ITS GAME, EVEN though it's not the young whippersnapper of the neighborhood anymore. As more chefs have flocked to The Heights to open establishments, Glass Wall has just kept on doing everything well. With a menu that uses seasonal ingredients in dishes like succotash ravioli (parmesan, ricotta, zucchini, corn, lima beans, green peas in a lemon-prosecco broth) or a sarsaparilla-braised short rib with Brussels sprouts and cheesy potato gratin, it's no wonder this "veteran" can still pack them in every night. Wine is also in abundance, with pairing suggestions next to every dish on the menu. Noise levels reach a roar around 8 pm every evening as the beautiful people shuffle into the cool-toned dining room.

GLORIA'S RESTAURANT
2616 LOUISIANA *at McGowen*
☎ (832) 360-1710 | MAP **F6** | 🍴🍴
GLORIASRESTAURANTS.COM

A HEARTWARMING STORY OF TWO IMMIGRANTS FROM EL Salvador has translated into a very successful upscale chain of Tex-Mex restaurants, and the first Houston location has opened since our last edition. Named after co-owner Gloria Fuentes, it's sleek and modern, with its own variation of enchiladas, combo plates and a few Salvadoran dishes like pupusas hinting at its heritage. The restaurant is popular in Dallas, which explains the cover charge that goes into effect after 10 pm, the dress code on salsa nights and the overall snazziness of the place despite the fact it serves really big burritos (not that there's anything wrong with that). Lunch and brunch are also served, and wines by the bottle are half-priced all day Sunday through Wednesday.

GOLDEN DUMPLING HOUSE

9896-B BELLAIRE BLVD., *just east of W. Sam Houston Parkway S. (Beltway 8)*

☎ (713) 270-9996 | MAP **C7** 🍴

I F LITTLE WRAPPERS STUFFED WITH ALL MANNER OF INGREDI-ents are your thing, Golden Dumpling House is the place. Counter service makes for easy split checks and group dining. The staff is happy to suggest dishes to try, and though you may end up with a plethora of leftovers, it will still most likely fall within the $10/person range. Dumplings come steamed, fried and blistering hot, filled with savory pork and vegetables or the deluxe version and house specialty dumplings with shrimp, pork and vegetables. There are also steamed buns and deep-fried versions that remind us of Southern fried pie, only filled with leeks and scallions. And that sour smell that greets you at the entrance? Don't turn up your nose: It's just the cabbage leaves that line the dumpling steamers. Nothing else is afoot here except great deals and impeccable dumplings. Cash only.

GOOD DOG HOT DOGS

903 STUDEWOOD | MAP **E5** *at E. 9th St.*

J OINING THE GROWING LIST OF FOOD TRUCKS-TURNED-RES-taurant-incubators, Good Dog Hot Dogs has gained legions of rabid fans with their brand of fully loaded hot dogs with toppings like home-made condiments (ketchup, roasted garlic aioli, whole grain mustard and dill relish, to name just a few), bacon, caramelized onions, muen-ster cheese, cream cheese, guaca-mole, beef and chorizo chili. Now they've finally made the big jump to a permanent building. Aptly located in The Heights, Good Dog took over the Big Mamou location and plans to offer beer, wine and coffee as well as an expanded menu when they open in the Fall 2013.

GOODE CO. TAQUERIA & HAMBURGERS

4902 KIRBY *at Westpark*

☎ (713) 520-9153 | MAP **E7** 🍴
GOODECOMPANY.COM

T ACOS AND BURGERS AND BREAKFAST, OH MY! IT'S A trifecta that's hard to beat, espe-cially considering that it's stamped with the trusted Goode Co. moni-ker. Old-fashioned country break-fasts featuring game meats like quail or venison and Mexican-style egg dishes are hearty and portioned as if everyone ate like a linebacker. (So just skip lunch to compensate). As the day progresses, the burg-ers and Tex-Mex favorites (tacos, enchiladas and fajitas) are more apt and readily available. There's an entire section devoted to Goode Co.'s mesquite grill with proteins ranging from catfish to border quail. The Texas kitsch is just enough without going overboard, and the longnecks sitting in tin buckets of ice are a nice touch.

RESTAURANTS

GOODE CO. TEXAS BAR-B-Q

5109 KIRBY *at Westpark*
☎ (713) 522-2530 | MAP **E7** | 🍴
multiple locations
GOODECOMPANY.COM

A BARBECUE MECCA BEFORE TEXAS BARBECUE BECAME somewhat of a national obsession, this Goode Co. version of smoked meats is worthy of its popularity. Though some barbecue snobs turn their noses up at the brisket (they claim it isn't fatty or tender enough), it's undisputed that the Czech sausage, smoked chicken, citrus-tinged turkey breast and pork ribs are mighty good. Sides are lacking in flavor, but just pour a little barbecue sauce on everything and focus on the meat. The pecan pies are legendary (buy one for the Thanksgiving feast), and the jalapeño cheese bread is just as remarkable. The Kirby location is fun to sit outside among the twinkling lights strung across tree branches, and the Katy Freeway location is designed to look like an old-timey saloon. There's now a Highway 290 location, too.

GOODE CO. TEXAS SEAFOOD

2621 WESTPARK *west of Kirby*
☎ (713) 523-7154 | MAP **E7** | 🍴
multiple locations
GOODECOMPANY.COM

T HERE IS YET ANOTHER WING OF GOODE CO. DOING GREAT things, this time in the world of seafood. With mostly Gulf Coast items taking precedence over all else, some are fried but others are grilled over mesquite—a cooking technique Goode Co. has perfected throughout all of its venues. Fried oysters are always right on the money, and the campechana, which comes in a sundae glass packed all the way to the top, is the best example of the dish in town. A little sweet, a little rich (avocado chunks are plentiful), a little piquant (minced red onions give it that punch) and packed with shrimp, there's nothing better to go with the stout frozen margaritas from the bar. Both locations stay at capacity. The original Westpark location is housed in an old train car and getting an expansion and a space reorganization, while the Katy Freeway location is tucked into a shopping center with an antique wooden boat as its dining room centerpiece.

GORDITAS AGUASCALIENTES

6102 BISSONNET *between Renwick & Hillcroft*
☎ (713) 541-4560 | MAP **D7** | 🍴
multiple locations

W ORKING-CLASS MEXICAN IS THE BEST WAY TO DESCRIBE what Gorditas Aguascalientes puts on tables at their various locations. Gorditas are, of course, something to add to your must-try list, as are the *barbacoa* (succulent long-cooked meat from the head of a cow) burritos that are as authentic as they come. *Tortas* (Mexican sandwiches) are also included in the list of good things here, along with the tacos stuffed with *nopales* (prickly pear cactus), *rajas* (poblano strips) and *chicharrónes* (fried pork skin). As any self-respecting Mexican restaurant open in the morning would, Aguascalientes serves breakfast tacos as well as a rich warm drink called *atole*, which mixes masa, cinnamon and chocolate. We leave you with two more words: homemade tortillas.

GORO & GUN

306 MAIN *at Congress*
☎ (832) 708-6195 | MAP **F6** | ⟨fork/knife⟩

A MAIN PLAYER IN THE DOWN-
TOWN MAIN STREET RESUR-
gence of businesses, Goro & Gun is
the brick-and-mortar transformation of The Modular, a one-time
food truck operated by Joshua
Martinez. It was originally billed
as a ramen joint when it opened in
early 2013, but a few months later
it feels much more like a hipster
bar that happens to have two types
of ramen on the menu. In truth, it's
not the Japanese-style noodle soup
that gets the most praise, it's the
funky flair of dishes like flash-fried
Brussels sprouts or fish-sauced
chicken wings. In any case, the food
acts more as a bolster to the tasty
cocktails from the large bar, which
makes for a unique and very upbeat
atmosphere for an area of town that
is finally getting its due.

GRAPPINO DI NINO

2817 W. DALLAS *between Waugh
& Montrose*
☎ (713) 528-7002 | MAP **E6** | ⟨fork/knife⟩
NINOS-VINCENTS.COM

A DJACENT TO BOTH VINCENT'S
AND NINO'S (TWO FELLOW
Mandola family establishments),
what began as a grotto-like patio
bar has evolved into a full-fledged
restaurant. The little Montrose
enclave sports a very casual, simple
menu, filled with *pizzette*, small
plates, pastas, salads and such,
all designed to share over a bottle
of wine. It's an environment that
invites lingering with live bands
most nights and al fresco dining.
There are also private rooms for
event dining here.

GRATIFI KITCHEN + BAR

302 FAIRVIEW *at Taft*
☎ (832) 203-5950 | MAP **E6** | ⟨fork/knife⟩
GRATIFIKITCHENANDBAR.COM

T HE NEIGHBORHOOD MONTROSE
RESTAURANT WITH THE FAN-
tastic patio used to be called
Ziggy's, and its niche was "healthy"
foods and burgers with offbeat
proteins like ostrich or kangaroo.
Keeping up with the times, ownership closed a branch in downtown
and subsequently rebranded their
Montrose location as Gratifi (pro-
nounce it like "gratify"). In all hon-
esty, not much has changed from
their original offerings with burgers
and sandwiches and homey plates
of meatloaf, salads and breakfast
items still on the menu with added
pizzas and emphasis on the "bar" that
serves a great selection of craft beer.
The large patio is dog friendly and a
great place for people watching.

GREEN SEED VEGAN

4320 ALMEDA *at Wheeler*
☎ (713) 487-8346 | MAP **E6** | ⟨fork/knife⟩
GREENSEEDVEGAN.COM

I T'S AS IF THE OWNERS OF GREEN
SEED VEGAN TOOK EVERY DIETARY
restriction and challenged themselves to overcome every one of
them. And that they have. Starting
out as a popular food truck serving
vegan fare as well as gluten-free
and non-GMO items, they've
moved into the big-time world of
brick and mortar thanks in part to
a $13,000 crowd-funded campaign
via Kickstarter. Popular items that
appeal to both mainstream and
strict vegan guests are the "Dirty
Burque" burger compiled with a
buckwheat patty studded with fresh
vegetables, cauliflower nuggets,
raw brownies and dill fries. Fresh

juices, smoothies and teas are also available.

GRIMALDI'S PIZZERIA

20 WATERWAY *at Timberloch, The Woodlands*
☎ (281) 465-3500 | 🍴
multiple locations
GRIMALDISPIZZERIA.COM

PLACED STRATEGICALLY IN FAMILY-FRIENDLY SUBURBAN areas, part of Grimaldi's appeal is the fact that everyone can enjoy a meal here, even the rowdiest of kids. Coal ovens are the cooking mechanism for the New York-style pies that come topped generously with traditional ingredients. Options are limited—only pies with two types of sauce (red or garlicky white) and a few starter salads—but there's no shame in specialization.

The Grove

GROTTO

4715 WESTHEIMER *just inside Loop 610*
☎ (713) 622-3663 | MAP **D6** | 🍴
multiple locations
GROTTORESTAURANTS.COM

ORIGINALLY FOUNDED BY HOUSTON RESTAURATEUR Tony Vallone of the famous Tony's, Grotto has grown into five locations including one in Atlantic City and another in Las Vegas. The other three are in and around Houston. The formula for higher-end Italian includes a sprawling dining room with vibrant murals and, during peak hours, a roaring level of noise. Neopolitan-inspired dishes built around scratch-made pastas line the menu, and the antipasti bar is equally impressive. The *pappardelle alla campagnola* with chicken and

zesty *sugo rosa* sauce remains a crowd favorite. Brunch is offered and business lunches are affordable and efficient at $17 or less per person, including salad or soup.

THE GROVE

1611 LAMAR *at Crawford,*
on Discovery Green
☎ (713) 337-7321 | MAP **F6** | 🍴
THEGROVEHOUSTON.COM

BILLED AS HAVING "RUSTIC AMERICAN CUISINE," THE Grove could also be considered a "locavore" restaurant, using many a Texas ingredient. And while the food is lovely most of the time (there have been reports of inconsistency), the real reason to visit is its enchanting modern location right in the middle of Discovery Green. Plenty of windows allow the scenery of downtown's skyline and the "green" of Discovery Green inside, while patio and rooftop seating puts guests directly into the park environment. Night is magical with the high-rises lighting up and sparkly lights hanging from the trees. Sipping a house cocktail or a glass of wine and sharing a plate of local ricotta *gnudi* (small pasta-like dumplings) out here will make you forget all the traffic and hassle of city living and remember the reasons you love Houston.

GUADALAJARA BAR & GRILL

2925 SOUTHWEST FWY. (HWY. 59) *between Kirby & Buffalo Speedway*
☎ (713) 942-0772 | MAP **D7** | 🍴
multiple locations
GUAD.COM

IT'S BIG, IT'S BUSTLING, IT'S TEX-MEX. WITH THAT LABEL COMES giant mounds of grilled meat and vegetables (fajitas have a menu all of their own), bacon-wrapped shrimp, Texas quail and snapper Veracruz. Adding to the non-stop energy is the sizable bar churning out the margaritas and Mexican *cervezas,* along with a happy-hour appetizer menu that fills seats and helps stressed out workers unwind from their busy days. Different locations around town cater to different clientele; the downtown "Del Centro" spot is known for quick lunch service for business people, and the West Houston and Inner Loop restaurants are kept packed with families and large parties.

HARRY'S

318 TUAM *at Bagby*
☎ (713) 528-0918 | MAP **E6** | 🍴
HARRYSRESTAURANTCAFE.COM

THIS UNDER-THE-RADAR DINER FIRST BEGAN SERVING UP Southern blue-plate specials in 1948. In 2002 the owners decided to expand the menu to incorporate a fusion of Latin, European and Mediterranean dishes. Not open for dinner, the lunch menu is served till 2:30 pm (3 pm on the weekends) and includes entrees like fried shrimp tacos, chicken souvalki, Southern fried chicken and Greek lasagne. And in keeping with the owners' Greek heritage, you can find feta cheese on about everything including the favorite feta fries dusted in parsley. Need another reason to visit? Breakfast all day, everyday.

HAVEN

2502 ALGERIAN WAY *east of Kirby*
☎ (713) 581-6101 | MAP **E7** | 🍴
HAVENHOUSTON.COM

CHEF RANDY EVANS, A BRENNAN'S VETERAN AND HOUSTON PIONEER in local and environmentally responsible dining, has created a menu that incorporates elegant twists on classic Southern dishes. Start with either the fried green tomatoes or the shrimp corndogs with Tabasco mash remoulade and finish with the filet of beef with crescenza cheese grits to experience Southern food elevation. Don't let the white tablecloths intimidate you: There are lunch specials five days a week for just $10 and include deliciousness like wild boar Frito pie on Wednesday and fried chicken on Thursday. With little lights draped over the lush patio and an affordable wine list, you might feel as if you are relaxing on a Texas ranch, with better food of course. Note: Haven won My Table's Houston Culinary Award for Best New Restaurant in 2010.

HEARSAY GASTRO LOUNGE

218 TRAVIS *at Congress*

☎ (713) 225-8079 | MAP **F6** | ¶¶

HEARSAYHOUSTON.COM

THIS LOUNGE'S IMPRESSIVE CEILINGS, EXPOSED BRICK AND lavish chandelier all tucked inside the second-oldest commercial building in town inspire a feeling of Old World elegance. You might even want to raise your pinky when sipping a cocktail. With its upscale comfort food and a fine cocktail program, this historical building is a perfect place to come for an after-work drink or a nightcap. And why not partake of some of the edibles while you are at it? The bacon burger with rosemary fries is the most popular item, and we also recommend the mahi-mahi tacos and smoked duck quesadillas.

Hearsay Gastro Lounge

HIMALAYA

6652 SOUTHWEST FWY.
(HWY. 59) *just west of Hillcroft*
☎ (713) 532-2837 | MAP **C7** | ❙
HIMALAYARESTAURANTHOUSTON.COM

IN THE SAME SHOPPING CENTER AS INDIA GROCERS AND LONDON Sizzler, it is only fitting that you can find a restaurant serving up cultural cuisine to round out the ethnic variations. And at Himalaya you can expect delicious Indian and Pakistani dishes offered by chef/owner Kaiser Lashkari. Don't know where to start? Come at lunch and order the lavish lunch special, which is served in one of those old-style cafeteria trays that haunt your elementary school memories. Things like tomato-rich chicken tikka masala and lamb biryani fill the sections of these trays. You should probably also order a side of the garlic naan, which comes out piping hot. Don't let chef Lashkari intimidate you when he's barking orders from his desk smack in the middle of the dining room. Heck, you'll probably be too busy devouring the authentically delicious food to even notice.

HOBBIT CAFE

2243 RICHMOND *between Greenbriar & Kirby*
☎ (713) 526-5460 | MAP **E7** | ❙
MYHOBBITCAFE.COM

AFTER DEVOURING BOWLS OF GUACAMOLE, YOU MIGHT FIND yourself thinking there is something good in this world, and it is worth fighting for. This *Lord of the Rings*-themed cafe first began in 1972 as a refuge for hippies and vegetarians searching for healthful food in a city dominated by sauce-drenched barbecue and sizzling fajitas. While the creaky, converted house now has plenty of meat-centric dishes, the funky ambiance has not gone anywhere. The menu is expansive and eclectic, with dishes like the salmon burger doused in creamy dill sauce, the Jamaican jerk chicken and delectable vegetarian fare. Don't expect noteworthy sides, however. Shredded carrots and black beans just don't cut it when sitting next to an avocado burger. Healthful-shmeathful. We would prefer a side of thick-cut fries without the extra cost.

HOLLISTER GRILL

1741 HOLLISTER *at Long Point*
☎ (713) 973-1741 | MAP **C5** | ❙❙
THEHOLLISTERGRILL.COM

THIS BYOB RESTAURANT IN SPRING BRANCH USED TO GO unnoticed by many inside-the-Loop foodies. The interior design is not something that will draw guests back. But the friendly service, BYOB option and large portions will do the trick. The Spring Branch location offers a casual lunch spot with home-style dishes like burgers and pastas and then transforms into a fine-dining venue for dinner, the shrimp and scallop risotto being one of our favorite dishes. With a devoted neighborhood crowd, it is best to make a reservation since it can fill up quickly during the evenings.

HOLLYWOOD VIETNAMESE & CHINESE

2409 MONTROSE *just south of Fairview*
☎ (713) 523-8808 | MAP **E6** | ❙
HOLLYVIET.COM

WHERE BETTER TO WATCH THE ABSURDITY OF LATE-NIGHT Montrose than on a patio colorfully adorned with decorations and aglow with neon lights? There is no doubt

RESTAURANTS

you will find better Vietnamese food in Houston, but there are some good options at this welcoming, non-judgmental eatery. We suggest the black pepper tofu and the "Vietnamese fajitas," grilled meats wrapped in rice paper. Come with a daring or, perhaps, tipsy mindset in order to choose dishes off of the enormous and culturally comprehensive menu. We don't recommend many of the Chinese entrees, but people watching and late-night munching is almost always enjoyed at this Montrose landmark.

HONDURAS MAYA CAFE & BAR

5945 BELLAIRE BLVD. *at Renwick*
☎ (713) 668-5002 | MAP **C7** | ⅋

HONDURASMAYACAFEBAR.COM

BEFORE YOU HAVE THE CHANCE TO ENJOY THE *BALEADAS*, FLUFFY and thick tortilla pockets smeared with refried beans and your choice of stuffing, you could be drifting into food coma from the endless baskets of chips and black bean dip sprinkled with salty cheese. This mom-and-pop cafe is much needed and appreciated in the city's entirely too small Honduran dining scene. If tired of Tex-Mex breakfast, try this cafe's traditional breakfast that is served with avocadoes, plantains, eggs and refried beans for something outside your breakfast comfort zone. Come in on a Friday for karaoke night and enjoy a refreshing margarita alongside the *lomito de res*, a platter of steak and sautéed peppers, or the *camarones Maya*, shrimp in lemon butter sauce. Maybe the ethnic flavors (or tequila) will put you in the singing mood.

HOT POT CITY

8300 W. SAM HOUSTON PKWY. S. (BELTWAY 8) *at Beechnut in Beltway Plaza*
☎ (832) 328-3888 | MAP **B7** | ⅋

HOTPOTCITYHOUSTON.COM

KIND OF LIKE A DESIGN-IT-YOUR-SELF FAJITA DINNER, THIS HOT pot restaurant gives you plenty of options to customize a hot pot to your liking. Start with the base, just as you would select flour or corn tortillas, and choose the broth you would like everything to marinate and cook in. Of the five types to choose from, our favorites are the spicy Mongolian and subtle Japanese shabu. The protein options go far beyond chicken or beef with options like lamb, pork, head-on shrimp and fresh cuttlefish. Next choose your starch, which include options like udon, vermicelli and "Canada noodles." To finish the interactive dining experience, throw in all the veggies you would like. When the temperate drops, a hot pot might just have you cheersing to the Chinese New Year. Who needs Christmas anyway?

HOUSE OF PIES

3112 KIRBY *between Richmond & W. Alabama*
☎ (713) 528-3816 | MAP **E7** | ⅋
multiple locations
HOUSEOFPIES.COM

THIS ICONIC 24-HOUR DINER WHERE YOU CAN ORDER A three-egg omelet and a slice of heavenly chocolate cream pie puts up no front. The decor is not themed or extravagant, and the menu sticks with the diner classics. Want to just sit and work on your laptop? This ain't no hipster coffeehouse, kids. There is a minimum charge per hour for sitting at a table if you don't order food. The name is no coincidence, either. The real reason this place is busy both day and night is for homemade pie varieties. The Bayou Goo with pecan crust, layers of sweet cream cheese and vanilla custard swirled with chocolate chunks is one of those classics, along with Texas pecan, lemon meringue and peach. The next time you are barhopping in Rice Village and the munchies strike, remember that a slice of pie is right nearby. All pies may also be purchased whole to take home; the line at Thanksgiving is pure madness.

HUBCAP GRILL

1111 PRAIRIE *at San Jacinto*
☎ (713) 223-5885 | MAP **F6** | 🍴
multiple locations
HUBCAPGRILL.COM

WITH TWO BRICK-AND-MORTAR LOCATIONS AND ONE ROAMING food truck, you can easily fulfill your muffaletta burger fix. If you didn't already know about this hand-formed patty topped with a house-made olive mix and Swiss cheese, why, you're welcome. Some other indulgently savory options include the Philly cheesesteak burger topped with thinly sliced rib-eye, grilled onions, bell peppers and Swiss cheese and the Sticky burger made with crunchy peanut butter and bacon. The original Downtown location is tiny and appropriately embellished with hubcaps everywhere. With an intense lunch rush, it may be worth your time to head to The Heights location and enjoy more elbow room for proper burger gripping.

HUGO'S

1600 WESTHEIMER *at Mandell*
☎ (713) 524-7744 | MAP **E6** | 🍴
HUGOSRESTAURANT.NET

IN A CITY WHERE TEX-MEX IS ALSO KNOWN AS MEXICAN FOOD, HUGO Ortega's restaurant is where the division between the two becomes quite clear. Ortega has created dishes that transport diners to cities such as Oaxaca (the birthplace of mole) and Puebla (the birthplace of Ortega himself). Don't come here if looking for fajitas, burritos or cheese enchiladas. This authentic Mexican restaurant is serving up dishes like octopus al carbon, pork cooked in banana leaf and roasted goat meat pulled from the bone, not to mention less-common dishes such as *chapulines* (crisp-sautéed grasshoppers to fold into tortillas). The much-praised Sunday brunch with traditional Mexican music and an outstanding buffet (including desserts like fresh hot *churros*) entices Saturday late-nighters out of bed and into the Sunday daylight. One more reason to come: The valets will wash your car for a smallish charge.

HUNAN GARDEN

4331 KINGWOOD DR. *in HEB Shopping Center, Kingwood*
☎ (281) 360-2668 | 🍴
multiple locations
HUNANGARDENRESTAURANT.COM

WHEN IN KINGWOOD, ORDER FROM HUNAN GARDEN. LOCAL Chowhound and restaurant owner Jenny Wang has made this the go-to spot for Chinese delivery/take-out in the Kingwood area. Don't let the strip center location fool you. The menu offers all of the chicken, beef, seafood and vegetable dishes one could want along with lo mein and fried rice varieties. With many appetizers and soups to choose from, the hot and sour soup is a favorite among many and highly recommended. Open 364 days a year, you can have delicious Chinese delivered to your door every day except Thanksgiving. *Note:* There is also a Rosenberg location.

HUNGRY'S

2356 RICE BLVD. *at Greenbriar*
☎ (713) 523-8652 | MAP **E7** | 🍴
multiple locations
HUNGRYSCAFE.COM

THESE BISTROS HAVE BEEN NEIGH-BORHOOD FAVORITES FOR decades. The comfortable bistro balances the need for casual dining and the want for inspired American cuisine right around the corner. The hardy weekend brunch menu serves up a variety of dishes such as eggs Florentine, *migas* and Belgian waffles. But a favorite on the menu is the crabcake eggs Benedict served on fresh-baked ciabatta bread. Don't forget to order a mimosa—strawberry and raspberry options available—to accompany your meal. Note: As we go to press with this edition, the Rice Village location of Hungry's is expanding. The restaurant has retained Jim Herd Architects (Haven, Underbelly) to build a new 9,000-square-foot building. Among the additions: a second-floor lounge space with an extensive wine menu and bar bites, plus a landscaped garden on the south side of the property facing Rice Boulevard.

HUYNH

912 ST. EMANUEL *at Walker*
☎ (713) 224-8964 | MAP **F6** | 🍴
HUYNHRESTAURANTHOUSTON.COM

AMIDST THE CLOSED-DOWN STORE-FRONTS OF EAST DOWNTOWN (or EaDo, as the civic promoters like

to call it) sits this nice family-run Vietnamese restaurant. The family spends their time cooking, so they let you decide what beer and wine to drink with its BYOB policy. It is easy to love this place, especially the pho, with its complex broth and handsome portions of meat and noodles. Don't worry about ordering the wrong item, they will all impress and you will most likely be back to order your second choice. To help narrow the selection, we suggest the pulled duck salad, the fried noodle pancakes and the Phoenix chicken served with a fried egg and spicy-sweet dipping sauce. To discourage a food coma and complete the experience, order an iced coffee made with imported Vietnamese beans.

IBIZA

2450 LOUISIANA *at McGowen*
☎ (713) 524-0004 | MAP **E6** | 🍴
IBIZAFOODANDWINEBAR.COM

THE LARGE OPEN KITCHEN THAT CURVES AROUND CHEF CHARLES Clark and manager Grant Cooper's Mediterranean-inspired restaurant allows diners to gaze into the citadel of Spanish, French and Mediterranean cuisine. You and your date can sip on very reasonably priced wine and enjoy separate entrees or share a few tapas-sized dishes with each other. Both options provide plenty of choices. Some entrees to consider: the six-hour lamb shank laced with Spanish mint oil and pan-seared foie gras and the Moroccan grilled shrimp sitting atop succulently savory goat cheese polenta. And no matter what, you should always order the appetizer of grilled shrimp with smoked jalapeño butter resting on crabmeat cornbread. Nice patio dining is a bonus.

INDIKA

516 WESTHEIMER *west of Taft*
☎ (713) 524-2170 | MAP **E6** | 🍴
INDIKAUSA.COM

FOR PROGRESSIVE INDIAN CUISINE THAT SWEEPS ASIDE YOUR EXPEC-tations, check out the menu at Anita Jaisinghani's Indika. Jaisinghani, who also owns Pondicheri, was one of the seven finalists for 2013's Houston Culinary Awards Chef of the Year, so it is no surprise that you will be surprised when dining at her restaurant. The sea bass in coconut kari leaf broth or the fish in coconut, mint and cilantro marinade are just two of the many unexpected dishes that Jaisinghani generates. Inspired by her mature rich flavors? In the past you could take advantage of her cooking classes offered at the restaurant the fourth Sunday of each month. How-ever, during 2013 Jaisinghani is taking a break from teaching in order to focus on writing her Indika cookbook.

IRMA'S

22 N. CHENEVERT *at Commerce*
☎ (713) 222-0767 | MAP **F6** | 🍴

FOR THOSE WHO LIKE THE OPTION OF CHOICE, THIS RESTAURANT might not be quite right for you. For those who don't mind eating whatever owner Irma Galvan decides to cook that day—like half of down-town's stockbrokers, oil executives, politicians and lawyers, it seems—head over on your next lunch break. While there is not a printed menu to tell you about the lunch specials or different variations of enchiladas, you will no doubt be served some-thing authentic, flavorful and home-cooked. Alongside your food order, don't forget to order the secret-rec-ipe lemonade that seems to impress and perplex diners throughout each

sip. (Or, heck, have a margarita.) Seriously good dishes include the guacamole, charro beans, chicken and spinach enchiladas and the pork ribs in tomatillo sauce. The funky spot is only open for breakfast and lunch unless the Astros have an evening game at neighboring Min-ute Made Park. Look for the lovely little spot of color in the under-whelming neighborhood. Galvan has a secure parking lot, too.

ISTANBUL GRILL

5613 MORNINGSIDE *just north of University*
☎ (713) 526-2800 | MAP **E7** | 🍴
ISTANBULGRILL.COM

YOU NEED NOT TRAVEL FURTHER THAN RICE VILLAGE TO EXPERI-ence some seriously authentic Turkish food. Whether to refuel after shop-ping or pub-crawling, this restaurant offers savory, fulfilling dishes such as the Turkish pizza, or *pide*, topped with things like cheese, Turkish sausage, ground lamb and eggs. We also recommend the *iskender kebab*, thin-sliced *doner* on buttered *pide* bread. Before you leave, you might also want to try the lamb, as it is a favor-ite of many diners. Make sure to go on a cheat day because you don't want to skip dessert: The bread pudding is exceptional. Istanbul is a true Turkish delight.

JANG GUEM TOFU HOUSE

9896 BELLAIRE BLVD. *at W. Sam Houston Parkway S. (Beltway 8)*
☎ (713) 773-2229 | MAP **B7** | 🍴

LIKE MANY HIDDEN CHINATOWN GEMS, THIS KOREAN RESTAURANT is tucked away in an inconspicuous strip center and can easily go unno-ticed among the huge number of like restaurants in the area. But Jang Guem stands apart from the other Korean restaurants because of its tofu soup varieties and commendable service. You can even customize the tofu soup with your preferred level of spice. Don't let the neon signage discourage your visit; inside the restaurant is adorned with warm yellow wallpaper that creates an inviting ambiance. Other notable dishes are the Korean barbecue platter and the fried seafood-and-green-onion pancake.

JASMINE ASIAN CUISINE

9938 BELLAIRE BLVD. *at W. Sam Houston Parkway S. (Beltway 8)*
☎ (713) 272-8188 | MAP **B7** | ¶¶
JASMINEASIANRESTAURANT.COM

I T IS BEST TO COME HERE WITH AN AMBITIOUS AND HUNGRY CROWD, because, while you can order a variety of delicious dishes, the real reason to patronize this Asian restaurant is for the seven courses of beef (or fish), a tradition in Vietnamese dining. With dark wood and paper fans suspended from the ceiling, it is the ideal serene environment for such a colossal food endeavor. You and your party will cook a portion of the meat tableside, while the other portion is brought to you already cooked with sides of fish sauce, rice paper wrappers and pickled vegetables. And since you've gathered the crowd already, you might as well order the whole fried catfish that has maraschino cherries cheekily placed over the eyes.

JASPER'S

9595 SIX PINES *at Lake Woodlands Dr., The Woodlands*
☎ (281) 298-6600 | ¶¶
JASPERS-RESTAURANT.COM

W ITH HIS TRADEMARK "BACK-YARD GOURMET," IT IS NO wonder chef Kent Rathbun has had success with his restaurants in Dallas, Austin, Plano and The Woodlands. Who doesn't want sophisticated American comfort food? When dining at Jasper's, Rathbun hopes it will be "like eating at my house." A house specialty (pun intended) is the fall-off-the-bone baby-back ribs, which pair nicely with the fantastic house-made potato chips with a subtle drizzle of blue cheese. The smoked bacon cheeseburger comes with onions braised in Shiner Bock and, if you are feeling fancy, you can request the burger be made with Kobe beef.

JAX GRILL

1613 SHEPHERD *between I-10 West and Washington*
☎ (713) 861-5529 | MAP **E6** | ¶¶
multiple locations
JAXGRILLHOUSTON.COM

T HE PERFECT STOP AFTER SPORTS, WHETHER YOU WERE WATCHING or playing, these Cajun-accented roadhouse diners serve up good food and a spirited environment. Gumbo and bacon-wrapped shrimp are goosed with a jalapeño kick, and you won't be disappointed in the fried catfish, chicken quesadillas or the chicken corn chowder soup. Specify how you want your burger cooked, as they can be dry in our experience. The Shepherd location can get a little rowdy on weekend nights, and, in general, the Bellaire location is more family-oriented.

JIMMY G'S

307 N. SAM HOUSTON PKWY.
E. (BELTWAY 8) *east of North Fwy.*
(I-45 North)
☎ (281) 931-7654 | MAP **E2** | ⑂
JIMMYG.COM

IF HEADED TO JIMMY G'S CAJUN SEA-
FOOD RESTAURANT, CHANCES ARE
you're either traveling to or from
Bush Intercontinental Airport or you
are hoping to widen your oyster hori-
zons. This seafood restaurant often
serves as a stopover for travelers, as
the kitchen does indeed grill some
tasty oysters. With no secret special
recipe, these oysters are simply
grilled on a gas grill and doused in
garlic butter and parmesan. If they
can grill 'em, they can fry 'em, too,
right? If the season is right, the
fried oyster (or crawfish) po'boy
can also be worth the drive. Also
fine eating: the crawfish bisque and
shrimp and oyster embrochette.

JONATHAN'S THE RUB

9061 GAYLORD *at Corbindale*
☎ (713) 465-8200 | MAP **C6** | ⑂⑂
JONATHANSTHERUB.COM

COME WITH FRIENDS, UNCORK YOUR
OWN BOTTLE OF WINE FOR A $7
corkage fee, get comfortable and prepare for the large portion of comfort
food you are about to ingest. Chef/
owner Jonathan Levine has created a
simple, rustic menu with dishes like
the nicely brined pork chop, a burger
on a slightly sweet but sturdy bun
and macaroni and five cheeses that
will leave you feeling warm and cozy.
(Or is that warm and comatose?)
Anything that "the rub" touches is
gold, and they put it on everything
from the garlic bread to the spice-
rubbed salmon. While the prices may
be a bit high, you will walk out of
this neighborhood joint with enough

leftovers for tomorrow's lunch. Oh,
and every meal begins with cheesy
bread. Let's hope your relationship
with Jonathan's is built around the
food and not the location because
this eatery is planning a move
and expansion in 2014.

JOYCE'S SEAFOOD & STEAKS

6415 SAN FELIPE *at Winrock*
☎ (713) 975-9902 | MAP **C6** | ⑂⑂
JOYCESSEAFOOD.COM

SET BACK FROM ITS SAN FELIPE
ADDRESS AND FACING WINROCK,
Joyce's has been one of Houston's
best-kept seafood secrets for a couple
decades now. Blending cuisines of
the Gulf Coast, Southern Louisiana
and Mexico, the kitchen puts out
eclectic dishes such as oyster shooters on tortilla chips with chipotle
aioli. Despite the cheesy decor (dark
blue walls, mounted deep-sea game
fish) reminiscent of a Galveston
Seawall tourist trap, the sparkling
fresh raw oysters, grilled fish tacos,
gumbo and crabcakes with poblano
pepper sauce are reasons to keep
coming back.

JULIA'S BISTRO

3722 MAIN *at Alabama*
☎ (713) 807-0090 | MAP **E7** | ⑂⑂
JULIASBISTRO.COM

ACHROME FINISH TO THE CHAIRS
PAIRED WITH SATURATED WALL
colors of magenta, ruby and coral
make this Nuevo Latino eatery an
energetic dining experience, and you
can expect the same vibrancy from
the menu. The white tablecloths
suggest your meal will be pricey, but
with flavorful dishes like the chipotle
Caesar topped with manchego
cheese, pulled pork taquitos and the
pork sandwich with plenty of a spicy

RESTAURANTS

mustard sauce, you can excuse the slightly high bill. Located right next to the MetroRail and lacking any noise barriers in the restaurant, it can get a little noisy.

JUS' MAC

2617 YALE *at E. 26th*
☎ (713) 622-8646 | MAP **E5** | 🍴
multiple locations
JUSMAC.COM

THIS MAC 'N' CHEESE EATERY PUTS NO LIMIT ON THE CHOICE OF TOP-pings or cheese to add to your personalized skillet of noodles. In fact, they encourage the shameless addition of toppings like poblano peppers, buffalo chicken, taco fixings and breakfast items. Everything is better with a fried egg, right? The cheese choices are practically endless with options including an American blend, colby jack, mozzarella, parmesan, blue and goat cheese. You can order a panini or a salad if you must, but we might judge you. Since the tiny Heights restaurant can fill up quickly, the owners decided to open a second location in Sugar Land, and a third location has been announced for Montrose. Keep an eye on Jus' Mac: A franchise operation is about to be born.

JUST DINNER

1915 DUNLAVY *at Welch*
☎ (713) 807-0077 | MAP **E6** | 🍴🍴
JUSTDINNERHOUSTON.COM

OWNER LILA RIVAS' COZY NIGHT-TIME RESTAURANT IS LOCATED in a renovated bungalow across the street from the Guild Shop and is a great choice for date night. The atmosphere will inspire romance, and since this spot is BYOB your pocketbook will also feel the love. With a garden outside, chef Daniel

Toro uses his own local ingredients as much as possible, and there is a level of refinement in his dishes. Toro believes "less is more," which can be seen in dishes like the crab-cake that relies on the natural sweetness of the crabmeat and the filet mignon that has a modest-sized topping of Gorgonzola butter.

KAHN'S DELI

2429 RICE BLVD. *between Kirby*
& Morningside
☎ (713) 529-2891 | MAP **E7** | 🍴
KAHNSDELI.COM

THIS LITTLE RICE VILLAGE HOLE-IN-THE-WALL HAS GONE THROUGH A series of changes since it first opened in 1948 under the name Alfred's, and so it continues. The newest owner is making some big changes to the interior, including a new paint job, and tweaking the menu. Even the website is under construction as this edition goes to press. But the overstuffed deli sandwiches—there are five kinds of Reuben alone—are not going anywhere. Pastrami, knockwurst, chicken salad and corned beef come piled high on Slow Dough buns. We also like the impressive list of craft beers.

KANEYAMA

9527 WESTHEIMER *east*
of S. Gessner
☎ (713) 784-5168 | MAP **C7** | 🍴🍴
KANEYAMA-HOUSTON.US

SERVING UP AUTHENTIC (I.E. LESS TRENDY) JAPANESE CUISINE IN West Houston since 1994, this restaurant and sushi bar offer diners a calming Japanese experience that is enhanced by kimono-wearing hostesses and traditional tatami private room dining. But sitting at the sushi bar lends to a visual interactive experience not worth missing. Owner

Keeper Lin describes the sushi preparation as "art for consumption," and the raw fish preparation, such as the sea urchin and salmon, is extraordinary. Come in between 4 and 7 pm on Monday through Thursday for 20 percent off all of the sushi rolls.

KANOMWAN

736 1/2 TELEPHONE *near S. Lockwood*
☎ (713) 923-4230 | MAP **F7** | 🍴

IT'S ONLY FITTING THAT MANY OF THE DISHES AT THIS RESTAURANT ARE fiery hot, just like late owner Darawan Charoenrat's famously prickly personality. Regarded by many foodies as one of the city's two most authentic Thai restaurants—the other is Vieng Thai in Spring Branch—the kitchen fires up the menu with liberal amounts of chiles. It is best to come with an adventurous crowd and also take advantage of the BYOB policy that lasts until 8:30 pm. Some recommendations are the deep-fried pork toasts, the whole fried snapper with chili sauce and the dangerously hot green curry with chicken. We warned you.

KASRA PERSIAN GRILL

9741 WESTHEIMER *at Gessner*
☎ (713) 975-1810 | MAP **C7** | 🍴
KASRAHOUSTON.COM

ANOTHER OF THOSE ANONYMOUS STRIP-MALL SPOTS THAT WOULD be passed by without prior knowledge, this noteworthy Persian restaurant is a favorite among the local ex-pat community. You know your dining experience is headed in the right direction when you are served complimentary hot flatbread with a small dish of feta cheese and herbs. And if you are doing things right, the garlicky hummus will be the first thing you order. Don't leave without tasting the fork-tender lamb shank in sour cherry sauce and the delicately spiced *kubideh* kebabs sitting atop a pile of tasty dill rice. Just because it is inconspicuously tucked back into a corner, still expect a crowded restaurant because the neighborhood residents and Persian foodies know what's up.

KATA ROBATA

3600 KIRBY *at Richmond*
☎ (713) 526-8858 | MAP **E7** | 🍴
KATAROBATA.COM

WHILE THE QUALITY OF THE SUSHI AND SUSHI RICE MAKE most dishes enjoyable, the reason to dine at this upscale sushi spot is for the innovative and stylish dishes created by sushi master Manabu Horiuchi. The fresh sushi is always delicious whether dressed with a crunch of salt and tart yuzu or a bolder dab of foie gras. For a memorable dining experience, the *omakase* (chef's choice tasting menu) is the way to go if your bank account allows. With a great signature cocktail and sake list, this Japanese restaurant welcomes both diners and drinkers. Come in early for the happy hour and taste the deliciousness at very reasonable prices.

KATCH 22

700 DURHAM *just south of Washington*
☎ (832) 804-7281 | MAP **E6** | 🍴
KATCH22HOUSTON.COM

KORY CLEMENS, SON OF FORMER ASTROS PLAYER ROGER CLEMENS, is the executive chef at the new (circa 2013) Katch 22. In business with the scion of another Houston dynasty—the Mandola family of restaurateurs—Clemens and partner

Luke Mandola have transformed the short-lived Convivio into a casual restaurant and sporty bar. Note the Clemens family baseball memorabilia while you scan the menu that includes wings, pizza, sliders, fish tacos and bacon-wrapped quail bites.

KATZ'S DELI
616 WESTHEIMER EAST OF MONTROSE
☎ (713) 521-3838 | MAP **E6** | 🍴
multiple locations
ILOVEKATZS.COM

Hankering for a reuben sandwich at 3 am? This is your spot. This New York-style deli, set right in the middle of the Montrose bar scene, is a favorite haunt among the late-night crowd. We love that sandwiches come in three sizes: skinny, "klassic" and the overstuffed New York. Come here for breakfast, too, including blintzes, sweet _matzo brei_ (imagine kosher-style French toast), bagel and lox, pancakes, egg-and-meat platters, corned beef hash and much more. Katz's Never Kloses" on Westheimer, but The Woodlands location does close at night.

KENNY & ZIGGY'S
2327 POST OAK BLVD. _between Westheimer & San Felipe_
☎ (713) 871-8883 | MAP **D6** | 🍴
KENNYANDZIGGYS.COM

A popular lunch spot for Jew-ish families, galleria-area shoppers, lovers of chicken soup and businessmen, this New York-style deli has been packing them in since its opening in 1999 because of things like house-baked breads and cakes, meats cured and pickled on site and smoked fish that is over-nighted from New York. Owner Ziggy Gruber's personality is as big as his towering

sandwiches, which include options like pastrami, corned beef, roasted brisket and much, much more. Feeling a cold coming? The chicken matzo ball soup is rumored to be a cure for all ailments. Overall, a fun restaurant for top-notch deli food and Jewish classics like cheese blintzes, fried _kreplach_ (filled dumplings), borscht, stuffed cabbage, noodle kugel, knishes and chopped liver.

KERALA KITCHEN
732 MURPHY ROAD _south of Avenue E, Stafford_
☎ (281) 499-7381 | 🍴
KERALAKITCHENHOUSTON.COM

Kerala kitchen is as bare-bone as can be. Four tables hold 20 people max, in front of a counter where you order and where take-out orders are dispensed. The only available drinks are water and Coke. You'll eat off disposable plates. Plastic spoons are available upon request, but since every other person we saw there was Indian, most customers eat in the traditional manner, using the fingers of one's right hand to scoop the food. There are no menus, and the day's dishes are listed on a dry erase board to the left of the register. Recommended: _avival_ vegetable curry with a ground coconut base and "beef fry" dry curry with _kalan_ (a tangy yogurt-based vegetable curry).

KHUN KAY THAI CAFE
1209 MONTROSE _at W. Clay_
☎ (713) 524-9614 | MAP **E6** | 🍴
KHUNKAYTHAICAFE.COM

There were a few tears among fans, including us at _MY TABLE_ magazine, back in 2008 when co-owners/cousins Supatra Yooto and Kay Soodjai closed their Golden Room, a tiny jewel box of a Thai restaurant that sat on this same lot. But then they opened the fast-casual Khun Kay Thai Cafe, and people have taken a liking to it, too. ("Khun Kay" is a Thai honorific, something like "Mrs. Kay.") It's equipped with a walk-up counter for ordering, a sunny yellow dining room and a menu full of Thai classics (plus some seasonal chalkboard specials). Not only can you order your favorite Thai entree, but with five levels of heat to choose from, you can also customize the spiciness of your dish. Nearly everything can be made with tofu or imitation duck, too, making this a vegetarian's dream. Limited free delivery in the neighborhood.

KHYBER NORTH INDIAN GRILL

2510 RICHMOND *east of Kirby*
☎ (713) 942-9424 | MAP **E7** | ¶¶

THIS MIGHT NOT BE THE GRITTIEST, MOST AUTHENTIC INDIAN REST-aurant in Houston, but we can appreciate Khyber for what it is: a solid inside-the-Loop Indian restaurant that has been continually serving Houstonians a taste of the culture's cuisine for a couple of decades. With so many ethnic restaurants popping up, our taste buds are becoming spoiled with authentic flavors and dishes, but this is a good choice if you are looking to slowly introduce yourself to the flavors of Indian cuisine. The lamb *korma* is a consistent favorite. And who doesn't like tandoori chicken, saag paneer or hot buttery naan? Even though the kitchen can have its good days and lackluster days, owner Mickey Kapoor's lunch buffet is still pulling customers in.

KILLEN'S STEAKHOUSE

2804 S. MAIN *south of CR 518, Pearland*
☎ (281) 485-0844 | ¶¶
KILLENSSTEAKHOUSE.COM

REGARDLESS OF HOW MANY TIMES THE ODOMETER SPINS AROUND, chef/owner Ronnie Killen's steakhouse makes a long car ride with your in-laws well worth it. Given his casual Western-themed dining room, Le Cordon Bleu-trained Killen doesn't expect you to come dressed to the nines, but the food—including the Allen Brothers USDA Prime beef—will make you feel fancy. Presented with nothing else on the plate, the gently seasoned, perfectly grilled steaks are reason enough to come to this middle-of-sorta-nowhere steakhouse. Add an order of Killen's legendary creamed corn to your dinner, and that's mighty fine eating. Note 1: The well-curated wine list includes several half-bottles and magnums. Note 2: As this book goes to press, Killen is readying his long-anticipated Killen's Barbecue at 3613 E. Broadway in Pearland. Throughout 2013 he's been offering a barbecue pop-up on weekend mornings at the steakhouse.

KIM SON

2001 JEFFERSON *at Chartres*
☎ (713) 222-2461 | MAP **F6** | ¶¶
multiple locations
KIMSON.COM

FLEEING VIETNAM IN 1980, "MAMA LA" (AKA KIM SU TRAN LA) ARRIVED in Houston with her husband and seven children with an ambitious dream to open a restaurant with a menu devoted to her mother-in-law's 250 recipes. In 2013, her unassuming restaurant has blossomed into numerous locations and brands (including Little Kim Son and Kim Son Cafe) all over the city and beyond, with each spot possessing its own charm. Back in the 1980s, most Houstonians had their first taste of Vietnamese food at either Kim Son or Mai's. The enormous downtown Jefferson Street location is still the frequent site of weddings and other celebrations in the Vietnamese and Chinese community.

KIRAN'S

4100 WESTHEIMER *east of Mid Lane*
☎ (713) 960-8472 | MAP **D6** | ¶¶¶
KIRANSHOUSTON.COM

OWNER/CHEF KIRAN VERMA'S DINNER-ONLY RESTAURANT GIVES diners a taste of traditional Indian cuisine but with a decidedly modern accent. Meat and seafood are high quality, sauces are lighter, vegetables are gently cooked (not overcooked). Mimicking the style of her cooking, the decor resembles a traditional Indian restaurant, but it is elegantly enhanced with dark wood paneling and white tablecloths. Dishes like the portobello mushroom stuffed with creamy paneer, various curries or a mixed grill of tandoori chicken, lamb and prawn served with mint and pomegranate chutney will please, as will the menu of *chaat* (Indian street snacks) to enjoy with cocktails. Due to popular demand, the restaurant has expanded its once-a-month afternoon tea with an exotic colonial Indian twist to a weekly ritual on Saturdays 2 to 4 pm.

KOREAN NOODLE HOUSE

1415 MURRAY BAY ST. *just north of Long Point*
☎ (713) 463-8870 | MAP **C5** | ¶

IT'S CALLED "HOUSE" FOR A REASON. AFTER WALKING DOWN THE SIDEWALK to the restaurant, lined on each side with soy sauce buckets used as planters, one truly has the feeling of walking into somebody's house—a feeling that nearly every "ethnic" restaurant strives for, but that Korean Noodle House actually achieves. The menu is small, with English translations available. But there's really only one dish you need to know about: the noodle dumpling soup. Order it. There's a bit of a language barrier, so patience is a must. Also, there's no alcohol, so BYOB.

KRIS BISTRO

7070 ALLENSBY *just north of Loop 610 at I-45 North, inside Culinaire Institute LeNôtre*
☎ (713) 358-5079 | MAP **E5** | ¶¶
KRISBISTRO.COM

THIS TEACHING/LEARNING FACILITY REPRESENTS ONE OF THE BEST price-value spots to enter the Houston French restaurant scene recently. Kris Bistro, focusing on modestly priced modern French dishes (most under $20) and equally modestly priced French wines, is a jewel worth the trip. It is a collaboration between namesake chef Kristopher Jakob and Alain LeNôtre, owner, instructor and chef of Culinaire Institute LeNôtre. The cozy wine lounge and sophisticated dining room are located within the culinary school and provide views of the kitchen. Menu items include *moules marinières*, grilled salmon Provençal, free-range feta-stuffed chicken and hanger steak with Borde-

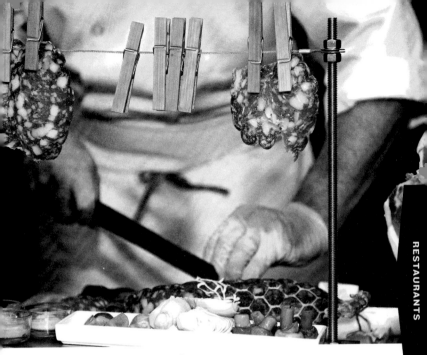

House-made charcuterie at Kris Bistro

laise sauce. The charcuterie service is outstanding.

KUBO'S SUSHI BAR & GRILL

2414 UNIVERSITY BLVD.
(upstairs) at Morningside
☎ (713) 528-7878 | MAP **E7** | ⑂
KUBOS-SUSHI.COM

DISCREETLY LOCATED ON THE SECOND LEVEL OF THE VILLAGE Arcade shopping center, Kubo's exterior doesn't grab many glances. But inside, the elegant atmosphere promises big things. The sushi here has always been outstanding, and Kubo's is one of the city's most-admired Japanese restaurants. As of 2013, there's been an additional attraction in the way of the nine-course *kaiseki* (seasonal meal) prepared by executive chef Eigo Yamaguchi, who came to Houston via Kyoto and

will personally plan and prepare the entire traditional dining ritual. The *kaiseki* requires reservations at least one week in advance and is limited to party of eight or fewer. It will cost at least $120 per person.

LA BALANCE

20680 WESTHEIMER PKWY #10
at S. Fry Rd., Katy
☎ (281) 206-7974 | ⑂
LABALANCECUISINE.COM

A NEW ADDITION TO THE KATY AREA JUST OPENED IN AUGUST 2013. We have not had a chance to visit as of press time, but chef Jose Hernandez, former pastry chef at Philippe, has foodies buzzing about his rustic yet modern French-based menu. Starters include escargot and terrine of foie gras. The entrees are equally classic with dishes like salmon with mushroom cream sauce, *steak frites, boeuf bourguignon* and the pork tenderloin with bordelaise sauce and plums. Tasting menus are available upon request, and desserts are (naturally) exceptional.

LA CASA DEL CABALLO

322 WESTHEIMER *at Taft*
☎ (832) 623-6467 | MAP **E6** | 🍴
LACASADELCABALLO.COM

MONTROSE ISN'T EXACTLY KNOWN FOR MEAT—THAT IS, GREAT steakhouses—so the owner of Mexican steakhouse La Casa de Caballo decided to change that. While La Casa de Caballo has none of the kitschy funk of the old tenant, La Strada, the new build-out enhanced the casual elegance of the oblong building. In other words, the place is dead sexy. Tiles of red and black glass adorn a dining alcove. A chrome bust of a horse sits on a leather bar, while a huge portrait of another hangs on the wall. Steaks come with sides, including fried potatoes (crispy, delicious and perfectly salted), refried beans (with bacon) and either flour or corn tortillas. Carlos Abedrop, who also owns a steakhouse in Saltillo, Mexico, is the owner.

LA FISHERIA

4705 INKER *just east of Shepherd*
☎ (713) 802-1712 | MAP **E6** | 🍴
LAFISHERIAHOUSTON.COM

THIS CHEERFUL BLUE AND ORANGE RESTAURANT FROM LATIN AMERIcan reality-TV chef Aquiles Chávez (you'll recognize him by the Salvador Dali moustache) has taken over the spot that used to be Pagoda Vietnamese. The menu is built around sparkling fresh seafood, especially ceviche-style dishes. The website is still under construction, and English is in limited supply. But you'll enjoy

the hospitality, brisk margaritas and happy-casual setting. *Note:* In Summer 2013 La Fisheria enacted a policy not allowing children under the age of eight in the restaurant after 7 pm. As expected, the policy has both its supporters and haters.

LA FOGATA

11630 S. WILCREST *at Southwest Fwy. (Hwy. 59)*
☎ (281) 495-7424 | MAP **B8** | 🍴

FOR NEARLY 20 YEARS, THIS FAMILY-RUN HAPPY HOLE-IN-THE WALL has been serving the best Colombian-style empanadas in town. Everything else on the extensive menu is pretty good, too. We recommend the soups, chorizos and *bandeja paisa* ("country platter" from northwest Colombia that includes steak, chicharrón, beans, fried egg, rice, plantains, avocado, etc.)

LA GRIGLIA

2002 W. GRAY *at McDuffie*
☎ (713) 526-4700 | MAP **E6** | 🍴
LAGRIGLIARESTAURANT.COM

FOUNDED BY TONY VALLONE AND NOW A PART OF THE LANDRY'S restaurant empire, this see-and-be-seen Italian restaurant is still adorned with a riot of mosaic tiling, lively wall murals and perhaps the loudest and most intensely colored carpeting in town. In fact, there's something about La Griglia that makes us think of Beverly Hills and movie star dining—some of the menu's dishes are even named for favorite customers, such as Trout 'Shelby' and Beef 'Morty.' The polished service is old school, the wine glasses are nice quality, and the patio on the east side of the building is a hidden-away retreat (should you be avoiding the paparazzi). Meals always begin with a basket of complimentary pizza bread. Follow with a pasta and then a veal chop or piece of nice fish. The shrimp and crab cheesecake, such a revelation when this restaurant was founded in 1991, is still on the menu after all these years.

LA GUADALUPANA BAKERY & CAFE

2109 DUNLAVY *north of Fairview*
☎ (713) 522-2301 | MAP **E6** | ⑂

I**F THERE EVER WERE A SMELL THAT COULD CURE A HANGOVER, IT WOULD** be La Guadalupana's house-roasted cinnamon coffee. This pocket-sized spot—it's a take-out bakery on the left, cafe on the right—is known for some mean *migas*, *machaca norteña* (a *migas* alternative made with scrambled eggs and dried beef), breakfast *tortas* (sandwiches) and Mexican pastries. Owner Trancito Diaz was once a pastry chef at the Houston Country Club, which explains the sweet treats. Breakfast is served all day, but, happily for us, the lunch and dinner options are also noteworthy, with the green chicken enchiladas being our current favorite. Want a beer with your lunch? La Guadalupana is BYOB.

LA MEXICANA

1018 FAIRVIEW *at Montrose*
☎ (713) 521-0963 | MAP **E6** | ⑂
LAMEXICANARESTAURANT.COM

B**IG AND RAMBLING IN A CHARM-INGLY DISORGANIZED AND ORGANIC** way, "La Mex" is the real deal, being much closer to authentic Mexican than many other Houston Tex-Mex restaurants. The breakfast menu is a long-time favorite with Montrose locals and offers options like *huevos rancheros*, *chilaquiles* and breakfast tacos a plenty. But the margaritas, which can be kept classic or made

with fruit like raspberries and strawberries, are a good reason to stop in for lunch or dinner. The lengthy menu is loaded with grilled meats, including fajitas by the pound, tamales, *milanezas* and soups. In fine weather, ask for a table outside under the huge palapa.

LA VISTA

1936 FOUNTAIN VIEW
at San Felipe
☎ (713) 787-9899 | MAP **D6** | ⑂
FATBUTTER.COM

T**HIS NEIGHBORHOOD JOINT IS KNOWN FOR TWO THINGS: ITS** BYOB policy (it was one of the earliest BYOB advocates in Houston) and the delicious bread that is served before every meal. The menu reads equally American and Italian—shrimp and grits share menu space with gnocchi. Well-prepared classics like spaghetti with meatballs, ceviche, meatloaf, center cut pork chop, salmon and grilled veggie platter appeal to the loyal locals who squeeze in. Lunch is served weekdays; dinner is served every evening starting at 5:30. Watching your diet? The kitchen has a "lite" program and offers pre-packaged portion-control foods for take-away.

LANKFORD GROCERY

88 DENNIS *at Genesee*
☎ (713) 522-9555 | MAP **E6** | ⑂
LANKFORDGROCERY.COM

66 T**HE HUNCH"—GUY FIERI'S TRADE-MARK POSTURE FOR EATING** oozing, dripping burgers—is a necessity at this burger joint. In fact, the celebrity chef put "the hunch" into action when he visited Lankford on one of Food Network's *Diners, Drive-ins and Dives* episodes. So get your

elbows up and place a two-handed grip around these hand-formed, coarse-ground patties sandwiched between two buns and toppings like bacon, chopped habaneros and fried eggs. Not a burger-eater? There is a whole slate of diner-style breakfasts as well as sandwiches and a daily blue-plate special. (Love those Wednesday enchiladas!) Originally an actual grocery store, Lankford is strictly a cafe now, albeit a much-loved Houston institution. The little white house with distinctive red trim fills up quickly at lunch. Make sure to bring cash because credit cards are not accepted.

LAREDO TAQUERIA

915 SNOVER *at Washington*
☎ (713) 861-7279 | MAP **E6** | 🍴

IF YOU FIND YOURSELF WAKING UP IN THE WASHINGTON AVENUE AREA after a night out, stumble on over to the no-frills Laredo Taqueria for breakfast tacos. There might be a long line, but we promise a bean and spicy potato taco will have you feeling rejuvenated. Woke up too late for breakfast? The chicken *mole* taco is a delicious choice for lunch, and the leftover bar change in your pocket can probably cover the $2 cost. The *barbacoa* (cow cheek) and *nopales* (cactus) tacos are also excellent choices. There are larger combo plates that come with a side of rice and beans or even tamales for those whose stomachs are extra ambitious.

LAST CONCERT CAFE

1403 NANCE *west of McKee*
☎ (713) 226-8563 | MAP **F6** | 🍴
LASTCONCERT.COM

WHILE THE TEX-MEX FOOD HERE IS NOT SOMETHING TO WRITE home about, this Houston classic,

located in the warehouse district just northeast of Downtown, is where hippies come to hula-hoop, oldies come to listen to a rock cover band and youngsters come to drink with their toes in the sand. (Yup, this is probably one of the few places you can touch sand inside the Loop.) The restaurant and music venue relies on its this-is-what-I'd-make-at-home food to keep patrons satisfied, such as the stewed beef tacos sprinkled with shredded cheese and black bean tostadas. After dinner, walk around the venue with a beer in hand and enjoy some reggae music while shopping the multiple vendors selling their handmade crafts. *Note:* There's no signage, and you have to knock to be admitted. Look for the red door.

LATIN BITES CAFE

5709 WOODWAY *between Chimney Rock & Bering*
☎ (713) 229-8369 | MAP **D6** | 🍴
LATINBITESCAFE.COM

CHEF ROBERTO CASTRE'S PERUVIAN-INSPIRED *TIRADITO*-STYLE sashimi dishes and ceviches practically quiver with their subtle combinations of sparkling seafood and chiles tossed variously with fruit, sweet potato or *choclo* (oversized corn kernels). Just as worthy are the cooked dishes, some of them in remarkable Easter-egg colors. Don't miss the pisco specialties from the bar, either. The room is often packed with well-dressed Latin Americans from all over the city, though the Tanglewood neighborhood has also quickly adopted Latin Bites as its own.

LAURENZO'S PRIME RIB
4412 WASHINGTON *at Patterson*
☎ (713) 880-5111 | MAP **E6** | 🍴
LAURENZOS.NET

WHEN THEY LAUNCHED IT IN 2010, THE NINFA LAURENZO family may have seemed undecided about which way to take their menu at this eatery—should they offer the Mexican food of their famous matriarch or Italian food to reflect their father's heritage? The veteran restaurateurs knew if they offered Texas-sized portions, people wouldn't complain. So while the menu features dishes like shrimp scampi, burgers and quesadillas, you come for the prime rib and you stay for the margaritas. Other specialties include the French dip sandwich, house-smoked salmon and the creamed corn. The weekend brunch menu offers several variations on eggs Benedict, but there are also choices like crêpe pancakes and French toast. The only complaint you might have walking out of this prime rib house is the amount of food you were served. And that's not a bad complaint to have.

LE MISTRAL
1400 ELDRIDGE *near Briar Forest*
☎ (832) 379-8322 | MAP **A6** | 🍴
LEMISTRALHOUSTON.COM

FOR A LONG TIME LE MISTRAL WAS ONE OF A MEAGER NUMBER OF French restaurants in Houston. In 2013 there are suddenly many. But even with all the French newcomers since our last edition (including Etoile, La Balance, Bistro des Arts, L'Olivier and Salé-Sucré) the Provence-inspired Le Mistral remains among the best. Chef David Denis runs the kitchen, and his brother Sylvain runs the front of the house and wine list. The handsome setting (just 50 yards or so from the original location) is very swank, as is the menu. The escargot and seared foie gras are always excellent starters. Follow with cassoulet, the entrecôte grillée, Australian lamb chops, salmon or... We could go on, but know that Le Mistral was rated by Zagat as having the best food in Houston in 2012.

LEE'S SANDWICHES
11210 BELLAIRE BLVD. *at Boone*
☎ (281) 933-9988 | MAP **B7** | 🍴
multiple locations
LEESANDWICHES.COM

SKIP YOUR NORMAL MORNING CUP OF JOE AND HEAD TO THIS DRIVE-thru Vietnamese sandwich shop where you should pass on the sandwiches and order the Vietnamese iced coffee. Along with this delicious perk-me-up, order a flaky, buttery croissant for a perfect on-the-go breakfast. The name may suggest a specialty in sandwiches, but in actuality, you won't be too impressed. Instead, order a *pâté chaud* (a stuffed flaky pastry) for a quick lunch and don't forget a cream puff for a late afternoon treat.

LES GIVRAL'S
2704 MILAM *at Drew*
☎ (713) 529-1736 | MAP **F6** | 🍴
multiple locations
LESGIVRALS.COM

WITH MULTIPLE LOCATIONS (AND VARIATIONS ON THE NAME), you won't find much consistency among the locations except for the basic menu categories. Head to the Milam location to enjoy *banh mi* sandwiches, pho or *bún* (vermicelli bowls) and to the Washington location for a drink at the full bar and to gawk at the spectacular interior design. The *banh mi* sandwiches are available with many options like shredded chicken, meatball, tofu and (our favorite) the chargrilled barbecued pork. With most sandwiches costing less than $3, don't hesitate to add a fried egg.

LIBERTY KITCHEN & OYSTER BAR

1050 STUDEWOOD *at 11th Street*
☎ (713) 802-0533 | MAP **E5** | 🍴
LIBERTYKITCHENOYSTERBAR.COM

FOR A GULF COAST CITY, WE DON'T HAVE NEARLY ENOUGH OYSTER bars. So we were awfully happy that Liberty Kitchen saw fit to add "& Oyster Bar" to its name. The kitchen is under the direction of chef Lance Fegen (founding chef at Glass Wall and BRC), and if the food is not graceful, it is very good, with big flavors and hearty portions. Think: oyster stew (shades of Grand Central Oyster Bar!) and gumbo, lots of hefty "guy food" (burgers, cedar-plank salmon, po'boys) and breakfast all day long. It looks and feels casual—kind of shack-like— though the prices are a little higher than you expect. A spin-off will open on San Felipe by the railroad tracks in late 2013.

LINE & LARIAT

220 MAIN *at Congress in Hotel Icon*
☎ (832) 667-4470 | MAP **F6** | 🍴
HOTELICON.COM/DINING

FIRST IT WAS BANK, THEN VOICE AND NOW THE SOARING GORGEOUS dining room in the Hotel Icon is Line & Lariat. The menu is an all-star line-up of Houston-centric favorite dishes, ranging from shrimp-crab campechana, braised pork tostada and bayou gumbo to fried Gulf shrimp with cheddar grits, grilled flatiron steak and seasonal game. We're hoping this incarnation has traction.

LITTLE BIG'S

2703 MONTROSE *at Westheimer*
☎ (713) 521-2447 | MAP **E6** | 🍴
LITTLEBIGSHOUSTON.COM

A HUGE BURGER AND FRIES MAY SEEM UNPLEASANT WHEN SWEATing in the Houston heat. So at this predominately outdoor eatery, chef Bryan Caswell (of Reef and El Real) miniaturized the menu by offering sliders and maximized the experience by offering grown-up milkshakes. After you chow down on your order of sliders—choose among beef with caramelized onions, fried chicken, pulled pork or black bean—slurp down the white Russian-inspired shake named The Dude. Open until 3 am on the weekends, this shake could serve as the perfect nightcap and also satisfy any munchies. Don't pass up the hand-cut fries with a spicy sriracha remoulade. You must abide.

LITTLE BITTY BURGER BARN

5503 PINEMONT *east of Antoine*
☎ (713) 683-6700 | MAP **D5** | 🍴
LITTLEBITTYBURGERBARN.COM

IF YOU CONSIDER YOURSELF A BURGER AFICIONADO AND AN H-TOWN enthusiast, Little Bitty is worth your visit. The never-frozen patties, which may be a bit thinner than at other joints, are sandwiched between toasted buns with all the usual-suspect toppings. Set in a trailer, this honest-to-God dive also serves up patty melts, double-decker BLTs, chicken-fried chicken sandwiches and a Juicy Lucy burger that oozes with different melted cheeses, including blue cheese. Good news for vegetarians: There are also veggie burgers and black bean burgers. Still not full? Try the "Big A$$ Root Beer Float." Kids eat free on Wednesday evenings.

LITTLE SHEEP MONGOLIAN HOT POT

5901-A WESTHEIMER
at Fountain View
☎ (713) 975-0687 | MAP **D7** | 🍴
LITTLESHEEPHOTPOT.COM

CHOOSE YOUR BROTH—WE REC-OMMEND THE SPICY ORIGINAL. Choose your favorite cuts of meat—we suggest the sliced lamb shoulder, a specialty here. Next, choose from a variety of veggies, dumplings, mushrooms, noodles and tofu. Since the broth at this international chain is so unique and flavorful, we recommend choosing mushrooms, which soak up all the Mongolian flavors that make this one of our favorite hot pot stops. To fully enjoy your interactive meal, an order of the fluffy sesame pancake is almost required for dipping. The more people you bring, the more sampling is possible.

LOCAL FOODS

2424 DUNSTAN *in the Village*
next to Benjy's
☎ (713) 521-7800 | MAP **E7** | 🍴
HOUSTONLOCALFOODS.COM

A NEW FARM-TO-TABLE COUNTER CONCEPT BY RESTAURATEUR Benjy Levit and chef Dylan Murray, Local Foods takes a page from the Revival Market playbook. It's located in the old Antone's space adjacent to Benjy's in the Village. Unlike Revival, Local Foods is not a meat market or produce stand; rather it's a take-away eatery that focuses on local foods, including seafood, eggs, produce, breads, dairy and beer. Great sandwiches and salads. A second location is set to open in the old Taco Milagro location on Kirby at Westheimer.

LOLA

1102 YALE *at E. 11th*
☎ (713) 426-5652 | MAP **E5** | 🍴
EATLOLA.COM

EVERYONE CAN APPRECIATE A BYOB DINER. THIS HAPPY ADDITION TO The Heights' eateries is one that draws in early risers, late sleepers and just plain hungry folks. The retro-styled diner serves both its breakfast and lunch/dinner menus all day, offering patrons a wide range of dishes to choose from. Craving savory and sweet? The chicken and waffles will hit the spot. Want a dish that will induce your afternoon nap? The "Day After Thanksgiving" sandwich with turkey, cranberry sauce, dressing and gravy should do the trick. You may not be blown away by some of the dishes, but with such an expansive menu that includes gluten-free, vegetarian and healthy options, Lola is a good spot to have in the neighborhood.

L'OLIVIER

240 WESTHEIMER *between Bagby & Taft*
☎ (713) 360-6313 | MAP **E6** | 🍴🍴
LOLIVIERHOUSTON.COM

FROM CHEF OLIVIER CIESIELSKI (A CHEF ALUM OF TONY'S), THIS casual French bistro took over the space that used to house an adult DVD store. It is understated, with an exposed brick wall, metal tables and Eames-style plastic molded chairs. The serving ware is beautiful and our recent meal there was very fine. We swooned over the chicken liver pâté, beef tartare and jar of pork rillettes, each served with warm, buttery croutons. There was the farmer's salad with lardons and topped with a jiggly poached egg. The meal's highlight was salmon risotto, also topped with

RESTAURANTS

Fresh fish at L'Olivier

one of those perfectly poached eggs and studded with nubbins of smoked salmon. Of special note is the fresh seafood, which provides grilled branzino, harissa-crusted tuna steak and bouillabaisse.

LONDON SIZZLER

6690 SOUTHWEST FWY. (HWY. 59) *at Hillcroft*
☎ (713) 783-2754 | MAP **C7** | 🍴
LONDONSIZZLER.COM

THIS BRITISH-STYLE INDIAN RESTAURANT TAKES WHAT IS GOOD IN the world—sizzlers, tandooris, curries—and pairs it with a refreshing English beer. Just imagine: one Newcastle Brown Ale, an order of chicken tikka masala and a side of garlic naan to dunk in the spicy sauce. The fresh, made-to-order menu also features North African influences, which make for unexpected and complex flavors. We recommend the meat sizzlers, vindaloo and the crispy *mogo*

(cassava sticks with a hot chili dip). London Sizzler also has an array of vegetarian dishes, our favorite being the masala *bhindi*, okra stir-fried with spices. The restaurant has a decently nice wine, beer and spirits menu along with flat screens perfect for a night of watching football. And we mean both the Texans *and* the Dynamo.

LOPEZ MEXICAN RESTAURANT

11606 S. WILCREST *at Southwest Fwy. (Hwy. 59)*
☎ (281) 495-2436 | MAP **C8** | 🍴
VIVALOPEZ.COM

SERVING DELICIOUS OLD-SCHOOL TEX-MEX IN THE SUBURBS THAT bump up against Sugar Land and Stafford, this big, handsome, family-run establishment packs them in, which can be one of the few downfalls here. But the consistent kitchen with go-to items like fajitas, cheesy enchiladas and combo plates (along with Mr. Lopez himself wandering the restaurant checking on tables) make up for the noise and packed house. You really can't go wrong with the *chile rellenos*, ground beef and cheese stuffed into two poblano peppers and then battered and fried. Fun margarita varieties are another reason to visit: classic, spicy habanero, strawberry, mango and more. After eats and drinks, you will be in serious need of a siesta.

LOVING HUT

2825 S. KIRKWOOD *north of Richmond*
☎ (281) 531-8882 | MAP **B6** | ❘❙
LOVINGHUT.US/HOUSTON

THIS INTERNATIONAL VEGAN CHAIN FOUNDED BY VIETNAMESE ENTREpreneur Ching Hai has made its way to West Houston and is on its way to building a cult-like popularity even among meat-eaters. The animal-product-free menu does not lack variety, with categories that include soups, salads, Western favorites (e.g. a burger, spaghetti with savory sauce, "Golden Nuggets"), fried rice, noodle entrees and desserts. The spring rolls are a good starting point, but the sushi roll appetizers are intriguing. You will have to come more than once to discover your preferred entree, but the Silken Moonlight fried noodle plate made with a variety of vegetables is our recommendation. As the Loving Hut website says, *Be Vegan, Make Peace.*

LUCILLE'S

5512 LABRANCH *just north of Binz*
☎ (713) 568-2505 | MAP **E7** | ❙❘❙
LUCILLESHOUSTON.COM

THIS MUSEUM DISTRICT RESTAURANT IS NAMED AFTER CHEF/

owner Chris Williams' great-grandmother, who was a noted cook, owned a restaurant way-back-when and left behind a plethora of her original Southern recipes. Williams, who previously worked at Max's Wine Dive, serves Southern comfort foods with European accents. He has put that Max's background to good use on behalf of the wine list, too, pulling together a selection of bottles at various price points. At a recent lunch, the hit was "pork and beans," but not what you're accustomed to eating. This was a long-braised pork shank on top of a medley of colorful favas, English peas, halved cherry tomatoes and black lentils, all pulled together by a sweet-sour agridolce reduction.

LUCIO'S

905 TAFT *near W. Dallas*
☎ (713) 523-9958 | MAP **E6** | ❙❘❙❙
LUCIOSBYOB.COM

WHILE THE BREATHLESSLY EXALTED THE PASS & PROVIsions may be an intimidating next-door neighbor, Lucio's well-executed menu, BYOB policy and homely decor are reasons this restaurant consistently has patrons flowing in through its doors, armed with wine bottles and ready for a good time. The classic American menu includes options such as poached sturgeon, vegetable terrine, hanger steak and a duo of duck. We suggest you start with the spinach and artichoke dip served with fried pita bread. And the prosciutto-wrapped pork chop and seared scallops served on butternut squash risotto are as good as they sound.

LYNN'S STEAKHOUSE

955 1/2 DAIRY ASHFORD *south of Katy Fwy. (I-10 West)*
☎ (281) 870-0807 | MAP **B6** | 🍴
LYNNSSTEAKHOUSE.COM

PAIR A JUICY NEW YORK STRIP WITH AN EXTENSIVE, AWARD-winning wine list and classic steak-house setting and you have the recipe for Lynn's long success. (It will be 30 years old in 2015.) If you can get past the dated decor—which you most definitely should—you can marvel at the savory-crusted strips that are brushed with salted butter and perfectly seared on a 1,600-degree grill. To the side of the meat, there are also noteworthy mentions such as fat onion rings, caprese salad and rich spinach au gratin.

MF SUSHI

5887 WESTHEIMER *at Fountainview*
☎ (832) 530-4321 | MAP **D6** | 🍴
MFSUSHIHOUSTON.COM

CHEF CHRIS KINJO, WHO RELO-CATED HERE FROM ATLANTA IN late 2012, opened to rave reviews from many of the city's serious sushi fans. (*Bon Appétit* had previously named his Atlanta restaurant one of the country's top 10 sushi restaurants in 2009.) However, recurring complaints about uneven service and menu items being unavailable plagued the restaurant's reputation on Houston social media websites. Our own experience, however, was top-notch, so there you have it. The initials? There's a goofy back-story that they stand for "magic fingers."

Lucille's

MADRAS PAVILION

3910 KIRBY *north of Southwest Fwy. (Hwy. 59)*
☎ (713) 521-2617 | MAP **E7** | ⑪
multiple locations
MADRASPAVILION.US

THIS RESTAURANT DRAWS IN A VARIED CROWD WITH ITS SOUTH Indian cuisine, kosher kitchen and ample vegetarian dishes (the Sugar Land location is not kosher). While the decor lacks any appeal, the lunchtime buffet is reason enough to visit. The big crêpe-like *dosa* is included in the buffet price and arrives piping hot from the kitchen after you let the waiter know how spicy you want it. Things to try from the steam table include the *channa masala* (chickpeas), *palak paneer* (homemade cottage cheese cubes cooked with seasoned spinach), *medhu vada* (rather bland unsweet doughnut, good for mopping up sauces) and vegetable *korma* (simmered in coconut cream). The staff is welcoming and happy to answer questions.

MAHARAJA BHOG RESTAURANT

8338 SOUTHWEST FWY. (HWY. 59) *between Beechnut and S. Gessner*
☎ (713) 771-2464 | MAP **C7** | ⑪
MAHARAJABHOG.COM

THIS IS FUN! SIT DOWN AT YOUR TABLE, AND YOU WILL RECEIVE a thali plate containing one large and eight small bowls waiting to be filled. There is no menu here, and everything is all-you-can-eat, all deliciously vegetarian, all for one set price. Not only do you have no menu choices, what is served changes on a daily basis. There are some 300 dishes in the restaurant's repertoire, so you could eat here every day for a month and not have the same dish twice. For Indian food newbies who might be intimidated by menus filled with unfamiliar dishes, it's a relaxed way to try small quantities of lots of different things. In Summer 2013, there were just four Maharaja Bhog restaurants in the world, and only one in the Western hemisphere: here in Houston.

MAINE-LY SANDWICHES

10745 NORTH FWY. (I-45 NORTH) *south of N. Sam Houston Parkway E. (Beltway 8)*
☎ (281) 820-8920 | MAP **E3** | ⑪
multiple locations
MAINELYSANDWICHES.COM

FOR INNER-LOOPERS WHO HAVE TRAVELED THE DISTANCE AND experienced the awesomeness that is a lobster roll in Texas, you will weep happy tears to learn that a second location of Maine-ly Sandwiches just opened as we go to press with this edition, and it is much, much closer. Sugarbaby's on South Shepherd Drive—the hot-pink spot once known for cupcakes and girly gifts—is that second location. Italian sandwiches, soups and desserts fill up the menu, but the reason to come is for the lobster roll—a buttered and toasted roll holds the lobster meat, which is perfectly coated in mayo and gently seasoned with salt and pepper. Have a cup of lobster chowder on the side.

MAI'S RESTAURANT

3403 MILAM *south of Elgin*
☎ (713) 520-5300 | MAP **F6** | ⑪
MAISHOUSTON.COM

AFTER A FEBRUARY 2010 FIRE DESTROYED THE RESTAURANT, owner Mai Nguyen transformed the interior of her family's well-worn restaurant into something of the

RESTAURANTS

fancier sort with sea-foam green walls, bamboo accents and a full bar. You can now enjoy a Pinot Noir or cocktail while browsing through the revamped menu, which has been edited down to a much more manageable length. While it may seem as if everything has changed inside this iconic Vietnamese spot, the food largely remains the same, if somewhat inconsistent. The eggrolls, summer rolls and *xoi chien thit nurong* (sticky rice patties and grilled pork) are great ways to start. We suggest any entree prepared with garlic, our favorite being the *bo luc lac* (garlic beef stir-fried with jalapeños and onions).

MALA SICHUAN BISTRO

9348 BELLAIRE BLVD. *between Ranchester & Corporate*
☎ (713) 995-1889 | MAP **C7** | 🍴

THE 2013 DARLING OF SERIOUS FOODIES IS THIS TRIM AND TIDY little Chinese spot in the northwest corner of the Metropole Center. It strikes a nice balance between being accessible to non-Chinese (the menu includes English translations, the service is friendly, use of the word "bistro") while feeling and tasting authentic. We especially liked the house special cold noodles, steamed ribs (hacked into small pieces for gnawing, served on the weekends only) with crushed rice and eggplants in spicy garlic sauce. Next time we'll screw up our courage to try red oil rabbit, "Top Notch Pot of the Outlaws," perhaps even the crispy and spicy pork intestines. No wine or beer is sold, but there is satisfying jasmine tea. Cori Xiong is the owner.

MANENA'S PASTRY SHOP

11018 WESTHEIMER *at Wilcrest*
☎ (713) 278-7139 | MAP **B7** | 🍴
MANENAS.COM

AN UNSUSPECTING STRIP MALL LOCATION STRIKES AGAIN— except this time with empanadas. This family-owned Argentine bakery offers up goodies of all sorts. Come in on a cheat day and indulge in some *alfajores* (caramel sandwich cookies); come in during your lunch hour and order one of the sandwiches *de miga* built with crustless white bread and interesting fillings; and most importantly, come in any time and grub on the delicately baked, delicious empanadas. Of the six varieties offered, our favorite is the *humita*, with creamy corn and red peppers.

MARIA SELMA

1617 RICHMOND *between Mandell & Dunlavy*
☎ (713) 528-4920 | MAP **E7** | 🍴
MARIASELMA.COM

START THE WEEKEND WITH A BREAKFAST OF *CHILAQUILES* AND *huevos rancheros* or begin the night with chips and salsa and shots of tequila from the extensive collection. Whatever the reason for visiting Maria Selma, the palapa out front is the place to be. With a ceiling fan above you and dried palm leaves blocking out the sun, this patio is perfect for dining, drinking and relaxing. The menu touches down in many parts of Mexico and includes *sopas* (soups), *tortas* (sandwiches), enchiladas and seafood, with tropical touches in dishes such as grilled pineapple with roasted pork. The chips are a bit thicker than at other Tex-Mex restaurants, but we enjoy them quite a bit. Owners Rene

Hidalgo and Joseph Varon named their restaurant after Varon's mother, Maria.

MARK'S AMERICAN CUISINE

1658 WESTHEIMER *east of Dunlavy*
☎ (713) 523-3800 | MAP **E6** | 🍴
MARKS1658.COM

YOU WILL BE PRAISING THE HEAVENS AFTER A VISIT TO THIS temple of fine dining. Chef/owner Mark Cox, who was executive chef at Tony's for several years, creates innovative American dishes at his restaurant housed in a beautifully renovated church set on a, *uh*, lively strip of Lower Westheimer. Cox and wife Lisa took advantage of the building and its vaulted ceilings and choir loft to transform the space into a graceful restaurant equipped with a balcony dining room. In a city full of every kind of food imaginable, Cox's upscale menus are as exciting as the day he opened in 1997. The menus change daily, so subsequent church visits are just as inspiring. Sitting amongst Montrose resale shops and tattoo parlors, Mark's is the quintessence of Houston fine dining.

MARTINEZ CAFE

1302 LORRAINE *east of Main*
☎ (713) 229-8490 | MAP **F6** | 🍴

THIS MODEST MEXICAN SPOT FEELS LIKE OLD HOUSTON, A HOUSTON before Metro trains, city-sponsored bicycle loan program or The Woodlands: It's where your father and grandfather might have stopped for a bag of tacos to take home. The menu is much the same today. Have a seat and order the cheese enchiladas (our personal favorite), *carne guisada* (Mexican beef stew) or flautas. The kitchen serves breakfast and lunch every day 7 am to 4 pm.

MARY'Z MEDITERRANEAN CUISINE

5825 RICHMOND *east of Fountain View*
☎ (832) 251-1955 | MAP **C7** | 🍴
MARYZCUISINE.COM

COME FOR THE PATIO AND A HOOKAH, STAY FOR THE GIANT MEZZA combination platter that arrives with hummus, falafel, stuffed grape leaves, *kibbie* (minced meat with bulgur) and more. This expansive Lebanese restaurant offers an array of flavored hookah tobacco but has more going for it than the handsome glass water pipes. The food here is great. The *foul moudammas* (seasoned fava beans) and aforementioned *kibbie* are particularly good starters. The chicken shawarma with pickles and tomatoes rolled in pita bread is a delicious sandwich, and for a bigger entree, the vegetable dishes are the way to go. This is a great place for a large celebratory meal, especially if there's a chance the group could get a little rowdy.

MASRAFF'S

1753 POST OAK BLVD. *south of San Felipe*
☎ (713) 355-1975 | MAP **D6** | 🍴
MASRAFFS.COM

WE APPRECIATE A FINE DINING RESTAURANT THAT PUTS AS much attention and energy into its decor as it does its menu. Father and son owners Tony and Russell Masraff did just that at their new location in The Galleria area, a contemporary study in neutral tones. A faux tree log runs across the ceiling in the dining room/bar area emitting flames, and a waterfall adds tranquility to the outdoor patio. And for the food, it is just as fancy. Some standouts are the seared foie gras with pears, ahi tuna salad with an unreasonable amount of bacon, bison ribeye, seared scallops and chilled crab salad. For dessert: Order the hot fresh-from-the-fryer donut holes with your coffee.

MAX'S WINE DIVE

4720 WASHINGTON *at Shepherd*
☎ (713) 880-8737 | MAP **E6** | 🍴
multiple locations
MAXSWINEDIVE.COM

S ERVING UP SOME OF THE BEST FRIED CHICKEN IN THE CITY, THERE is no better place than Max's to enjoy a glass of sparkling wine and a plate of the hot, crispy poultry. Many were skeptical of the combination, but since the arrival of many chef-driven comfort food joints across town, Max's has only grown in popularity. How can you elevate the already perfect fried egg sandwich? Chef Michael Pellegrino figured it out: Add truffle aioli, gruyère, then a bit more truffle oil and *voilà!* And with fancy hotdogs trending everywhere, Max's "Haute" dog piled high with onion strings and chili is certainly worth your visit. The small shotgun space fills up quickly, but with a second location opening soon in Montrose, your craving for fried chicken and really good wine will be more easily satisfied.

McCORMICK & SCHMICK'S

1151-01 UPTOWN PARK
at Post Oak Blvd
☎ (713) 840-7900 | MAP **D6** | 🍴
multiple locations
MCCORMICKANDSCHMICKS.COM

A HAPPY-HOUR MENU TO PLEASE YOUNG PROFESSIONALS AND AN upscale main menu to satisfy affluent businessmen, this Portland chain is practically two restaurants in one. If watching your checkbook but still craving the fine dining experience, the weekday happy hour 4 to 7 pm and 9 to 10 pm will satisfy both demands. Bruschetta and crispy shrimp croutons for $3? Baja fish tacos for $6 or a cheeseburger for $4? This is all possible in the bar area. If headed to the main dining room, know that the main menu has more varieties of raw oysters, harvested in the cold waters of the northern Pacific and Atlantic, than any other Houston restaurant.

MEZZANOTTE

13215 GRANT *at Louetta, Cypress*
☎ (832) 717-7870 | 🍴
MEZZANOTTERISTORANTE.COM

Y OU MAY HESITATE TO CHECK OUT A STRIP CENTER SPOT BECAUSE of its far-from-the-Loop Cypress location, but your curiosity would be rewarded at this imaginative Italian restaurant. The next time you find yourself in the area and your stomach starts rumbling, visit Gerry and Adri-ana Sarmiento's handsome dining room for the elegantly plated dishes and affordable yet interesting wine list. Live entertainment and bold red tones create a sense of energy that pairs well with dishes like osso buco or veal chop. We also recommend the classic pastas such as pumpkin-filled ravioli, *bucatini all'amatriciana* (a simple red sauce with pancetta), fettuccini carbonara and an especially good lasagne.

MI PUEBLITO

9425 RICHMOND *between Fondren & S. Gessner*
☎ (713) 334-4594 | MAP **C7** | ¶¶
MIPUEBLITOHOUSTON.COM

SINCE 1998, MI PUEBLITO HAS BEEN THE FAVORITE OF MOST Houston Colombians. All of the dishes are superb, especially the grilled meats and *ajiaco* (a rich chicken and potato soup famous in Bogotá and served with heavy cream, avocado and capers). This is one of the only Colombian restaurants with a full-service bar. Ask for *un trago de aguardiente*, a shot of Colombia's notorious anise-flavored firewater.

MIA BELLA TRATTORIA

1201 SAN JACINTO *at Dallas*
☎ (832) 319-6675 | MAP **F6** | ¶¶
multiple locations
MIABELLATRATTORIA.COM

THIS ITALIAN-WITH-A-TWIST RESTAURANT IS THE PLACE TO COME if your group can't seem to decide on a specific cuisine or restaurant. Serious meat-eaters with you? The New York strip will satisfy. Those wanting a dish with a modern twist? The wild mushroom strudel with goat cheese has unexpected flavors. And lastly, there are plenty of classic Italian dishes such as gnocchi and four-cheese ravioli for those who like to keep things simple. The lunch is worth trying because of the create-your-own pasta dish, with nine kinds of pasta, 11 sauce varieties and 12 different ingredients to throw into the mix.

MIA'S

3131 ARGONNE *behind Carrabba's on Kirby*
☎ (713) 522-6427 | MAP **E7** | ¶¶
MIASTABLE.COM

THIS IS A NEW AND UNEXPECTED CONCEPT FROM THE CARRABBA'S folks and part of a much-bigger development-in-the-making on Kirby Drive. The Mia's concept—it's named for Johnny Carrabba's daughter Mia—is about burgers, pulled pork, chicken strips, milkshakes and beer. It is the family-friendly (e.g. free soft-serve cones) part of the group of restaurants being built and resembles a Hill Country ranch house. Pluses include a nice live oak-shaded patio that is dog friendly and plenty of self-parking, including a brand-new garage across the street.

MICHIRU SUSHI

3800 SOUTHWEST FWY. (HWY. 59) *at Timmons*
☎ (832) 203-7082 | MAP **D7** | ¶¶
multiple locations
MICHIRUSUSHI.COM

HERE IS ANOTHER EXAMPLE OF A SUBURBAN RESTAURANT OPENING an inside-the-Loop location. In this case, it's a Webster sushi/Asian fusion restaurant that has opened near the Lakewood Church. On a recent lunch visit, the place was nearly empty, but the food was fresh and beautifully presented. Of special note is the "tuna dumpling," which is a piece of raw tuna pounded until very thin, then topped with more seasoned tuna and "crunch." The pounded tuna is then pulled up around its filling and tied off. In other words, it's tuna-filled tuna. Very imaginative and delicious.

MISSION BURRITO

2245 W. ALABAMA *east of Kirby*
☎ (713) 529-0535 | MAP **E7** | ❚
multiple locations
MISSIONBURRITOS.COM

YOU'RE EITHER A MISSION BURRITO ADVOCATE OR A FREEBIRDS advocate. Both have their arguments, but Mission Burrito's wide variety of filling ingredients, a number of vibrant salsas and a delicious queso make this build-your-own burrito joint a worthy competitor. We can all agree that a sauce can make or break a meal, and with a drizzle (or torrential downpour) of the cilantro dressing, your burrito will be magically enhanced. If your date isn't in the mood for a big-as-your-head burrito, the fish tacos or tortilla soup may facilitate your convincing.

MO'S A PLACE FOR STEAKS

1801 POST OAK BLVD.
south of San Felipe
☎ (713) 877-0720 | MAP **D6** | ❚❚❚
MOSAPLACEFORSTEAKS.COM

THIS STEAKHOUSE OFFERS DINERS PLENTY OF OPTIONS FROM APPE-tizers and sushi to steaks and chef specialties. The multiple-choice selection continues with the sauces: Chimichurri, brandy peppercorn, béarnaise, hollandaise or a red wine sauce can accompany the signature bone-in "cowboy cut" ribeye, filet or whichever cut of meat you choose (including a 4-ounce filet for lighter appetites). Other steakhouse classics are available as well, such as the tuna tartar, crabcake appetizer and creamed spinach. You will feel as if you're dining in a sleek Vegas-style lounge when getting comfortable in the leather chairs, except at this lounge you can also chow down on meat.

MOCKINGBIRD BISTRO WINE BAR

1985 WELCH *at McDuffie*
☎ (713) 533-0200 | MAP **E6** | ❚❚❚
MOCKINGBIRDBISTRO.COM

A SEXY GOTHIC INTERIOR LIT BY MEDIEVAL-LOOKING CHANDELIERS, a Texas-Provence menu that takes advantage of Houston's fresh markets and a large bar for nibbling bargain-priced bar bites have kept this restaurant, which is no longer exactly trendy, still buzzing with devoted diners. If anything, it grows more revered by the year. The cuisine features Texas ingredients with a French Riviera twist. You won't be disappointed with a starter of baby calamari served with two dipping sauces, house-made gravlax or the duck trio (foie gras *torchon*, rillettes and mousse). Or start with one of the kitchen's famous charcuterie platters for the table. Outstanding entrees include trout, *steak frites* and double-cut Kurobuta pork chops with boudin blanc dirty rice. We can't let you go without confiding our very favorite thing on the menu: the hamburger topped with stilton cheese and sided with truffled fries. An evening at this bistro will inspire romance, especially if you end with the sensual bitter-sweet chocolate torte served warm. Mockingbird chef/owner John Sheely had the soft opening of his brand-new Osteria Mazzantini just as this book was being laid out.

MOLINA'S

4720 WASHINGTON *at Shepherd*
☎ (713) 862-0013 | MAP **E6** | ❚❚
multiple locations
MOLINASRESTAURANTS.COM

THE HOUSE'S SPECIAL JOSE'S DIP HAS A CULT-LIKE FOLLOWING ALL of its own. This bowl of delightfully gooey queso with a gift of ground beef at the center just waiting to be mixed in attracts crowds of all varieties. In fact, this small chain of local Tex-Mex restaurants, now 70-plus years old, has fans (famously including George and Barbara Bush) for its entire menu, which is served up in a friendly cantina environment. The menu is expansive, with plenty of tacos, chalupas, enchiladas and fajitas, so everyone in your crowd will be satisfied. The *enchiladas de tejas*, stuffed with cheese and bathed in chili con carne, is as delicious as you might imagine.

MONARCH

5701 MAIN *at Binz, in Hotel ZaZa*
☎ (713) 526-1991 | MAP **F6** | 🍴
MONARCHRESTAURANTHOUSTON.COM

HOUSED IN THE UNCONVENTIONAL HOTEL ACROSS THE STREET FROM the Museum of Fine Arts—Hotel ZaZa reminds us of a retro black-and-white Hollywood movie—the dramatically decorated restaurant actually serves a rather conventional menu. Chef Jonathan Jones' menu includes shrimp and grits, Mediterranean capellini with tomatoes, capers and olives, a wedge salad and grilled ahi burger. The restaurant, which is perfectly sited in the Museum District, is the ideal place for a glass of Champagne after looking at art or to launch a chic evening. If the weather is tolerable, sit outside and inhale one of our city's very finest views of glorious old live oaks and the Mecom Fountain.

MOON TOWER INN

3004 CANAL *at N. Ennis*
☎ (832) 266-0105 | MAP **F6** | 🍴
DAMNGOODFOODCOLDASSBEER.COM

AS THE WEBSITE NOT SO SUBTLY SUGGESTS, GET OFF THE COUCH and head to this professional neighborhood cookout. This is a meat-eaters haven with venison, boar, buffalo and lamb hotdogs snuggled in Slow Dough pretzel buns and served with a bag of Zapp's potato chips. There are plenty of different toppings and sauces to choose from, such as black pepper ketchup and stout beer sauerkraut. Owners Evan Shannon and Brandon Young created a cozy backyard for patrons with a basketball hoop, picnic tables and even occasional movie nights. Don't forget about the inexpensive craft beer and the oozy, indulgent sandwiches like the classic grilled cheese.

MORTON'S

5000 WESTHEIMER *(upstairs) at Post Oak Blvd.*
☎ (713) 629-1946 | MAP **D6** | 🍴
multiple locations
MORTONS.COM

WHEN YOU ARE WITHIN WALKING DISTANCE OF A HALF-DOZEN hotels and have a nationally recognized brand, business will be good no matter the (lack of) attention you might get from the locals. There is definitely an experience to be had at Morton's from the Leroy Neiman prints and celebrity photos on the walls to the meat and live lobster shown tableside. Don't come here if you are on a health kick because, while you can order more healthful chicken and fish entrees, the richly caloric side dishes will crush your diet.

RESTAURANTS

Black magic cake at Mr. Peeples

MR. PEEPLES

1911 BAGBY *at Pierce*

☎ (713) 652-0711 | MAP **E6** | 🍴

MRPEEPLES.COM

LANDMARK HOSPITALITY GROUP (THEY ALSO HAVE 51FIFTEEN AND Hearsay Gastro Lounge) unveiled Mr. Peeples just as we were finishing up this edition of the guidebook. The luxuriously appointed restaurant and banquet space opened in the refurbished Boy Scouts of America Building in Midtown and combines a luxurious Las Vegas sensibility (e.g. huge crystal chandeliers) with an edgy urban sensibility (e.g. graffiti is worked into the design). The first-floor restaurant, under the direction of Pedro Silva, specializes in steaks and seafood. There are also private dining rooms available as well as cheeky little curtained-off spaces in the lounge. Plans call for the basement to become an upscale lounge.

NAM GANG

1411 GESSNER *north of Long Point*

☎ (713) 467-8801 | MAP **C5** | 🍴

LIKE ANY TRUE TEXAS CARNIVORE, YOU WON'T MIND WALKING OUT OF this do-it-yourself Korean restaurant smelling like grilled meat. Just note that the fragrance of kimchi may also linger on your clothes. Gas-fired grills (and a couple of less common coal grills) make this a unique spot for a foursome, and we love the *banchan* (all the various little side dishes and types of kimchi that come with every meal). Bring good company because they will have to be your main source of entertainment: There is a definite language barrier with the servers. But though the waitresses might not chat you up, they will keep an eye on you to make sure your meal is progressing well. No matter how many times we visit, we crack up when our server whips out scissors to cut up our meat. The sweet vodka-like *soju* will cool your palate after all the spicy vegetables, marinated *kalbi* (beef short ribs) and *bulgogi* (thin-cut ribeye).

NARA

2800 KIRBY *south of Westheimer, in West Ave* | MAP **E6**

TAKING OVER THE SHORT-LIVED KATSUYA, THIS NEWCOMER IS from veteran chef/restaurateur Donald Chang, who once had another restaurant named Nara on the West Side back in the 1990s. Chang, who also owns Uptown Sushi, will launch his modern Korean-inspired restaurant in late 2013. This new Nara will feature a complete revisioning of the exotic Katsuya space by architect Isaac Preminger, we're told, and the high-energy interior will place an emphasis on increased comfort and an opportunity to see the chefs in action. The entrance to Katsuya will also be pushed back to create an exterior patio for Nara with a separate outdoor menu. The Bun Bar, featuring rice flour buns stuffed with a variety of ingredients and other casual fare, will be unique to the outside patio and bar.

NARIN'S BOMBAY BRASSERIE

3005 W. LOOP SOUTH *at Richmond*

☎ (713) 622-2005 | MAP **D7** | 🍴

NARINSBOMBAYBRASSERIE.COM

ANOTHER DAY, ANOTHER INDIAN RESTAURANT TO CHECK OUT IN Houston. The white-tablecloth dining room at Narin's is paired with hand-carved Indian panels for an authentic atmosphere, and the foyer bar provides space for cocktail sipping and appetizer nibbling. While you are satisfying your Indian fix, you might as well give in to your fried craving with the tasty chicken *pakoras* (deep-fried nuggets). The menu is full of North Indian cuisine, with some dishes adding variety to the mix such as the pan-fried calamari sautéed with hot cherry peppers. There are plenty of traditional options on the menu, including an assortment of vegetarian dishes.

NATACHEE'S SUPPER 'N PUNCH

3622 MAIN *at Alabama*
☎ (713) 524-7203 | MAP **F6** | ‖
NATACHEES.COM

ON THE SAME STREET AS THE CONTI-NENTAL CLUB AND TACOS À GO-GO, Natachee's down-home country cookin' adds variety to the eclectic block. Before heading to a concert, make a stop at this eatery for filling comfort food and boozy punches. You won't go wrong with an order of the fried pickles to start, and the pulled pork nachos are a great follow-up. The chicken BLT is juicy, zesty and (best of all) bacon-y, and with a whole menu of burgers and nearly 20 different sides to choose from, the options are practically endless. To wash it down, order one of the eight different punches. Since the patio is equipped with plenty of picnic tables, it is easy to accommodate your concert entourage. Lest we forget: You can get breakfast here, too.

NELORE CHURRASCARIA

4412 MONTROSE *south of Richmond*
☎ (713) 395-1050 | MAP **E7** | ‖
NELORESTEAKHOUSE.COM

YOU KNOW WHAT TO EXPECT WHEN ENTERING A BRAZILIAN STEAK-house—meat, meat and more meat. This steakhouse offers 15 cuts of beef, chicken and pork and distin-guishes itself from similar establish-ments by offering guests a cozy atmosphere and a bit cheaper menu. The *gauchos*, or Brazilian cowboys, circulate through the restaurant slicing meat onto diners' plates, which could lead to you becoming acquainted with a skewer of bacon wrapped filet or garlicky rump roast. Be careful not to fill up on the puffy and cheesy Brazilian bread that accompanies the meal, and note that the traditional churrascaria salad bar is a bit more moderate than at other larger operations.

NEW YORK BAGEL & COFFEE SHOP

9724 HILLCROFT *near S. Braeswood*
☎ (713) 723-5879 | MAP **C8** | ‖

THIS IS TWO SPOTS IN ONE. ONE SIDE IS A VINTAGE LUNCHEONETTE THAT lives up to the "New York" in its name and has been a staple for the Houston Jewish community for years. You can order breakfast as well as kosher-style corned beef, salami and pastrami, latkes, matzoh ball soup and more. What's really special here, however, is the fish. Options include lox (regular or Nova), chubs, sable, kippered salmon and whitefish salad. They open early (6 am) and close in the late afternoon. Don't be a schmuck and leave without a bag of bagels to share with everyone at the office or at home. They're made and sold in the adjacent shop. The only problem is deciding which bagel and cream cheese spread to get that day. Cranberry walnut with pineapple cream cheese or the jalapeño bagel with onion cream cheese? Heck, just get a dozen of everything bagels. No one will complain.

NIDDA THAI
1226 WESTHEIMER *at Commonwealth*
☎ (713) 522-8895 | MAP **E6** | 🍴
NIDDATHAI.COM

THIS IS WESTHEIMER'S MOST RELI-ABLE THAI SPOT AND IT IS SITUATED right next door to what could maybe be Westheimer's most reliable X-rated shop, Erotic Cabaret. But there is no judgment in this neigh-borhood, so if you need a new pair of fishnets after your Thai meal, just walk next door. But first lunch: There are two eggplant dishes that come highly recommended—the sautéed eggplant with Thai chili and basil sauce and the *chu chee* eggplant, lightly battered slices cooked with red curry. For some-thing to awaken your senses and fill you with warmth, try the *tom yum gai*, a hot and sour chicken soup practically electric with lemongrass.

NIELSEN'S DELICATESSEN
4500 RICHMOND *at Mid Lane*
☎ (713) 963-8005 | MAP **D7** | 🍴

IF YOU LIKE TO SLATHER MAYO ON ALL THINGS EDIBLE, THIS MODEST delicatessen is where you need to come to realize homemade far sur-passes store-bought. The much-loved Ellen Nielsen Andersen passed away in early 2008, but her family carries on the Nielsen's tradition, including the homemade mayonnaise that has been whipped up daily since the store first opened. Anything that the mayo touches is richly enhanced, such as the beloved chicken salad, egg salad and deviled eggs. The fresh meats and cheeses, which are also available by weight, make for delicious sandwiches, our favorite being the corned beef on rye with the homemade liver paste.

NIKO NIKO'S
2520 MONTROSE *north of Westheimer*
☎ (713) 528-4976 | MAP **E6** | 🍴
multiple locations
NIKONIKOS.COM

HOUSTONIANS WILL ALWAYS CARRY A TORCH FOR THIS GREEK restaurant. While the menu is not cheap and the long line that grows during peak times is intimidating, locals seem to believe that patience makes the stomach grow fonder. You may have seen owner Dimitrios Fetokakis frying up *loukoumades* (Greek honey balls) with Guy Fieri on *Diners, Drive-Ins and Dives*, but we believe the best reason to visit is for the bright chicken-lemon avgolemono soup. The roasted potatoes and classic gyro are also good orders, as is the pork chop. The newish Market Square to-go kiosk is a great gathering place for the downtown community with outdoor seating. We love that Fetokakis maintains the grass, flowers and trees on the boulevard median in front of his Montrose location.

NINO'S
2817 W. DALLAS *between Montrose & Waugh*
☎ (713) 522-5120 | MAP **E6** | 🍴
NINOS-VINCENTS.COM

YOU MAY NOT CRAVE ROAST CHICKEN AT THE MOMENT, BUT ONCE YOU

RESTAURANTS

try Nino's acclaimed wood-roasted chicken and garlic mashers, you will have rotisserie goodness on your mind often. The straightforward Italian-American menu prepared with quality ingredients also offers other good options like crisp pizzas, lavishly sauced pastas and some of the best osso buco in the city. The Vincent Mandola family has created its own restaurant village of a sort, here on W. Dallas, consisting of Vincent's, Nino's and Grappino all around a sort of "town square" with music, fountains and great food.

NIPPON

4464 MONTROSE *between Richmond & W. Alabama*
☎ (713) 523-3939 | MAP **E7** | 🍴
NIPPON-SUSHI.COM

THERE IS SOMETHING INHERENTLY REASSURING ABOUT A JAPANESE restaurant full of diners of Japanese heritage. At family-owned Nippon, that is what you can expect, along with rich and flavorful ramen and fresh, simple fish. From the outside, this place can go unnoticed, but the regulars don't seem to mind that hipster foodies and the media overlook their secret spot. The understated decor of dark wood and paper lanterns mimic the simplicity of the sushi. You won't find too many crazy specialty rolls, but the basics including hamachi, eel and mackerel are consistently fresh. The parking, located behind the restaurant, is challenging and often insufficient.

NOE RESTAURANT

4 RIVERWAY *just off Woodway, in the Omni Hotel*
☎ (713) 871-8177 | MAP **D6** | 🍴
NOERESTAURANT.COM

THE IN-HOUSE RESTAURANT FOR THIS ELEGANT TUCKED-AWAY OMNI Hotel serves up New American fare with "Pan Asian undertones." The current menu features dishes such as curried lobster carbonara and pan-seared diver scallops with green tea lemon rice. The restaurant offers those with special diets the opportunity to customize meals to fit dietary needs and even provides a few dishes that are already vegetarian, gluten-free and/or dairy-free. Noe is an attempt to intertwine sustainable cooking with all the contemporary trends one would find at a fine-dining restaurant.

OAK LEAF SMOKEHOUSE

1000 TELEPHONE ROAD *near Stimson (east of I-45)*
☎ (713) 487-8987 | MAP **F7** | 🍴
OAKLEAFSMOKEHOUSE.COM

TAKING OVER THE LOCATION THAT WAS PETE'S BBQ BRISKET & SEA-food, Brian Lewis and Lisa Kuhfeldt aim to not only do barbecue and its side dishes well, but they want to present a "multilingual" barbecue menu, if you will: Carolina-style barbecue, Memphis-style, Kansas City-style. For now, however, this newcomer is focusing on Texas.

OCEAN PALACE

11215 BELLAIRE BLVD. *west of Wilcrest*
☎ (281) 988-8898 | MAP **B7** | 🍴

BEFORE SO MANY OTHER DIM SUM SPOTS POPPED UP, FOLKS MOSTLY went to Ocean Palace. Houston's mecca of dim sum still has its loyal diners that fill the restaurant's two levels, the downstairs for nightly dinners and the upstairs on weekend mornings. Pick and choose your dishes off the dim sum carts, with the staples such as *ha gao* (shrimp dumplings in delicate wrappers), *shu mai* (pork dumplings), egg custard tarts and puffy fried taro always being an option. We can't go to Ocean Palace without ordering the pan-fried daikon cake, and we suggest you do the same. Still hungry? Take your clipboard to the hot foods bar for some fried noodles or a bowl of congee.

THE OCEANAIRE SEAFOOD ROOM

5061 WESTHEIMER *in The Galleria*
☎ (832) 487-8862 | MAP **D6** | 🍴
THEOCEANAIRE.COM

MANY PEOPLE WOULDN'T KNOW THAT THIS RESTAURANT WAS formerly a Minnesota-based chain. That is because Landry's took ownership and locally enhanced the menu with plenty of Gulf seafood. Chef Trevor White's menu changes daily and also features other geographical regions with dishes like Alaskan salmon, ahi tuna and Chesapeake Bay-style crabcakes. While the decor is elegant—it puts us in mind of a Baltimore seafood house—The Galleria location brings in casually dressed shoppers during the day. The raw bar is great for a quick lunch between shops, especially if you enjoy slurping up some cold-water oysters from both the East and West Coasts.

ODGEN'S HOPS & HARVEST

GATEWAY MEMORIAL CITY MAP **C6**

CHEF BRADLEY OGDEN'S NEWEST CREATION CELEBRATES THE SEAsons with a menu devoted to farm-to-table comfort food. This upscale pub, which is set to open in late Fall 2013, will feature 50 draft beers (many of which come from the Houston area), handcrafted cocktails and a decent selection of wines on tap.

OISHII

3764 RICHMOND *at Timmons*
☎ (713) 621-8628 | MAP **D7** | 🍴
OISHIIHOUSTON.COM

THE GOOD: THIS IS ONE OF HOUSTON'S BEST SUSHI HAPPY HOURS. The bad: This is one of Houston's most popular sushi happy hours, so you are practically guaranteed a curb-side wait at this little sushi spot. You will find much better sushi in the city, but for the price you can't do any better. From 3 to 7 pm on weekdays and 3 to 6 pm on Saturdays, $4 appetizers are buy-one-get-one-free. We suggest the vegetable tempura appetizer or roll, the spicy salmon roll and the gyoza. But you won't be able to sneak out with any leftovers. The menu explicitly states, "No to-go boxes for happy hour."

OLIVETTE

111 N. POST OAK LANE *between Woodway & Memorial, in The Houstonian Hotel*
☎ (713) 685-6713 | MAP **D6** | 🍴
HOUSTONIAN.COM

IF YOU WANT TO GET AWAY FOR AN EVENING, A DINNER AT THIS RESTAUrant located inside a posh hotel and spa might temporarily satisfy your vacation yearning. Before entering the Tuscan-themed restaurant, you will drive through the Houstonian's lush landscape, give your car to the valet and then walk by the handsome hunting lodge-style main room. (Plan to sit there after dinner with a nightcap and soak up the ambiance.) Giveaways make any getaway better, and the complimentary warm bread, hummus and olives are Olivette's arrival gifts. Indulge in chef Neal Cox's contemporary American menu such as the sweet corn soup, steaks, seafood and crispy artichokes with seared scallops. The menu's Southwest Caesar Salad? It won the annual Caesar Salad Competition (held every October) so many times that Olivette was banned from competing for a few years in order to give everyone else in town a chance.

ONION CREEK

3106 WHITE OAK *west of Studewood*
☎ (713) 880-0706 | MAP **E5** | 🍴
ONIONCREEKCAFE.COM

I**F YOU'RE FEELING A TRIP TO AUSTIN MIGHT BE NECESSARY, TAKE OFF YOUR** crazy cap and just head to Onion Creek, which does its best to channel the hipster city's eccentricity. Relax on the pleasant patio with a local beer while munching down one of the sandwich or burger varieties. Conveniently located next to Fitzgerald's and Heights Vinyl, this is the perfect stop before a night of live music considering the Austin-y atmosphere. The eatery opens at 7 am to serve as your neighborhood coffeeshop and stays open late, often with a DJ spinning, to entertain as the local bar. The food won't change your life, but it can definitely cure a hangover.

OPORTO CAFE

3833 RICHMOND *at Weslayan*
☎ (713) 621-1114 | MAP **D7** | 🍴
OPORTO.US

A **SHORT WALK FROM EDWARDS GREENWAY PLAZA, THIS WINE AND** tapas bar is a good choice for happy hour drinks and eats before you head to a movie date night. While the focus during lunch is sandwiches and salads, which is ideal for the business crowd, the dinner service is focused around small plates. Enjoy a glass from the affordable yet serious wine list along with stuffed pequillo peppers or garlicky shrimp in piri-piri oil. A crowd favorite dish is the chicken curry empanadas. Pretend you're European and come here for a snack and glass of wine.

ORIGINAL MARINI'S EMPANADA HOUSE

10001 WESTHEIMER *near Briarpark*
☎ (713) 266-2729 | MAP **C6** | 🍴
multiple locations
ORIGINALMARINISEMPANADA.COM

T**HE MARINI FAMILY'S ORIGINAL MONTROSE-AREA EMPANADA** house (founded in 1971) burned down in 1985 and was slow to reopen. In 2004 a location in Katy finally reappeared, followed in 2007 by the Carillon Center branch. The Marinis enlarged the menu, with options such as churrasco sandwiches and Argentinean wines, but we did not need any persuasion to return. The menu is dominated by savory and sweet Argentine turnovers: The Gaucho is a classic, stuffed with beef, boiled eggs, olives and onions, but the Demichelli with avocado, tomato, bell peppers, cheese and mushrooms is perfect for vegetarians. Don't leave without trying a sweet version, such as the Elvis Melbis stuffed with peanut butter, diced banana and dulce de leche served at the Westheimer location.

THE ORIGINAL NINFA'S

2704 NAVIGATION *east of the S. Jensen exchange*
☎ (713) 228-1175 | MAP **F6** | ⑪
NINFAS.COM

YOU CAN'T CALL YOURSELF A TRUE HOUSTONIAN UNLESS YOU HAVE visited The Original Ninfa's on Navigation multiple times. This restaurant is something we can call our own. To give back to its loyal diners, the restaurant installed a breezy patio with its own bar and tequila program. It gets better. The bar program was crafted by Bobby Heugel of Anvil, and many of the selections go perfectly with the bar's oozy fajita burger. Here is how your first order at this Houston institution should go: margarita, *queso flameado* with chorizo, margarita, classic beef fajitas and then another margarita. Bring a designated driver.

OSTERIA MAZZANTINI

2200 POST OAK BLVD. *between San Felipe & Westheimer*
☎ (713) 993-9898 | MAP **D6** | ⑪
OSTERIAMAZZANTINI.COM

LIKE HE DOESN'T WORK HARD ENOUGH ALREADY: MOCKINGBIRD Bistro chef/owner John Sheely has decided it's time to spread his wings and open a second restaurant with an entirely new concept. He hired Paul K. Lewis (previously with Cullen's) as the executive chef, and the two have crafted a menu full of rustic Italian cuisine inspired by Sheely's Italian heritage. You can expect fresh-made pastas and hand-tossed pizzas as

well as entrees such as whole grilled snapper and grilled pork chops. It's set to open the week after we finish editing this book in the new BBVA Compass Plaza, so we haven't been yet. But we'll go out on a limb: Osteria Mazzantini will be one of 2013's best new restaurants.

OTILIA'S

7710 LONG POINT *between Antoine & Wirt*
☎ (713) 681-7203 | MAP **D5** | ⑪
OTILIASMEXICAN.COM

WE ARE STILL HOPING FOR A REVIVAL OF THIS ONCE-RAVED-about Mexican restaurant. They serve up authentic interior Mexican cuisine like shredded Yucatan-style pork and enchiladas with mole. We used to dream about the *chiles en nogada* (stuffed poblano peppers draped with cream sauce and sprinkled with pomegranate seeds). But it seems that once the building was renovated and expanded, the price of the dishes also increased. Some have suggested that the prices are a bit too high. We believe that Houstonians will pay for a good gordita. If you haven't been to Otilia's in a while, this family-run spot deserves another look.

OUISIE'S TABLE

3939 SAN FELIPE *near Willowick*
☎ (713) 528-2264 | MAP **D6** | ⑪
OUISIESTABLE.COM

THIS STATELY GRAY SALTBOX IS WHERE LADIES COME TO LUNCH, brunch and shamelessly munch. Elouise Adams Jones, aka Ouisie, is a local pioneer among women chefs and has created a gorgeous space for women (and men, too) to enjoy delicious Southern and seafood dishes. Ouisie's chicken-fried steak comes

Oxheart's Karen Man and Justin Yu

with a side of black-eyed peas, corn pudding and serious girl power. Other menu highlights are the brandied oysters, shrimp and cheese grits, seafood crêpes and pan-roasted chicken. About two years ago Jones began serving weekday breakfast, too, and the restaurant quickly became a popular rendezvous spot for power breakfasts. One other feature to note: There's a beautiful little garden that is ideal for brunch or cocktails.

OXHEART

1302 NANCE *at Richey*
☎ (832) 830-8592 | MAP **F6** | 🍴
OXHEARTHOUSTON.COM

OUR REVIEWER CALLED OXHEART "AN ASTONISHING HYBRID—ONE part purveyor of high-end *haute cuisine*, one part funky mom-and-pop cafe." Just how good is it? Oxheart was named one of 2012's 10 best new restaurants in the country by *Bon Appétit*. Located among the rehabbed lofts and industrial detritus of the warehouse district just north of downtown, it is a collaboration of chef Justin Yu and his wife/pastry chef Karen Man. (Sommelier Justin Vann helped open the restaurant but has since moved on.) Everything in the space is locally handmade as much as possible (even the knives), and the foodstuffs are, of course, local too, sourced from Utility Research Garden, Louisiana Foods, Revival Meats and others. It is very small, just 30 seats, and open for dinner only. The chef offers only three *prix fixe* menu options each evening—one is vegetarian, one includes a couple of meat courses and one is a "tasting menu" that pretty much encompasses the first two. You can count on an enormously inventive and a meticulous (one almost wants to say obsessive) approach to your dinner. Don't miss it.

PALAZZO'S TRATTORIA

10455 BRIAR FOREST *at W. Sam Houston Parkway S. (Beltway 8)*
☎ (713) 785-8800 | MAP **D6** | 🍴
multiple locations
PALAZZOSCAFE.COM

WHILE YOU MIGHT NOT CRAVE AMERICANIZED ITALIAN OFTEN, there is something so satisfying about a meal that took you three minutes to order via phone. During the holidays, this kitchen gets hit with order after order for the "Palazzo Pans" of piping hot pasta, which you have probably enjoyed at a neighbor's Christmas party. The pastas and pizzas are consistently tasty, but the veal dishes (try the piccata) are worth a trip to eat in at the restaurant. If looking for a more intimate first experience, head to John and Stassa Moore's original Palazzo's at 2620 Briar Ridge, but the bigger, fancier Briar Forest version is great for large crowds and families.

THE PALM

6100 WESTHEIMER *between Fountain View & S. Voss*
☎ (713) 977-2544 | MAP **D6** | 🍴
THEPALM.COM

THE 2013 RENOVATION AND EXPANSION—IT COST A MERE $5 million—of the circa 1978 Houston edition of the Palm added a new roof, more seats and fresh walls ready for their local caricatures. At the time of the grand reopening in July, the management announced that the Houston renovation is the prototype for redesign of all the group's restaurants across the country. The classic steakhouse menu along with Italian favorites remains more or less the same, but there's nothing wrong with that. The biggest lobsters in Houston swim in the Palm's tanks.

PAPPADEAUX SEAFOOD KITCHEN

2410 RICHMOND *east of Kirby*
☎ (713) 527-9137 | MAP **E7** | 🍴
multiple locations
PAPPADEAUX.COM

WHERE DO YOU *GEAUX* FOR SEAFOOD? COUNTLESS LOCALS reply, "Pappadeaux." You can expect fresh seafood with a Cajun twist and mighty fine portions. When you're devouring the gooey shrimp and crawfish fondeaux, you might even forget about the crazy themed decor that surrounds you. The restaurant can get deafening, but diners just can't get enough of the crawfish étouffée, fried shrimp or grilled fish. If there's "Pappas" in the name, you can anticipate a wait for a table.

PAPPAS BROS. STEAKHOUSE

5839 WESTHEIMER *at Bering*
☎ (713) 780-7352 | MAP **C7** | 🍴
PAPPASBROS.COM

TO BE TAKEN SERIOUSLY, ANY RESTAURANT EMPIRE MUST ATTEMPT a steakhouse. Luckily for Houstonians, the Pappas brothers knew exactly what they were doing. The restaurant is sheathed in handsome dark paneling, the classic steakhouse setting for enjoying a martini, wedge salad and bloody-rare USDA Prime steak. Cozy up in one of the booths for date night or intimate celebrations—the 500-plus labels on the award-winning wine list will impress a new business partner. If it's you and your significant other, order the porterhouse for two. Add on asparagus, skillet potatoes and/or creamed spinach. Expensive but worth it.

RESTAURANTS

PAPPAS SEAFOOD HOUSE

3001 S. SHEPHERD
near W. Alabama
☎ (713) 522-4595 | MAP **E7** | 🍴
multiple locations
PAPPASSEAFOOD.COM

WHAT DO GREEKS KNOW ABOUT GULF COAST SEAFOOD? QUITE A lot, apparently. They also know a thing or two about Texas-sized portions. The restaurant brags about "portions as big as the ocean," which is only a slight exaggeration. The redfish "on the half shell" is truly amazing. It might ruin any other redfish dish for you. But the menu has boatloads of other options, too, from fried calamari and stuffed flounder to all kinds of oysters and shrimp. Combining the owners' Greek heritage with a beloved Texas expression, their Greek salad is definitely bigger in Texas.

PAPPASITO'S CANTINA

6445 RICHMOND *at Hillcroft*
☎ (713) 784-5253 | MAP **C7** | 🍴
multiple locations
PAPPASITOS.COM

IT'S A BIT OF A LETDOWN IF A TEX-MEX SPOT DOESN'T BRING BOTH RED and green salsas to the table. At this cantina, you get both, and they are some of our favorites in town. You may be full by the time your entree arrives, but if stuffing your face with chips and salsa is what you have to do to distract yourself from the loud background music and general din, then go right ahead. We've definitely done it a few times, but we have learned our lesson. We know to save room for the Plato Del Mar, a combo of fajitas and bacon-wrapped shrimp on a large sizzling platter. The cheese enchiladas seem to have changed for the better in the last few years.

New gravy recipe, Pappasito's? Since you're eating your calories, order the Skinny Margarita made with agave, tequila and lime juice to even things out.

PASHA

2325 UNIVERSITY
west of Greenbriar
☎ (713) 592-0020 | MAP **E7** | 🍴
EPASHA.COM

INSIDE THIS CONVERTED HOUSE, YOU'LL SEE WHITE TABLECLOTHS AND LOVELY pomegranate colored walls, but the attitude at Mustafa Ozsoy's Turkish restaurant is actually quite casual. If you've never tried Turkish food before, it is easy to fall in love with. There are plenty of good choices, which is exactly why we order (and suggest you do the same) the mixed grill plate. It really is the easiest decision since you get a tasting of all the goodness: *doner* (carved meat, something like shawarma), shish kebab and *adana* (a ground meat kebab), which all arrive on a golden platter with sides.

THE PASS & PROVISIONS

807 TAFT *between W. Dallas & Allen Pkwy.*
☎ (713) 628-9020 | MAP **E6** | 🍴
PASSANDPROVISIONS.COM

CHEF/OWNERS TERRENCE GALLIVAN AND SETH SIEGEL-GARDNER have created two restaurants in one. Both opened in late 2012. Provisions opened first and is the more casual spot, serving lunch and dinner. It's praised for its excellent pizzas, bone marrow brioche and crazy twists on everyday foods. (Order the smoked salmon, and be charmed by what you get.) The Pass, open for dinner only, is the more formal concept and opened about two months later.

Chefs Seth Siegel-Gardner and Terrence Gallivan at The Pass and Provisions

It instantly became 2012-2013's must-go-to restaurant, offering five- or eight-course prix-fixe menus. Our magazine's blogger was beside herself, noting "the chef team dishes out a fantasy cuisine that will turn your culinary expectations inside out. Imagine cocktails that have been changed into gummy candies and mushroom forests that seem to only be missing the little woodland fairies to make them complete. There's no fruit-flavored, lickable paper being served, but we're sure the magicians at The Pass are working on how to make that elegant and practical." As we go to press, The Pass has already been named to numerous local and national "best-of" lists, and the madness is not over yet.

PATRENELLA'S

813 JACKSON HILL *south of Washington*
☎ (713) 863-8223 | MAP **E6** | 🍴
PATRENELLAS.NET

L OCATED A BLOCK AWAY FROM WASHINGTON AVENUE IN A CHEERY white and red 1938 house built by owner Sammy Patrenella's father, the feeling of family resonates as soon as you step inside. The menu focuses on hearty Americanized Italian cuisine, and the kitchen puts out consistently good dishes. A popular starter is Sammy's eggplant—four pieces of eggplant lightly fried and topped with cheese and marinara. So simple yet tasty. Something we always love to see, a big and well-kept vegetable garden, is just outside the back door. With its fresh herbs and tomatoes, it's no wonder the simple marinara tastes so flavorful.

PAULIE'S

1834 WESTHEIMER *east of Hazard*
☎ (713) 807-7271 | MAP **E6** | 🍴
PAULIESRESTAURANT.COM

THERE IS NOTHING MORE TO ASK
FOR FROM A NEIGHBORHOOD
restaurant—house-made pastas, a
Greenway Coffee program, delicious
shortbread cookies and an all-Italian
wine program. (Texas-grown wines
made with Italian varietals are also
served.) Owner Paul Petronella
always wanted to offer house-made
pasta, but it wasn't until he found the
right machine that it became possible
to do so. Now, he's not only making
his own pastas but supplying other
local chefs with his freshly made
pastas as well. On the home front,
his menu includes a messy shrimp
BLT and the satisfying fettuccini
alfredo. A new favorite is the *bucatini
all'amatriciana* made with hollow
spaghetti-like tubes and topped with
smoked bacon, garlic, cherry tomatoes, chili flakes and pecorino. This
pasta dish is decidedly spicy, but the
bursts of tomato and rich bacon help
to cool your mouth. Tip: Even if you
are starving, a "small" pasta portion
is usually plenty.

PEKING CUISINE

8332 SOUTHWEST FWY.
(HWY. 59) *at Gessner*
☎ (713) 988-5838 | MAP **C7** | 🍴
PEKING-CUISINE.COM

YOU COME HERE FOR THE DUCK,
AND WHATEVER ELSE YOU MIGHT
enjoy while here is just an added
bonus. Best to call hours or days in
advance because the Peking Duck
Dinner runs out, and a trip to the
outskirts of Chinatown isn't the same
without it. The slow-roasted meat
with extra crispy skin is served with
crêpes, hoisin sauce and scallions.

If they are sold out, the menu, which
specializes in Northern Chinese cuisine,
does have plenty of other pork, seafood,
chicken and vegetable options. The
salted baked shrimp is a good consolation choice. But you should plan for
a second visit to try the duck.

PERBACCO

700 MILAM *at Capitol, in the
Pennzoil Tower*
☎ (713) 224-2422 | MAP **F6** | 🍴
PERBACCOHOUSTON.COM

IF HEADING TO A SHOW AT JONES HALL
OR THE ALLEY, AN INTIMATE ITALIAN
dinner at Perbacco is almost required.
This quaint, unassuming restaurant
deserves more attention than it gets.
A meal starts with the garlicky olive
oil concoction for bread dipping and
should continue with an order of one
of the nightly specials. An equally
satisfying meal would be a simple
salad and gnocchi, and many diners
rave about the cheesy lasagne. If you
work downtown, the counter-service
lunch is worth checking out, though
it can get crowded quickly.

PERRY'S STEAKHOUSE & GRILLE

2115 TOWN SQUARE PLACE
*at Southwest Fwy. (Hwy. 59),
Sugar Land*
☎ (281) 565-2727 | MAP **A9** | 🍴
multiple locations
PERRYSRESTAURANTS.COM

IF WE NEEDED ANOTHER REASON TO
LOVE FRIDAYS, PERRY'S STEAKHOUSE
gave it to us: their Friday lunch pork
chop special. Seeing as how we
would willingly and happily pay full
price for this monstrous, caramelized hunk of meat, paying only $12 is
something worth celebrating. Chris
Perry's pork chop has changed lives,
but his dry-aged steak is no joke

either. The steak goes through a three-step process: caramelizing with signature spices, char-grilling to trap natural juices and finishing with garlic butter. Tasty appetizers like bacon-wrapped scallops round out the dining experience. The Perry's restaurants, founded in Southeast Houston in 1979, get bigger and more upscale every year.

PHILIPPE RESTAURANT
1800 POST OAK BLVD. *between Westheimer & San Felipe*
☎ (713) 439-1000 | MAP **D6** | 🍴
PHILIPPEHOUSTON.COM

CHEF PHILIPPE SCHMIT, THE ROGU-ISHLY HANDSOME RESTAURANT namesake and self-described French Cowboy, successfully integrated his classically trained French sensibility with Houstonians' love of bold flavor and impressive portions. The perfect examples: the spicy duck confit tamales, lamb meatballs, pulled pork ravioli or the grilled trout served on a dramatically long, narrow platter. Alas, Schmit left the restaurant in late 2013. Chef de cuisine Manuel Pucha has since taken over the kitchen and not missed a beat. The dramatic staircase, flickering candles and reflective glass accents might make you feel as if you are about to melt down your debit card, but the paper placemats on your table hint at the restaurant's relative affordability.

PHO BINH I
10928 BEAMER *south of Fuqua*
☎ (281) 484-3963 | MAP **H9** | 🍴
multiple locations
PHOBINH.COM

IT IS SAFE TO SAY THAT MANY OF HOUSTON'S BEST ETHNIC REST-aurants are found in not-the-best locations. Located south of Hobby Airport, this modest trailer with minimal inside seating has been serving up some of the city's most authentic pho since 1983. We willingly cope with extremely limited parking and wait times for tables because we know the reward of the food within. A bowl of the broth would be satisfying enough, but delicate rice noodles, succulent beef and fresh jalapeño complete the experience. Some of the other locations' menus are bigger, with Vietnamese sandwiches, egg rolls and grill dishes, but we recommend the original Beamer location for the pho.

PHO DANH
11209 BELLAIRE *west of Wilcrest, in Hong Kong City Mall*
☎ (281) 879-9940 | MAP **A8** | 🍴
multiple locations

HONG KONG CITY MALL IS THE HOME TO QUITE A FEW RESTAU-rants, markets, bakeries and little cafes, one of which is Pho Danh—usually packed and always serving noodle soup and only noodle soup. The broth is layered with flavors of beef, onion and star anise that compliment your choice of meat. Brisket, flank steak, beef tenderloin and meatballs are among the options, but the *bun bo hue* (a spicy version full of shrimp flavor and cubes of congealed pork blood) is an adventure of sorts. If feeling inspired after your meal, you can grocery-shop the nearby Hong Kong Food Market and attempt to recreate your favorite rendition of pho at home.

PHO GA DAKAO

11778 BELLAIRE *near Kirkwood*
☎ (281) 879-5899 | MAP **B7** | 🍴

THERE ARE PEOPLE IN THE WORLD WHO DO NOT EAT RED MEAT. AND while we may not understand them, this Houston mom-and-pop shop luckily allows those people to indulge in the goodness that is pho. *Pho ga*, the restaurant's namesake, is the chicken-based equivalent to the beef-broth pho. The chicken and fixings is the main feature, with the broth (still delicious) in a smaller bowl on the side. Pour in however much you would like and enjoy your bowl of *pho ga*, which at this restaurant is equally delicious as pho.

PIATTO RISTORANTE

4925 W. ALABAMA *just off Post Oak Blvd.*
☎ (713) 871-9722 | MAP **D7** | 🍴
multiple locations
PIATTORISTORANTE.COM

CHEF/OWNER JOHN MARION CARRABBA'S PIATTO CERTAINLY lives up to the expectations that come with the name "Carrabba." The menu is large and the food is consistently delicious. To guarantee a memorable dining experience choose from these two starters: the asparagus that is lightly breaded, fried and topped with jump lump crabmeat and a lemon butter sauce or the fried calamari, also lightly breaded and fried, but served with pepperoncini peppers and a lemon butter sauce. The restaurant itself is intimate and casual and not too loud, which is the prefect environment for enjoying a romantic dinner with a companion or a big bowl of pasta and glass of wine just by yourself.

PICO'S MEX MEX

5941 BELLAIRE BLVD. *at Renwick*
☎ (713) 662-8383 | MAP **D7** | 🍴
PICOS.NET

PICO'S GIVES US EVERYTHING WE COULD EVER NEED FROM A MEX-Mex—i.e. interior Mexican cuisine—restaurant: dreamy salsa, dangerously good margaritas and mole sauce that demands to be taken seriously. We strongly suggest you order some nachos or quesadillas for a starter if you are going to have the 48-ounce *mucho grande* margarita, which we also recommend. (Go big or go home, right?) Our favorite entree is the *cochinita pibil* (pork cooked in banana leaves served with pickled onions), but the *chiles en nogada*, the classic stuffed-chile dish topped with walnut cream sauce, is another noteworthy dish worth trying if you've never had it. And our prayers are being answered: Soon we will no longer have to travel to Southwest Houston for our Mex-Mex fix. Pico's is opening a second location at Kirby and Richmond in the building that used to be a Ninfa's. Olé!

PIERSON & CO. BBQ

5110 T.C. JESTER *north of W. Tidwell*
☎ (713) 683-6997 | MAP **D4** | 🍴

ANYONE WHO HAS TASTED HIS RIBS OR HAD A GLIMPSE OF HIS contagious smile wept the day that barbecue pit master Clarence Pierson announced he would have to close Pierson & Co. BBQ because of knee surgery. And we surely all felt a tear of joyous anticipation roll down our cheek when it was first rumored via a relative's post that Clarence Pierson would be reopening his shop soon. According to the *Houston Chronicle*, J.C. Reid of the Houston BBQ Festival has spoken with Pierson and confirmed the reopening and the target date of September 2013. Same location, same mouth-watering brisket, same smoky ribs. Fingers crossed.

PINK'S PIZZA

403 HEIGHTS BLVD. *at W. 14th*
☎ (713) 864-7465 | MAP **E6** | ¶
multiple locations
PINKSPIZZA.COM

IF YOU ENJOY THE FINER THINGS IN LIFE, PINK'S PIZZA IS FOR YOU. AND by finer things we mean not having to put on pants, not having to leave your house (or better yet your couch) and being able to eat fresh, fancy and tasty food. Prosciutto and gorgonzola anyone? Order a pizza from Pink's and expect pizzas with names like The Deuce but with ingredients like goat cheese, spinach, portobellos, roasted garlic and pesto. This mini Houston chain takes a bit longer to deliver, but good things come to those who wait. You won't be disappointed with the Mediterranean-accented Big Sleep that is topped with roasted garlic, double feta, sun-dried tomatoes, marinated artichokes and chicken breast.

PIOLA

3201 LOUISIANA *just south of Elgin*
☎ (713) 524-8222 | MAP **F6** | ¶
PIOLA.IT

HOUSTON HAS BEEN STRUGGLING TO PRODUCE TRUE ITALIAN-STYLE pizza for a while now and finally decided to outsource, gladly welcoming this worldwide chain based in Treviso, Italy, to the Midtown area. Everyone can appreciate a crispy thin crust, especially when toppings like smoked salmon and brie can be placed on top without worry of a sagging slice. Everyone can also appreciate a good happy hour or weekly special, and Piola has two worth mentioning: free appetizers with any alcohol purchase during weekday happy hour and all-you-can-eat gnocchi for $15 on the 29th of every month. It seems these Italians really understand what Texans want: booze and buffets.

PIQUEO

13215 GRANT *at Louetta, Cypress*
☎ (281) 257-9097 | ¶
PIQUEO.COM

WHILE NEXT-DOOR MEZZANOTTE (FOUNDED IN 2005) HAS MADE a name for itself in Italian cuisine, Piqueo (founded in 2011) is Gerry and Adriana Sarmiento's effort to return to his Peruvian roots. Peruvian food is difficult to find in Houston, so it is a testament to their passion and excellence that the restaurant has been so warmly embraced in suburbia. The menu includes such traditional dishes as empanadas, gently cooked octopus topped with aioli, *anticuchos* (grilled beef heart), various ceviches, *chupe de camarones* (traditional shrimp chowder) and grilled meats. Come for $5 tapas on Wednesday evenings.

PISTOLERO'S

1517 WESTHEIMER *at Ridgewood*
☎ (281) 974-3860 | MAP **E6** | ¶
PISTOLEROSHOUSTON.COM

THIS TEQUILA-AND-TACOS CONCEPT FROM BOONDOCKS/ROYAL OAK owner Shawn Bermudez and chef Brandon Schillings (he was a founder/owner of Pola Artisan Cheeses) is a makeover of Nabi, the short-lived Asian fusion spot, and opened in

RESTAURANTS

Prego

early 2013. The room has been opened up, and there is a liberal use of barn wood, dozens of Mexican-themed artifacts on the wall along with velvet paintings of Mexican heroes. A tiled bar has large glass dispensers of infused tequila dotting its length. Among our favorite dishes: a *sope* (like a very thick corn tortilla) with a fried egg on top of tender, juicy, spicy, smoky pork spiked with a rich, creamy poblano sauce, the oxtail taco topped with tomato jam and a portobello mushroom taco dressed with cauliflower puree.

PIZARO'S PIZZA NAPOLETANA

14028 MEMORIAL *at Kirkwood*
☎ (281) 589-7277 | MAP **B6** | 🍴
PIZAROSPIZZA.COM

PIZARO'S PIZZA OWNERS BILL AND
GLORIA HUTCHINSON DEFTLY

bring together authentic ingredients (e.g. "00" imported Italian flour) and a custom-made 900-degree wood-fired oven to produce excellent Neapolitan style pizza in West Houston. Bill learned the art of pizza in Italy and is a VPN-certified pizza master. The smartly edited menu offers seven traditional and five specialty pizzas. Pizaro's makes their dough and sauce in-house daily. Bonus: Pizaro's is BYOB with no corkage fee.

PIZZITOLA'S BAR-B-CUE

1703 SHEPHERD *just south of Katy Fwy. (I-10 West)*
☎ (713) 227-2283 | MAP **E6** | 🍴

WHILE THE NAME OF THIS REST-
AURANT SEEMS TO BE HAVING
a bit of an identity crisis, it all makes sense when you learn that Italian-American Jerome Pizzatola took over this 1934 barbecue restaurant and

has been continuing the original own-ers' "pit style" cooking ever since. Seasoned very lightly, the fall-off-the-bone pork ribs are some of the best in the city, and diners also love the moist and tender brisket, both of which are delicious without extra sauce. Finish the experience with Jerry's mother's banana pudding.

POLLO BRAVO

6015 HILLCROFT *at Southwest Fwy. (Hwy. 59)*
☎ (713) 541-0069 | MAP **D7** | 🍴
multiple locations
ELPOLLOBRAVO.COM

THERE ARE A COUPLE OF SPECIALTIES AT THIS PERUVIAN RESTAURANT, but one dish in particular keeps peo-ple coming back: rotisserie chicken with green tomatillo salsa. All of the dishes served here are hearty and comforting, but the chicken is juicy, flavorful and even better when doused in the green sauce. If want-ing to expand beyond the chicken, order the Gordo Combo that comes with a whole chicken, *salchipapa* (a hot dog and frozen French fry combo that's oddly good), avocado salad, sweet plantains, rice and pinto beans. You can have your chicken, eat it and try other dishes, too. It's the best of both worlds.

POLONIA

1900 BLALOCK *at Campbell*
☎ (713) 464-9900 | MAP **C5** | 🍴
POLONIARESTAURANT.COM

HOUSTON IS A MELTING POT OF ETHNICITIES, WHICH BECOMES evident as you cross off different ethnic cuisines from your list. It is not often you come across a Polish res-taurant in this part of the world, but we are lucky that the one we have is excellent. If it is your first visit, the sample platter is the way to go to get a wide taste of the culture's cuisine. It is piled high with all the Polish clas-sics: *pierogi* (a bit like ravioli), stuffed cabbage rolls, kielbasa, meatloaf, duck leg and *bigos* (a Polish hunter stew). The potato pancake served with a side of sour cream and chased with a tankard of Pilsner Urquell might just be the perfect meal.

PONDICHERI

2800 KIRBY *at Westheimer, in West Ave*
☎ (713) 522-2022 | MAP **E6** | 🍴
PONDICHERICAFE.COM

THERE IS NOTHING QUITE LIKE A CASUAL VERSION OF A DELICIOUS fine-dining restaurant. Chef Anita Jaisinghani opened the doors to her second restaurant, Pondicheri, in early 2011. It celebrates classic street foods of India with innovative touches, just like her flagship restau-rant Indika does. The lunch/dinner menu features dishes like unctuous beef shank and oxtail curry, but the real ingenuity is found in the break-fast menu with dishes like *roti* stuffed with scrambled masala eggs topped with green chutney. As a pastry chef in her earlier days, Jaisinghani's desserts are also something to check out. We recommend the Bournavita ice cream sandwiches and chile-spiked chocolate chip cookies.

POSCÓL VINOTECA E SALUMERIA

1609 WESTHEIMER *at Mandell*
☎ (713) 529-2797 | MAP **E6** | 🍴
POSCOLHOUSTON.COM

DROP IN FOR A GLASS OF WINE WITH FRIENDS AND PASS AROUND dozens of little dishes or come with your special someone for a bottle of wine and bowl of risotto. Whatever the reason for your visit, you will enjoy chef Marco Wiles' rendition of a typical wine bar you might stumble upon in the streets of Venice. The name hints at its strengths—wine and house-cured meats—but we also recommend the braised octopus with cannelloni beans and any of the risottos. There are no pizzas at this Italian spot, but there are flatbreads to satisfy your need for cheesy dough. As we go to press, word is that Wiles is relocating Poscól to a larger space.

PREGO

2520 AMHERST *east of Kirby*
☎ (713) 529-2420 | MAP **E7** | 🍴
PREGO-HOUSTON.COM

AFTER YOUR FIRST MEAL AT PREGO, YOU WILL LONG FOR THE STATUS as a regular at this neighborhood trattoria. In fact, most of the diners here *are* regulars and receive a warm "welcome back" from bartenders and servers as they walk through the narrow restaurant to their favorite table. We always start with chef John Watt's cornmeal-crusted oysters with pancetta and chive sauce and then order our very favorite lasagne, made with layers of house-made noodles, veal meatballs, mozzarella, tomato sauce and pesto. Another favorite is the *zucca risotto* with caramelized butternut squash, jumbo shrimp, house-made pancetta and scallions. This neighborhood favorite can be as dressy as you would like—casual Village shoppers stop in for lunch and groups make reservations for a formal celebration. Is your party looking for privacy? Walk through the kitchen and you'll find Houston's most hidden private room. Pastry chef Matthew Zoch, who has been with Prego for a year now, has made the dessert course at this restaurant practically mandatory.

PRONTO CUCININO

1401 MONTROSE *near W. Gray*
☎ (713) 528-8646 | MAP **E6** | 🍴
multiple locations
NINOS-VINCENTS.COM

VINCENT MANDOLA CREATED PRONTO FOR A CASUAL, COUNTER-service alternative to his three more upscale restaurants. The most popular dishes from Vincent's, Nino's and Grappino are on the menu, curb-side service is available and your children will always be welcomed. Just because it's fast-casual dining doesn't mean the flavor will be lost—the pastas are rich, the pizza squares are crisp and the brick-oven rotisserie spins out delicious, moist chickens. It seems Vincent Mandola has found his latest niche—serving food *pronto*.

PUNK'S SIMPLE SOUTHERN FOOD

5212 MORNINGSIDE *at Dunstan*
☎ (713) 524-7865 | MAP **E7** | 🍴

COMING SOON: CLARK COOPER CONCEPTS AND CHEF BRANDI Key are introducing a new concept that will "capture the spirit of the South" once open in early 2014. The menu will feature classic Southern dishes with sophisticated twists from chef Key, marrying "decades-old tradition with Southern swagger." Expect dishes like fried green tomato and crab salad, Southern fish and chips, pulled pork sliders, smothered pork chops and ice cold oysters served with a special "punk" sauce.

Grilled okra at Punk's Simple Southern Food

QUATTRO

1300 LAMAR _at San Jacinto, in
the Four Seasons Hotel_
☎ (713) 276-4700 | MAP **F6** | ¶↑¶
QUATTRORESTAURANTHOUSTON.COM

IF "AUTHENTIC" IS AN ADJECTIVE
YOU OFTEN EMPLOY WHEN DES-
cribing your favorite dining options,
Quattro takes it to heart. Located
inside the Four Seasons Hotel, this
Italian option is all about making
food that's true to its source and
hiring a young chef directly from
Italy. Maurizio Ferrarese is making
the food of his homeland in dishes
like the _cavatelli con anatra_ (pasta
topped with a slow-cooked duck
ragout with wild mushrooms), a veal
osso buco served with gorgonzola,
black truffle polenta and a variety of
seasonal dishes that change often.
Being a hotel restaurant, there are
also the given breakfast, lunch and
kids' menus, but dinner is where the
restaurant is able to let its hair down
and have a little more fun. Bright
blocks of color and beaded metal
curtains brighten things up to make
what has the possibility to become a
stodgy restaurant much more playful.

QUEEN VIC PUB
& KITCHEN

2712 RICHMOND _west of Kirby_
☎ (713) 533-0022 | MAP **E7** | ¶↑
THEQUEENVICPUB.COM

THE INDIAN-ENGLISH HYBRID
OF PUB FOOD SERVED HERE IS
stellar. Much like the dishes found in
London pubs, which integrated curries and Indian ingredients into their
food for reasons an anthropologist
would probably be happy to expand
upon, the menu is a mix of hearty
food like short rib _samosas_ (stuffed
and fried Indian-spiced pastries), a
Scotch egg doused in curry, mulliga-

tawny (the soup made famous in an
episode of _Seinfeld_) made with lentils
and coconut milk, shepherd's pie and
some tasty burgers. Cocktails are
somewhat of a specialty here, with
exotic Indian spices sometimes in the
mix, but a cold ale always goes nicely
with the curries. Wine is carefully
curated, which makes sense, as the
couple behind this place also owns
Oporto Wine Bar.

RA SUSHI

3908 WESTHEIMER
west of Weslayan
☎ (713) 621-5800 | MAP **D7** | ¶↑¶
multiple locations
RASUSHI.COM

SINGLES READY TO MINGLE
PONY UP TO THE GIANT BAR
in this Highland Village sushi hotspot.
(Things are slightly more subdued
at its CityCentre location.) With
blaring dance music, booze-y punch
drinks and sometimes even a little
sushi, fine young things flirt, gossip,
laugh and have a generally good
time. RA caters to an audience that
doesn't mind that the most popular
roll is named "Viva Las Vegas" and
combines crab, cream cheese, eel
sauce and a tempura crunch, but
sushi purists probably won't be
impressed. But that's how RA dif-
ferentiates itself: a young, pulsating
energy where nothing is taken too
seriously. That's not to say that
the food isn't good, because it is,
especially the cooked dishes like
tempura and stir-fries. But the real
reason most visit RA is for a good
time, and that's exactly what
you'll get.

RADICAL EATS

507 WESTHEIMER *near Taft*
☎ (713) 697-8719 | MAP **E6** | ❚
RADICALEATS.COM

RADICAL EATS, WHICH USED TO LAY CLAIM TO THE TITLE OF "Houston's Only Vegan Taqueria" underwent some radical changes in 2013. After moving from their first brick-and-mortar location on the North Side to a larger, swankier and more accessible Montrose address (formerly the site of Roots Bistro), owner Staci Davis also announced the menu would no longer contain exclusively vegan dishes. While the famous vegan tamales that started it all and other Mexican dishes remain, Davis is evolving to include sustainably raised meats to appeal to omnivores. Knowing Radical Eats' talent to transform only plant-based ingredients into appealing Mexican favorites, it can only get better from here.

RAGIN' CAJUN

4302 RICHMOND *west of Weslayan*
☎ (713) 623-6321 | MAP **D7** | ❚
multiple locations
RAGIN-CAJUN.COM

FOR A CITY SO CLOSE TO THE BORDER OF LOUISIANA TO HAVE so few selections of true Cajun food is practically a crime. Perhaps it's because not many have had the gall to compete with the Mandola family's Ragin' Cajun. Whether it's for Louisiana sports-watching (Geaux Tigers!) or just getting down and dirty with a flat of boiled crawfish in the spring, the restaurants always manage to seem packed. Crab gumbo, po'boys, muffalettas, hot boudin, crawfish pie and red beans and rice are at the ready to feed the hungry masses, who often cram in together at long tables, making friends along the way. But be warned, prices do reflect the fact that there isn't much competition between here and Louisiana. Adjacent to the Richmond location is the LA Bar, a great choice for an Abita beer and barbecued oysters.

RAINBOW LODGE

2011 ELLA *at T.C. Jester*
☎ (713) 861-8666 | MAP **E5** | ❚❚
RAINBOW-LODGE.COM

APPROPRIATELY TERMED A "LODGE," THIS RESTAURANT feels, tastes and looks like a vacation home in the Rocky Mountains. Set inside a 100-year-old log cabin in The Heights and overlooking White Oak Bayou (their patio is like a mini-upscale camping trip in itself), the cuisine focuses on wild game while the atmosphere lulls guests to relax and just enjoy. Venison, quail, lamb, wild boar, antelope and bison have all been spotted on the menu at one time or another and are prepared to respect the flavor of the meat, though delicately refined enough for this white-tablecloth environment. Duck gumbo makes a great starter, and the kitchen has a deft touch with its house-made charcuterie. Trust us: A martini seems to taste even better when served in the open fall air overlooking the lush back "yard" of the lodge.

RAVEN GRILL

1916 BISSONNET *at Hazard*
☎ (713) 521-2027 | MAP **E7** | ❚❚
THERAVENGRILL.COM

FOR WRITERS, IT'S ALWAYS EXCITING TO FIND AN EDGAR Allan Poe reference in unexpected places. For food lovers, it's always

RESTAURANTS

Grilled swordfish at Reef

exciting to find a comfortable spot for everyday dining in the West University area. Rob and Sara Cromie's Raven Grill is therefore exciting to both groups with a name that pays tribute to nearby Poe Elementary and food that is both expertly prepared over a green mesquite fire and great for any night of the week. Southwestern is a running theme with blue corn-crusted catfish, chipotle-honey glazed pork chops and several variations of enchiladas, with nightly specials to entice as well. Home-style food keeps regulars coming back, despite the dire parking situation, which can be a headache during peak hours. On mild days, ask to be seated on the patio.

RDG + BAR ANNIE
1800 POST OAK BLVD.
between Westheimer & San Felipe
☎ (713) 840-1111 | MAP **D6** | ⑪
RDGBARANNIE.COM

CALL IT THE NEXT GENERA-TION SCHILLER DEL GRANDE restaurant if you will, but the French-Southwestern food done with high-concept flair is still the centerpiece of RDG + Bar Annie. What replaced the iconic Cafe Annie in 2009 has become a place for glitz and glamour and Gulf crabmeat tostadas. It's the same Galleria location, give or take 100 yards, so of course there are certain standards to uphold. And the valet line out front is proof that chef Robert Del Grande still has "it." Upstairs RDG is the more formal option, serving Del Grande's classic black bean terrine as well as grilled fish, steaks, quail and pheasant. The balcony terrace is one of the city's most beautiful outdoor spaces, so ask for a table here for brunch (order the beignets!), a pre-theatre burger or a nightcap. Bar Annie is usually packed with a well-heeled crowd.

REEF

2600 TRAVIS *at McGowen*
☎ (713) 526-8282 | MAP **E6** | 🍴

REEFHOUSTON.COM

THERE'S A REASON CHEF BRYAN CASWELL HAS BECOME A nationally known culinary figure, and it's not just because of his boyish good looks. Reef is the restaurant that started Houston's current design trend for an open industrial look and a menu trend that brings together so many of the city's disparate cuisines. Caswell's version of Gulf Coast cuisine mixes with Vietnamese, Mexican, Southern and other global influences to make for some really tasty food. Dishes like the crispy skinned snapper with sweet and sour chard and tomato brown butter, redfish on the "half-shell" with fried mac 'n' cheese and a snapper carpaccio prove Caswell is not just another pretty face. Located on the east side of the building is Reef's 3rd Bar where a separate, drink-friendly menu offers sliders and shrimp shooters. The well-priced and well-curated wine list is another laudable feature of this contemporary Houston classic.

REGGAE HUT

4814 ALMEDA *at Wentworth*
☎ (713) 520-7171 | MAP **E7** | 🍴

REGGAEHUTCAFE.COM

A JAMAICAN SPOT WITH HUMBLE BUT ARTSY DIGS WITH MURALS by local artist Tierney Malone, Reggae Hut is just right. Not too big, not too small, the menu covers all the Caribbean favorites like patties stuffed with seasoned ground beef, pigeon peas, jerk chicken, oxtail stew and goat curry. With the aromas and flavors of allspice and thyme, the food has a lot of heart, which probably comes from owner Marcus Davis' commitment to food that soothes the soul as well as the appetite. (He also commands the impressive Breakfast Klub ship known for its Southern soul food.) Service is friendly and guests order at the counter, many for take-out orders. Try the homemade ginger beer while you're here.

REGINELLI'S PIZZERIA

12389 KINGSRIDE LANE *just west of Gessner*
☎ (713) 468-2727 | MAP **C6** | 🍴

REGINELLIS.COM

IF YOU LIKE YOUR PIZZA CRUSTS STURDY ENOUGH TO HOLD UP under the thickest of toppings, try Reginelli's. The New Orleans-founded pizzeria had 17 years to perfect their hand-tossed method before moving into Houston in February 2013. (They partnered with Alex Brennan-Martin of Brennan's for the expansion.) Their signature thicker-crusted pies are served alongside the pastas, salads, sandwiches and calzones that made them so popular in their home state of Louisiana. Cool, modern interiors, a very affordable wine list and no-corkage-fee BYOB policy make it the place for casual Italian any night of the week.

RESTAURANTS

THE REMINGTON

1919 BRIAR OAKS LN. *north of San Felipe, in the St. Regis Hotel*
☎ (713) 403-2631 | MAP **D6** | ᵇ¹ᵏ
STREGISHOUSTONHOTEL.COM

WHEN MONEY IS NO OBJECT AND IT'S TIME TO GLAM IT up, The Remington should be on your short list for reservations. Ideal for special-occasion dining, this posh restaurant inside the St. Regis Hotel spares no expense (nor will you) when it comes to, well, everything. The dining room itself is quite lively with red walls, immaculately dressed tables—fresh flowers are a nice touch—and plenty of natural light during the day as well as an intimate patio for dining al fresco. New American cuisine from chef John Signorelli is elegant and refined with many Texas influences, though ingredients are sourced from all corners of the United States. Lobster bisque is a favorite with guests, but many of the dishes change with the seasons. One of our favorite features here is the elegantly presented afternoon tea served with scones, finger sandwiches and tea or, if you prefer, Champagne.

RESIE'S CHICKEN & WAFFLES

233 W. GREENS RD. *west of the North Fwy. (I-45 North)*
☎ (281) 248-4392 | MAP **E2** | ᵇᵏ
RESIESCHICKENANDWAFFLES.NET

FANS OF THAT UTTERLY SOUTHERN COMBINATION OF FRIED chicken wings and fluffy waffles regularly trek to this happy spot. "Smothered" chicken (fried wings covered in a brown gravy), burgers, fried fish and grilled chicken are other options with sides like hot water cornbread, collard greens, candied yams and macaroni and cheese. If you find yourself here on a Friday, don't pass up the daily gumbo special full of shrimp, okra and sausage.

RESTAURANT CINQ

3410 MONTROSE *south of Westheimer, in La Colombe d'Or Hotel*
☎ (713) 524-7999 | MAP **E6** | ᵇ¹ᵏ
LACOLOMBEDOR.COM

THE CLASSICALLY BEAUTIFUL DINING ROOM AT RESTAURANT Cinq (inside the boutique La Colombe d'Or Hotel with a mere five rooms) has played host to many an anniversary and business celebration. Its romantic charms include plenty of nooks for intimate dinners, stately gilded accents, chandeliers and service that befits its high-end appointments. Cinq's menu also contains the refined classics like rack of lamb and filet mignon, but it has recently undergone a transformation to include more modern dishes as well. Chamomile-poached veal sweetbreads, braised goat from local purveyor Black Hill Farms and seared scallops with sea urchin butter, kimchi vinegar and shishito peppers liven up what used to be a fairly stodgy selection. Interestingly, Cinq's current executive chef German Mosquera is a vegan—he obviously has no problems playing around with meat.

RIOJA

11920 WESTHEIMER *at S. Kirkwood*
☎ (281) 531-5569 | MAP **B7** | ᵇ¹ᵏ
RIOJARESTAURANT.COM

THE PAELLA AT RIOJA IS FAMOUSLY CHOCK FULL OF ALL THE GOOD stuff: Squid, mussels, chicken and chunks of house-made chorizo nestled in a bed of short-grain Valencia rice, the whole steamed in a bath of saffron-tinged broth and rife with the flavors of Spain. The house boasts a large selection of Spanish wines, which includes options that won't break the bank. Also wine-friendly are the cold and hot tapas selections, ranging from seared Portuguese sardines to piquillo peppers stuffed with codfish to fried black Spanish sausages. The rustic interior is pleasant for date night, topped off with the sounds of live music Thursday through Saturday.

RISTORANTE CAVOUR

1080 UPTOWN PARK *north of San Felipe, in Hotel Granduca*
☎ (713) 418-1104 | MAP **D6** | 🍴
GRANDUCAHOUSTON.COM

INSIDE GALLERIA-AREA BOUTIQUE HOTEL GRANDUCA, EVERYTHING about this gorgeous jewel box of a restaurant invites ooh-ing and ahh-ing. Soft lighting, sage green walls and luxuriously upholstered chairs set a regal scene where service is stately and the menu is Northern Italian. Baked monkfish tail and breaded branzino are among the seafood selections while house-made pastas like the pumpkin and chestnut gnocchi are not to be missed. Brunch follows a more American trend with eggs Benedict but Italian touches like the mascarpone-topped waffles bring it all back around.

ROOST

1972 FAIRVIEW *at Hazard*
☎ (713) 523-7667 | MAP **E6** | 🍴
ILOVEROOST.COM

OWNER/CHEF KEVIN NADERI (PREVIOUSLY AT HAVEN) IS doing great things inside a humble neighborhood space that is as small

as it is charming. The limited seating seems to only increase demand, and Naderi's grounded, farm-to-table cuisine is worth the wait. A starter of cauliflower dressed with a creamy miso sauce and garnished with roasted pine nuts, scallions and shaved *bonito* (smoked dried tuna) has become an iconic Houston dish in a short time, and mains like the flatiron steak with a pecan *romesco* sauce, roasted mushrooms and chimichurri are equally pleasing to the palate. It's home-style food with surprising flavors, and there's nothing quite like it anywhere else in town. Dinner only.

RUDI LECHNER'S

2503 S. GESSNER *north of Westheimer*
☎ (713) 782-118 | MAP **D6** | 🍴
RUDILECHNERS.COM

GERMAN CUISINE ISN'T KNOWN FOR BEING REFINED, BUT THAT'S exactly why it's so beloved. Such is the case at Rudi Lechner's, which attracts sausage-lovers from all over the region to its West Side location replete with German charm and vigor. Oompah bands are often found, as are the polka dancers enjoying them, working off heavy meals of golden-fried *wienerschnitzel*, sauerkraut and Austrian potatoes or goulash. There are those ubiquitous sausages, *sauerbraten* (a sweet and sour beef pot roast) and garlic-and-caraway roasted pork loin as well. To experience it all, come on a Wednesday evening for the weekly Oktoberfest buffet. Top it off with a *bier* served in a glass boot, and you've got a full-blown party.

RESTAURANTS

RUGGLES GREEN

2311 W. ALABAMA *east of Kirby*
☎ (713) 533-0777 | MAP **E7** | 🍴
multiple locations
RUGGLESGREEN.COM

HIPPIE FOOD ISN'T JUST FOR HIPPIES ANYMORE. LABELED as "green"—meaning eco-friendly—and full of options free of gluten, meat and dairy, Ruggles Green thrives on the theory that healthful, sustainable food can actually taste good. And all walks of life who visit the small chain of Houston restaurants tend to agree. Grub like quinoa mac 'n' cheese, smoked chicken pizza and grilled egg and cheese sandwich are constructed with a variety of organic, preservative-free and hormone-free ingredients, and the "hempanadas" (made with the very-much-legal hemp flour) stuffed with beef and raisins contain lots of protein but definitely no GMOs. Counter-service makes for easy-breezy ordering, and the Green Restaurant Association certifications make for a clear conscience.

SAIGON PAGOLAC

9600 BELLAIRE BLVD.
at Corporate
☎ (713) 988-6106 | MAP **C7** | 🍴

AT SAIGON PAGOLAC, THERE ARE THE VARIOUS NOODLE dishes—some topped with thinly sliced charcoal-grilled pork, others with meatballs, etc.—and there are steaming bowls of pho, that fragrant Vietnamese soup that acts as a cure for every ill. But the real magnet drawing guests from all over town is their famous "Seven Courses of Beef" menu. It's available a la carte, but to really experience the extravagance, order all seven. The feast starts with thinly sliced pieces of beef poached in a boiling bath of vinegar-based broth done right on the table and continues with various meatball, sausage, grilled and soup variations. And while you're experimenting with extravagance, you might as well try the whole grilled fish, which takes a little time, but comes out spectacularly topped with peanuts, crispy pork skin and scallions.

SALDIVIA'S SOUTH AMERICAN GRILL

10234 WESTHEIMER *east of W. Sam Houston Parkway S. (Beltway 8)*
☎ (713) 782-9494 | MAP **B7** | 🍴
SALDIVIAS.COM

FAMILY-RUN SALDIVIA'S IS AN UN-STUFFY STEAKHOUSE THAT offers a South American twist on a meat-heavy meal. Jars of chimichurri sauce (an Argentine-Uruguayan condiment made from parsley, garlic, olive oil and vinegar) adorn every table, tempting you to spoon it on anything and everything on the menu. Try the house specialty, *entraña*, a Uruguayan skirt steak served with Spanish rice and more chimichurri. If you're willing to share, the *parrillada completa*, or mixed grill, comes with enough meat to feed three or four people. Appetizers of empanadas and grilled sweetbreads are interesting and accompany a bottle of well-priced South American wine very nicely.

SALÉ-SUCRÉ

2916 WHITE OAK *west of Studewood*
☎ (713) 623-1406 | MAP **E6** | 🍴
SALESUCRE-TX.COM

THE HOUSTON TRADITION OF ADORABLE FRENCH BISTROS continues, this time with one in the very happening Heights area along White Oak. The name, which means "savory-sweet," hints at its selection of crêpes, soups, salads and desserts, which are equally satisfying to ladies who lunch or a special date night with the significant other. Locally sourced ingredients are utilized in their dishes when possible, which could range from a trio of pâtés to a fresh tomato soup to hand-cut steak tartar and steak frites. The menu is nicely compact without sacrificing options, the wine list is exclusively French, and there's a full bar to complement those sweet and savory crêpes everyone loves to order here.

SAMMY'S WILD GAME GRILL

3715 WASHINGTON *at Yale*
☎ (713) 868-1345 | MAP **E6** | ¶
SAMMYSWILDGAMEGRILL.COM

THERE ARE HAMBURGER/HOT DOG JOINTS AND THEN THERE'S Sammy's Wild Game Grill. Taking the all-beef patty lovers for a spin, Sammy's uses buffalo, antelope, yak, venison, pheasant, wild boar, kangaroo, llama, lamb, elk and ostrich in various dishes like sausage dogs, burgers and even salads. There *is* Angus beef, grilled chicken and portobellos for those not feeling so adventurous, but where's the fun in that? Conveniently, there's also a drive-thru option, so you can try your first bite of a camel meat sausage (you never know what the chef will want to experiment with in any given week) in the privacy of your own home.

SANDONG NOODLE HOUSE

9938 BELLAIRE BLVD. *at W. Sam Houston Parkway S. (Beltway 8)*
☎ (713) 988-8802 | MAP **B7** | ¶

WITH HANDMADE NOODLES AND TAIWANESE PREP-arations of said noodles, Sandong is one of the most authentic places to slurp a bowl of soup. Though it moved a couple years ago to a larger space to accommodate its growing clientele, Sandong has still managed to maintain the grungy Chinatown look. Those in the know never pass up the pan-seared dumplings with their crispy brown bottoms and juicy fillings made better by build-your-own dipping sauce using the hot chili oil, vinegar and soy sauce placed on each table. The beef noodle soup is also a winner, garnished with pickled mustard greens and the best cure for the common cold. The cashier tends to be a little on the surly side, but keep a smile on your face and remember how delicious those dumplings were.

SEASONS 52

4410 WESTHEIMER *between Mid Lane & Loop 610*
☎ (713) 621-5452 | MAP **D6** | ¶¶
SEASONS52.COM

COMBINING UPSCALE DINING WITH SEASONAL INGREDIENTS and a guarantee that no dish will come in over 475 calories (which sounds like a lot but really isn't comparatively), this Florida-based chain is almost guilt-free. Luckily, there is an extensive wine list that includes 60 choices by the glass, just in case you feel like misbehaving ever so slightly. The flatbreads here are especially appealing with toppings like cremini mushrooms, grilled steak,

RESTAURANTS

blue cheese, spinach and caramelized onions and can be combined with a flight of wines at a bargain price during their Flights & Flatbreads happy hour. Grilled lamb, pork, chicken and fish round out the entrees while the dessert menu consists of twee little shot glasses packed with tiny renditions of Key lime pie, carrot cake and the like.

SHABU HOUSE

9889 BELLAIRE BLVD. *at W. Sam Houston Parkway S. (Beltway 8)*
☎ (713) 995-5428 | MAP **B7** | 🍴
SHABUSHABUHOUSTON.COM

IF COOKING YOUR OWN SOUP SOUNDS LIKE A GOOD IDEA (though clean-up is thankfully the restaurant's responsibility), Shabu House should be on your to-do list. Shabu shabu—the style of cuisine here—translates to "swish swish" in Japanese, presumably from the motion you'll be making with your chopsticks to stir up the boiling broth occasionally. Choose from one of three soup bases—traditional Japanese dashi, a spicy version or a tomato broth—and then onto the meats and vegetables. Seafood isn't always the freshest, but the well-marbled beef tastes marvelous in a pot with taro, Napa cabbage, tofu and mushrooms. Each person in the closet-sized restaurant gets their own hot pot to tend, so swish-swish as much as you'd like.

SHADE

250 WEST 19TH *near Yale*
☎ (713) 863-7500 | MAP **E5** | 🍴
SHADEHEIGHTS.COM

IT'S EASY TO BECOME A REGULAR AT SHADE. LOCATED IN ONE OF THE most picturesque and walkable areas

of Houston with a happy hour that's practically highway robbery, the menu of upmarket globally-inspired dishes begs for repeat visits. Chef/owner Claire Smith has made plenty of fans with her highly curated menus, and dishes like fried shrimp and bacon-cheese grits doused with just enough Frank's RedHot sauce get just as much attention as the filet mignon. The open dining room rides the line between cozy and modern and hosts many a date night or business lunch with a weekly brunch for good measure. Coming back to the happy hour: The cornmeal-crusted oysters with jalapeño ranch and mixed greens goes nicely with a $7 martini.

SHAWARMA KING

3121 HILLCROFT *at Richmond*
☎ (713) 784-8882 | MAP **C7** | 🍴
SHAWARMAKINGONLINE.COM

IT'S DIFFICULT TO LIVE UP TO A ROYAL STATUS, BUT IN THE WORLD of Mediterranean delis, Shawarma King is mighty. The modest Hillcroft restaurant doesn't flaunt its charm in the setting but instead saves it all for the food. The shawarma is well seasoned and stays moist inside its fresh pita. All the normal accompaniments of shredded lettuce, tomato, pickles and tahini complement the slow-roasted meat. The falafel here is also praise-worthy, being freshly fried and very crisp. Middle Eastern sides like hummus, babaganoush, tabouli, stuffed grape leaves and spinach pies are also available to round out a meal. Lunch hour can be a bit hectic, but the friendly faces behind the counter make the experience much more tolerable.

SHEPHERD PARK DRAUGHT HOUSE

3402 N. SHEPHERD *at 34th*
☎ (832) 767-1380 | MAP **E5** | 🍴
SHEPHERDPARKTX.COM

IT'S A TINY GARDEN OAKS SPACE, THOUGH ALL OF IT IS UTILIZED well. The rock-n-roll theme, complete with a goth-looking lounge area up front with a couch that could easily be found in the dungeon of a dominatrix, is something unexpected for this neighborhood pub but works nonetheless. The draw is the selection of craft beers on tap (fill your growler here), but the food isn't too shabby either. The parent company of Shepherd Park is behind Lola's in The Heights, Witchcraft Tavern and the pizza chain Pink's (there's one right next door in fact), so they've had plenty of experience creating broadly-liked menus. Here, the burgers never disappoint, with juicy, thick patties cooked to medium, and entrees like the jerk chicken, Shepherd Park pie (their riff on a shepherd's pie) and Korean short rib tacos seem to be reliable, too. The common denominator is every dish's ability to pair nicely with a cold pint.

SHIVA INDIAN RESTAURANT

2514 TIMES *east of Kirby*
☎ (713) 523-4753 | MAP **E7** | 🍴
multiple locations
SHIVARESTAURANT.COM

THE DINING ROOM FEELS A LITTLE ON THE FANCY SIDE— perhaps because it's nothing like the bare-bones decor often found in similar Hillcroft establishments—but don't be fooled. This is a casual, welcoming restaurant. Serving Rice Village patrons comforting Indian food classics like *saag paneer* (stewed

mixed greens with cheese) and hot *naan* (flatbread) since 1990, this restaurant knows what their customers want. Curries galore, tandoori-grilled items, clay pot-cooked meats, chicken, lamb, shrimp, fish and a vegetable section that reads like a novel gives plenty to choose from. Lunch is an inexpensive buffet, ideal for newbies to Indian cuisine ready to explore, and the newer Sugar Land location is a bit more polished than the original.

SICHUAN KING

9114 BELLAIRE BLVD. *east of Ranchester*
☎ (713) 771-6868 | MAP **C7** | 🍴

GATHER YOUR INTESTINAL FORTITUDE AND A SENSE OF adventure before heading to Sichuan King (aka Sichuan Cuisine). Spicy, tongue-numbing, fire-breathing cuisine has been perfected here, and chili heads are all about it. *Ma po* tofu with spicy minced meat, crispy chicken with three chilies and incendiary lamb and celery stir-fry are nothing short of invigorating, if not somewhat of a discomfort several hours down the road. The smoked tea duck also gets raves for its spicy, juicy and smoky flavor combinations. The interior is fairly bland and typical Chinese dining hall-esque, but the food is quite the opposite.

SINH SINH

9788 BELLAIRE BLVD. *east of W. Sam Houston Parkway S. (Beltway 8)*
☎ (713) 541-0888 | MAP **B7** | 🍴

IT'S A SIT-DOWN RESTAURANT WITH CHINESE BARBECUE, AND each side of Sinh Sinh has its benefits. Hanging lewdly behind the glass are whole ducks with glistening lacquered skin and barbecued pork with a skin that is so crispy, it seems defiant of the laws of physics. The barbecue can be eaten at the table, but it is mostly ordered by the pound for take-out. Whole pigs and ducks can be pre-ordered for special occasions and make for a dramatic buffet for at-home parties. As far as the dining-in aspect, service is a common complaint. But if you can overlook the sometimes-inattentive servers, ordering a plate of seafood can be a fun adventure. Tanks of living fish, lobsters, crabs and other sea creatures provide the ingredients, so you know it's of optimum freshness. Sinh Sinh is also known for late-night dining with a kitchen that doesn't close until 2 am (and sometimes even later).

SMITH & WOLLENSKY

4007 WESTHEIMER *at Drexel*
☎ (713) 621-7555 | MAP **D7** | 🍴
SMITHANDWOLLENSKY.COM

WHEN AN ICONIC AMERICAN STEAKHOUSE COMES TO mind, Smith & Wollensky is one of the top contenders for the title. With branches throughout the United States—including this one in Houston's posh Highland Village shopping mecca—the restaurant group has developed a loyal following. Luxury is at the forefront with truffled mac 'n' cheese and a surf and turf that requires two servers to push a silver cart and meticulously shell a giant lobster (that was flown in earlier that day) tableside. You'll pay for the pleasure, but what a pampering it is. The wedge salad, shellfish tower and Cajun-marinated ribeye that's as large as it is flavorful are also popular here. The wine list with around 600 selections is predominantly from American producers (sorry, France) for a slightly different approach, and

any one of them is a treat to sip on the large balcony as the sun sets over Houston.

SNAP KITCHEN

3600 KIRBY *at Richmond*
☎ (713) 526-5700 | MAP **E7** | 🍴
multiple locations
SNAPKITCHEN.COM

AN IMPORT FROM AUSTIN THAT TAKES AIM AT THE HEALTH NUTS among us, this is a chef-driven take-away spot that emphasizes flavor as much as nutrition. There are hummus-filled deviled eggs, bison hash, Asian chicken salad, quinoa "fried rice" and curry-dusted cauliflower "steak." Serving breakfast, lunch and dinner, Snap Kitchen also tosses salads to-order and has a three-week diet regimen for the seriously committed. A blueberry crumble made with steel-cut oats, almonds, berries and agave nectar with a creamy marshmallow topping was our dessert of choice.

SOMA SUSHI

4820 WASHINGTON *between Shepherd & Durham*
☎ (713) 861-2726 | MAP **E6** | 🍴
SOMASUSHI.COM

SOMA IS THE YOUNGER SIBLING TO ITS SISTER ESTABLISHMENTS Azuma Sushi and Kata Robata. As such, it is still partying in college while the older siblings have since graduated to the status of young professionals. The scene here is set with black and red interiors and high-decibel noise levels as well as a prime location along Houston's youthful Washington Avenue. The food, however, is refined and creative with top-notch sushi, including daily "exotic" selections, a chef's tasting menu and some of the best ramen and Japanese soups in town. (Just because she parties doesn't mean she can't make straight A's.) It's a mixture of fun and serious that hits the mark and continues to evolve over time.

SORREL URBAN BISTRO

2202 W. ALABAMA *at Greenbriar*
☎ (713) 677-0391 | MAP **E6** | ⑪
SORRELHOUSTON.COM

BILLED AS "FARM-TO-TABLE" AND "ORGANICALLY FOCUSED," Sorrel thanks all their local purveyors on each printed menu. Names you might recognize include Gundermann Acres and Atkinson Farms and a whole host of others. These ingredients go into seasonal cocktails as well as the rotating menu items, which change daily according to what's available. In addition to higher-end preparation of farmers' market goodies, there is a separate charcuterie menu, which goes well with their selection of wines (some on tap). Brunch and Sunday dinners are also thrown in the mix. Interestingly, there are closed-circuit television cameras in the kitchen, and the live feed is displayed on monitors in the dining room for a sneak peek. Whether you find it creepy or fascinating is another story entirely.

SORRENTO

415 WESTHEIMER *between Taft & Montrose*
☎ (713) 527-0609 | MAP **E6** |
SORRENTOHOUSTON.COM

THE SMALL PLEASURES OF A WELL-APPOINTED TABLE AND GOOD service can turn a whole week around. And, for a price, so can a good Italian meal. Abbas Hussein's Sorrento offers just the indulgence for such occasions with dark woods, hand-painted murals and neo-Italian cuisine. Lobster bisque is stellar, salads are well-dressed and the tasting menu of osso buco ravioli, burrata and heirloom tomato salad, pan-seared onaga and orange confit preserve panna cotta is decadent in the best way. Mature crowds tend to fill the tables here, which means a civilized time should be had by all.

SPANISH FLOWERS

4701 N. MAIN *at Airline*
☎ (713) 869-1706 | MAP **E5** | ⑪
SPANISH-FLOWERS.COM

SPANISH FLOWERS IS A 24-HOURS-OF-TEX-MEX LEGEND IN HOUSTON. You can stop by any time of the day or night for a fix of enchiladas, tostadas de *carnitas* or *mole* poblano. If it's covered in cheese, chances are, it's going to be delicious. Tortillas are fresh and hot, and lunch specials are cheap, though admittedly, a bowl of chile con queso never tastes as good before midnight (and before a few margaritas). Breakfast comes in both Mexican and American varieties, allowing those with poor decision skills to indulge in both mango pancakes and breakfast enchiladas in one sitting.

SPANISH VILLAGE

4720 ALMEDA *at Blodgett*
☎ (713) 523-2861 | MAP **E7** | ⑪
SPANISHVILLAGERESTAURANT.COM

A LITTLE BIT FUNKY, A LITTLE BIT FUN, A LOT OF CHRISTMAS LIGHTS and some of the best margaritas (made with real lime juice) around—these are just a few ways that fans describe Spanish Village. Call it vintage Tex-Mex or call it kitschy, but don't call it bland. While those margaritas are tasty, there's no bar to speak of, and you can only have

RESTAURANTS

Chef Monica Pope of Sparrow Bar + Cookshop

one if you also order food, which isn't such a bad policy. The *chile relleno*, pork *carnitas* or special enchiladas do it up right and—surprise!—the Southern fried chicken is also a hit. This sentimental favorite is a place where Houstonians have been going since birth, and it will certainly remain as such as long as the already well-worn building (is it leaning or does it just look that way?) can handle the crowds.

SPARROW BAR + COOKSHOP

3701 TRAVIS *just north of Alabama*
☎ (713) 524-6922 | MAP **E6** | 🍴
SPARROWHOUSTON.COM

WHEN "NORMAL" PEOPLE NEED A CHANGE, THEY MIGHT CUT their hair, repaint the living room or even buy a new car. When chefs—at least Monica Pope—need something different, they change the concept of their restaurant. Despite her success under the T'afia name, Pope launched a new restaurant in the same space in 2012 and hence we have Sparrow. Pope's focus on local and sustainable still comes in as a priority, but the dishes and some of the dining room have been modified to spruce things up a bit. Seasonal menus run wild with global influences: crispy duck leg confit with Thai-style mushroom ragout, coffee-rubbed veal sweetbreads with grits and pickled mustard seeds and okra, duo of goat and lamb ribs rubbed with guajillo chile and served with a mustard sauce. It's an exciting menu, though there have been complaints that portion size can be unpredictable with certain dishes. A definite positive result of the overhaul is a ramped-up cocktail program.

STAR PIZZA

2111 NORFOLK *at S. Shepherd*
☎ (713) 523-0800 | MAP **E7** | 🍴
multiple locations
STARPIZZA.COM

PIZZA STIRS UP PASSIONS IN PEOPLE WHO ARE AS RIOTOUS and extreme as those who incite revolutions. Luckily for Star Pizza, it's almost universally beloved by Houston. Known for deep-dish, Chicago-style pizza with toppings (or are they fillings in this case?) of whole garlic cloves and spinach in the Joe's or the meaty goodness of ground beef, Italian sausage, pepperoni, mushrooms, onions, and green peppers in the Starburst, offered on either a whole wheat or regular crust. Thin-crust and individual focaccia pizzas are also available for the anti-Chicago crowd. With such a laid-back atmosphere and locations that feel almost like second homes, it's surprising that anyone would choose take-out or delivery, but both are readily available if you must catch the season finale of *The Walking Dead* and don't have time to cook.

STRAITS

800 W. SAM HOUSTON PKWY. N. (BELTWAY 8) *in CityCentre*
☎ (713) 365-9922 | MAP **B6** | 🍴
STRAITSRESTAURANTS.COM

THE FORMULA AT STRAITS (AN UPSCALE CHAIN) TAKES Singaporean food, puts it into a format that feels comfortable to those who've never had it and then kicks up the glitz with a dark and sleek interior design. Right at home in the CityCentre development, known for upscale shopping and dining, Straits is more than just another pretty face. With many dishes meant to be shared family-style, sticky tamarind beef and

RESTAURANTS

crabs doused in chili sauce impress both visually and with their bold flavors. There's also an array of beef, wok-fired seafood and poultry items as well as a raw bar and small plates like Indonesian corn croquettes, satay skewers, *roti prata* (griddled flatbread with curry dipping sauce) and the kitchen's signature chicken lollipops. The patio is a hip spot to share a few small plates, sip mojitos and people watch.

SULLIVAN'S STEAKHOUSE
4608 WESTHEIMER *west of Mid Lane*
☎ (713) 961-0333 | MAP **D6** | 🍴
SULLIVANSSTEAKHOUSE.COM

THIS CLASSIC STEAKHOUSE AND PIANO BAR, WHICH IS owned by Del Frisco's Restaurant Group, has a lower profile than its flashy Galleria sibling. It's more of a neighborhood steakhouse where diners stop in for the $49 prix-fixe offering called The Sure Thing. Dining at the bar is popular with the regulars who contentedly order hand-shaken martinis, a wedge salad, oysters on the half-shell and bone-in ribeye with all the sides.

SUSHI JIN
14670 MEMORIAL *west of N. Dairy Ashford*
☎ (281) 493-2932 | MAP **A6** | 🍴

QUIETLY TRADITIONAL AND MERCIFULLY OVERLOOKED BY the hordes of 20-somethings who prefer outsized rolls slathered with cream cheese and sprinkled with tempura "crunch," Sushi Jin's secret is its über-fresh seafood, with some fish only hours out of the water and flown in as often as possible. The reason: Owner Bill Nakanishi used to own a seafood import company, and his customers still expect the freshest possible. The best way to experience what Sushi Jin has to offer is to put yourself in the care of the sushi chefs. They'll take what's freshest and create a masterpiece of Canadian salmon or caramelized scallops or whatever's in-season that moment. Just a hint at its authenticity are the groups of Japanese businessmen closing deals, though there are a wide range of local patrons at this West-Side gem, too.

SUSHI MIYAGI
10600 BELLAIRE BLVD.
between Rogerdale & Wilcrest
☎ (281) 933-9112 | MAP **B7** | 🍴

NONDESCRIPT MIGHT BE THE BEST WAY TO DESCRIBE SUSHI Miyagi's curbside appeal. With a simple "Sushi" sign on the outside of this strip-mall tenant in Chinatown, tiny family-run Sushi Miyagi proclaims its specialty to the world. If you don't get here before the weekend dinner rush, chances are you may not be able to eat here. (Disappointing as that may be, there's always the consolation of Golden Dim Sum next door.) If you do get a coveted seat, get started with the *agedashi* tofu, which is deep fried and served in a savory broth with dancing *bonito* (smoked tuna) flakes on top and then move on to the sushi. Created painstakingly by Mr. Miyagi himself, it's fresh and authentic and served lovingly by the staff and sometimes even Mrs. Miyagi, whose artwork adorns the walls here. There are fancy, Westernized rolls here, but the true experience lies in the traditional sushi and sashimi.

SWEET PARIS CRÊPERIE & CAFE

2420 RICE BLVD. *between Morningside & Kelvin*
☎ (713) 360-6266 | MAP **E7** | ❢
SWEETPARIS.COM

IT'S AS IF THE ONLY THING MISS-ING FROM RICE VILLAGE WAS AN adorable little crêperie until Sweet Paris arrived. With a menu developed alongside actual French chefs, the crêpes here are made with a light and fluffy batter and filled with savory and sweet ingredients that can be as simple as Nutella or as playful as you'd like. (Keeping in mind those with a different set of dietary concerns, the kitchen can also whip up an egg- and dairy-free batter.) Sweet Paris also offers panini, cheese plates and shaved-ice desserts as well as coffee, hot chocolate, beer, wine, sangria and wine-based cocktails. The fast-casual concept means efficient service, and WiFi means lingering is welcome.

SYLVIA'S ENCHILADA KITCHEN

12637 WESTHEIMER *near Dairy Ashford*
☎ (281) 679-8300 | MAP **A7** | ❢❢
multiple locations
SYLVIASENCHILADAKITCHEN.COM

IF ENCHILADAS IS IN THE NAME OF YOUR RESTAURANT, THEY better be good. No need to worry because Sylvia's has proven itself as the go-to for this comforting Tex-Mex dish for years. There are nearly 20 varieties that range from the not-often-seen-in-Houston stacked El Paso-style enchiladas doused in chili gravy to the rich, earthy chicken *mole*. The restaurant's enchiladas aren't the only beloved thing about Sylvia's. Owner Sylvia Casares is a community figure herself who experienced just how much Houstonians had come to love her after receiving letters, calls and expressions of support after she suffered a gunshot wound in 2012. Fully recovered and back in the restaurants, Casares is proof that feeding people good food is a labor of love. She used her downtime recovering to work on a cookbook.

TACOS À GO-GO

3704 MAIN *just north of Alabama*
☎ (713) 807-8226 | MAP **E6** | ❢
multiple locations
TACOSAGOGO.COM

IT'S TACOS WITH A SIDE OF PERSON-ALITY AT TACOS À GO-GO. THE quirky set-up with a rockabilly, Mexican, retro feel is just kitschy enough. As for the food, it's just what you'd expect at a rocking taco joint: *picadillo* (flavorful ground beef), veggie, spicy pork, shredded chicken, beef fajita, lamb barbacoa and more all served in whole wheat, flour, corn or crispy tortillas. The salsa bar is a fun experiment to see how far your taste buds can go down the scale of spice, and the sangria helps cool things down. An added bonus here—though some might say the main event— are breakfast tacos that are served all day.

TAN TAN

6816 RANCHESTER
at Bellaire Blvd.
☎ (713) 771-1268 | MAP **C7** | ❢
multiple locations
TANTANRESTAURANT.COM

THERE ARE TWO REASONS TO VISIT TAN TAN. THE FIRST IS FOR FAST, hearty and inexpensive Asian comfort food. The second is for late night/ early morning dining after an evening of partying, as the place stays open

RESTAURANTS

until 3 am. The two sometimes merge together, but both crowds come for a taste of their popular *banh bot chien* (fried rice cake), noodle soups and hot pots. With servicing large crowds down to a science, servers in uniform use headsets for efficiency, and the dining area holds enough people to keep wait times down. Their second location on Westheimer is just as tasty but lacks that certain China-town charm so prevalent at the original.

TANGO & MALBEC

2800 SAGE *at W. Alabama*
☎ (713) 629-8646 | MAP **D7** | 🍴

TANGOMALBEC.COM

LOCATED IN THE SHADOW OF THE GALLERIA, TANGO & MALBEC features a wide-ranging menu that has its roots in Argentina and Uruguay—which means plenty of beef with South American accents. The kitchen is so serious about its cuisine, the owners built a special grill that uses hot coals instead of an open fire, which is more authentic to the Argentinian way of cooking. Recommended dishes include any of their *parrilla* (grilled) options, slow-poached veal tongue that is sliced thinly and served with a cool vinai-grette, crispy sweetbreads served on a sizzling platter and Peruvian-style ceviche. Those familiar with Argentinian culture will also see the Italian influence with house-made pastas, *Milanesa*-style dishes (thin cuts breaded, fried and topped with tomato sauce and mozzarella) on the menu as well as a Caprese-style salad. Tango dancers perform on Saturday night.

TASTE OF TEXAS

10505 KATY FWY. (I-10 WEST)
between Gessner & Beltway 8
☎ (713) 932-6901 | MAP **B6** | 🍴

TASTEOFTEXAS.COM

TASTE OF TEXAS IS ALMOST AS BIG AS TEXAS. THE FAMILY-RUN, sprawling giant of a steakhouse has grown mighty big since its founding in 1977. Perhaps the key to such exponential growth is its comfortable setting (think Hill Country ranch house) and upscale food. With steaks that aren't for the faint of heart (a 32-oz porterhouse, 38-oz tomahawk ribeye and 24-oz bone-in ribeye all grace the menu) that also come with all the trimmings, they're catering to the big boys and girls who aren't afraid of a big slab of red meat. However, that doesn't mean it isn't family friendly (it is) or not accessible to non-red-meat-eaters (it is that, too). Other dishes include pecan-crusted chicken breast stuffed with goat cheese, a grilled-veggie plate and a salad bar. It's especially fun to take out-of-town guests for a look at the restaurant's onsite museum with as much Texas memorabilia as you can handle.

TEALA'S

3210 W. DALLAS *west of Waugh*
☎ (713) 520-9292 | MAP **E6** | 🍴

TEALAS.COM

TEALA'S MAY BE ONE OF THOSE PLACES YOU SPOT DRIVING BY and think, "What a cute-looking spot. I need to remember this next time we go out to dinner." Let this be your reminder to give it a chance. Good for sipping fruity margaritas—the mango is especially enticing—in a wooden bar area with a sexy vibe, Teala's is not so great for the Tex-Mex staples you might be expecting.

Opt instead for their Yucatan specialties like *cochinita pibil* (roasted pork) with cucumber salad or the chicken in a peanut *mole* sauce. While service can be hit-or-miss and valet-only is a downside, River Oaks regulars don't seem to mind one bit. The patio facing West Dallas is a very pleasant place to while away the brunch hour.

TEOTIHUACÁN

1511 AIRLINE *just north of N. Main*
☎ (713) 426-4420 | MAP **E5** | 🍴
multiple locations
TEOMEXICANCAFE.COM

IF YOU DRIVE PAST THE AIRLINE LOCATION OF TEOTIHUACAN, YOU may want to invest in an eye exam. It's impossible to miss with a hot-pink/bright-orange façade and its name spelled out in giant letters on the awning. The other locations aren't quite as colorful, but the food at each sets a high bar for inexpensive Mexican favorites. Platters of sizzling chargrilled meats come flying through the kitchen doors, with beef, quail, chicken or shrimp as your options. Also known for its fresh corn tortillas and paper-thin chips perfect for scooping up their vibrant salsas, it's hard to go wrong here. Even the charro beans and above-average rice score points. Breakfast is a popular time to visit, with large dishes and large crowds moving in and out, it's quite a way to begin the day.

TEX-CHICK

712 FAIRVIEW *east of Montrose*
☎ (713) 528-4708 | MAP **E6** | 🍴
PUERTORRICANRESTAURANT.COM

IT'S A TINY RESTAURANT WITH A STORIED HISTORY, FROM WHERE IT got its interesting name to how the current owner came to be. There's not enough room here for the entire

saga, but just know there's a lot of heart and soul in both the restaurant and the food. In what feels like your grandmother's kitchen—yes, it's about that big—Puerto Rican food like *mofongo* (a fried ball of plantains with garlic and pork rind), *pastel-arroz habichuela* (similar to tamales), *arroz con gandules* (white rice and pigeon peas), fried pork chop and *carne guisada* (beef stew) is churned out for the regular crowds. The menu is simple and hearty and full of Puerto Rican spirit. Only open until 4 pm Monday through Wednesday and 6 pm Thursday through Saturday.

THAI STICKS

4319 MONTROSE *south of Richmond*
☎ (713) 529-4500 | MAP **E7** | 🍴
THAISTICKSHOUSTON.COM

THERE'S AN UPSCALE VERSION OF JUST ABOUT ANY TYPE OF FOOD, so why not Thai? If you can get past the idea of eating massaman curry in a setting other than a grungy strip mall, Thai Sticks might be the place to visit. Basil chicken, a roasted half duck seasoned with ginger sauce, lamb kebabs, tamarind mahi mahi and scallops and green curry are just a few dishes to speak of, and all of them at elevated prices, but you'll get great service, white tablecloths and beautifully plated dishes, which isn't the case at many a casual Thai spot. Added bonus: extensive wine and martini selections available.

THANH PHUONG

3236 E. BROADWAY *near E. Walnut, Pearland*
☎ (281) 412-7868 | 🍴
THANHPHUONGRESTAURANT.COM

WHAT'S SO SPECIAL ABOUT A SMALL VIETNAMESE RESTAUrant in a strip mall in Pearland? Well, quite a bit, actually. A recent change in ownership spruced things up mightily, with added dishes utilizing game meats. There are still the Vietnamese standards that existed before—pho, vermicelli dishes, *bo luc lac* (stir-fried beef)—but the rabbit, wild boar, venison and frog leg plates get the most raves. Venison carpaccio seems to be the most widely enjoyed, with raw slices of deer meat dressed in a citrus-fish sauce combination and garnished with scallions and crushed peanuts. It's not your typical Vietnamese restaurant, and that's exactly why it's so exciting. Patience required should you wish to view their menu online: It's 14 pages and very slow to load.

THIS IS IT!

2712 BLODGETT *between Alabama & Southmore*
☎ (713) 521-2920 | MAP **E7** | ❙

HOUSTONTHISISIT.COM

THE LADIES WHO SERVE AT THE THIS IS IT! STEAM TABLE DISH up the best soul food in Houston. Open for lunch and dinner, (and breakfast, too, 7 to 10 am Monday through Saturday), This Is It! is owned by Craig Joseph and his wife. Joseph is the grandson of Frank and Mattie Jones, who first opened the restaurant in 1959. With a rotating menu that includes meatloaf, yams, mac 'n' cheese, ham hocks, braised oxtails, chitlins, ribs, smothered pork chops and much more. For around $10, you get three heaping sides, an entree and cornbread, and the ladies who dish it up usually know what you'll like and how much you should have. This is pure Southern comfort.

TILA'S

1111 S. SHEPHERD *just south of W. Dallas*
☎ (713) 522-7654 | MAP **E6** | ❙❙

TILAS.COM

THIS ITTY-BITTY MEXICAN RESTAU- RANT SITS ON ITS OWN LITTLE oddly situated island of land at the eastern edge of River Oaks. Maybe it's the island mentality that inspires Tila's cheeky advertising, with quips like, "Every flauta is hand-rolled with exotic Mexican spices by genuine Mayan Virgins. Or Carlos, *depending on who's available*." That quirkiness spills into the snug dining room with countless art pieces that give it a lively Mexico City feel, and the strong margaritas help that along. The bar is lined with more than 60 tequilas to keep guests refreshed. Every meal starts with complimentary tortilla and plantain chips with red and green salsas. The menu is a refreshing departure from the usual Tex-Mex with offerings such as an avocado stuffed with marinated shrimp, crab-meat tostadas, *milaneza* (breaded cutlet, either pork or chicken) and *chile en nogada* (roasted poblano stuffed with chicken, topped with a creamy walnut sauce and pomegran-ate seeds). Breakfast is served on the weekends, and there's a charming patio in front.

TINY BOXWOOD'S

3614 W. ALABAMA *between Buffalo Speedway & Weslayan*
☎ (713) 622-4224 | MAP **D7** | ❙❙
multiple locations
TINYBOXWOODS.COM

TINY BOXWOOD'S DOESN'T MERELY SOUND LIKE A "PRECIOUS" KIND of restaurant, it actually is one. The original is built in the middle of a high-end garden/landscape design company, so it feels like a place you'd find nestled among the highly manicured gardens of jolly old England. As far as the menu goes, it's as equally precious as everything else. Of course there's a mid-afternoon tea service—there's a certain feminine appeal to such civility—and brunch, but also lunch and dinner, where dishes like a smoky goat lamb burger (with ground lamb, goat cheese, aioli and pomme frites) and the salmon Provençal salad are two of the heartiest selections available. It's not for the giant-portion-loving crowd, but there is something to be said for refined food from a refined menu being served in a refined environment. Just ask the ladies who lunch. It's one of their favorite locales.

TONY MANDOLA'S

1212 WAUGH *at W. Dallas*
☎ (713) 528-3474 | MAP **E6** | ¶¶
TONYMANDOLAS.COM

TONY MANDOLA HAS REALLY, TRULY ARRIVED. HOW DO WE know? All he had to do was place his name on a restaurant, and people instinctively flocked here from day one. It does help that the ambiance and service are top-notch, too. Mandola has certainly earned his reputation in Houston, having served Gulf Coast cuisine to many over the years. Replacing Tony Mandola's Gulf Coast Kitchen (where Brasserie 19 is now) with this new larger spot and losing the longer name, this Mandola's still focuses on seafood and Louisiana favorites but many with a twist. For instance, you'll find what is quite possibly the only gumbo pizza served in the world— imagine a dark roux (in place of tomato sauce) with crabmeat, mozzarella and parmesan cheese. Still the same as it always was:

the crowd of Houston movers and shakers who frequent the place for a chance to be seen and enjoy a reliably good Gulf Coast meal.

TONY'S

3755 RICHMOND *at Timmons, in Greenway Plaza*
☎ (713) 622-6778 | MAP **D7** | ¶¶
TONYSHOUSTON.COM

RESTAURANT TRENDS COME AND GO, HOT CHEFS IMPLODE, CERTAIN neighborhoods peak and then the crowds move on to the next best dining destination, this is all true. But in Houston one thing remains stalwart. Tony's is that constant—and has been since the early 1980s. Unctuous, fresh and delicately stuffed pastas, tender veal and impeccable seafood (call ahead to order the whole fish baked in salt) are just some of Tony's attractions, not to mention the always excellent service, award-winning wine selection and intriguing setting outfitted with *important* art. Owner Tony Vallone has become an expert at not only overseeing his namesake restaurant but also spoiling Houston's rich, famous and powerful with indulgences and an attention to detail that is unmatched. Tony's chef alums who have gone on to open their own important Houston restaurants are countless and include Mark Cox (chef/owner of Mark's American Cuisine) and Marco Wiles (chef/owner of Da Marco).

TOOKIE'S

1202 BAYPORT BLVD. *near Hwy.146 and NASA Rd., Seabrook*
☎ (281) 942-9334 | ¶

HURRICANE IKE KNOCKED TOOKIE'S OUT IN 2008, AND IT took three years for it to come back

RESTAURANTS

Gulf Coast oysters at Tony Mandola's

and reopen. Since then, this iconic (if now much cleaner) burger joint has reclaimed its reputation for interesting burgers and great sides. Charred beef patties anchor a straightforward hamburger that makes you appreciate simplicity. "The Squealer," which adds ground bacon to the beef patty, is the menu favorite, but the bean burger has its followers, too. Try also the wine-marinated burger, jalapeño poppers (called Pelican Eggs here), enormous onion rings and crisp-on-the-outside, creamy-on-the-inside French fries. The atmosphere is festive—which is to say loud—and there's a miniature train that runs through the dining room, adding to the din. On a fine day you'll want to sit outside: There's still a large deck cooled by sea breezes.

TORCHY'S TACOS
2411 S. SHEPHERD *just north of Westheimer*
☎ (713) 595-8226 | MAP **E6** | 🍴
multiple locations
TORCHYSTACOS.COM

WHEN "COOL" AUSTIN RESTAURANTS START MIGRATING TO Houston, does that mean we've arrived? In any case, Torchy's Tacos, an Austin cult-classic, opened here in 2011; a third location in The Heights is already in the works for late 2013. Rabid fans line up at all hours of the day for their unusual tacos that include messy breakfast versions. The most famous is the "Dirty Sanchez" (if you don't get the reference, feel free to look it up on UrbanDictionary.com, but don't say we didn't warn you), which includes scrambled eggs, fried poblano chiles, guacamole, pickled carrots, shredded cheese and poblano sauce. There's also the "Trailer Park" that includes fried chicken, green chiles, poblano

sauce, pico and lettuce. Their queso might be one of the best things on the menu, and the soda fountain is a trip all its own.

TQLA
4601 WASHINGTON *east of Shepherd*
☎ (281) 501-3237 | MAP **E6** | 🍴
TQLA.COM

AT TQLA, IT'S UNCLEAR WHERE THE TEQUILA BAR STARTS AND the restaurant ends. All the merrier, since the nearly-200 tequilas make for a better restaurant, and the upscale Southwestern and coastal Mexican cuisine makes for a better bar. The low-lit restaurant with its glowing fire-hues offset by dark furniture is both sexy and vibrant, which is a siren song for the young professionals who so enjoy the Washington Avenue scene. It also attracts foodies with items such as blue corn-crusted oysters with chorizo cream and a wild mushroom tamale with a roasted corn and sun-dried tomato salsa. The third group are the tequila aficionados, who come to sip the añejo tequilas and survey the scene.

RESTAURANTS

TRADIÇAO BRAZILIAN STEAKHOUSE

12000 SOUTHWEST FWY. (HWY. 59). *at Dorrance, Stafford*
☎ (281) 277-9292 | 🍴
multiple locations
TRADICAOBRAZILIANSTEAKHOUSE.COM

NEVER-ENDING MEAT: IT'S THE CONCEPT BEHIND THIS INDEPEN-dently owned rodizio grill in the prosperous Fort Bend suburbs. Rodizio service is characterized by servers—called "gauchos" or the loose equivalent to a cowboy in South American terms—who pass by with skewers of meat, ready to slice them directly onto your plate. A little coaster with a red side (stop!) and green side (go!) silently announce to the servers who is ready for more meat and who might be entering a carnivorous coma. There are also the Brazilian cheese puffs that are conveniently gluten-free and a lavish salad bar. The price point is more approachable than other restaurants of this type, though still not cheap. Service is commendable, and it is recommended you plan a nap immediately after your visit.

TREEBEARDS

315 TRAVIS *between Congress & Preston*
☎ (713) 228-2622 | MAP **F6** | 🍴
multiple locations
TREEBEARDS.COM

GETTING A CRAVING FOR TREE-BEARDS FOR DINNER IS LIKE the tragedy of driving to a Chick-Fil-A on Sunday, only to remember they're closed that day of the week. This is because Treebeards is a lunch-only establishment. We'll have to forgive them, however, because the food here is so good and comforting, no one could stay mad

for long. With the main location on Market Square, it's become such a downtown staple that they now have branches in the Cloister at Christ Church Cathedral, two spots in the tunnels and The Shops in Houston Center. Cafeteria-style grub consists of Southern/Cajun favorites like blackened catfish, meatloaf, pot roast, red beans and rice, gumbo, jambalaya, dirty rice and some of the richest shrimp étouffée known to man (the secret is in the butter). Meat and two—even the sides are commendable here—is a popular choice with a very affordable price tag.

TRENZA

2800 KIRBY *at Westheimer, in West Ave* | MAP **E6**
TRENZAHOUSTON.COM

IF YOU'RE A FAN OF FOOD NETWORK PROGRAMMING, YOU MAY RECOG-nize Trenza's founder/chef Susie Jimenez. The lovely young lady was a finalist in the 2011 season of *Next Food Network Star* and has been busy planning a Houston restaurant since exiting the show. Originally based in Colorado, Jimenez now refers to herself as a "part-time" Houstonian and is opening her first restaurant here in the swanky West Ave development in late 2013. Presumably she'll travel between the two states. The announced menu will be a mix of Mexican and Indian cuisine. Hopefully you'll be able to flip through these very pages in Fall 2013 while simultaneously enjoying chicken tikka masala enchiladas and a curried yellow tomato bloody Mary.

TREVÍSIO

6550 BERTNER *(top floor) at Moursund, in the Medical Center*
☎ (713) 749-0400 | MAP **E7** | ¶¶
TREVISIORESTAURANT.COM

THE RARITY OF FINDING GOUR-
MET FOOD ATOP A PARKING
garage makes this Medical Center
stunner that much more interesting ...
as do the two exterior 65-foot water-
falls that announce you have arrived
at your destination. The expansive
interior offers a grand view of the
Medical Center (and beyond), and
private rooms offer plenty of confer-
ence amenities for business meetings
and pharmaceutical presentations.
As for the food, it's a menu full of
upscale Italian with contemporary
touches. Pastas like the duck-stuffed
tortellini in a toasted pistachio bianco
sauce and wood-grilled meats like
the free-range lamb chops with a

Chianti reduction are indulgently rich,
though there are plenty of salad and
soup options for a lighter touch.

TRINITI

2815 S. SHEPHERD *at Kipling*
☎ (713) 527-9090 | MAP **E7** | ¶¶
TRINITIRESTAURANT.COM

TRINITI IS, FIRST, A FEAST FOR THE
EYES. THE RESTAURANT IS SO
stunning it earned a James Beard
Award nomination for its archi-
tecture firm in 2012. Very modern
with clean lines, dramatic lighting
elements and modern art on the
walls, it feels almost like it should be
hosting an art gallery rather than a
restaurant, though the bar and newly
added lounge area up front make
it feel warmer and more inviting to
happy-hour patrons. As for chef Ryan
Hildebrand's food—which is ever-
evolving since the restaurant's 2011

RESTAURANTS

Uchi

opening—it's a mix of high-concept techniques (think sous-vide, meticulous plating, modern) and seasonal ingredients. Any given menu might have plates of ribeye artfully plated with a potato "mosaic," spring onion yogurt vinaigrette, bone marrow chip and wild mushrooms and other delightfully inventive dishes. Not everything hits the mark, but when it does, it's a fantastic bullseye.

TRIPLE A

2526 AIRLINE _just inside Loop 610_
☎ (713) 861-3422 | MAP **E5** | 🍴
TRIPLEARESTAURANT.COM

TRIPLE A IS A CLASSIC OLD-FASHIONED DINER, ONE OF HOUSTON'S favorites. That's all it aspires to be and always has been. Established in 1942, not much has changed since. The patrons may have cycled through the many stages of life, and a few stoplights have been added to the road out front (though the condition of the street just seems to continue to deteriorate), but the retro building and all-American breakfasts haven't been alerted that it's now well into the 2000s. Eggs, sausage, bacon, toast, biscuits and, of course, pancakes from the griddle are why people come to appease their appetites in the morning. Lunch and dinner also feature diner classics with a famous chicken-fried steak, Southern-fried chicken and seafood, sandwiches and hamburgers.

TRULUCK'S

5350 WESTHEIMER _west of Sage_
☎ (713) 783-7270 | MAP **C7** | 🍴
TRULUCKS.COM

IF YOU'VE EVER EATEN A STONE CRAB CLAW IN HOUSTON, CHANCES ARE it was at Truluck's. In season, these sustainably harvested treats (they're taken from the crab, which is then released alive to regenerate the claw) can cause quite a frenzy at this upscale seafood house. The Truluck's chain is known for other seafood and crabs as well: Red king crab, Dungeness crab and the all-you-can-eat crab Mondays (while in season) are proof of such. Crabcake sliders, blackened redfish Pontchartrain (a rich Creole sauce of shrimp, crawfish tails and blue crab), steaks and other dishes that change along with what ingredients are available lure the I-don't-really-feel-like-getting-messy-eating-crab crowds as well. The outstanding wine list and fun cocktails make for a very bounteous experience, especially when paired with a chilled seafood platter.

TWO SAINTS RESTAURANT

12460 MEMORIAL _west of Gessner_
☎ (713) 465-8967 | MAP **C6** | 🍴🍴
TWOSAINTSRESTAURANT.COM

TWO SAINTS IS THE BEST OF BOTH WORLDS BY OFFERING FINE dining in a neighborhood setting. That fine dining comes in the form of kicked-up comfort classics like the truffled onion rings, a pan-seared half chicken and a humorously named "Oh For The Love O' Mac 'N' Cheese" that comes fully loaded with four cheeses, fresh jalapeños, thick-cut bacon and parmesan bread crumbs. Conveniently BYOB, it makes sense once you know that owner Joe Rippey also owns the nearby wine shop/bar Vine Wine Room. Weeknight dining is a prix-fixe affair with four courses at a very affordable price, while weekend dining (Friday and Saturday) gets you the full menu to select from. There's also a chef's tasting option on weekends for yet another fixed price.

UCHI

904 WESTHEIMER *just east of Montrose*
☎ (713) 522-4808 | MAP **E6** | ¶¶¶
UCHIRESTAURANTS.COM/HOUSTON

FROM THE "JAPANESE FARMHOUSE" DESIGN THAT COMPLETELY revamped and revived the former Felix Mexican Restaurant location to the near-perfect bites of food that employ every inch of the palate to the impressively educated servers, Uchi is just about flawless. Austin owner/chef and James Beard Award winner Tyson Cole runs a tight team of highly trained chefs who create tiny masterpieces—this isn't a place you'll leave moaning for elastic waist-bands—elaborately and painstakingly built for the ideal balance of texture, flavor, temperature and aesthetics. The menu is rife with seafood, both cooked and raw, but there are also a surprising number of dishes that employ vegetables (Brussels sprouts are otherworldly here), meat and grains brilliantly. Desserts are equally inventive and the perfect ending to a perfect meal.

UDIPI CAFE

5959 HILLCROFT *near Southwest Fwy. (Hwy. 59)*
☎ (713) 334-5555 | MAP **C7** | ¶
multiple locations
UDIPICAFEUSA.COM

YOU NEVER KNOW WHEN THE CRAVING FOR AN INDIAN BUFFET will strike, so it's always good to have a few choices at the ready. If you're near Hillcroft, Sugar Land, Katy or even as far as Dallas, Udipi is always an option. The menu contains only vegetarian dishes from the South of India (no onions or garlic, however) that are comprised mostly of legumes, grains, vegetables and fruit. Its Hillcroft location remains the most modest, but then again, so are most restaurants on Hillcroft. In addition to the very-inexpensive vegetarian lunch buffets, Udipi is the place to order *dosas*, lentil-rice crepes filled with a variety of sauces and vegetables.

UNDERBELLY

1100 WESTHEIMER *at Waugh*
☎ (713) 528-9800 | MAP **E6** | ¶¶¶
UNDERBELLYHOUSTON.COM

UNDERBELLY COULD EASILY BE THE POSTER CHILD FOR THE NEW generation of Houston restaurants. At its helm is the beloved chef Chris Shepherd, with his friendly demeanor in the front of house and his multi-cultural approach to cuisine in the back of house (though the two intermingle with the extremely open kitchen). Shepherd's dishes are a mash-up of local, seasonal ingre-dients and cooking techniques and flavors borrowed from Houston's rainbow of ethnicities: Vietnamese, Cajun, Chinese, Thai, Korean and more. And that's not even taking into account his in-house butcher shop, which allows Shepherd to bring in whole animals, or his in-house curing room. It really is the story of Houston food, whether it's the beloved spicy braised goat over Korean dumplings or a whole fish served family-style. The only drawback is the confusing plate sizes, which range from tiny to massive and a few in-between. It's always best to get a server's input before placing your full order.

RESTAURANTS

UP

3995 WESTHEIMER *(3rd floor)*
at Drexel, in Highland Village
☎ (713) 640-5416 | MAP **D7** | 🍴
UPRESTAURANT.COM

IT'S A BIRD, IT'S A PLANE, IT'S…
DEFINITELY NOT SUPERMAN. IT'S
Up, the fine-dining restaurant on the
third floor, just above Cole Haan in
Highland Village. Named for its location on top of the shopping center,
it could just as easily refer to the
upward mobility of its financially
confident clientele or its gorgeous
balcony or perhaps just the fact
that things are always looking "up"
after a martini at the bar. Coolly
contemporary with neutral tones
and floor-to-ceiling windows, it feels
like a luxury hotel setting as much
as it does a restaurant. Cuisine is all
over the place, with dishes like paella
right next to lobster ravioli, Hong
Kong-style red snapper and sushi.
The thing they all have in common
is decadence. The crowd is actually
a good mixture of young and mature
but always well heeled and usually
sipping a glass of vino.

UPTOWN SUSHI

1131 UPTOWN PARK BLVD.
north of San Felipe
☎ (713) 871-1200 | MAP **D6** | 🍴
UPTOWN-SUSHI.COM

THE SUSHI BAR IS THE CENTER
OF EVERYTHING AT THIS ASIAN-
fusion Galleria-area restaurant. Set
up like a stage in the style of a theater
in the round, scenesters start filing
into their booths and tables in the
L.A.-inspired decor to watch the
action unfold. Techno beats and a
late-night crowd mean fine young
things are a majority of the clientele, and they all enjoy the various
specialty rolls that are prepared by a
team of five sushi chefs during peak
hours. The popular Lickety Split roll
combines tuna, crawfish, cucumber
and sprouts inside with spicy tuna,
yellowtail, salmon and avocado
outside. (The rolls are large, so order
progressively.) Cocktails are always
the preferred drink of choice, so
much so that the restaurant has been
recognized with a Houston Culinary
Award for Best Bar Service. Dress to
impress, and if you're single certainly
be ready to mingle.

VAN LOC

3010 MILAM *north of Elgin*
☎ (713) 528-6441 | MAP **E6** | 🍴
VANLOCRESTAURANT.COM

LET'S JUST CUT TO THE CHASE
HERE. VAN LOC ISN'T GOING TO
win any awards for service or design,
the former is cold and the latter
is dull brown. However, there is a
reason it's included in this book:
summer rolls with ideal texture,
perfectly cooked vermicelli in a
soup of shrimp and pork, clay-pot
catfish, barbecued pork, whole fried
fish and *bo luc lac* (sauteed beef).
But wait, there's more. Tofu fried
with chile peppers, garlic and scallions pleases both meat and non-
meat eaters and most dishes come
in at under $12. Fun fact: "Van loc"
means "lots of luck" in Vietnamese.

VIC & ANTHONY'S

1510 TEXAS *at LaBranch*
☎ (713) 228-1111 | MAP **F6** | 🍴
VICANDANTHONYS.COM

SOME MAY SCOFF AT THE SERI-
OUSNESS OF LANDRY'S RES-
taurant group, but they have never
had the pleasure of dining at Vic
& Anthony's. It's truly a premier
steakhouse for which Landry's CEO
Tilman Fertitta put in the research by

traveling the country with his father Vic and his cousin Anthony, visiting steakhouses and putting all of his favorite aspects into one brand. The end result is a two-story, Craftsman-style setting with fine wood, wrought ironwork and dramatic chandeliers, impeccable service and exemplary steakhouse classics. Oyster service will not only include a piquant cocktail sauce and horseradish, but the luxurious touch of a mignonette brings it to another level. Then there are the bone-in ribeyes cooked to a perfect medium rare or the creamed spinach or the onion strings or the caviar to start. It's all very over-the-top in the best possible way. Speaking of over-the-top, special events can include anything from a burger Friday to a meal of 40-day dry-aged Kobe beef directly from Japan. Also impressive are the 1,000-plus wines, including plenty available by the glass. Nothing is too luxurious or indulgent for Vic & Anthony's, and that's exactly how we like it.

VIENG THAI

6929 LONG POINT *between Silber & Antoine*
☎ (713) 688-9910 | MAP **D5** | 🍴

WHEN CHEFS TELL YOU THEY LIKE TO EAT AT A RESTAURANT, YOU listen. Vieng Thai is one of those restaurants. Service is so-so, atmosphere is modest and the neighborhood is slightly sketchy, but the food... oh, the food. It's fully spiced, so take advantage of their BYOB policy and bring some cooling beverages along. Their *tom ka gai* coconut milk soup, beef *panaeng* curry, *pad sar-to*, which is shrimp sautéed in chili paste with *sar-tor* (also called "stink beans"), are all so full of flavor they'll make you want to shout it to the rooftops. But the must-have here

is the *som tam*, a green papaya salad that includes chilies, palm sugar and tiny dried shrimp—a mix of sweet, salty, tangy and spice that builds with each bite, finally reaching a climax of heat. You'll most likely be dewy before you've made it halfway through, but consider it the culinary version of a sweat lodge and keep plowing through.

VINCENT'S

2701 W. DALLAS *between Montrose & Waugh*
☎ (713) 528-4313 | MAP **E6** | 🍴
NINOS-VINCENTS.COM

LOCATED IN THE MINI-ITALIAN VILLAGE CREATED BY VINCENT Mandola, his wife and two daughters, Vincent's is part of a trio. The other siblings are Nino's and Grappino di Nino, and they're all exceptional in their own little realm. Vincent's may be best known for a dish of simple roasted chicken seasoned with lemon and garlic and served with artful mashed potatoes and seasonal vegetables. It's down-home grand-motherly cooking in a very Italian setting. There are the pizzas and pastas, sure, but the Veal Vincent, coated in parmigiano with lemon butter and artichoke hearts is also a scene stealer. Service is always part of the pleasure, as is the courtyard all establishments share.

WHITE OAK KITCHEN + DRINKS

5011 WESTHEIMER *in the Westin Hotel, in The Galleria*
☎ (713) 960-6588 | MAP **D6** | 🍴
WHITEOAKHOUSTON.COM

A LITTLE SHOPPING AT THE GALLERIA CAN WORK UP A big appetite. Thankfully, there are now some refined options that do not include the wild energy and huge crowds of The Cheesecake Factory or the fast-casual options in the food court. Instead, try this all-at-once rustic and vibrant spot inside the Westin. Gorgeously appointed, its siren song of adult beverages is hard to resist after maneuvering through The Galleria crowds. Inviting you to stay even longer is an extensive menu of New American bistro-y dishes that run the gamut from Asian to Southwest to gluten-free. Also inviting? A Sunday brunch and an everyday happy hour from 3 to 8 pm.

WILLIE G'S

1605 POST OAK BLVD.
north of San Felipe
☎ (713) 840-7190 | MAP **D6** | 🍴
WILLIEGS.COM

PART OF WHAT MAKES HOUSTON SUCH A GREAT DINING DESTInation is its proximity to the coast. The bounty of the ocean always makes a tasty dish, and Willie G's has been working with the freshest ingredients since day one. Now a part of the Landry's restaurant group, not much has changed. There's still flounder, grouper, golden tile, swordfish, rainbow trout, redfish and oysters when in season, and it's all fresh-caught. Typical dishes like the snapper Hemingway, which is cracker crumb-breaded and topped with lump crab, and the zesty shrimp remoulade are always crowd pleasers. Other not-to-miss seafood house classics are the iced seafood tower (perfect with a martini) and the wedge salad with blue cheese. Oysters on the half shell in season are a rite of passage, and the service is among the best in its class. The decent wine list tops things off.

YILDIZLAR

2929 SOUTHWEST FWY. (HWY. 59) *east of Buffalo Speedway*
☎ (713) 524-7735 | MAP **E7** | 🍴

FUNNY NAME, GREAT FOOD. DON'T FRET OVER YOUR PRONUNCIATION, just get here and try some of the Mediterranean food. It's typical kabobs, gyros, falafel, babaganoush, hummus and the like, but it's well done and in a casual, counter-service setting. It won't change the world or anything, but it will satisfy the meanest craving for a fresh hot falafel. The chicken shawarma sandwich is also a staple, as is the combination plate that covers all the bases with a variety that spans 10 different foods. Homemade spinach pies are not to be missed, but unless you enjoy a lingering floral taste, do skip the rose water.

YUM YUM CHA

2435 TIMES BLVD. *between Morningside & Kirby*
☎ (713) 527-8455 | MAP **E7** | 🍴
YUMYUMCHACAFE.COM

NO PUSHCARTS HERE INSIDE THIS SMALL DIM SUM PARLOR; INSTEAD there are flipbook menus with photos of the dishes. With 50-plus items on the regular menu along with daily chalkboard specials, there's plenty to try out, especially since the serving sizes are smaller, as dim sum traditionally tends to be. Shrimp and chive dumplings, turnip cake, steamed buns, potstickers and even a few adventurous items like chicken feet or beef stomach keep things interesting and tasty. If the place is crowded, the manager will take your name and call you on your cell when a table opens up. A few things to note: Even after all these years the AC is still insufficient during summer months,

Chef Jamie Zelko of Zelko Bistro

so avoid tables by the window. And service is slow, so don't order in stages.

ZABAK'S

5901 WESTHEIMER *at Fountain View*
☎ (713) 977-7676 | MAP **C7** | 🍴
ZABAKS.COM

THERE ISN'T MAGIC DUST IN THE FALAFELS AT ZABAK'S, SO WHAT is it that makes them so unusually delicious? Co-owner Peter Zabak simply says it's a mixture of garbanzo beans, jalapeños, onions and a blend of spices—though he wouldn't dish which ones exactly—all ground together, formed into patties, deep fried to order and served inside a pita or as stand-alone entities. Whatever the case may be, this is a dish that defines Houston inasmuch as it might be the best example the city has to offer. It's taken numerous titles in the world of falafel, so we're not the only ones who think they're grand. It's all made that much better by the family-run environment, with friendly service and warm hospitality.

ZELKO BISTRO

705 E. 11TH *west of Studemont*
☎ (713) 880-8691 | MAP **E5** | 🍴
ZELKOBISTRO.COM

THIS LITTLE HEIGHTS BISTRO BE-CAME AN INSTANT NEIGHBOR-hood favorite the day it opened in 2010. Chef Jamie Zelko—who won the 2007 Houston Culinary Award for Up-and-Coming Chef of the Year—has been providing diners with consistently good upscale comfort food in this cozy bungalow, and that's as good a business plan as any. Top it off with her commitment to serve sustainable, local ingredients and how could anyone not like it? The

wine list—many of the bottles are produced by women—is priced to move inventory, which is a win-win for everyone and especially good for pairings. The dining room can get packed on weeknights, but it's just a testament to the good thing Zelko has churned up in the neighbor-hood. Luckily, there's a nice covered patio for overflow. Note: Don't leave without buying a jar of Zelko's honey harvested from her own hives.

ZYDECO LOUISIANA DINER

1119 PEASE *at San Jacinto*
☎ (713) 759-2001 | MAP **F6** | 🍴
ZYDECOLOUISIANADINER.COM

A LITTLE PIECE OF LOUISIANA HAS BEEN A PART OF HOUSTON'S downtown for three decades now. Not in the hip resurgence of Market Square Park, not in a fancy develop-ment, but just in a simple, well-worn location not far from the South Texas College of Law. Zydeco serves up Cajun soul food to a crowd of law-yers, downtown office workers and those craving a fried oyster po'boy. Meat-and-three steam-table specials will stick to your ribs with stuffed pork chops, jambalaya, chicken fric-assee, chicken and sausage Creole and fried chicken (depending on the day of the week), and gumbo is always a safe bet. The crawfish étouffée always brings patrons back for more, and the side dishes them-selves could stand alone. Moist cornbread, black-eyed peas, stewed okra and creamy garlic mashed potatoes are just a sample of offer-ings. Lunch only.

Index

INDEX

INDEX

INDEX BY LOCATION

INDEX BY LOCATION

buy 9/16 —
free   10 yr exten war   999⁰⁰   )
1-800-303-6578   'Lynnzie
Generac —
"Quality Computers"   9/16 AM
936-756-4971